M O Z A M B I Q U E

The Africanization of a European Institution

M O Z A M

ALLEN F. ISAACMAN

BIQUE

The Africanization of

a European Institution

THE ZAMBESI PRAZOS, 1750–1902

The University of Wisconsin Press

MADISON, MILWAUKEE, & LONDON

Published 1972
The University of Wisconsin Press
Box 1379, Madison, Wisconsin 53701

The University of Wisconsin Press, Ltd.
70 Great Russell St., London

First Printing

Printed in the United States of America
North Central Publishing, St. Paul, Minnesota

ISBN 0-299-06110-8; LC 72-176413

TO

my wife Barbara

TO

the people of Mozambique

Contents

List of Maps

List of Tables

Preface

During the early part of the seventeenth century the Portuguese government established several crown estates, or *prazos da coroa*, in the lower
Zambesi Valley of Mozambique. These institutions have been alter-
nately described as a transplanted Portuguese feudal system, as a modified plantation system, and as a European tribute system. While there is
widespread agreement that the *prazos* played an important role in the
historical development of Mozambique, few scholars have attempted to
assess the significance of the institution. Almost all the literature displays
a distinct Euro-centric bias and treats the prazos as an alien institution
within the larger framework of the expansion of Europe.

This study seeks to correct these deficiencies through a comprehensive
examination of the prazos over two centuries. It attempts, however, to
go beyond merely "filling in the gaps" and to redefine the prazos as an
African institution operating in its Zambesian milieu. This departs substantially from the standard approach which Alexandre Lobato first
posited in his pioneering work *Evolução Administrativa e Económica de
Moçambique.* He defined the prazos as estates which the crown distributed to female inhabitants of the Zambesi or to prospective immigrants for a period of three generations. Theoretically, these could only
be transmitted through the female line. The recipients had specific obligations to the state, of which the most important was a tax, or *foro*, to
be paid annually.[1]

Before suggesting an alternate approach, it seems useful to examine
the limitations inherent in the legalistic interpretation which Lobato and
other historians have employed. The most obvious shortcoming is the
emphasis upon the relatively insignificant relationship between the
crown and the estateholder, known as the *prazero*,[2] rather than upon
the nature of the institution itself. Such basic problems as the political
relationship between the prazero and the indigenous African chiefs, or

the ethnic and cultural composition of the peoples who lived on the prazos and their impact on the Portuguese are ignored. Apart from overlooking or oversimplifying questions dealing with the organization and operation of the institution, such a static approach fails to explain change. Although the theoretical relationship between the crown and the prazeros remained constant for 150 years, there is no reason to assume that immutable political and social patterns developed in the Zambezi Valley.

This study examines the prazos as a functioning institution within an African environment. From this perspective a prazo can be defined as an operative system with the following characteristics: (1) a European, Indian, or *mestizo* overlord holding a number of privileges and prerogatives which had formerly belonged to the land chief, or *mambo*;[3] (2) a *colono*, or free African, population living in its traditional manner on its historic lands; (3) a slave population with diverse origins owing primary loyalty to the prazero; (4) theoretically fixed frontiers based on the historic boundaries of the indigenous unit before the arrival of the prazero; and (5) a contractual relationship between the prazero and the crown. Of all these characteristics the legal relationship between the prazero and the king had the least relevance and in many cases did not even exist. There were numerous examples of estateholders who failed to fulfill their part of the contract and acted independently of the government. These illegal activities ranged from the common refusal to pay the foro to military resistance when the prazero felt the state impinging upon his autonomy. Similarily, a number of prazeros established functioning prazos without the requisite grants (known as *aforamentos*). Others with legal titles were unable to acquire recognition from the local African leaders and were therefore forced to retire from "their" land. Finally, even after the prazos had been legally abolished in 1832, a substantial number continued to function throughout the nineteenth century.

Unlike the legalistic approach, this study emphasizes the internal dynamics of the institution and its impact on the historical development of the lower Zambesi Valley. Among the major questions posed in subsequent chapters are the following: How did an alien Portuguese or mestizo achieve a modicum of political control over the local Zambesian chieftaincies? What were the principal organizational principles around which the prazos developed? What impact, if any, did the Portuguese presence have on the cultural makeup and social institutions of the indigenous population? How did the institution survive for 150 years and what types of structural changes did it undergo? Finally, this study seeks to achieve a degree of universality by means of a comparative analysis of certain Zambesian institutions and historical processes with those of other areas of Africa.

The material presented in this analysis comes primarily from written records and oral testimonies. Ethnographic data, linguistic evidence, and published archaeological records provided valuable information which complemented the written texts and traditions.

Primary sources, both printed and archival, are quite abundant and generally accessible. Published travel accounts, chronicles, diaries, and official correspondences are available for every century. They are particularly important in the period before 1650 for which the archival data are quite uneven. The most important collections of published sources are *Documentos sobre os Portugueses em Moçambique e na África Central 1497–1840*, and G. M. Theal, ed., *Records of South-East Africa*. The Portuguese archives, especially the Arquivo Histórico Ultramarino, Arquivo Nacional da Torre de Tombo, Biblioteca Nacional, and Biblioteca Pública de Ajuda, house impressive collections of documents as does the Arquivo Histórico de Moçambique, located in Lourenço Marques.

The written data suffer from a number of inherent defects. Since they are the records of foreigners who rarely had more than a superficial knowledge of the culture or language of the Zambesi peoples, these descriptions of the life styles of the indigenous population were generally distorted and colored by ethnocentric assumptions. A substantial proportion of the documents focus only on the Portuguese and mestizo community and ignore all aspects of African life, except as they impinged on the presence of the Portuguese. Many of the official reports and petitions tended to extol the virtues of the authors and, for this reason alone, must be treated with care. Despite these limitations, the written texts are invaluable. They provide detailed descriptions of important aspects of the prazeros' life, of the recurring conflict between the estate owners and the Portuguese government, and of the factors which ultimately led to the demise of the prazo system. They also are the principal source of valuable statistical material, and they can be used to corroborate and date events recalled by the Zambesi elders.

This type of study, however, could not have been completed without the collection of oral data. The testimonies lack a fixed structure and suffer from such characteristic problems as the manipulation of historical charters, the embellishment of past events, and the absence of an absolute chronology. Nevertheless, through textual analysis, comparison and cross checking of conflicting testimonies, group interviews, and careful assessment of the informants' biases, distortions and weaknesses in the oral texts can be minimized. These are the same techniques required of all sound historical research. (See Appendix A for a note on the collection of oral data.)

The information extrapolated from the oral accounts provides a new dimension absent in the written accounts. The testimonies explain in great detail how the Africans perceived the prazero's political role and how his presence affected both the royal family and commoners. Such fundamental questions as the nature of the social and cultural institutions of the Zambesi peoples and the impact of the prazero on these institutions can only be answered by the oral sources. They also contain essential information about the economic systems which operated on the prazos. In short, the oral testimonies provide graphic accounts of how the system actually functioned rather than the way in which it was legally defined in Lisbon or perceived by most local chroniclers.

Any monograph treating such a complex institution over 150 years must necessarily be selective in the questions posed. A wide range of significant problems which a historian interested in European expansion might have stressed have been generally ignored. Several considerations, apart from manageability, dictated this decision. The most important was a belief that the historiography of Mozambique needed to be redirected. An overemphasis upon the Portuguese presence at the expense of the activities of the indigenous population has helped generate a series of racially and culturally arrogant myths. Inextricably intertwined with this Euro-centric bias was an elitist approach which focused on governors, judges, generals and, in passing, on African leaders. Obviously, this is not the stuff from which meaningful social histories are written.

Those historians interested in Portuguese studies or European expansion might examine the prazos within this larger frame of reference. A detailed analysis of the prazos as a transplanted feudal institution or as the basis of a Portuguese settler colony would make an important contribution to our knowledge of that country's overseas experience. Both the writings of Alexandre Lobato and M. D. D. Newitt have made valuable contributions in this area. A comparison of the historical development of the prazos with either the *donações* of Brazil or the parallel system in Goa would be an interesting addition to the growing field of comparative history. The prazos also could be examined in conjunction with the growth of other European settler colonies and the ensuing frontier-metropolis conflict. Although valuable, such works must invariably constitute something less than a study of the prazos.

Minneapolis   A.F.I.
October, 1971

ACKNOWLEDGMENTS

It would be impossible to thank properly the numerous individuals who provided valuable assistance during the course of this study. I would, however, like to extend my gratitude to Padre A. da Silva Rego for his invaluable aid, to Harold Scheub, Philip D. Curtin, and Peter Carroll, all of whom made a number of penetrating criticisms of the manuscript, and especially to Jan Vansina, whose guidance and knowledge has been a source of inspiration. I would also like to thank Lynn Sheridan who made the first maps. The Foreign Area Fellowship Program provided generous assistance which enabled me to spend twenty months in Africa and Portugal completing the research for this project. To my informants and interpreters, my profound thanks. In the final analysis this represents a joint effort with my wife Barbara who acted as a full-time researcher, field worker, and reader. It is to her that I dedicate this work with all my love.

Glossary of African Terms

Achikunda: warrior slaves on the prazos
Akaporo: adopted dependents or "domestic slaves" of the indigenous
    Zambesian peoples
Badzo: slave official on the prazos
Bare: inland mining site
Chipante: preferential form or marriage
Chuma: bride price
Inhacoda: female slave chief
Inhacuaua: positional title of local Zambesian political authority
Inhamucangamiza: forced sale of agricultural products on the prazos
Iyanga: Lunda warrior-settlers
Kazembe: variant form of mukazambo
Mabandazi: slaves who worked in and around the prazeros' homes
Mambo: indigenous land chiefs
Manchilla: domestically woven cloth
Massa: porridge made from grain
Mazi-a-mango: holy water presented by the Portuguese at the corona-
    tion of the Barue king
Mbuemba: ritual stick which the Sena mambo employed during the
    rain ceremony
Mfumu: indigenous political authority
Mhondoro: religious medium who invoked the ancestor spirits
Mitete: symbolic act through which a person voluntarily enslaved
    himself
Mizimu: ancestor spirits
Mucate: female slave leader
Mukazambo: male slave leader
Mungaba: subordinate female slave official
Mupanga: Sena slave dealer who stole children from the Manganja

Muropa: symbolic gift generally consisting of a small number of beads
       which was paid for the blood of a newly acquired slave

Musitu: independent slave communities

Mutsonko: annual tax paid to the mambo or prazero

Mutupu: clan name

Muzinda: royal village

Muzungu: racially mixed Afro-Portuguese

Mwini dziko: Malawian land chief

Mwini mudzi: Malawian village headman

Npaza: symbolic gift indicating a male's willingness to marry his pro-
       spective bride

Nphete: symbolic gift indicating a male's willingness to marry his pro-
       spective bride

Nsaka: slave regiments

Pombe: beer made from fermented grain

Rusambo: symbolic gift which marked the end of a slave trading
       transaction

Samacoa: African official appointed by the Portuguese to work on the
       new prazos

Sangira: African official appointed by the Portuguese to work on the
       new prazos

Tsachikunda: slave official on the prazos

Tsantamba: Tawara mambo's walking stick

M O Z A M B I Q U E

The Africanization of a European Institution

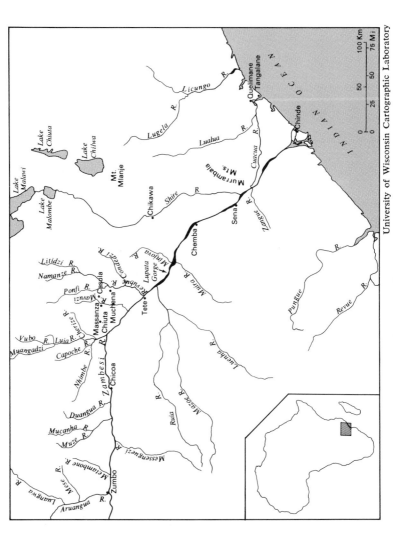

MAP 1 *Principal Landmarks of the Zambesi.*

University of Wisconsin Cartographic Laboratory

1

The African Background: Peoples and Polities of the Greatest Zambesi to ca. 1700

THE EARLIEST INHABITANTS OF THE ZAMBESI

When Portuguese traders first settled in the Zambesi during the middle of the sixteenth century, they found an indigenous population characterized by ethnic and cultural diversity. Successive groups of African migrants had already settled throughout this region. Both north and south of the river a similar demographic pattern seems to have developed. Groups of iron-age Bantu conquered the bands of Anões,[1] or bushmen, and were themselves subsequently incorporated into the larger Malawian and Karanga kingdoms. (See Maps 2, 3, and 4.)

Traditions collected in this region universally recognize the Anões as the earliest inhabitants of the Zambesi. They lived in either rock shelters or holes dug in the ground. Lacking gardens, the Anões relied solely on the fruits they gathered, the small animals and eggs they collected, and the game they hunted and snared. Their principal weapons were short wooden spears used to kill prey. Because of their small numbers and limited technology, they were easily driven south by the first iron-age peoples who migrated into the area.[2]

It is impossible to identify with precision the earliest agriculturalists and to date their arrival. In the Tete region, known as Chedima, oral traditions indicate that three or four groups had migrated into the Zambesi well before the Karanga conquerors who founded the famous kingdom of the Muenemutapa. Perhaps the earliest were the Zimba, who are sometimes credited with introducing iron utensils.[3] Tawara

3

informants recall that when their ancestors arrived in this area, they encountered and subdued scattered groups of Pimbe and Dema as well as Zimba.[4] The Tawara settled in the area adjacent to Tete, where they were divided into a number of independent chieftaincies until they were conquered by the warriors of the Muenemutapa sometime in the fifteenth century.

South of Tete, in the area adjacent to the confluence of the Luenha and Zambesi rivers, lived the Tonga, whose origin remains obscure.[5] Since the term "Tonga" does not necessarily refer to an ethnically homogeneous people and was used in the Zambesi to signify any conquered or tributary group, it is difficult to trace their early history. A logical hypothesis of their origin is that members of the alien Chilendje clan had subjugated an unknown riverine people and incorporated them into Tonga chieftaincies. This would explain why kingship remained the sole monopoly of the Chilendje clan. An equally acceptable explanation, propounded by some Tonga elders, is that those who bear the clan name Chilendje are the direct descendants of the first Tonga to arrive in the Zambesi and those who belong to all other clans were the members of stranger groups who were subsequently assimilated.[6] Emphasis on the element of first arrival serves to legitimize both the royal clan's claim to be the rightful owners of the land and their dominant position in Tonga society.

Tonga informants recalled that, before the arrival of the Europeans, their territory was divided into a number of independent chieftaincies. A land chief, known as mambo, who had important religious as well as political functions, governed the respective polities. Assisting the mambo was a council of elders and a group of village headmen, or *afumu*, who were generally the senior members of the dominant local lineage. Where the chieftaincy encompassed a particularly large area, the mambo often appointed several territorial chiefs from among his junior kinsmen to supervise the outlying regions.[7] Scattered Portuguese accounts confirm the existence of these early Tonga polities.[8]

The Sena and related peoples [9] lived between the present-day village of Sena and the mouth of the Zambesi River. Their political organization closely parallelled that of the Tonga, the principal difference being the absence of a dominant royal clan in Sena society. This anomaly seems to suggest a migration of unrelated peoples rather than a movement of a conquering elite or a homogeneous ethnic group. Although it is impossible to date the arrival of the Sena, early Portuguese sources mention several chiefs living in the vicinity of the village of Sena and local Sena traditions note that their ancestors conquered the Anões well before the arrival of the Europeans.[10]

It is far more difficult to establish the identity of the first agriculturalists who lived on the northern banks of the Zambesi. Malawian traditions emphatically deny the presence of an iron-age people prior to their own arrival.[11] This allegation, however, does not preclude the existence of an earlier sedentary Bantu population, since it is in the interest of the Malawi to manipulate history in order to legitimize their ownership of the land. Acknowledgment of the presence of the Anões does not undermine this position, since the Anões merely gathered the products of the land and never remained in one area for a long period of time.

There are, nevertheless, several suggestions that agriculturalists were residing in the region before the arrival of the Malawi. Preliminary diggings in eastern Zambia reveal pots and iron of pre-Malawian origin.[12] Furthermore, Malawi traditions attribute to the Anões culture traits, including sophisticated hut sites and iron workings, that are clearly alien to their life style.[13] It is conceivable that these accounts actually refer to agriculturalists whom the Malawians conquered and assimilated. There is also the intriguing fact that the Banda, an important Malawi clan, monopolize the role of raincallers and are well represented in chieftaincy positions at the local level because of their close affinity with the land. This could be explained by their arrival prior to the Malawian immigrants who conquered and assimilated them.[14] Finally, accounts recorded north of the Zambesi differentiate between the Malawian invaders and the indigenous Bantu population.[15] From superficial descriptions the area seems to have been divided into relatively small chieftaincies not unlike those on the southern bank.

This limited description is all that can be surmised from our very sketchy knowledge of early Zambesian history. The most important characteristics of this period were the absence of any major state systems and the corresponding proliferation of relatively small chieftaincies on both banks of the Zambesi.

THE KARANGA CONQUEST OF THE ZAMBESI AND THE FOUNDATION OF THE KINGDOM OF THE MUENEMUTAPA

The Karanga, who are generally credited with having built the complex Acropolis at Zimbabwe, migrated into present-day Rhodesia some time before the fourteenth century and perhaps even as early as the end of the first millennium.[16] Excavations throughout the southern half of

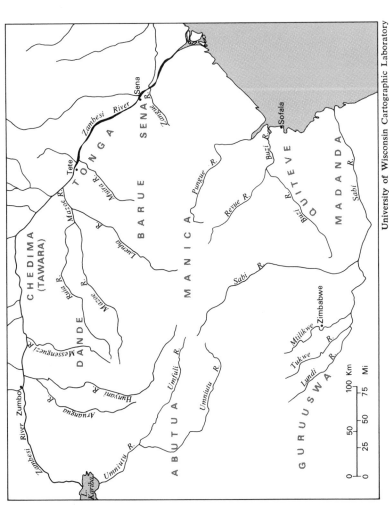

MAP 2 The Karanga States.

University of Wisconsin Cartographic Laboratory

Rhodesia indicate that Karanga groups moved southward from Zimbabwe at least as far as the confluence of the Shashi and Limpopo rivers in the region known as Guruuswa. By the beginning of the fifteenth century Mtota Nyatsimba, first remembered Karanga king, established his capital in this region (see Map 2).

From Guruuswa the Karanga expanded northward into the lower Zambesi, probably in search of salt and new land.[17] In the second quarter of the fifteenth century Mtota and his followers conquered the Pimbe, Dema, Zimba, and Tawara. From this victory, he received the praise name Muenemutapa, or master pillager, and his Karanga warriors became known as the Korekore, or locusts, because of the manner in which they consumed the land. During this expansion Mtota moved the capital from Guruuswa to Dande. Mtota died before the conquest of the Zambesi had been completed, and left to his youngest son Matope the fulfillment of the expansion. By about 1480 Matope governed the entire area from Tete to the mouth of the Zambesi.[18] The Karanga expansion continued even after the annexation of the chieftaincies on the southern bank of the Zambesi. By the first third of the sixteenth century, the Karanga kingdom embraced the areas of Barue, Quiteve, Manica, and Sedanda (see Map 3) and was probably the most powerful polity in southern or central Africa.[19]

The vast domains of the Muenemutapa appear to have been divided into three types of administrative units. In the outlying regions of Manica, Barue, Quiteve, and Sedanda, immediate descendants of Mtota and Matope ruled as provincial chiefs. The Muenemutapa delegated complete authority over all internal matters to them. They selected and distributed land to all subordinate chiefs and received appropriate tribute and taxes, and, in return, were responsible for the general health and well-being of their territory. Despite their relatively autonomous positions, they had clearly defined obligations to the reigning Muenemutapa. They were expected to acknowledge his supreme authority, to pay him a periodic tax, and to supply men in time of national emergency.[20]

The Muenemutapa personally governed the core of the empire, which spanned the region known as Dande and Chedima. He divided these lands into various territorial units which were distributed to patrilineal relatives, to those lieutenants who had participated in the conquest and, perhaps, to some senior wives.[21] These officials received the title of mambo and they and their descendants were granted perpetual ownership of the land. The amambo in turn appointed district and local chiefs from among their patrilineal relatives.[22] These subordinates also received the title of mambo or *muanamambo*, which literally meant "son of the chief."

Both at the territorial and the local level the respective amambo collected taxes and tribute, received symbolic gifts, and consulted the ancestor spirits, or *mizimu*.[23] Their direct responsibilities to the Muenemutapa varied, depending on their position in the political hierarchy. Generally, these obligations paralleled those of the provincial chiefs. The close proximity of the royal capital, however, enabled the Muenemutapa to exert much greater control over these subjects.

The strip bordering on the Zambesi from the confluence of the Luenha to the Indian Ocean was probably no more than a fringe area over which the Karanga exerted some form of indirect rule. The evidence indicates that, unlike what occurred in the area to the north, the indigenous Sena and Tonga land chiefs continued to rule as long as they recognized the ultimate authority of the Muenemutapa and periodically transmitted taxes to his royal capital.[24] The fact that Tonga and Sena traditions make no mention of the Muenemutapa suggests that his direct influence was rather limited. It is, nevertheless, possible that the Karanga king appointed junior relatives to govern strategic areas or to supervise the activities of the indigenous Tonga and Sena amambo.[25]

The Muenemutapa appointed principal members of the royal family to govern important regions, thereby adding to the stability and strength of the state. Such mechanisms reduced the possibility that the non-Karanga subjects would revolt or fail to meet their obligations and also removed a number of potential successors who might have become involved in court intrigue. The availability of a powerful army enabled the Muenemutapa to enforce his authority and to contain most subversive activities.[26]

Karanga religious institutions and rituals reinforced the position of kingship. Ancestor worship closely identified the reigning Muenemutapa with the supernatural. The king was not only the principal spiritual link with the royal mizimu but he himself became a national ancestor spirit upon his death. On the appropriate religious occasions, and in times of crises, only the Muenemutapa and the royal *svikiro* mediums had access to the deceased kings who had power to intercede with the supreme diety, or *murungu*. Because these religious mediums were closely associated with the royal family, they served as a powerful corporate group defending the status quo. The annual rekindling of the royal torch also reaffirmed the Muenemutapa's role as the principal secular and religious authority in the kingdom. At a designated time the Muenemutapa sent out trusted agents to the capitals of the

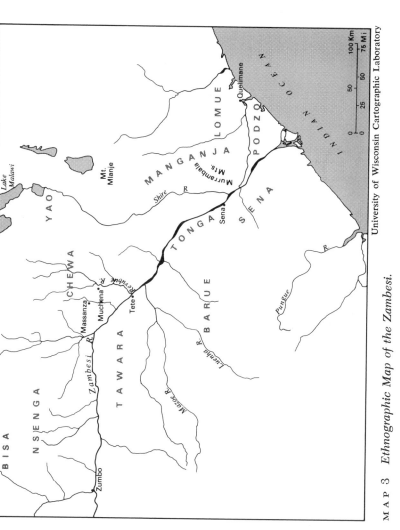

MAP 3 *Ethnographic Map of the Zambesi.*

University of Wisconsin Cartographic Laboratory

principal regional and territorial chiefs ordering them to extinguish their royal fires and to proceed to the royal Zimbabwe where they would be rekindled as part of a larger ritual of fidelity. At the death of the reigning Muenemutapa, all fires were extinguished until the selection of his successor, at which time the vassal chiefs were expected to return to the Zimbabwe and ignite their royal flames from that of the new Muenemutapa. Failure to fulfill either ritual obligation was tantamount to treason, and the army would be sent to punish the guilty party.[27]

Despite these unifying rituals and institutions, a number of factors militated against the growth of a highly integrated and centralized state. Among the most important of these were the overextension of the lines of communication, the inability of the army to police the vast regions of the state, and the recurring political intrigue and succession crises at the capital. These exacerbated the internal tensions and centrifugal tendencies in a society which lacked ethnic and cultural homogeneity.[28]

Given these structural weaknesses, it is not surprising that in the period immediately following the final phase of Karanga expansion the Muenemutapa was unable to contain the rebellious activities within his domain. The principal threat came from Changamira, a former shepherd who had been given a region in the central Zezuru plateau as a reward for his outstanding service. Shortly after establishing control over this area, he declared himself independent and, with the help of dissident members of the royal family, began to conquer the areas to the south and west. He built his capital at Abutua and carved out the independent Rozvi state which bore his name. When the Muenemutapa demanded that Changamira drink a toxic potion, the Rozvi king attacked the royal capital, killed the Karanga king, and usurped the throne for several years before he was defeated and killed in battle. Although his heirs never again gained national ascendancy, they transformed Abutua into a great military power which proved to be a constant threat to the Karanga rulers in the succeeding centuries.[29]

Centrifugal pressures within the kingdom increased substantially during the sixteenth century. Some time between Changamira's defection and 1580, Manica, Quiteve, and Sedanda effectively established their independence, although they continued to satisfy certain ritual obligations.[30] During this century Barue also revolted. In 1612 Muenemutapa Gatsi Rusere tried unsuccessfully to reincorporate Barue into the larger Karanga state.[31] A similar pattern occurred in the lower Zambesi where the Muenemutapa's basis of authority was even more precarious. Tonga and Sena chiefs refused to acknowledge his sovereignty and effectively resisted all attempts to reestablish Karanga hegemony.[32] Only the core area appears to have remained intact, and even here the reigning Muenemutapa had to guard against the subversive activities of rebellious kinsmen.

The rapid decline of the Karanga state increased the relative importance of Barue, Quiteve, and Manica. Having achieved their independence, they expanded the frontiers of their territories to include areas which had formerly belonged to their Karanga overlord. They also benefited from the growing trade with the Arabs and the Portuguese, who competed fiercely for their gold and ivory.[33]

Despite these early successes, the newly independent kingdoms were by no means secure. Manica, constantly threatened by the armies of Changamira, was ultimately conquered in the 1690s. Rivalries between Quiteve and Manica, the military campaigns of the Muenemutapa, and the rebellious activities of the Tonga resulted in a series of costly military confrontations.[34]

Apart from these external threats, there is some evidence that they suffered, albeit less severely, from the same types of structural weakness as the Karanga. This would not be surprising, since these states seem to have been organized along lines similar to those of the Muenemutapa. In the seventeenth century there are scattered reports of prolonged succession struggles in Quiteve and the inability of the king to control the outlying districts. Similarily, the ease with which individual Portuguese gained control over the frontier areas of Barue and Manica suggests the weakness of the central authority.[35]

THE MALAWIAN EXPANSION

While the Karanga were expanding the frontiers of their kingdom, Malawi immigrants were involved in a similar process of state formation in the area to the north of the Zambesi. Most traditions indicate that the early Malawians, under the leadership of Kalonga Chinkhole, migrated from the Katanga region in the fifteenth or sixteenth century.[36] By 1614 they arrived at their present home, Mankhoma, adjacent to the southern tip of Lake Malawi.[37]

Having established his capital at Mankhoma, Kalonga (the positional title which all Chinkole's successors adopted) sent his principal matrilineal kinsmen to subjugate and govern the entire region north of the Zambesi. Kaphwiti and Lundu migrated south to the Shire area, and Undi moved westward with his followers conquering the areas north of Tete (see Map 4).[38]

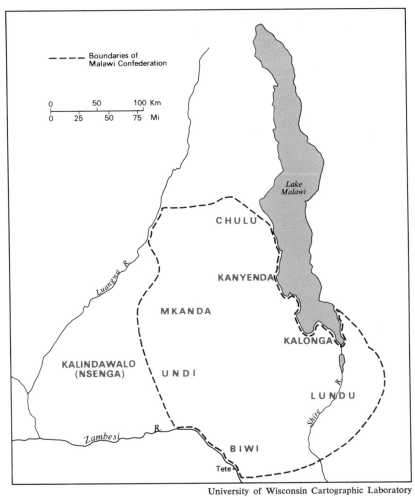

University of Wisconsin Cartographic Laboratory

MAP 4   *The Malawi Confederation.* Source: Harry Langworthy, "A History of Undi to 1890" (Ph.D. diss., Boston University, 1969), Map 1, "The Malawi Area."

Long-distance trade seems to have served as the principal underpinning for the Malawi economy. In the sixteenth and seventeenth centuries the Zambesian entrepôts of Quelimane, Sena, and Tete and the island of Mozambique served as major outlets for Malawian products. Kalonga appears to have retained a theoretical monopoly over the external sale of ivory, which was the most important trading commodity.

The king granted charters for such trade to several territorial chiefs. But as his authority diminished it became a common practice for the more distant chiefs to trade freely without his approbation.[39]

Apart from their commercial links with the Zambesi, successive Malawian kings seem to have emerged as important power brokers in the politics of the region. By the beginning of the seventeenth century Malawi's military might had reached its apogee. In 1608, for example, Kalonga Mazura sent 4000 troops to help defeat the enemies of the Muenemutapa.[40] Fifteen years later, he again dispatched an expedition to the southern bank of the Zambesi, hoping to take advantage of the impending succession crisis in the kingdom of the Muenemutapa.[41] In 1630 and 1631 Malawian troops, reputedly numbering 20,000, were again instrumental in crushing a major Karanga revolt.[42]

Thirty years later Kalonga's domain reportedly embraced the area from the Nsenga homelands in the west to the East African coast and the entire region along the Indian Ocean from the Zambesi to Mozambique Island.[43] Yet, by the middle of the following century, the entire Malawian state had collapsed.[44] While the exact cause remains unknown, succession crises, the defection of Kalonga's royal mother and sister, the lack of control over the principal raincaller, Makewana, and increased centrifugal pressure were all contributing factors.[45]

Kalonga's state was not the only Malawian polity to undergo successive phases of expansion, consolidation, and decline in the seventeenth and early eighteenth centuries. A similar pattern characterized Manganja.[46] Some time in the sixteenth century, Kalonga sent two junior kinsmen, Kaphwiti and Lundu, south to incorporate the lands on the banks of the Shire. Kaphwiti, who was the senior of the two, settled with his followers near the northern part of Lake Chilwa and had only limited contact with the Zambesi region to the south. Lundu and his supporters migrated further south to the lower Shire and established a capital at Chikawa.[47]

By the middle of the seventeenth century Lundu governed an area whose southern border extended along the Zambesi for more than 150 miles and whose northern frontier encompassed the area inland from Quelimane and perhaps as far up the coast as Angoche. At one point Lundu even refused to recognize Kalonga as his superior, despite the fact that the Malawian king was at the height of his power. Even after Lundu was subdued, he and his successors still retained control over Manganja.[48]

Lundu's power deteriorated in subsequent decades. By the middle of the eighteenth century, Manganja no longer remained a dominant Zambesian power. Local accounts described the southern part of Manganja as being divided into a number of relatively autonomous chieftaincies. Although Lundu still retained vestiges of authority, he was either unwilling or unable to defend these frontier districts against attack. While it is impossible to determine the exact cause or causes for Lundu's decline, they were probably similar to those which affected Kalonga — recurring succession struggles, the ascension of one or a number of relatively weak leaders, the defection of frontier provinces, and increased Yao competition.[49]

The decline of Kalonga and Lundu left Undi, king of the Chewa, as the most powerful Malawian ruler. Some time before 1614 he had departed from Mankhoma and had established his royal capital at Mano (see Map 3).[50] During this formative period Undi appointed his closest matrilineal kinsmen as governors of important territorial units. Chewa chiefs were also sent west to establish their hegemony over the neighboring Nsenga.

The Undi reigned at the apex of the political system, serving as supreme ruler and owner of the land. The provincial chiefs, who were generally immediate kinsmen of Undi, acted at the next level of authority. They were acknowledged as *mwini dziko*, since they were the perpetual owners of all the land within their domains. They also carried the title of mambo, which throughout the Zambesi signified a major land chief. Each province contained a number of territorial chiefs who were also recognized as owners of the land although they were differentiated from their superiors by the positional title of *mfumu*. While in most cases Undi appointed distant kinsmen to these positions, he also rewarded a number of nonrelated followers for performing outstanding service. At the lowest level of authority were the village headmen known both as *mwini mudzi* and mfumu, who were the senior guardians of the local matrilineal segment.[51]

The various chiefs enjoyed a relatively autonomous position with complete jurisdiction over internal matters. They assigned land to subordinates, received annual tribute, resolved the principal disputes, directed the rain and first fruits ceremonies, and were responsible for the defense of their areas. Each had a royal council composed of junior relatives and principal subordinates. The council members assisted the chief in judicial and administrative matters.[52]

Unlike other central African polities, the Chewa lacked specialized officeholders in either the political or military spheres.[53] Undi relied solely on his council and his territorial and local representatives. He derived his religious and secular powers from his position as ultimate owner of the land. He had the theoretical right to appoint and remove all subordinate chiefs and was the principal link with the royal ancestors who were considered the national guardians. The mechanism of positional succession reinforced his ties to the ancestors since each reigning Undi was thought to be the embodiment of all his predecessors. As owner of the land, Undi received the larger tusk of any elephant which died within his domain, as well as periodic taxes and labor services. The ivory payment was not only a symbolic recognition of his ultimate authority but enabled him to trade for prestigious imported products, part of which he redistributed to his principal subordinates.[54]

Despite these theoretical powers, Undi's actual control outside the core area was often quite limited. The decentralized political system and the lack of a national army permitted internal conflicts and allowed powerful chiefs to secede, often to be faced with similar problems within their own domains. Added to these structural weaknesses was each Undi's dependence on the powerful raincaller, Makewana. Because of her supernatural origin she could consult directly with the dieties and had greater control over the elements than did Undi, who had to rely on the goodwill of the royal ancestors for divine assistance. Unlike the svikiro mediums in the Muenemutapa's kingdom, Makewana and her subordinate raincallers did not always exercise their authority in a manner designed to bolster the institution of kingship. Given these challenges to centralized authority, it is not surprising that the Chewa state probably began to decline shortly after it was established.[55]

Nowhere was this centrifugal tendency more pronounced than in Makanga, a region bordering on the northern bank of the Zambesi. By the middle of the eighteenth century, this province, under the leadership of Biwi, had broken away from the central government. Written sources treat Undi's supposed subordinate Biwi as if he were autonomous. Within Makanga, however, Biwi seems to have suffered a corresponding decline in power. Although still recognized as being more important than the neighboring chiefs, his effective authority seems to have been restricted to a relatively limited area.[56]

THE PORTUGUESE ARRIVAL IN THE ZAMBESI

The Portuguese had founded their first settlement in Mozambique at Sofala in 1505. Within twenty years individual merchants and adventurers migrated inland in order to dislodge the Arab traders and to gain access to the reputed gold mines of the Queen of Sheba. They established commercial and administrative centers at intermittent points along the Zambesi, of which the most important were located at Sena and Tete (see Map 2). By the end of the century they had effectively eliminated their Arab competitors and had discovered that gold was not nearly so abundant as they had thought. The Zambesi, nevertheless, offered a number of commercial advantages as well as the opportunity to acquire large tracts of fertile land. As a result, a small but continuous migration of Portuguese occurred throughout the seventeenth century.[57]

This influx took place at a particularly auspicious time. The inability of the Muenemutapa and the Malawian kings to retain effective control over the margins of the Zambesi created a power vacuum in this region. In part, this phenomenon can be explained in terms of the peculiar geopolitical position of the Zambesi, which fell just outside the frontier of a number of states and was considered to be an unimportant area. The willingness of Undi, Muenemutapa, and the King of Quiteve to part with their holdings in this zone during the seventeenth century confirms its minor significance. It also suggests the impossibility of containing the fissiparous pressures which characterized political relations in the Zambesi. The subsequent process of prazo formation only makes sense in light of these conditions, which continued to exist until the nineteenth century.

2

The Process of Prazo Formation: An Historical Overview, ca. 1650 to ca. 1850

Historians of the prazos have advanced a number of hypotheses to explain the origin of the institution. These can be divided into three schools: first, that they were an Arabic institution introduced by early Muslim traders; second, that they were the product of a simple conquest-substitution process in which individual Portuguese replaced local African chiefs; third, that they were a transplanted Portuguese feudal institution. Apart from specific weaknesses, all three explanations suffer from a lack of understanding of Zambesian institutions, an overemphasis on alien military exploits, and an implicit assumption that the historical development of an individual estate paralleled that of the system as a whole. (See Appendix B for an historiographical note.)

There is, however, no correlation between the stability of the system and the life span of the component estates. Individual prazos underwent recurring phases of formation, consolidation, and decline, which varied substantially in detail and duration. Prazo formation, therefore, cannot be viewed as an isolated phenomenon which occurred at one point in time. Instead it needs to be seen as a continuing process in which Portuguese, mestizo, or Indian colonists acquired recognition as political chiefs over an African population. As a result these alien overlords gained specific prerogatives which had previously belonged to the Zambesi chiefs. The existence of similar indigenous political relations facilitated this transfer of power to the prazero. This authority role was probably not very different from the earlier pattern that had existed between the Tonga, Sena, and Chewa chiefs and their alien Karanga and Malawi rulers.

A number of local factors as well as the personal relationship between the prazero and the indigenous authorities determined the acceptability of the overlord. These factors varied considerably over time. The one important constant was that this recognition occurred in a relatively fluid political climate marked by the absence of any form of state system.

Through conquest, or threats of punitive action, a number of prazeros gained control over small Tonga, Sena, and Malawian chieftaincies on the margins of the Zambesi. The basis of the prazero's power was his large *achikunda*,[1] or slave, army, which he acquired through slave raids, purchase, and the indigenous practice of voluntary enslavement.[2] It was not uncommon for such powerful early prazeros as António Lobo da Silva to own 4000 to 5000 slaves,[3] and one prazero was reputed to have 15,000 slaves.[4]

It is more difficult to assess the effect of firearms in altering the balance of power. There is little doubt that they had certain advantages over the hunting bow, and the various types of spears and knives which the indigenous populations possessed.[5] Since the guns were relatively primitive, however, they probably provided little technological superiority. During this early period, moreover, it is questionable whether guns were widely distributed among the achikunda and whether the Portuguese were able to retain a monopoly on firearms. What seems most probable is that the guns merely added to the general power advantage which the early prazeros already enjoyed over the small Zambesi chieftaincies.[6]

Perhaps the highpoint of the prazeros' military activity occurred in the middle of the seventeenth century when such powerful estate owners as Lourenço de Mattos (known by his African name, Maponda), Sisnando Bayão (Massuampaca), António Lobo da Silva (Nhema), and Manoel Paes de Pinha conquered many of the Sena-Tonga chieftaincies and made substantial inroads in the areas north of the Zambesi. They did not, however, limit their military activities to the smaller chieftaincies adjacent to the Zambesi. During this expansive phase Lobo da Silva conquered Barue, Bayão annexed a portion of Quiteve, and Manica became part of the informal empire of several powerful prazeros.[7]

As a result of changing conditions in the Zambesi Valley, the Portuguese gradually lost their preeminent military position. The inherently unstable nature of the prazos and recurring inter-prazo wars led to the decline of most of the families which had dominated the region in the seventeenth century.[8] Despite the high price of warfare, fierce military and political competition continued into the eighteenth century. According to an anonymous document dating from the early eighteenth century, these hostilities frequently resulted in the destruction of both warring parties,[9] and by 1730 most of the remaining great prazos were in decay and others were totally abandoned.[10]

Their demise and Lisbon's attempt to increase the settler population led to the proliferation of a number of smaller prazos in the period after 1750. These new estate owners, however, lacked the military power of their predecessors. Although there were still a few older families who could send several thousand slaves to conquer a neighboring chieftaincy, the vast majority of the newer prazeros rarely owned more than a few hundred slaves.[11] Furthermore, throughout the latter part of the eighteenth century and early part of the nineteenth, there was a progressive decline in the size of the slave population on the prazos, which can be traced to the emergence of the Brazilian slave trade. By 1826, the majority of the prazeros in Sena had only twenty to thirty slaves.[12]

While military action remained an important component of prazo formation, simple conquest was rarely effective in the eighteenth and nineteenth centuries. The apparent resurgence of Quiteve, Barue, and the kingdom of the Muenemutapa not only eliminated the possibility of Portuguese military expansion, but also led to the conquest of a number of prazos bordering on their frontiers.[13]

The prazeros' intimate involvement in local African politics seems to have been equally important in the overall process of prazo formation. As a result of unstable political relationships, recurring conflicts, and the general power vacuum, individual prazeros acquired a disproportionate amount of influence. By adeptly manipulating their power or by actively allying themselves with one of the combatants, they were able to establish or extend their authority. On several occasions Undi, Macombe, the king of Barue, Chikanga, the king of Quiteve, and the Muenemutapa sought the assistance of powerful prazeros or inland traders. In compensation for military aid or for assurances of future protection, they offered the prazeros outlying regions of their kingdoms which were generally in revolt or of questionable loyalty.

These gifts, as well as the land purchases of later prazeros,[14] carried with them the same abstract political prerogatives which the king had formerly transmitted to his district chiefs. The prazero still required the recognition of the descendants of the founding lineage, however, to govern effectively. There are numerous examples of chiefs who refused to accept such overlordship; they either migrated to another area [15] or actively resisted the bid for power.[16]

The relationship between Sisnando Bayão and the king of Quiteve illustrates the intimate connection between early prazeros and African sovereigns. Bayão, or Massuampaca, was *capitão* of Sena and the Rios de Cuama and was generally depicted as the archetype of the conquering prazero.[17] It is significant, therefore, that he did not acquire his most important possession, Prazo Cheringoma, simply through conquest. Around 1640, dissident members of the royal family of Quiteve forced King Berenha to abdicate his throne. Simultaneously, a number of vassal Tonga chieftaincies revolted. In desperation, Berenha sought the aid of Bayão, who helped eliminate both threats. Berenha rewarded Bayão with Cheringoma, which was an outlying area of Quiteve.[18]

The origin of Prazo Makanga serves as an instructive comparison with that of Prazo Cheringoma. Although the general process of formation was similar, it occurred more than a century later among the fragmented Southern Chewa rather than in the relatively centralized Karanga kingdom of Quiteve. This case reveals the types of local factors which were operative throughout the Zambesi and suggests some of the benefits which subordniate chiefs hoped to acquire from a prazero's presence.

Despite several accounts which emphasize the conquest factor, it is apparent that other pressures were operative. Padre Courtois, who had an opportunity to converse with the principal elders of Makanga, offered a different version of the ascension of the Pereiras.[19]

The first to rule the territory of Makanga, the homelands of the Muzimba, was the Goan merchant Pedro Caetano Pereira. After he established a trading center among the Muzimba, several chieftaincies came to ask him for assistance against the rebels who were continually attacking them. Pereira provided arms and powder and gained the trust of his new allies. His stature grew and he was able to assert himself throughout the territory and was recognized as Paramount Chief and received the name Chamatowa — the conqueror.[20]

According to oral traditions gathered in southern Makanga, the mestizo trader Pedro Caetano Pereira, established a very close relationship with Undi shortly after arriving in the area.[21] In a gesture of solidarity, Undi gave either the elder Pereira or his son, known more commonly by his African name, Chicucuru, a maternal relative in marriage. This marriage alliance and subsequent trading agreements proved mutually beneficial. The Pereiras acquired a new source of slaves and ivory, while Undi was able to reduce his dependency on the Yao traders coming from the coast. More important, at Undi's request, the Pereiras brought large quantities of guns and powder from Tete, which were distributed to loyal chiefs. With these new weapons Undi and his supporters crushed a number of revolts. In repayment, Undi gave the

Pereiras the secessionist fringe area known as Makanga. The gift not only carried the customary political rights which Undi conferred on all his territorial chiefs, but also explicitly gave them permission to subjugate hostile chieftaincies. The actual process of incorporation seems to have been conducted under the leadership of Chicucuru.[22]

Informants in Southern Makanga disagree as to how the local afumu received Chicucuru. According to some, the afumu were pleased to have his protection and appreciated the salt and other valuable gifts which he distributed.[23] Other informants relate that the afumu, who had been virtually independent of Undi, refused to recognize Chicucuru, and some, including Kamulankanje and Chidotta, were killed while resisting.[24] Biwi, on the other hand, realized the futility of this action and agreed to recognize Chicucuru's authority.[25] The apparent inconsistencies in the oral data, rather than limiting their value, probably suggest the varied responses to Chicucuru's arrival.

The fissiparous tendencies within the surrounding states also provided an excellent opportunity for prazeros and other inland Portuguese to ally with disenchanted local chiefs who sought independence from their respective sovereigns. This was particularly common when a minor chief felt oppressed or when a conflict with a superior jeopardized his position. Under these circumstances, he either offered his land and his people to an aspiring prazero in return for protection, or he fled to an existing prazo and gave his allegiance in return for land. As early as 1631 it was noted that persecuted vassals of the Muenemutapa had shifted their allegiance to Portuguese overlords.[26] Throughout the eighteenth and nineteenth centuries, many Tonga chiefs who had suffered under the harsh rule of the Barue sought asylum on surrounding Sena prazos. One Tonga mfumu, living on the frontiers of Barue, fled with his followers to Prazo Chemba where his paternal uncle Canzemba was mfumu. Many years earlier Canzemba had escaped from Barue and joined the prazo.[27] These examples indicate both that the prazero did not always initiate recruitment of independent afumu and that lineage relationships were a principal factor in attracting new groups to a prazo.

Similarly, after succession struggles it was common for the unsuccessful claimants or deposed chiefs to flee to nearby prazos. In the 1790s, Zenhenbe, a junior relative of Macombe, unsuccessfully attempted to usurp the king's position. When it became apparent that he lacked the necessary support, he led his followers to Prazo Sungue where they recognized the overlordship of the prazero.[28]

Offering asylum to discontented chiefs was only one way of forming a prazo relationship. Entering military alliances with the indigenous

Zambesi authorities let the prazeros extend their holdings. Threats from the Barue and the nineteenth-century Nguni invaders commonly motivated small Tonga and Sena chieftaincies to recognize the overlordship of a prazero in order to obtain protection.[29] Informants in the area of former Prazo Chemba recall that, after a discussion with the elders, mambo Maya allied his people with Gambete, or António Vaz, as a defense against the Nguni. In response to the same threat, five Tonga chiefs sought to reestablish their historical ties with the prazo system.[30]

Independent amambo and afumu derived other benefits from entering a prazo relationship. In order to acquire recognition, many prazeros found it necessary, or at least advisable, to offer such highly valued trade goods as cloth, salt, and bracelets to the Zambesi sovereigns and to the principal members of the royal family.[31] Imported cloth was very valuable: it replaced barkcloth as the standard item of dress, served as the principal trade commodity and, in some areas, had an important function in the rain ceremony.[32] Throughout the Zambesi the scarcity of salt made it particularly attractive and valuable.[33] These gifts enhanced the prestige of the indigenous authorities and through their selective redistribution helped to secure the loyalty of their principal subordinates.

Despite the recurring phenomenon of prazo formation and the stability of the institution as a whole, individual prazos exhibited a short life span. Inherent in the nature of the institution were two structural weaknesses which tended to undermine the prazero's authority. First, since the prazero lacked any traditional legitimacy, he operated from a poorly defined position which often brought him into conflict with the indigenous authorities whose cooperation he needed to retain his overlord position. Even when a prazero was able to acquire a certain sanction from the ruling family, it was of a personal rather than a structural nature. This meant both that the royal approval could be withdrawn and that each new prazero, whether relative or stranger, faced the same difficulties as his predecessors. Without the approbation of the mambo, the prazero had no alternative but to govern by force, and this invariably led either to armed opposition or to migrations from his land. Secondly, the prazero's reliance on his slave army compounded his tenuous position since the loyalty of the achikunda was not absolute. Under a strong slave leader, or *mukazambo*, the achikunda were a threat to any prazero who abused his position or, through carelessness or oversight, abdicated his authority.

In addition to these structural weaknesses, the threat of invasion persisted, especially for those prazos located on the frontiers of Barue, the Muenemutapa, and the Malawi states. Not only were they vulnerable to a planned attack, but they often found themselves invaded when a succession crisis or internal feud spilled onto their lands. Historic rivalries among prazo families proved to be the cause of additional turmoil and destruction.

A relatively unproductive agricultural system aggravated the latent instability of the prazos. Because the achikunda rarely farmed, the resources of the colonos were strained to satisfy the consumption requirements of the slave army. In the best years, agricultural production barely met these internal needs. The low level of production also meant that lack of rain or other natural disasters would lead to severe food shortages. Under these circumstances, competition for food increased the tensions between different groups on the prazos. The achikunda were particularly abusive during these periods and used their power to rob the colonos of their limited foodstuffs. Famines increased the propensity of the colonos to migrate from the prazos to areas in the interior in search of food and to free themselves from the burden of supporting the achikunda. It was even common for the prazero to free a number of slaves when he could no longer afford to feed them.[34]

Given these structural weaknesses, the threat of invasion, and the periodic famines, it is not surprising that the prazos were individually unstable. In the district of Sena, during the second half of the eighteenth century, for example, almost one-half of the estates had a life span of under ten years and many of these functioned for less than half this period.[35] Data from the early nineteenth century indicates a dramatic increase in the mortality rate.[36]

An overview of the Zambesi during this 200-year period suggests a very fluid situation. The general pattern seems to have been a relatively high turnover among prazeros and a relatively short life span of any one estate. While it is more difficult to describe precisely the situation among the Africans, the evidence indicates that the small chieftaincies periodically entered into and withdrew from the prazo system. Thus, although the Portuguese government regarded the entire lower Zambesi as crown land, the actual configuration of operating prazos varied from decade to decade and year to year.

3

The Political Organization of the Prazos
1750-1850

The ability of the prazeros to acquire local recognition depended upon their willingness to acknowledge the sanctity of the royal family and the legitimacy of the traditional political process. Rarely did they attempt to remove the aboriginal chiefs,[1] and there is no evidence that they sought to restructure the indigenous system. Instead, they imposed an entirely new set of political institutions on top of the existing structure. These formed the basis of a nontraditional administrative system which the prazero personally directed and staffed with his slaves. Before examining the division of authority on the prazos, it is necessary to sketch the broad outlines of the traditional political structure of the Zambesi peoples who were incorporated into the system.[2]

THE INDIGENOUS POLITICAL SYSTEM

By the middle of the seventeenth century the decline of the major Karanga and Malawi states had enabled a number of Zambesian chieftaincies to reassert their independence. Each indigenous polity was governed by a land chief,[3] whose legitimacy was based upon real or fabricated links with the founding lineage or subsequent conquering groups. Among the Southern Chewa, many of the afumu were aboriginal chiefs who were in power at the time of Undi's conquest. Because they chose not to resist the invaders, they were allowed to retain their positions. Others were followers of Undi who received territorial

24

gifts in exchange for their services. These aliens gained recognition as land chiefs through the depositions of the indigenous chiefs, marriage alliances, or perpetual kinship relationships.

Similarly, among the Tawara living in the area of Tete the mambo's position reflected his direct blood relationship with either the aboriginal lineage or the conquering Karanga group.[4] Sena and Tonga also used the principal of first-arrival to explain and legitimize the royal family's position. They claimed that their amambo were the first inhabitants of the area; subsequent stranger groups who migrated into the region recognized them as the rightful owners of the land.[5]

Although possessing similar patterns of organization, the Zambesi chieftaincies varied in their specific configurations. The larger chiefdoms were governed by a mambo who was assisted by a local chief, known as mfumu or inhacuau, and by village headmen. Most chieftaincies had only two levels of authority, with the mambo governing directly through the mfumu.[6]

The mambo delegated a limited amount of administrative and judicial authority to junior kinsmen and members of the dominant local lineage. The subordinates, or afumu, resolved minor disputes, transmitted and enforced the dictates of the mambo, and collected appropriate taxes. Junior relatives and village elders also provided various types of bureaucratic assistance when necessary.[7]

In addition to these local officials, the land chief received counsel from a body of advisers which met regularly at his *muzinda*, the royal village. It generally included the principal members of the royal family, the afumu, and respected elders. The council considered legal and political questions and suggested appropriate action to the mambo. There were also a group of messengers who transmitted the mambo's orders to his various subordinates. Among the Tawara, the messenger, or *tsantamba*, carried with him the mambo's walking stick as a sign of his legitimacy.[8] There is no evidence that any of these chieftaincies had a standing army.[9] In times of emergency, all male members of the chieftaincies united under the direction of their mfumu or mambo to defend their lands.

Among the Zambesi peoples, the land chief retained final judicial authority. With the assistance of his counsel, he decided all legal disputes which his subordinates could not resolve or which were outside the realm of their responsibility. Minor litigations, such as drunkenness, small thefts, and family quarrels were initially resolved at the local level. The displeased party, however, could appeal to the land chief for a redress of his grievances. The more serious cases, especially those which threatened to disrupt the internal stability of the chieftaincy, were brought directly to the land chief. These included accusations of murder, violent assault, and witchcraft.[10] The land chief also resolved quarrels among afumu or between different villages. The principal causes of these disturbances were boundary disputes, violation of hunting and fishing monopolies, crop destruction, and thievery.[11]

After the mambo resolved a case, he determined the amount of compensation to be paid to the victim or his lineage members.[12] In all cases brought before the land chief, the guilty party had to compensate the mambo as well as pay a fine for his misdeeds. Specified amounts of cloth, livestock, slaves, or some other valuable commodity were associated with different crimes. The mambo then distributed a portion of these goods to his counsellors and used the rest for his own needs.[13]

In addition to resolving serious crimes and local disputes, the land chief presided over all cases which posed a threat to his authority or involved the safety of the chieftaincy. Thus when a hunter failed to present the land chief with a specified portion of the game killed within the chieftaincy, he was brought before the mambo and fined.[14] Similarly, a subordinate official who was dishonest or disloyal could expect to be dismissed and punished in accordance with the seriousness of his act.[15]

As the direct descendant of the founding or conquering lineage, the Zambesi chiefs were the ultimate owners and guardians of the traditional lands. In this capacity, they had the sole right to alienate the territory within their chieftaincy. They initially distributed such grants to junior kinsmen and strangers who were willing to recognize their authority. These subordinates in turn allocated parcels to their own kinsmen or followers. The recipient alone could farm the lands, pick the trees, and hunt and gather within his designated area. He owned all the products of his labor and could sell them as he pleased. Despite the fact that his heirs had first claim to the land, he could neither sell nor lease it. When the land was vacated it automatically reverted back to the sovereign.[16]

All the inhabitants within the chieftaincy had to pay an annual tax or *mutsonko*, which reaffirmed the mambo's ownership of the land.[17] The tax seems to have been quite small, usually a bushel or two of sorghum or a comparable number of goats, sheep, or chickens. The mambo also received a series of symbolic gifts. These included the larger tusk of any elephant which died within his chieftaincy and the prescribed parts of any other animal killed on his lands.[18]

The land chief served as the principal link between the people and the royal ancestors' spirits, or mizimu. He performed a number of religious ceremonies to propitiate the mizimu and to gain their assistance and guidance. He organized and directed the rain ceremony, which was the most significant of his ritual responsibilities. With the assistance of his followers, he beseeched the mizimu to intercede directly with the murungu, or dieties, to assure abundant rainfall and the continued fertility of the land. The mizimu were the Africans' only link with the supernatural, and their gratification was crucial, therefore, to the well-being of the chieftaincy.[19]

In the early fall and during periods of famine, for example, the Sena mambo directed the women of his chieftaincy to make fresh beer and place it in a hole dug in the middle of the forest. Various other offerings were then placed around it. The elders then lay down in a circular pattern around the offerings while the younger people remained in the background and danced. When the beer fermented, the mambo was summoned from his muzinda. Upon his arrival, he dismissed his followers and ordered them to return to their villages without looking back toward the ritual area. He then covered the hole, picked up two ritual sticks, *mbuemba* and *nidcua,* and proceeded to summon the spirits of his ancestors. When he completed the invocation, he cast the two sticks on the covered hole and, according to tradition, it began to rain.[20] The Tonga, Tawara, and Chewa chiefs performed similar rituals at prescribed times of the year.[21]

In addition to the rain ceremony, the local land chiefs consulted the mizimu prior to making important decisions. Before migrating to new lands, for example, the chief and his advisors visited the prospective site and left a handful of grain in the center of the location for a twenty-four-hour period. If the grain remained intact, it meant that the mizimu were displeased and a new site was sought. Similarly, before going to war, the land chief and his followers prepared a great feast to the mizimu to discover the advisability of such an action and to seek their aid in battle. Offerings were also made before a major hunt to insure the success of the expedition and during first-fruit ceremonies at the harvest.[22]

The direct links with the royal ancestors legitimized the land chief's position and simultaneously reinforced his prestige and authority in secular matters. The people turned to the mambo for leadership and security with the knowledge that his special relationship to the mizimu provided them with an indirect nexus to the supernatural. Furthermore, at least some Tawara and Chewa chiefs were thought to have acquired powerful remedies against witchcraft and diseases as a result of their intimate ties with the mizimu.[23]

THE ROLE OF THE LAND CHIEF ON THE PRAZOS

The recognition of a prazero did not radically alter the intimate relationship between the land chief and the indigenous population. This role continuity can be explained in part by the relatively distant physical and political position of the prazero. A more important factor, however, was the prestige and obedience which only the mambo could command as both the legitimate heir of the royal lineage and the principal intermediary between his people and the mizimu. Although the land chief was no longer independent, and in certain important areas lacked ultimate authority, he always retained the status and influence embodied in kingship.[24] Even in the extreme cases where the prazero was able to reduce the land chief to total subservience, he still had to govern through the mambo.

On most estates the mambo continued to resolve all principal disputes and retained ultimate judicial authority. In theory, the colonos could appeal their decision to the prazero and even to the state-appointed judge. The Africans rarely followed this procedure, however, since they preferred to have their cases adjudicated within the traditional legal structures.

The royal family also retained its right to appoint the local afumu and select the new mambo.[25] There were a few scattered examples where the prazero attempted to arbitrarily remove a particular mambo or mfumu, but there is no evidence that this was done systematically.[26] In general, a mfumu or mambo was replaced only when he died or became physically unfit to govern. When a village headman passed away, members of his village gathered with the approval of the mambo and selected his heir.[27] If the village headman did not have any heirs, or if these were considered incompetent, another respected resident of the village was appointed. After the land chief confirmed the appointment, this information was forwarded to the prazero. Sometimes the new headman also visited him, but this was merely a token presentation.[28]

When the land chief died, the principal members of the royal family selected his successor in accordance with the customary rules of descent. The mambo then went to the prazero, who confirmed his appointment and presented the new land chief with a token gift.[29]

Any attempt to interfere in this process was met by opposition and, often, revolt. On Prazo Chemba, for example, when the prazero appointed one of his slaves as mambo, the indigenous population rebelled. Led by the royal family, they attempted to drive the prazero away. Only with the assistance of his large slave army did he defeat them.[30]

The prazero's dependence on brute force, even when successful, indicated his precarious position. Without at least the tacit cooperation of the aboriginal leaders, few prazeros could hope to retain their authority for a sustained period of time.

Among the Africans, the mambo continued to be recognized as guardian of the traditional lands. For this reason, they still paid him the annual mutsonko as well as the ivory tusks and specified parts of dead game. The taxes and tribute were then transferred to the prazero, whom the land chief recognized as his overlord. On most prazos, the members of the royal family were also required to present the prazero with a symbolic gift.[31] What is more significant is that the indigenous population generally presented additional taxes or gifts to the mambo as a sign of its continued loyalty and recognition of his authority.[32]

The prazero's presence in no way impinged upon the religious role of the land chief. He continued to organize the rain ceremony and to consult the mizimu.[33] On many estates the prazero acknowledged the mambo's religious preeminence. Not only was it common for him to seek the mambo's assistance in times of drought or famine, but the mizimu were often invoked before the prazero went to war.[34] Obviously, the extent to which prazeros transferred religious recognition to the land chief varied greatly from one to another and was related to their shifting world views.[35]

THE PRAZERO AS OVERLORD

As political chief, albeit a distant one, the prazero did acquire a number of privileges and prerogatives which had formerly belonged to the mambo. Because he lacked traditional legitimacy, however, his role was relatively undefined. The exact nature of his position and the amount of power he exerted depended on his personal relationship with the mambo and, to a lesser degree, on the size of his military force. Since both factors differed substantially from one prazo to another, they help to explain the varying degrees of authority which individual prazeros enjoyed.

Underlying the prazero's position was the land chief's recognition, at least in theory, of his suzerainty. This affirmation was usually consummated by a simple exchange of gifts as a sign of friendship and fidelity.[36] Occasionally it was consummated more dramatically by traditional rites of investiture which included a symbolic marriage between the mambo and the prazero and the exchange of gifts. After the ceremony, the mambo clapped his hands as a sign of loyalty and subordination.[37] These ceremonies occurred both when a new prazero arrived and when a new land chief was selected.

A number of prazeros entered marriage alliances with the royal family to reinforce their links with the mambo and to provide a basis of legitimacy for their heirs.[38] Other estateholders sought to legitimize their position by adopting the trappings of kingship. One early Portuguese estateholder reputedly could invoke the mizimu to bring the rains.[39] Pedro Caetano Pereira adopted the Undi's praise name, Chissaca, and was believed to have remedies derived from the ancestors which made him invincible,[40] and Gouveia carried a royal drum.[41] On the estates, the Africans acknowledged, at least overtly, the prazero's preeminent position. When, on rare occasions, he visited the village areas, the colonos greeted him with rhythmic handclapping, chants, and prostrations. These rituals of fidelity previously had been reserved solely for the mambo.[42]

By virtue of his position, the prazero acquired significant economic and political benefits relinquished by the mambo. The Zambesi chiefs

T A B L E 1   *Mutsonko Collected on Prazo Cheringoma*

Muzinda	Manchilla (arms' length?)	Chickens	Honey (pots)	Wax	Meat (pots)	Dried Fish	Massa
Bava	25	25	5	60	4	0	0
Urbuy	60	60	4	48	2	0	0
Samira	30	30	0	0	2	3000	30
Quisanza	12	12	0	0	2	1000	20
Cangane	38	38	0	0	2	1500	30
Queze	18	18	0	0	1	0	20
V'anca	9	9	1	12	1	0	20
Ondue	14	14	1	12	1	0	20
Rupangara	10	10	3	36	2	0	20
Inhaminga	5	5	1	12	1	0	20
Masanza	5	5	1	12	0	0	0
Chambo	3	3	1	12	0	0	0
Inhamgoma	5	5	1	12	0	0	0
Nhamute	5	5	1	12	1	0	0
Tendiri	11	11	1	12	1	0	0
Inhaputera	3	3	1	12	0	0	0
Chimxere	21	21	4	48	4	0	0
Inhamusapa	24	24	4	48	4	0	0
Bandori	7	7	0	0	0	0	0
Macaya	26	26	0	0	0	0	0

Source: A.N.T.T., Ministério do Reino, Maço 604: "Rendimento da ditta terra, a que se chama missonco, que hé o nésmo, que dizimos dos viveres, que produzem a terra" (unsigned, undated).

were no longer the ultimate recipients of the symbolic tribute. Although the hunters continued the historic practice of presenting the larger tusk and prescribed parts of the animal to the mambo, he forwarded these to the estate owner. The prazero then gave both the mambo and the hunter small gifts in return.[43]

The mambo also yielded his claim to the traditional taxes. The village headmen collected the mutsonko and then forwarded it to the mambo who passed it on to the prazero's personal agent.[44] In payment for this service, the prazero often redistributed a portion of the mutsonko to the mambo and his subordinates. On Prazo Tipue Segundo almost one-third of the *manchilla*, or locally fabricated cloth, which the prazero received was presented to the land chief.[45]

TABLE 2 *Annual Mutsonko Collected on Prazos Cheringoma and Teve Teve (Principal Products)*

Bares of Ivory	10
Arms' Length of Cloth	1257
Balls of Wax	20
Pots of Honey	48
Chickens	557
Pots of Oil	21
Dried Meat	28
Dried Fish	6000
Bushels of Sorghum	5000

Source: A.N.T.T., Ministério do Reino, Maço 604: "Rezumo Geral do Rendimento da Terra Chiringoma, e Teve Teve" (unsigned, undated).

The exact content of the mutsonko varied substantially from one prazo to another as did the amount and total value assessed each family. On some estates, the traditional payments were continued while on others the mutsonko were substantially increased.[46] One observer noted that the value of the mutsonko was in direct proportion to the military force which the prazero possessed.[47] Even within the same prazo, the actual tax collected varied from year to year and reflected both the relative economic prosperity of the local population and the ability of the prazero to assert his authority.[48] (See Tables 1 and 2.)

The prazero also acquired the right to settle people on "his" lands. He rarely disturbed the residence patterns of the indigenous population and usually selected unused lands to build villages for his achikunda. Stranger groups which were actively recruited to the prazo no longer sought permission from the land chief but negotiated directly with the prazero. While this reduced the mambo's authority within the prazos, it did not affect his status among his traditional followers.[49]

On some estates, the prazero gained ultimate judicial authority. On Prazo Caya, Henriques Ferrão judged all murders and other serious crimes which the mambo was unable to resolve. He also meted out punishment and collected a fine from the guilty party.[50] Lacerda noted that many other prazeros adjudicated in the most despotic and absolute manner.[51] The extent of the prazero's juridical involvement depended upon his relationship with the land chiefs. Where the prazero was well respected or particularly powerful he tended to retain greater control over important secular questions.[52] Such prazeros, however, were exceptional. On most estates the indigenous legal processes continued to be used to resolve all cases.[53]

THE NONTRADITIONAL ADMINISTRATIVE SYSTEM

The prazero exerted the greatest authority in those areas that directly affected the internal stability and security of the estate. To reinforce his overlord position, the prazero organized and directed a nontraditional administrative system staffed by slaves who, in theory, owed their ultimate allegiance to the prazero. The slaves supervised the traditional authorities and protected the vital interests of the prazero.

The most important position in this nontraditional administrative sector was that of the chuanga (pl., achuanga), who served as the principal intermediary between the alien overlord and the indigenous land chiefs. Apparently this position derived its origin from the neighboring peoples, and was only slightly modified to meet the particular needs of the estate owners.[54]

The prazero appointed a group of achuanga from among his most trusted slaves to oversee principal villages on his estate. The achuanga generally built their compounds on the outskirts of the royal villages. A small group of slave warriors often resided with the achuanga, serving to reinforce their authority. The principal responsibilities of the achuanga were to transmit the orders of the prazero, to see that they were enforced, and, most important, to spy on the indigenous authorities. The achuanga personally resolved minor infractions against the prazero. When they noted serious opposition or subversive activities, they sent word to the prazero. In this way the prazero was kept informed of the activities of the colonos on his estate.[55]

Although the achuanga lived apart from the local inhabitants and were theoretically not involved in the actual governing of the village or cluster of villages, their mere presence probably influenced all important decisions. It was not uncommon for the achuanga to enter the muzinda when an important question was being resolved or a new mfumu selected. Since the achuanga derived their local authority not from traditional legitimacy but from effective power, their relationship with the afumu was essentially a microcosm of the prazeros' position vis-à-vis the amambo.[56]

The achuanga also supervised the collection of the taxes at harvest time. Approximately one month before the harvest, they toured the area and tied a knot in a rope for each taxpayer. Then the mambo sent out trusted subordinates to the various villages or ordered the village household or lineage heads to bring the mutsonko to his compound. The achuanga either accompanied the subordinates or waited until all the taxes were collected. After comparing the actual mutsonko with the rope count, they sent both back to the prazero so he could make the same calculation. In addition, the achuanga visited the mambo or his subordinates to collect the ivory and other game which belonged to the prazero. For their loyalty, the achuanga received a portion of both.[57]

The prazeros also employed the achuanga as internal purchasing agents. In plentiful years, the achuanga bought the colonos' surplus sorghum, maize, rice, and other agricultural products. This was the *inhamucangamiza*, or forced sale, since the achuanga offered much less than the market value for these goods. Before the transactions began they presented the mambo and mfumu with specified amounts of cloth to enlist their support. The mambo and mfumu, however, generally resented this practice, not only because it angered their supporters, but also because they often had the biggest fields and therefore the most to lose. Despite local opposition, the achuanga could usually persuade or force the colonos to cooperate.[58]

As a means of enforcing his authority, the prazero deployed a slave army at strategic points on his estate. Its size ranged from twenty to thirty men on smaller prazos to several thousand on such large estates as Cheringoma, Gorongoza, and Luabo.[59] The slaves were divided into sections and each lived in a separate compound or village. A muka-zambo (pl., *akazambo*) or *kazembe* governed each regiment. They were personally appointed by and were ultimately responsible to the prazero. The akazambo were selected on the basis of their professed loyalty and outstanding service, their physical prowess as soldiers, and the respect and obedience which they commanded among the achikunda.[60]

Within each section, the position of the mukazambo approximated that of the mambo. "*Mucazambos* are almost similar to the *Manamam-bos* in the dominions of the lands of their landlords," one prazero wrote, "but they do not descend from royal blood."[61] With the assistance of a *badzo*, an assistant slave chief, and an unofficial council of elders, the mukazambo possessed nearly absolute political and judicial authority.[62] The prazero did, however, retain ultimate authority, which he asserted in cases that affected the internal security of the prazos. Moreover, the mukazambo's potential power was somewhat restricted, for, unlike the mambo, he could be dismissed or demoted within the slave hierarchy.[63]

Each regiment was divided into a number of squads, which were groups of ten to twelve slaves. A *tsachikunda*, or subchief, whom the prazero appointed, governed each unit. The tsachikunda was responsible only to the mukazambo of his slave section. Orders were transmitted from the slave chief to the various subchiefs. They in turn passed the orders on to their deputies. Like the mukazambo, any slave official who was inefficient or suspect could be removed.[64]

The achikunda emerged as a powerful military class, armed with European muskets, whose principal function was to police the local populations. Thus, when the chuanga reported that an individual or village had refused to obey the prazero, a slave squad was sent to punish the recalcitrant party. Similarly, when rebellion spread throughout the chieftaincy, the prazero dispatched entire slave sections to defeat the colonos and to punish or kill their mambo or afumu.[65]

In addition to quelling revolts, the achikunda were used to control migrations from the prazos. They were deployed on the frontiers of the estate to prevent individuals or entire chieftaincies from fleeing, and they were sent out to capture any who had escaped. Thus military power represented a significant, if secondary, component for the preservation of the system.

STABILIZING FACTORS IN THE POLITICAL SPHERE

Despite the broad similarities among prazos, the historical development of individual estates was rather uneven. Although many were marginal and had a relatively short life span, there were a small number of stable prazos whose owners continuously played an important role in the Zambesi. These prazeros possessed certain characteristics which, taken together, suggest the basic factors necessary for the perpetuation of the institution as a whole. Other than the acquisition of traditional legitimacy, there was no single attribute which insured stability. Some mixture of all was essential, but the relative importance of each varied from one prazero to another.

The integration of the prazero into the indigenous political system constituted the easiest means of acquiring legitimacy. This process, however, seems to have been an extremely rare phenomenon. The best-documented case is that of the Pereiras, who actually governed Makanga as the recognized royal family for more than one hundred years. Undi gave Chamatowa, eldest of the Pereiras, the secessionist area of Makanga in repayment for his assistance in putting down several revolts. This gift carried with it the same powers and privileges over the conquered lands that Undi had transmitted to his appointed territorial chiefs in the seventeenth century. Chamatowa enhanced his legitimacy when the Undi gave him his sister or niece in marriage, since his descendants could then claim direct links with the Chewa paramount chief. With the aid of a large achikunda army, he curtailed the secessionist tendencies of the local afumu. Through the adoption of African cultural and religious forms and numerous marriage alliances with local chiefs, the Pereiras became integrated into Chewa society. One nineteenth-century observer reported that Pedro Caetano Pereira lived "like the Africans and their chiefs, not only dressing as they do, but adopting their entire way of life, all their superstitions, even having houses full of all the types and qualities of things called remedies." [66]

Informants in Makanga were unable to differentiate between the seventh king of Makanga, Kankuni, who reigned from 1875 to 1886, and the subordinate afumu except by his complexion, which they characterized as "meio Africano." He dressed and lived like the local population, believed in witchcraft, practiced muabvi, had remedies, and knew how to propitiate the mizimu. [67]

The reign of the Pereiras was characterized by general stability, except for occasional succession crises among the various Pereira contenders to the throne. They had acquired the religious and political authority of a Chewa mambo and received the support and counsel of the other afumu. The latter played an active role in determining policy and in choosing the new king of Makanga from among the Pereiras. Even the Portuguese government, which obstinately refused to recognize them except in the capacity of prazeros, was forced to acknowledge them as the legitimate rulers in an 1875 treaty. [68]

Most prazeros, however, did not acquire this legitimacy and had to rely on the sanctions of the royal lineage. They acquired this recognition most effectively by establishing a satisfactory relationship with the mambo and principal headmen. Through prestigious gifts, especially cloth and arms, marriage alliances, and protection against internal opposition and external threats, many prazeros gained the allegiance, at least in the short run, of the indigenous leaders. [69] The gifts and protection the mambo received enhanced his prestige and bolstered his position. He was thus more willing to relinquish absolute authority to a prazero overlord.

Force served more effectively as a complement to, rather than as a substitute for royal sanction. Nevertheless, the absolute power advantage of such prazeros as Dona Ignez Pessoa de Almeida Castelo Branco of Cheringoma, Dona Ignez Garcia de Cardoza of Luabo, and Manoel Gonçalves Gil of Massangano gave them the option of imposing their wills upon the traditional elite. With several thousand slaves, moreover, neither a rebellious mukazambo nor the escape of a small number of slaves could threaten the prazero's authority. Even among the most powerful prazeros, however, the number who had sufficient force to meet every difficulty was quite small. Most had to rely on a relative military advantage, a judicious use of power, and at least the tacit cooperation of the traditional mambo.

The personal prestige of the prazero also contributed to his success. Prestige was derived from such disparate factors as the power of his slave army, his reputed physical prowess, and his possession of remedies which were thought to give him supernatural powers.[70] The evidence suggests that those prazeros who came closest to adopting an African style of life enjoyed the greatest status among the colonos living on their estates. This process of acculturation tended to increase their legitimacy by blurring the differences between the alien overlord and their indigenous subjects. The most successful nineteenth-century prazeros, like the Bongas, the Pereiras, Ferrão, Gambete, and Gouveia, underwent such changes.

The number of generations that one family lived on the same estate was both an indication of past stability and an important factor for future success. While not insuring a favorable relationship with the indigenous chiefs, permanent occupation increased the possibility of developing such a bond. Physical presence also reinforced the family's claim to the land and gave it an opportunity to acquire a large slave army and to establish an efficient administrative system. Finally, it meant that there was no disruptive transition from one prazero to another which might encourage the mambo to reassert his independence.

The history of the Bayão family of Prazo Cheringoma illustrates the significance of a lengthy occupation. Several years after receiving this area from the king of Quiteve, Bayão voluntarily offered it to the king of Portugal on the condition that the rights of settlement would always remain within his family. Except during two short periods, when the crown illegally expropriated the estate, members of his family governed Cheringoma until the 1830s, when Barue and Nguni forces

successively invaded their lands. Throughout this two-hundred-year period, Bayão descendants succeeded in building a large family empire
by adding numerous other prazos to their holdings. Perhaps the high
point of the family's history occurred in the mid-eighteenth century
during the reign of Dona Ignez Pessoa de Almeida Castelo Branco,
who personally owned several other estates besides Cheringoma
and who controlled a slave army of some 6000 achikunda soldiers.[71]

ABUSES AND THE REACTION OF THE AFRICANS

Although Prazos Cheringoma, Makanga and Luabo (see Map 5) were
relatively stable, most estates did not exhibit this quality. The prazero's
attempt to overstep his poorly defined position seems to have been the
immediate cause of dissension and instability on most prazos. According to Governor Lacerda, many prazeros and their achikunda committed acts of violence, imprisonment, and torture with impunity.[72]

These abuses were not limited to harsh physical punishment.
Throughout the eighteenth century prazeros arbitrarily enslaved colonos who lived on their estates. This treatment became particularly common in the latter part of this century when the slave trade increased in
importance.[73] Members of the indigenous population were often arrested for the slightest infraction and, after judging them guilty, prazeros enslaved them and their entire families. On one occasion, when
the owner of Prazo Caya received word of the death of one of his don-
keys, he ordered the driver and members of his family sent to Quelimane for export.[74]

Prazeros also introduced a number of economically exploitative practices, including the sale of agricultural products at deflated prices,
increased taxation, and forced labor. In addition, many retained a trading monopoly on their estates and compelled the indigenous population
to purchase European goods at highly inflated prices.[75]

The most serious transgression involved a variety of plots to undermine the position of the indigenous authorities. Although this does not
seem to have been a common phenomenon, there are a few documented cases. On Prazo Benga two achikunda were dispatched to the
royal muzinda where they ambushed and killed the mambo.[76] On one
occasion, a prazero tried to appoint his trusted mukazambo as mambo
and, on another, exiled the indigenous chief and personally appointed
a substitute from among the members of the royal family.[77] Such acts
invariably produced active opposition since they challenged the very
essence of kingship and the basic fabric of the chieftaincy. It was pre-

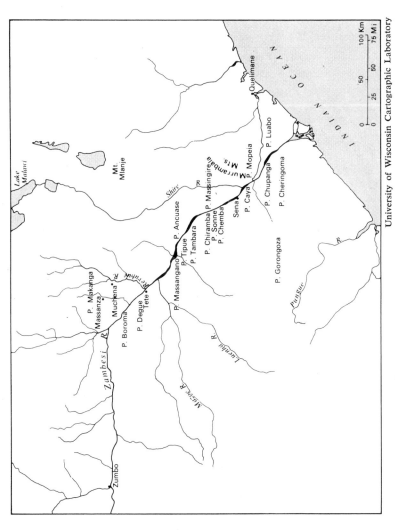

MAP 5 *Principal Zambesi Prazos, 1750–1900.*

University of Wisconsin Cartographic Laboratory

cisely because of the predictability of the Africans' reaction that prazeros rarely committed them.

The colonos were subjected not only to the planned exploitative actions of the prazero but to arbitrary and often spontaneous mistreat-
ment at the hands of the achikunda. Within the prazo, natural
competition existed between the two groups for the limited resources
and symbols of wealth. Ethnic differences and the achikundas' conscious desire to assert their position as the prazo's African elite reinforced the tension between them. Because they possessed superior
weapons and were deployed most often in remote areas, the achikunda
could terrorize or abuse the indigenous population without the knowledge of the prazero. They extorted tribute, robbed the fields, beat people, and stole women.[78]

The colonos employed a number of tactics to protest this persecution.
These included sending representatives and petitions to the government,[79] refusing to pay the mutsonko,[80] and withholding agricultural
products, trade items, and services.[81] These acts rarely alleviated their
grievances and often led to increased hardships. When their situation
became intolerable, they forcefully rejected the alien system and either
revolted or withdrew. In both cases, the motivation and the leadership
emanated from the ruling lineage and generally involved the entire
population.

The principal aim of revolt was to remove the alien overlord without losing their historic lands. This course of action seems to have been
most common on the smaller estates where the power relationship was
relatively favorable. Even the most important prazeros, however, were
not immune from revolt since the Zambesi chiefs often retained their
links with the royal lineages of surrounding states or were able to negotiate secret alliances with them. This situation was especially true in
the fringe areas, where the prazos bordered directly on independent
chieftaincies or states. On Prazo Sungue, for example, mambo Chirima
and his supporters covertly shifted their allegiance to Macombe and
the Barue. They sent valuable information which enabled Macombe
to effectively attack the estate and, as the Barue forces approached,
Chirima and his followers revolted.[82]

The colonos often had to contend with neighboring prazo slave armies and government irregulars as well as the achikunda deployed on
the estate. These temporary alliances reflected the prazeros' concern
about the resurgence of the Africans in the area around their estates.
A revolt in 1796 on the strategically located Prazo Massangano was
declared a national emergency, and, with the assistance of the Governor, a combined force gathered to crush it.[83] In addition to reestab-

lishing order, the prazeros and officials also used these expeditions to acquire slaves.[84]

Despite the union of prazeros and government, many of these revolts succeeded, and official reports during the second half of the eighteenth century indicated their widespread nature. In 1762 Governor Marco Coutinho de Montaury noted that a large number of prazeros had abandoned their estates because their colonos had revolted.[85] This assessment of local conditions in the Zambesi was quite similar to that of Governor António de Mello de Castro in 1780 and of Governor Truão at the beginning of the nineteenth century.[86]

Withdrawal was an unusually easy and more effective course of action. An alienated group of colonos frequently asserted their independence by migrating from their historic lands rather than by attempting to remove the prazero. Although the colonos were strongly attached to the land of their ancestors, their traditional pattern of shifting agriculture accustomed them to a mobile existence. The obvious difficulties and dangers of rebellion and the accessibility of the open frontiers explain why this strategy was so commonly employed.[87]

Having fled, the colonos had three alternatives. The first was to migrate to another prazo. Because of the fierce competition between prazeros, these newcomers, at least initially, were certain to be well received. The second alternative was to flee to a surrounding chieftaincy and recognize the overlordship of another mambo in return for permission to live on his land. Finally, they could migrate to unclaimed lands and reestablish an independent chieftaincy.[88]

Widespread withdrawal had a great impact upon the prazo system. One official observed that as a result of their dissatisfaction the colonos deserted en masse to the lands of surrounding chieftaincies, which increased their relative power with regard to the prazeros.[89] On many estates the indigenous population suffered a net decrease of as much as 80 or 90 percent, and there were several prazos reputed to have a total colono population of fewer than five families.[90]

Opposition was not limited to the free African population. The achikunda formed a powerful corporate group whose interest often conflicted with that of the prazeros. Since they were well armed, and had transferred their ultimate loyalty to the akazambo, the achikunda were a potential threat to every prazero. In order to stifle opposition, the prazero was particularly harsh on all disloyal slaves, which only tended to exacerbate the natural tensions and points of conflict.[91]

The manifestation of achikunda discontent ranged from disobeying specific orders to violent uprisings. Not surprisingly, the akazambo organized and directed most major internal resistance and played an important role during armed confrontations. Because the achikunda had no traditional attachments to the land, they tended ultimately to seek sanctuary outside the prazos. According to the annual report of the Governor of the Rivers of Sena (then the official Portuguese title for the area) in 1806, almost half of the twenty thousand slaves were listed as "absent." Despite the questionable validity of these statistics, they demonstrate the unstable character of this segment of prazo society.

Once free from the prazos, the slaves attempted to return to their traditional homes, joined other prazos as freemen, or established independent slave communities, or *musitu*, in the interior. Although there are few extant documents which relate to the formation of such musitu, they probably resembled the quilombos, runaway slave communities, of northeastern Brazil. Certainly their raison d'être, their frontier character, and their hostile relations with the surrounding Portuguese paralleled the Brazilian experience. Furthermore, one can assume that within musitu society the akazambo retained their neotraditional authority roles, much as African chiefs reasserted theirs in the Brazilian *sertão*.[92] This hypothesis does not preclude the possibility that ordinary slaves, by virtue of their power and prestige, could attract a large following of fugitives.[93]

These musitu presented a very serious problem for the prazeros both because they offered a sanctuary to other slaves and colonos and because they threatened the outlying prazos. The possession of European weapons reinforced the military power of these fugitive bands. On occasion they were also able to subvert the prazero's authority by inducing the indigenous population to revolt. Along with the expansive tendencies of the surrounding states, the runaway slaves continually challenged the stability of the prazo system and were instrumental in bringing about its ultimate demise.

CONCLUSION: THE PRAZOS AS A CENTRAL AFRICAN
POLITICAL INSTITUTION

The type of political system governing the prazos was not unique to the Zambesi Valley. In terms of its organization and limited functions, it was similar to institutions which other stranger groups in Central Africa established to rule subordinate populations. Although much smaller than these states, the prazos fit within the broad conceptual framework of Vansina's incorporative kingdoms, which possessed the following characteristics: (1) the recognition of an alien overlord; (2) the retention of the aboriginal chiefs who governed prior to the incorporation;

(3) the establishment of a dual administrative system — one traditional and the other nontraditional; (4) the appointment of alien overseers to keep a check on the traditional authorities.[94] A comparison with the Lunda kingdom of Kazembe reveals several structural similarities.[95] Among these are the division between alien political chief and indigenous land chief, the introduction of a nontraditional administrative system and the continuity of many aspects of the traditional political process.

Despite these functional and structural parallels, however, the historical development of the prazos and the Lunda state followed very different patterns: the prazos were unstable with short life spans, while Kazembe's empire had much greater longevity. The most obvious reason for this was that the prazeros were not, as a rule, integrated into African society. This shortcoming meant that they never gained traditional legitimacy and therefore lacked a clearly defined political role. In attempting to determine the limits of their authority, they often conflicted with the indigenous chiefs who were unwilling to abrogate traditional prerogatives. These conflicts invariably undermined the prazeros' position, which derived from the approval and cooperation of the mambo. The Lunda, on the other hand, established well-defined and relatively tension-free relationships with the Shila chiefs, through the mechanisms of positional succession and perpetual kinship. In this way, the indigenous chiefs were assimilated into Lunda society while the Lunda authorities acquired traditional legitimacy as political chiefs.

Equally important were the different relationships of the achikunda and *iyanga*, or Lunda warrior settlers, with their overlords and the indigenous populations. The achikundas' loyalty was uncertain and, unlike the iyanga, they posed a serious potential threat to the stability of the system. The relations of the achikunda with the colonos tended to increase tensions, and reinforced cultural and ethnic differences. After the Lunda expansion, however, the iyanga lived in relative peace with the Shila, and through their intimate relations with the indigenous population, they served as important carriers of Lunda culture and ideology.

4

The Composition and Organization of
Prazo Society, 1750-1850

In its broadest sense prazo society contained an indigenous and alien, or traditional and nontraditional population. More specifically, it was divided into four groups, each characterized by clearly defined recruitment patterns, residence systems, role obligations, and reference groups. The principal social units were the colonos, the vast majority of whom had descended from the indigenous inhabitants, their domestic slaves known as *akaporo*, the prazeros, and their slaves.[1]

COLONO SOCIETY

Both the oral data and the limited archival and ethnographic evidence suggest that the social organization of the colonos remained largely unaffected when they joined a prazo. This continuity does not imply that the life style of the indigenous population remained static, but rather that the changes which occurred were gradual and were not primarily related to the Portuguese presence. The absence of sustained interaction between the prazero and the colono community coupled with the relatively short life span of most estates help to explain this phenomenon.

The colonos living on prazos south of the Zambesi were divided into a number of exogamous clans. Apart from sharing a common name, or *mutupu*, and certain food prohibitions, membership in a particular clan had no effect on the daily lives of the colonos, since clans did not perform any corporate functions. In times of war or famine, for example, a colono would never seek or expect to receive assistance simply on the basis of a common mutupu.[2]

Within this framework of a noncorporate clan structure, the three-generation extended family with a patrilineal core constituted the principal social unit. Membership included a man and his nuclear family, his parents and their family. This localized segment served as the principal reference and corporate group for the individual; it determined his descent and residence patterns, acted in all legal matters, and provided a wide range of economic and social assistance.

Among the southern Zambesi colonos, descent was transmitted through the male line. When a child was born, he received his father's clan name and automatically became a member of the latter's patrilineage. While he often maintained contact with his mother's family, his most intimate relationships and greatest respect were reserved for his paternal kin. The child had the warmest relationship with his paternal grandparents, who played an important role in his early socialization, suggesting that the alliance of alternate generations was an underlying factor in preserving the stability of the patrilineage.[3]

Succession and inheritance patterns were also passed through the patrilineage. When a man died, his oldest brother, or half-brother, married the deceased's wives and took over as father of the children.[4] The kinship terminology, which equated the role and position of paternal uncle with that of the father facilitated this process of widow inheritance. If the brother or half-brother already had several wives, he often married only the senior wife of the deceased. The others were either distributed to junior members of the patrilineage or returned to their own patrilineage. In either case, all the children remained with the senior wife and the oldest brother. When the senior wife was very old, the brother might select a junior wife. This, however, had no effect on the children of the deceased, who were always inherited by the brother.

As part of the practice of false levirate, or widow inheritance, the brother received the property and all the material goods of the deceased. These were integrated into the "family" estate and were therefore not reserved for his nephews. He, of course, took on full financial responsibility for his new family.[5]

Marital patterns also varied somewhat among the patrilineal peoples living on the southern prazos. The Tawara, for example, generally practiced preferential marriages. Prospective wives were most often selected from among cross cousins or the wife's younger sisters. In marriages between relatives, known as *chipante*, the groom was exempted from paying the *nphete* and *npaza*, which symbolized his intent to marry the girl.[6] The Sena and Tonga, on the other hand, generally chose their spouses from outside the "family," and preferential marriage seems to have been relatively unimportant.[7] In such situations, the boy or his patrilineal relatives presented the prospective wife's parents with token gifts to formalize the marriage contract. None of the Zambesi peoples practiced prescribed marriages, and the unions of parallel cousins as well as other marriages involving members of the patrilineage were considered incestuous. These prohibitions necessitated marriages with other lineages, which strengthened the family's system of alliances.

The prospective husband also had to pay bride price, or *chuma*. It generally consisted of grain, copper bracelets, iron hoes, and a small piece of cloth. The bridewealth not only secured the husband's economic and sexual rights over his wife and enabled him to sue in case of adultery, but also insured the transference of the woman's fertility to the patrilineage. Barrenness therefore was a principal cause of divorce. Despite its limited economic value, the chuma had the important social function of perpetuating the patrilineage. It helped to guarantee the continuation of the husband's lineage, since a barren girl could be returned and the bride price used again to secure a fertile partner. If there were no complications, the girl's patrilineage was then able to use the chuma to obtain wives for its male members.[8]

Besides these payments, the prospective son-in-law had to provide bride service. Before the marriage, he was required to work in the field of the girl's parents, to build additional grain huts, and to do any other jobs which the father-in-law required. The usual length of service was from one to three years.[9]

Residence patterns were initially patrilocal. After the wedding, the groom took his bride to live in or adjacent to his father's compound. The father also provided his son with a small area to plant a field and helped the couple clear the area. Until the first harvest, the newlyweds relied on the boy's parents for food and other assistance. After a few years, the male sometimes selected additional wives. All were subordinate to the senior wife in prestige and authority. As the man's nuclear family grew, he generally moved from his father's compound and established his own nearby.

The patrilineal segment provided its members with economic and social assistance in times of crisis. During famines, when a colono lacked enough grain to feed his family or to pay the mutsonko, he sought help from his patrilineal kinsmen. At harvest time members of the lineage were expected to help collect the crops. When an individual was involved in a dispute, the lineage elders represented him before the mfumu or mambo. Conversely, when a man committed a crime, his patrilineage was held responsible for his action and often had to pay his fine to close the case.[10]

The lineage's social responsibility to its members continued until death when a proper burial was arranged for the deceased, who entered the world of the ancestors. Thereafter he was venerated and propitiated in the hope that he would serve as a familial guardian and link with the deities. In this way, the colonos acquired supernatural protection against the numerous hardships which threatened them.[11]

Although the colonos on the southern bank of the Zambesi were patrilineal, they exhibited some noticeable bilateral tendencies, the most significant of which was the universal prohibition of half-brother–half-sister marriages. In all instances, it was considered incestuous for the daughter and son of the same mother and different fathers to marry or to have sexual intercourse.[12] The obvious reason for this taboo was that they were considered to be related even though they belonged to different patrilineages.

The wife's patrilineage also had significant secondary social and economic functions. The maternal grandparents served as important socializing agents and often had a more relaxed relationship with their grandchildren than did their patrilineal counterparts. They also provided valuable economic insurance if the male's kinsmen were unable to assist. In the Zambesi, where there were frequent food shortages, the husband often had to rely on the aid of his wife's patrilineage to assure a sufficient food supply. The actual request was transmitted through his wife, since the husband generally had a very distant relationship with his in-laws. In addition, the wife's patrilineage served as a secondary supplier of labor which could be recruited at harvest time or in a crisis. Its role, however, was relatively undefined and depended upon the relationships between the two families as well as the proximity and affluence of the wife's family. Despite this assistance, the wife's patrilineage had neither corporate nor legal functions with regard to her husband and children and only limited responsibilities to her.[13]

The incorporation of the northern matrilineal peoples into the prazos does not seem to have had a significant impact on their system of social organization. Oral data collected among descendants of the colonos living on Prazo Makanga indicates that their customary descent, resident, and marital patterns remained unaltered.[14] Ethnographic comparisons with other Chewa groups who remained outside the prazo system confirms this conclusion.[15] This is particularly significant since

Makanga was one of the most stable prazos and the indigenous population could be expected to have undergone a more complete process of acculturation than colonos living on neighboring estates whose life span was substantially shorter.

Although ethnographic data is generally unavailable for the other matrilineal peoples, such as the Manganja and Podzo, who were integrated into the prazo system, evidence from the Chewa coupled with the minimal impact the prazero had in the neighboring patrilineal regions suggests that a similar phenomenon occurred among these peoples.

Throughout the Zambesi the prazero's cultural impact was nearly as minimal as his effect on the indigenous social organization. Indeed, as a group, they were essentially the converted rather than the converters. The principal Portuguese contribution seems to have been the introduction of certain material goods. These included specialized types of cloth and beads, a small number of guns, and, in certain areas, salt.[16] Although these artifacts improved the material conditions of the colonos, they did not radically alter the indigenous life style. In the more important cultural areas such as value systems and world view, the colonos remained totally unaffected. For example, in Tete, with a total estimated population of 50,000 there were 259 Africans and mestizos who were listed as Christians between 1812 and 1821, and only 18 of these were colonos.[17] The Portuguese failure to alter the life style of the colonos is attested to in the continual reports of disgruntled Zambesi *administradors* and more dramatically by the minute number of Africans who acquired the status of *assimilados* during the Salazar regime.

DOMESTIC SLAVERY ON THE PRAZO

The institution of domestic slavery, or more precisely adopted dependency, was equally unaffected by the establishment of the prazo system. This indigenous institution persisted in its customary form in Zambesian society when the colonos were incorporated into the prazos. The number of akaporo a man owned depended upon his wealth and status. It was most common for the mambo and mfumu to have the largest number of attached dependents, although wealthier members of the chieftaincy often rivaled them. A man was considered well-off and quite powerful if he owned ten akaporo, and most people were unable to purchase more than a few because they lacked a surplus of negotiable commodities to trade.[18]

Akaporo were most commonly acquired through commerce. The general pattern consisted of trade with neighboring ethnic groups. These relationships seem to have been relatively fixed. The direction of the trade reflected the relative prosperity, easy access to desirable European goods, and internal stability of the purchaser's ethnic group. The Sena colonos, for example, traded with the Manganja, but rarely with the Barue or Tonga. Sena informants explain the receptivity of the Manganja in terms of their general shortage of food and the great demand for locally fabricated and imported cloths.[19] Similarly, the Tawara purchased their akaporo primarily from the Chewa, who possessed a surplus of prisoners captured in inter-Chewa wars.[20]

A discussion of commercial relations between the Sena and Manganja suggests the complex nature of the trading process. A small group of traders went annually to designated Manganja villages where their local counterparts had gathered a number of slaves. These trading ventures usually took place just before the harvest when the scarcity of food increased the likelihood that the Manganja would sell their domestic slaves or even members of their own families to insure the survival of the rest of the lineage. After protracted negotiations, the ultimate price depended upon the dearth of food, the quality of the cloth, and the desirability of the akaporo. Some informants claimed that females were worth more because of their procreativity, while others declared that the price paid for a young man was higher because of his greater work capacity. Since the traders generally did not resell the slaves, the particular needs of each Sena lineage probably determined preferences. The average price per slave seems to have ranged between three and six meters of cloth and varying amounts of grain. Before their departure, the Sena traders presented the Manganja village headman with a small gift and gave each slave a piece of cloth and some food to secure its loyalty. The trading party waited until dark before leaving the Manganja village so that the captives would not know the route back from the prazos to their homeland.[21]

Another way of obtaining domestic slaves, especially women and children, was through robbery or war. Among the Sena it was common for men known as *mupanga* to cross the Zambesi and steal children from the Manganja. These thefts were committed before the harvest, when the high sorghum enabled the mupanga to approach a village undetected.[22] The various inter-state wars, as well as the more local feuds within the Zambesi also provided excellent opportunities to enslave members of the vanquished community. In general, only the elderly and disabled were spared, since they had limited social and economic value.[23]

Akaporo were also acquired from related peoples living on the prazo during periods of famine or drought. In such situations, it was common for a man to sell a member of his family or even to voluntarily attach himself to a wealthy colono or chief in exchange for food, clothing, and future security. The majority of slaves, wrote one prazero, "came to be captive from the times of famines, pestilence and locust, because their urgent needs obliged them to come and offer themselves as captives."[24] A man could also pawn his son for a specified period of time. In this situation, he was theoretically selling the boy's services in exchange for food or clothing. Failure to repay the debt within the prescribed period resulted in the permanent enslavement of the child.[25]

Finally, dependents were acquired as compensation for crimes committed against a person or lineage and as a penalty for illegal acts which threatened the authority or position of the land chief. Throughout the Zambesi, the family of a murderer was obligated to provide the victim's lineage with a specified number of slaves,[26] and, among the Chewa of Prazo Makanga, an admitted adulterer could satisfy his punishment by providing the husband with akaporo.[27] Acts of disobedience against the mambo generally resulted in the enslavement of the guilty party or the payment of a number of slaves to rectify the situation. One prazero observed that a man found guilty of robbing the mambo's field of even a few ears of corn would be enslaved.[28] The land chief also received slaves as recompense for his legal services.

The principal purpose of acquiring dependents was to expand and strengthen the lineage. Economic considerations, although important, were clearly secondary. Throughout the Zambesi prazos the akaporo were integrated into the kinship system as low status members. A young dependent generally received the clan name of his owner, which created symbolic familial links. An older dependent, already aware of his mutupu, was allowed to retain his clan identity. In both cases the akaporo were treated as family members despite the absence of any blood relationship. The dependents addressed their patron as father and developed an intimate relationship with him and the localized members of the lineage. The young akaporo lived in the compound of their owner who took full responsibility for their upbringing and protection. They had clearly defined tasks, which included working in the fields, collecting firewood and water, and guarding the herds. These tasks were generally required of all children.[29]

After the rites de passage, the *kaporo* was expected to take a spouse. Often he would marry a member of the lineage or another of his owner's dependents. These unions exhibited some of the characteristics of preferential marriages, since they kept the bridewealth within the family. The dependent, however, could marry outside of the lineage and, in such cases, his patron would provide the necessary bride price. Conversely, the owner received the bridewealth when one of his female akaporo was married to someone outside of the lineage. The new couple respected the customary rules of residence and built their homestead in or near the compound of the owner, who provided them with a small field to plant. Their children had an intimate relationship with the patron, who served in the capacity of an "adopted grandfather," just as he served as "adopted father" to the dependent.[30]

Recently acquired akaporo who had already passed puberty were generally integrated into the local lineage through marriage. It was especially common for the patron to marry his female dependents or to give them to his son or maternal nephew, depending on the descent system. Similarly, male akaporo often obtained the sisters or daughters of their owners. As in the case of the dependent brought up since childhood, the kaporo and his spouse followed the prescribed residence patterns, and the offspring were considered part of the lineage.[31]

As a valued member of the kinship system, the adopted dependents were not sold except during times of crisis. It is true, however, that because they lacked a blood relationship they were considered most expendable in an emergency. Most informants agreed that such an action was only taken when no other options existed.[32]

The principal characteristic of Zambesian domestic servitude was institutionalized manumission. Slave status was never more than one generation deep. This suggests the validity of the more specialized term, adopted dependents, which differentiates the Zambesian institution from a number of other African forms of servitude in which manumission was either postponed several generations or never institutionalized.[33] Among all the ethnic groups living on the prazos, when a dependent married her patron or his kinsmen, she and her future heirs were automatically manumitted. Similarly, when a male slave married the daughter, niece, or sister of the owner, he and his heirs gained a free status.[34] This process seems to have been most common among matrilineal peoples who were accustomed to assimilating male strangers. In Sena and Tonga society, the married male was legally free but his social position was rather ambiguous since junior kinsmen often treated him in a condescending manner.[35] This inferiority created tensions and served as the principal motivation to move outside the patron's village. Among the Tawara, male emancipation was much more limited. Because the male dependent generally married a female kaporo of the same owner, manumission was deferred an additional generation, and both husband and wife remained in a subordinate status. Their children, however, were always considered free, and were integrated into the lineage with full rights and privileges.[36]

While adopted dependents were automatically emancipated when they married free members of the society, there was not a general consensus on the status of two married akaporo. Since the responses did not follow ethnic lines, they could either reflect a certain amount of confusion on the part of some of the elders or more likely structural ambiguity within these societies. Most informants contended that the newlyweds were free,[37] while a minority held that it was only their children who acquired full status within the lineage.[38] In either case, even under the most extreme circumstances, the owner only had the right to the services of the slave he bought and not to that of the kaporo's heirs.

In addition to institutionalized manumission other channels of upward mobility were available, at least among the colonos living on the Sena prazos. If the principal heirs were deceased or scattered, a kaporo inherited his master's wealth. He would also inherit the dead man's wife or wives and take responsibility for his children. This pattern is clearly consistent with his position as an adopted but distant member of the kinship system. Dependents universally received gifts from their patrons as a sign of affection and a reward for their good service. By carefully saving or investing these gifts, one could accumulate enough wealth to purchase additional wives or his own akaporo, who had the same relationship to him as he had to his patron.[39]

THE SLAVES OF THE PRAZERO

An extremely different slave system, bearing only the most superficial resemblance to the indigenous African form, also existed on the prazos. It included the household slaves of the prazero and his achikunda. Because these slaves played a critical role both in the maintenance of internal stability and in defense, the prazero continually sought to augment their ranks.

The indigenous practice of voluntary enslavement assisted the prazeros in this search. In crises, colonos and neighboring peoples entered the service of the prazero as they had historically sold themselves to prosperous Africans. Strangers, orphans, and outcasts no longer attached to a traditional group willingly exchanged their freedom for future security. Others agreed to such an arrangement in order to repay outstanding debts. According to one prazero, the vast majority of his slaves had voluntarily joined during periods of famine.[40]

The actual process of voluntary enslavement varied substantially from one situation to another. In some cases, it involved careful selection and detailed negotiations between the prospective slave and the potential buyer. After choosing a desirable owner who was reputed to be wealthy and kind, the former went to the prazero's home and offered his services in exchange for specified goods. The prazero informed him that he was not only selling himself but his heirs and his immediate family as well, and pledged that neither the slave nor his family would ever be sold outside the prazo. If this was agreeable, they arranged a mutually satisfactory price, which usually included a specified amount of cloth and alcohol.[41]

Often a man became a slave through the symbolic act of destroying an article of very limited value which belonged to the prazero, such as a cup or a piece of cloth. This was commonly known as breaking a *mitete* and was a practice historically employed in the Zambesi. From the perspective of the future slave, he was entering a form of slavery not unlike the traditional pattern, with its safeguards and benefits, and many considered themselves far superior to the colonos. Others, who were forced to flee from one prazero, had no option but to join the slave army of another in exchange for sanctuary and protection.[42]

The prazero also acquired a number of slaves by virtue of his position as overlord. Every two years the mambo and afumu had to give him a slave as a symbol of their continued loyalty. Colonos sometimes paid the mutsonko in slaves instead of agricultural produce or manchilla. In addition, the prazero received slaves in payment for serious crimes committed on his lands as well as for judgments rendered in important legal cases.[43]

Wars and slave raids against the surrounding chieftaincies provided many estateholders with additional manpower.[44] The prazo armies from Tete, for example, frequently attacked neighboring Chewa polities. Perhaps the most vulnerable of these was Biwi, whose close proximity and weak military position made it an ideal target. During the second half of the eighteenth century, Biwi villages were under continual attack (see Chapter 7). The captured men, women, and children were either integrated into slave sections, exported, or sold in local auctions.[45]

Force was often directed against the local colono population as well. On many estates, Africans were arrested and enslaved on the slightest pretext. At least some prazeros enslaved the free relatives of their deceased slaves in order to meet their manpower requirements and others used colono uprisings as a pretext for the same end.[46]

Large numbers of slaves were also purchased from the surrounding

African peoples. Historically, the principal sources were the Malawi chieftaincies Nsenga and Yao. The prazeros rarely engaged in the actual trading process. Instead, they sent their specialized trading slaves, or *misambadzi*, into the interior to exchange cloth, beads, alcoholic beverages, and guns for both slaves and ivory.[47]

The families of deceased prazeros often sold their slaves before abandoning their estate or to satisfy outstanding debts. The principal estate owners in the region were invited to the home of the deceased for an auction. Slaves were generally sold in their neotraditional slave sections or *insaka*.[48] The slave's skills or his position of authority within the slave regiment determined his value. On Prazo Chemba, for example, an unskilled slave cost one-quarter the price of a slave chief.[49] Similarly, on Prazo Cheringoma, the assessed value of a warrior was only one-half that of a fisherman and one-tenth that of an iron worker or goldsmith.[50]

In addition to augmenting the slave population from external sources, the prazero benefited from the natural reproduction of his slave population. Unlike the status of the akaporo of the colonos, slavery was a permanent and inherited status. Barring any major political upheaval or natural disaster, there was a geometric increase in the slave population.[51]

The multiple patterns of recruitment fostered the development of an ethnically heterogeneous slave population whose homelands stretched from the hinterland of Sofala to Bisaland in present-day Zambia. While there are no systematic data on the origins of the slaves, there are a few detailed documents which provide invaluable information on this subject. The most significant is a list of 659 male slaves who were freed in the Tete area in 1856. Assuming that the prazeros did not emanicipate slaves according to their ethnic background, this document provides an excellent sample of the slave population on the Tete prazos. The ethnic diversity is reflected in the more than twenty definable ethnic groups; 85.4 percent of those were related to peoples living in the matrilineal belt north of the Zambesi, even though many of the Tete prazos were surrounded by patrilineal peoples. Malawian groups, primarily Chewa, Manganja, Chipeta, and Maravi, accounted for 398 or 61 percent of the total freed population. Of these, the Chewa were the most heavily represented, comprising nearly 58 percent of all Malawi slaves. The largest identifiable patrilineal group originated in Quiteve and included only 7 slaves. Slaves emancipated by a single owner exhibited the same ethnic diversity.[52]

Despite the ethnic diversity and the disparity in numbers of slaves, the same organizational principles governed from one prazo to another.

The slaves were divided into two broad functional groups: the *maban-dazi*, or *escravos da porta*, who worked in and around the prazero's home; and the more numerous *escravos fora da porta*, who were comprised primarily of warriors, mineworkers, and their spouses. The mabandazi constituted only a small percentage of the total slave population. Their absolute number rarely exceeded 50 and most often was between 15 and 30. On Prazo Cheringoma 26 out of the 946 slaves were mabandazi, while on the Dominican prazos in Quelimane there were 66 achikunda, 70 agriculturalists and fishermen, and 20 household slaves.[53] This latter category generally included the unskilled maids, cooks, breadmakers, carpenters, and iron and goldsmiths.

The residential patterns and social organization of the slaves varied according to their function on the prazos. The mabandazi and their families were organized into one section, or *nsaka*, which a slave captain governed. In general, they lived in a series of compounds adjacent to the prazero's home in what could be considered a nontraditional occupational village.[54]

The female slaves who lived and worked in the mining camps also seem to have been organized into occupational villages. Within the village each compound, composed of a female nsaka, was governed by a *mucate*, a female slave leader. At the head of several sections was a *mungaba* or female slave chief.[55] These were generally temporary residence patterns, since many of the mines were only seasonal. During the remainder of the year the miners lived with their husbands, who were probably the warrior slaves.

The achikunda were also divided into sections which served as their main residential units. Each nsaka formed a separate village or village segment where warriors lived with their families. Every chikunda possessed his own compound comprised of a number of huts for his various wives. The choicest location in the village was reserved for the tsachikunda, whose position was similar to that of a village headman. Several adjacent villages comprised the domain of a slave regiment under the auspices of a mukazambo. On the larger estates, at least one regiment was located near the prazero's home, and the others were deployed in strategic areas.[56]

Because of their ethnically heterogeneous membership, the chikunda regiments provide a unique example of the construction of a neotraditional social organization.[57] The members of each village formed a distinct corporate group which over time developed its own social identity and network of kinship relationships and laid the basis for the genesis of the present-day "chikunda people" of Zambia.[58]

The critical factor which seems to have determined the origin and nature of the chikunda social institutions was that a warrior and his male heirs retained permanent membership in a nsaka. Although the vast majority of the slaves came from matrilineal societies, this fixed residence pattern generated patrilineal tendencies. Initially, a chikunda had to rely on friendship until he could develop a network of kinship ties through marriage. When a slave married, his wife was brought into his village, which meant that residence patterns were always patrilocal. The implications of this shift for a matrilineal people were substantial.

An entirely new network of localized kinship relationships within the nsaka was created to take care of the functions which the matrilineage had previously performed. What emerged was a patrilineal extended family reinforced every generation by the fixed residence of the male population. Furthermore, since most of the prazos were in patrilineal areas, wives recruited from the indigenous population brought with them their patrilineal norms and were easily integrated into such a social system. This adjustment was probably more difficult for women coming from a matrilineal area, but since they were effectively cut off from their maternal kinsmen, they had no alternative but to accept the existing pattern.

A COMPARISON OF THE TWO SLAVE SYSTEMS

While there are certain superficial similarities between the kaporo and chikunda forms, a careful examination of the core characteristics indicates that they were two distinct systems. The fundamental difference between the two institutions was that the European considered his slaves to be property rather than kinsmen. As a result, the mabandazi and the achikunda lacked the basic rights and privileges generally associated with African domestic slavery. As chattels, the prazero could and did sell his slaves, despite the theoretical agreement between him and those slaves who voluntarily joined the estate. Moreover, when a slave died, the prazero as owner took control of all his worldly possessions. This practice was often extended to include his free relatives. The treatment of the slaves reflected the impersonal nature of their relationship with the prazero and the absence of institutional mechanisms to protect them from arbitrary and capricious actions. This motivated one nineteenth-century observer to draw an unfavorable comparison between prazo and plantation slavery.[59] Among my informants, there was universal agreement that the adopted dependents of the colonos were treated far better than their counterparts in the service of the prazero.[60]

Another significant difference was the lack of structural or institutional manumission. The status of the prazero's slaves was passed on to all future generations. The only time slaves were freed in significant numbers was during famines when the prazero could no longer afford to feed them.[61] The alternatives for the slaves were revolution or flight, both of which contained obvious dangers.

Upward mobility of any form was much more restricted among the European's slaves than among the akaporo. The adopted dependents had a number of opportunities to gain status and wealth. Economic possibilities ranged from a successful trading venture to inheriting the property of a rich owner. Similarly, the status position of the akaporo automatically increased as they achieved senior ranks within the lineage. Apart from the mukazambo, chuanga, and a small handful of other slave officials, the vast majority of the prazero's slaves remained frozen at the lowest social position and whatever material benefits they accrued could be arbitrarily confiscated. More precisely, the pyramidical stratification structure of the achikunda insured that only a small handful would progress to the second or third rung of the slave hierarchy.

In addition to the levels of stratification within the nonindigenous slave society, there are indications that two distinct European slave systems operated on the prazos. Unfortunately, the oral and written documentation dealing with the mabandazi is very sketchy, and it is therefore impossible to present a detailed comparison with the achikunda. Nevertheless, one can draw a few inferences about the nature of this form of slavery. Because of their role, which included caring for the children and serving as the personal valet to the prazero and his wife, the mabandazi probably developed a relatively intimate relationship with their owners. It is clear from their skills and the contact with the prazero and his family that they were the most affected by Portuguese culture. Scattered baptismal records indicate that this group provided the only segment of African society whose members became Catholics in any appreciable number.[62] Because of their positions and their adoption of Catholicism, the prazero probably felt a closer affinity to the mabandazi and was less likely to sell them.[63] Taken together, these scattered data suggest that the position of mabandazi might have approached that of a household slave on an American plantation and was appreciably different from that of the achikunda.

THE PRAZERO COMMUNITY

The prazeros lived in a social milieu which remained essentially outside African society. Historically, a small group of established prazero families had monopolized the power, wealth, and social positions in the Zambesi. In the seventeenth century, this elite included such men as Sisnando Bayão, António Lobo da Silva, Lourenço de Mattos, and Belchior de Sa Mella. Many were from respectable families in Portugal and received their estates as personal gifts from the king in return for various services.[64] They continued to identify with the metropolis, and sought to have their newly acquired positions and power reaffirmed through royal decrees and honors. One contemporary described António Lobo da Silva as a very rich and powerful man whose only unsatisfied desire remained the acquisition of a patent of nobility and the habit of the order of Christ.[65]

Throughout most of the eighteenth century these older families, joined by a number of enterprising new prazeros, formed a relatively closed Zambesi elite which monopolized the wealth, power, and prestige as completely as had their predecessors. Within this elite connections between the principal families were reinforced through marriage alliances. Multiple marriages, owing to premature deaths from tropical diseases and the adverse climate, increased this tendency. In the course of their lifetime many prazeros took two, three, or even four spouses. This pattern seems to have been more prevalent among the Zambesi *donas*, who for some reason had greater resistance to the climate than their male counterparts;[66] several of them continued their marital escapades until they were eighty years old, which gave them numerous opportunities to enter the proper marital unions.[67]

Perhaps the most successful power brokers were the descendants of Bayão, who controlled the important Cheringoma-Gorongoza complex. By carefully selecting their spouses, they expanded their web of alliances to include many of the prominent prazero families. The apogee occurred in the middle of the eighteenth century when Bernardo Caetano de Sa Botelho married the widow D. Catharina de Faria Leytão, who was the most powerful prazero in the district of Quelimane. In the succeeding decade, his daughter was betrothed to João Xavier Pinheiro de Aragão, one of the most important and feared prazeros in Sena. As a result of these unions, the resources of at least nine estates, and many thousand achikunda, were incorporated into one power bloc.[68]

The pattern of gift giving also tended to reinforce the closed nature of the elite by keeping the estates within the hands of a small number of prazeros, who often had several prazos. When the prominent prazeros did not have immediate kin, they apparently selected their heirs from their former spouses' families or intimate friends belonging to the Zambesi elite.[69]

Because of the narrow nature of the elite and the apparent reluctance

on the part of the racially mixed donas to marry Africans, it was necessary to selectively recruit prospective husbands from the larger Portuguese community, especially from among important government
officials. In the short period between 1750 and 1775, for example, three
Governors of the Rivers of Sena married into prazo families.[70] They
brought with them positions and titles, which the older families eagerly
sought.

Despite its small size, the prazero elite, was not a homogeneous or
united group. The constant struggle for the symbols of wealth and
power led to the emergence of competing elite segments based on
mutual interests and marriage alliances. Within each sub-group, the
same pressures existed, and the rivalries were often most intense among
members of the same family.[71]

The affluence of the elite was reflected in its life style, which most
observers characterized as vulgarly opulent and decadent. Prazeros
compensated for the hardships of living in the interior by surrounding
themselves with all the goods necessary to satisfy their material and
sensual needs. Their homes were often furnished in the latest styles;
their tables were loaded with exotic fruits and meats; and the prazero
smoked the best cigars and drank the finest wines. "The life of a
senhor . . . consists in eating, smoking, and sleeping being surrounded
by young negro women and giving himself up to continual sensuality." [72] The women led an equally frivolous existence, passing their
days beautifying themselves and being entertained by their male
slaves.[73]

A number of prazeros did not live in such splendor, nor did they
trace their ancestry to prominent Portuguese families. Many of the
smaller estates were owned by minor officials, soldiers, and *degredados*,
who belonged to the lower echelons of Portuguese society. Although
they tried to emulate the life style of their wealthier counterparts, their
marginal position and the closed nature of the elite limited their upward mobility.[74]

A proliferation of new estateholders in the second half of the
eighteenth century dramatically altered the composition of prazero society. In the period between 1750 and 1783, the number of estates
doubled as the crown sought to create a permanent European population in the Zambesi.[75] The recipients were drawn both from the lower
class residing in Portugal and from impoverished inhabitants of the
Zambesi. Typical of the new applicants was Dona Florencia de Brum
Rezenda, who was given a small estate so that she would no longer
remain destitute.[76] Simultaneously, the government began to limit the
number of prazos one individual could own by refusing to confirm ad-

ditional estates. Although this policy was initially implemented in the 1750s, it was not acted upon until the latter part of the century. Its long-term effect was to limit the holdings of some of the traditional families and, at the same time, make more land available to new prazeros.

The unhealthy climate and the dearth of unattached males severely limited the choice of husbands for the Zambesi donas and forced them to seek unions with men who were well below them in social standing. The least unacceptable were the wealthy Goan traders who began to reside in the Zambesi after the abolition of the trade restrictions in the middle of the eighteenth century. Initially, the marriage of a proper "Portuguese" female, who was in fact mestiza, to a Goan was considered scandalous. As the demographic pressures continued, it became more acceptable to marry Indians, although many of the stereotypes and prejudices persisted. By 1789 the Goans had attained a dominant social and economic position in prazero society. Their descendants retained this preeminence throughout the nineteenth century and were joined by a small number of lower-class Portuguese who also had been able to marry into the traditional families.[77]

T A B L E 3   *Births and Deaths in Sena, 1740–1801*

	Births (1740–1801)	Deaths (1775–1801)
Pardos (mestizos)	1340	179
White (incl. Goans)	188	120

Source: A.H.U., Moç., Cx. 40: "Rellação Circunstanciado de Nascimentos, Cazamentos, E Exlecimentos havidos nesta Fregazia de Santa Catharina da Villa de Senna" (unsigned, undated).

In addition to the class changes, the racial complexion of prazero society continued to darken each generation. The most important reason for this was the virtual absence of European women in the interior.[78] The inland Portuguese, therefore, cohabited with African women or with the mulatto offspring of previous interracial unions. The prevalence of malaria and the difficult climatic conditions produced a high mortality rate and a bad overseas image both of which also limited migration of males. The infusion of Portuguese blood was, therefore, marginal, and successive generations were absorbed into the growing mestizo community. They became the characteristic racial group in the Zambesi, and were collectively known by the African term *muzungu*.[79]

The best indication of these changes comes from a summarized parish record of Christian births and deaths in Sena (see Table 3).

Scattered racial and demographic data for Tete and Sena provide additional evidence of the direction of the change. They must, however, be taken only as suggestions, since the accuracy of the census and the use of unclear terms to define certain groups especially in the census of 1735 limit their reliability. Nevertheless, they do indicate certain patterns which are consistent with the other available data (see Table 4).

TABLE 4   *Racial Composition of Sena and Tete*

	1735		1777		1802	
	%	No.	%	No.	%	No.
Portuguese	22.8	188	14.6	103	23.3	253
Goans	16.2	147	18.5	130	—	—
Pardos [a]	60.0	489	66.9	471	76.6	666

Sources: A.H.U., Moç., Cx. 3: Jeronyme de Sau, "Rol dos Frequezes de Sta Maria deste Frequezia de Senna," 1735; A.H.U., Moç., Cx. 3: "Lista dos Christaons, e Frequezos de Tette da Administração dos Rios de Senna," E. Fr. Matheus de S. Thomas, 6 May 1735; A.H.U., Moç., Cx. 15: P[e] Manoel Pinto da Conceição, Vigário, 6 July 1777; A.H.U., Moç., Cx. 15: António José Lobo, 20 July 1777; A.H.U., Moç., Cx. 39: "Relazam Circunscriada dos Brancos E os Pardos E os Negros que existem nas tres villas dos Districto do Governo desses Rios de Sena, 1802" (unsigned, undated).

[a] The unclear categories in the 1735 census were "filhos da terra" and "rol de molhos." Both have been subsumed here under "pardos."

A census of the entire Zambesi in 1819, including the coastal town of Quelimane with its relatively high European population, corroborates the preponderance of muzungu. In that survey, the mestizos comprised 61.6 percent, the Europeans 12.9 percent, and the Indians 25.5 percent of the total Christian population.[80] Oral information from a slightly later period supports this conclusion; according to my informants, the vast majority of the prazeros were mixed or Indians, and only a small number were Portuguese.[81]

The relative decline of the "white" population occurred despite the crown's attempt to alter the growing racial imbalance. In 1755, legislation was passed reconfirming the dona's responsibility to marry only Portuguese men.[82] In theory, failure to fulfill this contractual obligation could result in loss of the estate. Similarly, a policy giving preferential consideration to "whites" who applied for prazos, especially women, was instituted at the end of the eighteenth century.

Inextricably related to the shifting racial pattern was the tendency of the prazeros to adopt African cultural forms. In general, the longer a family or individual remained in the Zambesi the more likely was acculturation. In most cases, the cultural conversion was incomplete, and the prazero retained some valued European traits and occasional links with European institutions.

There were two fundamental causes for this pattern of acculturation. First, the biological changes and reinforced blood relationships with Africans and mestizos meant that the indigenous way of life was no longer considered alien or barbarian. Sustained interaction with African relatives and with the household slaves reinforced this tendency.[83]

Second, the prazero, and especially his children, lacked any meaningful contact with European-oriented institutions. This isolation was due, in part, to the absence of schools and churches which perpetuated European ideas and values. The few clergy who were stationed in the Zambesi were totally immersed in commerce and had no time to fulfill either their religious or secular responsibilities.[84] One Governor characterized them as scandalous criminals whose only interest or desire was to accrue wealth and power.[85] A high church official preferred to blame the religious and educational failure on the dearth of churches rather than on the incompetence of the clergy: "They have never heard the mass, and know nothing of the doctrine, because there has been no one to teach them, since the *prazeros* often live seventy or eighty leagues apart and there are only a small number of priests scattered throughout the region."[86] His attempt to exonerate the clergy does, in fact, indicate the other reason for the prazero's cultural isolation. The enormous distances between one estate and another meant that the amount of interaction was quite limited for all members of the family, but especially for the children. This reinforced the tendency of the children, and often of their parents, to look within the prazo for companionship, explanations, and assistance. Thus their principal reference group was composed of a variety of different Africans and mestizos, all of whom were potential transmitters of indigenous cultural elements.

As might be expected, the prazeros quickly and universally adopted African artifacts, material goods, and techniques. Not only were these culturally neutral and therefore not a challenge to their customs, values, and mores, but they helped them to adapt to their new environment. It was quite common for the prazeros to dress in loincloths, to employ local hunting and fishing techniques, to eat African foods, and to live in an African style home.[87]

Of much greater significance were the changes in their world views. This shift indicated a definite modification of the value system which is at the core of man's culture. During times of crises the prazeros often sought African explanations and solutions.[88] Belief in witchcraft, for example, was almost universal. One observer reported a case in which a principal inhabitant of Sena killed four of her slaves because they had used magic to murder her sister,[89] and another "complained of a violent headache and added that his sister's slave whom he offered for the purpose of carrying the Royal treasury had bewitched him."[90] According to my informants, such well-known nineteenth-century prazeros as Gouveia, Bonga, Pereira, Gambete, and Ferrão all believed in witchcraft.[91] Individual prazeros also administered muabvi, or the poison ordeal, to discover and punish witches.[92] Among those reputed to have been involved in such practices was the Vicar General of the Rivers of Sena.[93] The prazeros relied heavily on diviners to assist them with their difficulties and to provide information about the future. It was common to consult a diviner before a long trip or an important business venture.[94] On other occasions, they were consulted to find the cause of illness and to provide supernatural remedies.[95] Herbalists were regularly called upon to prepare the right medicines to cure the prazero and his family.[96]

The fusing of indigenous ceremonies with certain Catholic rituals created syncretic religious forms. A church edict issued in Goa in 1771 denounced and prohibited the introduction of a number of "pagan" rites into the Catholic service and scorned the general tendency to adopt "primitive" ideas and beliefs. Specifically it charged that alien rituals had been introduced into the baptismal, that marital unions were confirmed by an exhibition of the linen or cloth which demonstrated the previous virginity of the bride, and that funeral services were terminated by the union of a female and a male slave in the bed of their deceased owner.[97] Although these religious and cosmological changes reflected specific aspects of the Africans' world view, certain similarities between medieval Catholicism, with its emphasis on spirits, demons, ghosts, and witches, and the religious beliefs of the indigenous population probably facilitated this transference.[98]

The lack of schools and general isolation resulted in a subtle type of cultural regression. As members of a European culture, the prazeros successively moved from a literate to a nonliterate state. This was especially true of the female population, which rarely knew any Portuguese. It is demonstrated by the numerous extant documents signed merely with an "x."[99] While some male members of the Portuguese community were also illiterate, most managed to maintain a minimum knowledge of written Portuguese, which they rarely used, except in official correspondence with the state. From an African perspective, the prazeros and their families can be seen as members of the preliterate indigenous culture who relied primarily on oral communication in Chi-Sena, Chi-Tawara, or whatever other local language was spoken on their estate.[100] In fact, all spoke one or a number of Zembesi dialects and used them as their principal form of communication.

The prazeros, to varying degrees, adopted selected aspects of the indigenous social system. Multi-marriages, for example, were the general pattern among the estateholders. "Polygamy is so common, that it has become acceptable. It is true that it rarely occurs in the town, but on the *prazos* there are not any *patricios* (as are called the children of this River who are a mixture of African, European or Canarian) who do not have three or more wives." [101] According to my informants these prazeros universally recognized the authority and prestige of the senior wife.[102] Gamitto described what appears to have been an extended matrilocal family, composed of a Portuguese father and mother, their married daughters and respective spouses and children, and their step-daughters, living in a series of adjacent compounds.[103] From oral data there are several indications that indigenous influences went far beyond simple polygamy and concubinage. Among the Bongas, who owned Prazo Massangano, for example, a type of false levirate was practiced, while the Pereiras, of Prazo Makanga, adopted a clan name, recognized their matrilineage and, employed the local pattern of descent (see Chapter 9 for a discussion of this process).

Prazo society was a composite of four interdependent yet socially distinct strata. Among the colonos historic kinship connections served as the basis of their social organization as they did for the akaporo, whose blood links were artificially fabricated. Residential patterns defined the basic social grouping of the achikunda, who constructed a neotraditional society based on a nexus of patrilineal kinship relationships. The apparent tendency for members of a prazero family to be widely dispersed suggests that the nuclear or a very shallow extended family formed the normal residential unit while localized segments of the Afro-Portuguese community served as the principal reference group. Interestingly, the lack of social interaction between the various strata living on the prazos was not reflected in the cultural sphere, where the alien achikunda, free Africans, akaporo, and prazeros all adopted the indigenous cultural forms to varying degrees.

5

The Economics of the Prazos: Production
1750-1850

Despite legislation designed to stimulate innovation and production, the traditional pattern of shifting agriculture prevailed on the prazos. One eighteenth-century observer described the limited utilization of the lands and the low output in the following manner: "One sees a piece of cultivated land, from which there is hardly enough to collect a small amount of sorghum and vegetables, it is communally owned and provides the annual sustenance for the *colonos*, all the rest remains bush."[1] When the land became worn out, it was allowed to lie fallow for a number of years. One governor estimated that less than 20 percent of the land on the prazos was cultivated at any given time, which, if correct, indicates a respite of approximately five years.[2] When a smaller estate could no longer support the colono population, the mambo called together the afumu and principal elders to select a new homeland. After examining alternatives and consulting the mizimu, they moved to a location where the land was more productive.

Sorghum, millet, and maize constituted the principal crops cultivated on the prazos. The Africans also planted beans, squash, melons, peppers, cassava, and smaller amounts of rice and sugar. On most estates the sugar and rice as well as the coffee which grew wild in the forest were forwarded to the prazero as part of the mutsonko.[3]

The initial preparation of the fields began in late July or August when the male colonos and their akaporo cleared the new areas of major obstructions and then burned the fields. They collected the ashes for later use as fertilizer. In October or November, just before the first rains, the women went to their respective plots and cleared and burned whatever shrubbery still remained. The only implement they used was an *enchada*, or short hoe.[4]

Having cleared and hoed the fields, they began to plant the crops according to a fixed time schedule. During the following months, the women cut the surrounding grass and weeded the fields in order to remove the parasites which often destroyed the crops. The moist, hot Zambesi climate provided an ideal environment for these parasites, and the colonos often had to abandon a portion of their fields in order to concentrate their labor on the most fertile sections. Another threat to the crops came from the francolin and the monkeys which periodically robbed the fields. All members of the family, but especially the older children, were expected to guard against these incursions. In some areas the men built platforms just before the harvest where they spent the night warding off such attacks. They also placed fires on the outskirts of the fields to keep elephants away.[5]

The first harvest occurred in late February and March when the colonos gathered the millet and the assorted fruits and vegetables planted in November. They collected the sorghum and maize in early May, and also planted a final crop of grain. All the members of the nuclear family helped gather these crops. They were joined by local lineage members and other villagers, especially if the crops were in danger. At the end of the harvest, the workers gathered for a party at which time the hostess served freshly brewed beer, known as *pombe*, made from recently harvested grains.

After collecting the grains, the women brought them back to the village, where they were stored. They periodically visited the granaries and took a portion of the sorghum or millet commensurate with the short-term needs of the family. The women reduced the cereals to a fine consistency by placing them in a wooden mortar and pounding with a large pestle.[6] They then prepared the grain, which served as the mainstay of their diet, in a variety of ways. A porridge, or *massa*, and a breadlike substance constituted the most common dishes. Beer was also brewed in large quantities from the fermented grains, and was consumed quite freely, especially after the harvest. Although many contemporary Portuguese observers considered this to be a wasteful use of limited food resources, there is no question that the pombe was a very important source of nutrients.[7]

Fruits and vegetables, domesticated animals, wild game, and fish provided the principal supplements to the cereal-based diet. Most colonos owned some chickens, pigs, sheep, and goats. Wealthier members of the local population also possessed a number of cattle. Along with hunted game and dried fish, the domesticated animals furnished the major protein intake for the Africans living on the prazos.

Apart from the foodstuffs, the colonos cultivated a substantial amount of cotton which the women wove into a variety of cloths known as manchilla. Manpower shortages and the lack of weavers, however, severely limited the total output.[8] The manchilla constituted the general form of dress on the prazos. They also served as the principal trade item and local commodity currency. The colonos fixed the value of akaporo, cattle, metal implements, and other specialized items at a prescribed number of manchilla, depending on the type and quality of the fabric. The manchilla were also used to satisfy the mutsonko. Most prazeros, in fact, required that a specified number of cloths be included in the annual tax. The fact that the colonos rarely fulfilled this part of the mutsonko obligation suggests the high value they placed on the cloth.[9] The manchilla which the prazero did receive were sent inland with the misambadzi, or trading agent, where they were in great demand.[10]

In the period immediately after the harvest, there was a tendency among the colonos and achikunda toward overconsumption. They brewed large quantities of pompe, feasted on such delicacies as fresh sorghum in milk, and ate many of the fresh fruits and vegetables which were available. Most contemporary prazeros and officials explained these actions in terms of a theory of "uneconomic man."[11] This line of reasoning obviously ignored the rhythmical life style of the colonos, the social and religious significance of the post-harvest period, and long-term storage difficulties.

Before the harvest, the Africans spent their time and energy preparing and guarding the fields and gathering forest products to sustain themselves. It was therefore natural for the colonos and the achikunda to compensate for their past difficulties by enjoying the relative abundance and security. More important, this period of relative inactivity enabled them to satisfy fundamental social and religious obligations. Beer parties were commonly held to repay the laborers who had assisted them during the harvest. The colonos consummated marriage alliances which extended their web of social relations. And localized lineage segments and chieftaincies took this opportunity to make offerings to the mizimu as part of the first-fruit ceremonies. Parties and feasts which may have been uneconomic, depending on the colonos' capacity to store the products over a prolonged period of time, accompanied all these activities. Even if this was a wasteful practice, social and religious responsibilities had a higher priority for the long-term well-being and perpetuation of the indigenous population than did consumption requirements.[12]

Overconsumption, along with the relatively low level of production, did lead to food shortages and seasonal famines, which were an integral part of the agricultural cycle.[13] The mutsonko requirements, the achikunda robberies, and the inhamucangamiza, or forced sale further depleted the limited reserve. The most critical time was the period between the planting and the first harvest. In addition to the seasonal famines, periodic droughts and pestilence resulted in major crop failures and prolonged food shortages. Scattered archival records suggest that these occurred with a certain degree of regularity. In the periods 1792 to 1796 and from 1822 to 1828, plant diseases and lack of rain were responsible for two major famines which reportedly killed thousands.[14]

During the dry season, as well as in times of more serious crises, the colonos, their akaporo, and the prazeros' slaves relied primarily on gathering wild vegetation to supplement the cassava and whatever cereals remained. Thorton, who passed through the Zambesi during one of the more serious food shortages, noted that almost the entire local population was in the forests searching for wild roots and the fruits and only a few remained to guard the drought-ridden fields.[15] The men would go into the woods in search of a variety of roots which they brought back to the village where the women pounded them and prepared a porridge. In addition, they collected wild fruits, especially small apples, mangoes, and berries.[16]

Hunting and fishing, normally secondary sources of food, became much more important. The dry-season hunts meshed well with the harvest schedule, since the men had a great deal of free time to allocate. Furthermore, the lack of rain provided favorable conditions for such activities. A variety of traps were set throughout the forests to snare such small animals as gazelles, francolin, and rodents. Expeditions armed with sticks, spears, and bows and arrows traversed the forests and rivers in search of larger game. Villages which relied heavily on fishing were often able to withstand short-term drought, since they could exchange their surplus of dried fish for small amounts of grain. Their relatively secure position, however, was jeopardized during a prolonged drought.[17] As the water level declined and the river beds dried out, the possibility of replenishing their catch was substantially reduced.

The famines rarely affected the prazeros personally. They were able to supplement the foods collected from the mutsonko and from their fields with a wide variety of imported foodstuffs. At worst, many prazeros had to suffer the indignity of eating cassava, which was considered "Kaffir food." The droughts nevertheless invariably weakened their position and, in extreme situations, threatened their authority. As a rule, these scarcities increased tensions between the various African groups competing for the limited food supplies. Thefts, quarrels, and even inter-village wars were quite common during such periods.[18] The achikunda were particularly abusive; they used their power to rob the colonos of their limited reserves. Instability on the prazos was even more pronounced during prolonged famines. At such times there was a sharp increase in colono migrations to the sertão. Both reduced the prazero's power and wealth considerably.

THE FAILURE TO ESTABLISH A PLANTATION ECONOMY

Although the crown envisioned the prazos as the basis for a future Zambesi plantation economy and issued decrees ordering the prazeros to grow coffee, sugar, tobacco, and other cash crops, the estateholders exhibited no interest in such economic activities. In the 1760s, for example, prazeros exported only insignificant amounts of rice and wheat. By 1806, the principal cash crop, sugar, accounted for less than 2 percent of the total value of exports. A decade and a half later they no longer exported sugar, and the total value of agricultural exports had declined to less than a quarter of the 1806 figure. The prazeros even failed to exploit the coffee and indigo which grew wild in the forests on many estates.[19]

There were several factors which made it impossible for the crown to stimulate agricultural production. The most important were the lack of any real economic incentive, the shortage of a fixed labor supply, and the unwillingness of the prazeros to introduce possible technological innovations.

Historically the prazeros had played an integral role as long-distance middlemen in the lucrative trade between the coast and the interior. Neither a governmental decree nor meaningless threats could make them divert capital from such a profitable venture to one that was so obviously precarious. From all perspectives, the Zambesi lacked the necessary preconditions for large-scale cash cropping. Overland transportation remained inefficient for bulky, low-value agricultural commodities, especially because pack animals could not be used in tse-tse fly zones. Shipping on the Zambesi proved hazardous and was limited to the rainy season. Apart from Quelimane and Mozambique Island, there were virtually no local markets and even these small population centers had very limited food requirements. Finally, the cost of shipping to Mozambique Island and the high export taxes at the customs house made most products noncompetitive in foreign markets.

Manpower requirements also presented a serious problem. The colonos, whose historic methods were geared to a subsistence economy, constituted the principal potential labor force. Moreover, their relatively mobile residence patterns meant that they could not be expected to provide a constant source of labor. The only other group which might have supplied the requisite labor was the achikunda, but their important military and political functions precluded an active role in agriculture.

The few attempts at commercial agriculture produced marginal results. The general unreceptiveness of the prazeros to contemporary agricultural techniques and equipment, and their total misuse of those which were adopted compounded the problems which they faced. Perhaps the most scathing commentary is to be found in Governor Botelho's description of sugar cultivation on the Tete prazos in the first quarter of the nineteenth century.

It is true that sugar is cultivated in Tete but only with difficulty and imperfections. They plant the cane out of season and without any attempt to distinguish the most appropriate and suitable lands for this endeavor; and the crop failure is then attributed to the quality of the land rather than the ignorance of the cultivator. If the production of sugar cane is poorly planned, it is no worse than the cultivation in which they use inappropriate machinery which neither conserves time nor manpower.[20]

He pointed out that a similar phenomenon existed in cotton production. Because the prazeros refused to adopt cotton seeders, amounts of twenty pounds, which could have been deseeded in a few hours, often took as long as two months.[21]

Not only were agricultural exports minimal, but the prazeros regularly imported many products which either could have been cultivated or which grew spontaneously in the forests. Among the most important of these were sugar and coffee.[22]

MINING

Unlike cash cropping, gold mining and, to a lesser degree, iron and copper extraction, did provide a valuable export commodity for a number of prazeros. On most estates female slaves periodically searched the river beds for alluvial deposits. On a few, like Prazo Cansunsa, rich mineral veins were discovered, and large numbers of female slaves worked them intensively.[23]

In general, the most successful mines were not located within the confines of the prazos but at the inland *bares* (mines) scattered throughout the interior. Most were situated north of the Zambesi River, since the principal southern chiefs prohibited the prazeros from working the mines in their land. The major bares were Manxinga, Queborabaça, Mano, and Java, located in Maravia, and Mixonga, Pamboa, and Malima, which were adjacent to Zumbo. The most important of these, Mano, rivaled the trading fair at Manica and Abutua as the principal source of gold in the Zambesi.[24]

The prazeros rarely owned the lands on which the bares were located. They generally leased the site for a specified time after negotiations with the local land chief and the representatives of Undi and Lundu in those areas over which they still retained effective control. In addition to rental fees, the prazero had to present a special gift as homage to the mizimu and pay taxes on all goods imported to the bares. The indigenous authorities also retained the option of stationing spies at the bares. They took this precaution to prevent the prazeros from undermining their authority in the surrounding region and to make certain that the appropriate taxes and gifts were paid.[25]

The prazeros selected the mining sites on the basis of information which their akazambo had received from members of the local population. The slave chief generally paid a substantial amount of cloth to find out the exact location of the mines. This inducement was necessary because many amambo and afumu were reluctant to negotiate with the prazeros. In some areas, such as Abutua, a royal decree expressly forbid such actions.[26] The belief that anyone who touched the gold would die served to reinforce this prohibition.[27] In such cases the prazeros were left with two options. Either they could send achikunda to seize the area, or they could respect the sovereignty and dictates of the traditional authorities. North of the Zambesi they forcibly annexed a number of bares, while in the southern region their unfavorable military position left them no alternative but to send traders to purchase the gold, copper, and iron from royal agents.

After acquiring the mining areas, the prazero dispatched several squads of female slaves to do the actual digging. Each was composed of six to ten women governed by an *inhacoda*. She was ultimately responsible to a mukazambo sent from the prazo to supervise the entire operation. The number of slaves ranged from about a thousand at the larger sites, such as Mano or Manxinga, to twenty to thirty at the smaller bares.[28] A group of achikunda resided at each bare. Their principal responsibility was to insure the security of the mining camp, since competition and disputes among prazeros often flared into armed warfare.[29] In addition, they guarded the camps against attacks from the surrounding chieftaincies. The causes of these confrontations ranged from the failure of the prazero to pay the annual rent to his involvement in local politics. Apart from their military role, the achikunda protected the caravans which brought goods to the camp and also periodically transported the gold back to the prazo.

The female slaves used three general methods to extract gold at the bares. During the rains, when it was impossible to dig, they went out daily and brought back several pounds of rock which they reduced to a very fine consistency by banging one against the other. The fragments were then washed through a trough, and the mineral particles removed. After the rainy season ended, each nsaka was sent to the various rivers and streams to collect any alluvial ores which had been washed ashore.

The most productive operations, however, were the dry season diggings. Each group worked a prescribed area and dug in large pits, ten to fifteen feet deep. The only implement used was a short hoe. The soils were brought to the surface and washed through two square trays, known as *zimba*, until all that remained were the residual grains of gold and other mineral particles.[30]

As in the case of agricultural production, there is no evidence that the prazeros made an effort to introduce any innovations. In fact, one observer noted in 1580 the same techniques that were being used in the middle of the nineteenth century.[31] The failure to introduce improvements may have limited the potential level of production. Nevertheless, a prazero with the good fortune to have acquired a rich site could mine a substantial amount of gold if he had a large number of slaves at his disposal. There are several documented cases of bare owners who received upwards of 500 ounces of gold annually. The principal sites were collectively estimated to have produced 3500 ounces of gold annually, or one-third of the total quantity exported during the 1760s when the trade was at its high point.[32] While no statistical data are available for most bares, the low overhead and the high price that gold commanded suggests that even the less productive mines provided a valuable secondary source of income for many prazeros.

A brisk commerce which took place at the bares supplemented the profits derived from mining. Most prazeros took advantage of their inland position to establish trade relations with the surrounding peoples. Generally they converted part of the area within the bare into a localized fair, where they exchanged Indian cloth, beads, and a variety of European manufactured products for ivory, wax, gold, slaves, and enough food to supplement the agricultural produce which the female slaves grew. These trading centers also served as staging areas for caravans travelling into areas which were not easily accessible from Tete.[33]

6

The Economics of the Prazos: Distribution
1750-1850

Trade continued to be the dominant economic activity within the Zambesi and the principal source of the prazeros' wealth. Throughout this zone and the adjacent region, there existed several networks with fixed markets, staging areas, and distribution centers. The prazeros served as the principal long-distance middlemen in this southern nexus of the Mozambique-India trading system.[1] In this capacity, they linked the Indian Ocean port of Quelimane with the vast interior, stretching at times from the Southern Lunda kingdom of Kazembe to the Rozvi kingdom of Changamira in present-day Rhodesia (see Map 6).

TRADE PATTERNS WITHIN THE PRAZO

On the prazos various trade systems operated at different levels. The indigenous commercial patterns, for example, continued to function independently of the prazero. These ranged from the exchange of specialized goods, such as metal crafts or fish, to a more general trade in cattle, surplus grains, locally fabricated cloths, and slaves. This system lacked fixed markets; producers or, in some cases, itinerant traders known as misambadzi carried their wares from village to village until all were sold. It is likely that the local commerce stretched beyond the frontiers of the individual prazos. The core area, however, remained the traditional chieftaincy upon which the prazo was built. Apart from these purely economic activities, redistribution of goods and services

72

occurred through a number of traditional mechanisms, such as bride price, the communal assistance at the harvest, and the residual mutsonko which the mambo continued to receive.[2]

A substantial trade between the prazero and the colonos also existed on each prazo. As in the case of many political chiefs in Central Africa, the prazero used his position and power to establish a virtual monopoly on all the principal trade goods purchased or sold within his territory. Thus he was able to obtain ivory, gold, and agricultural products at well below their market value. The inflated prices he charged for the imported cloths, beads, and alcoholic beverages which his agents sold to the indigenous population compounded his profits.[3]

When the prazero did not receive what he considered to be an adequate supply of trade goods, he ordered an inhamucangamiza or forced sale. Each chuanga informed the local mfumu or mambo that the prazero's trading agent, or misambadzi, would be arriving shortly to conduct the inhamucangamiza. This was often enforced with total disregard for the consumption requirements of the indigenous population. The mutsonko and the ivory tax also served as important mechanisms through which the prazero acquired a number of valuable goods.[4]

The agricultural products collected in the trade and through taxes enabled the prazero to remain relatively self-sufficient except during the most serious famines. The grains, especially millet and sorghum, provided him with an adequate food reserve to meet both his family's needs and the consumption requirements of the misambadzi and achikunda, neither of whom were entirely self-sufficient. On some estates, the colonos cultivated manioc especially for the slaves of the prazero. Surplus grains were also used to feed the members of the trading caravan during the initial phase of their journey.[5] The locally woven cloths which the prazero acquired served as the principal source of clothing for his family in place of the more costly imported materials. In addition, the prazero redistributed a portion of the highly valued manchilla as rewards to his slave leaders, helping to insure their continued loyalty.[6]

The internal trade also functioned as an important adjunct to the long-distance commercial system. The agricultural products reduced the prazeros' potential expenditures on food imports, while the gold, ivory, and wax exported to the coast provided capital which he reinvested in cloth and other goods traded in the interior. The manchilla, however, constituted the principal input into this trade system. The locally woven cloths enjoyed great popularity among the Nsenga, Chewa, Southern Lunda, and Karanga-related peoples. In exchange, the prazero received gold, ivory, copper, and slaves.[7] Because the pra-

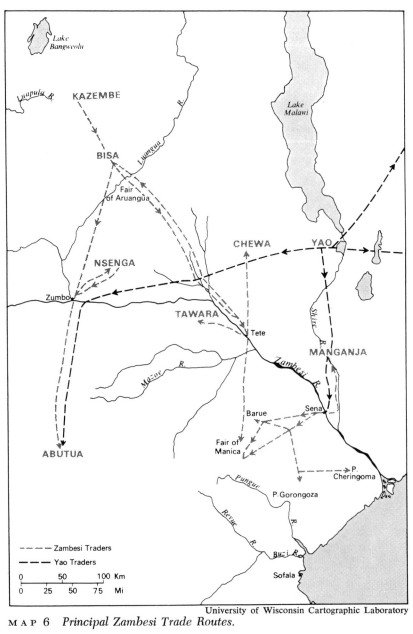

MAP 6   *Principal Zambesi Trade Routes.*

zeros purchased the manchilla at depressed prices, they could afford to sell them inexpensively and still make comfortable profits. According to several observers, Zambesi yarns surpassed the famed cloths of Goa as the single most important trade item.[8]

LONG-DISTANCE TRADE

From the time of their arrival in the Zambesi, the principal activity of the Portuguese had been the profitable long-distance trade with the various Karanga and Malawi chieftaincies. Their control of the commercial sphere dated back to the elimination of the Arab middlemen who dominated the Zambesi trade until the end of the sixteenth century. At this time the precursors of the early prazeros and other inland Portuguese rapidly moved in to fill the economic vacuum and redirected trade from the Swahili coast and the Persian Gulf to Goa, the administrative center for Mozambique.

The Indian Ocean monsoon indirectly regulated all aspects of the Mozambican-Goan trade pattern. In late January or February, shortly after the monsoon, ships began to arrive from India at Mozambique Island, which served as the national customs house for all goods imported to and exported from Portuguese East Africa. After the duties were paid, the goods were shipped on small craft to Quelimane and then inland via canoes and porters to Sena, the principal collection and distribution center for the entire region. Merchants then forwarded the imports to subordinate trading centers at Tete and Zumbo to be dispersed throughout the interior. This pattern continued until May or June when the direction of the trade was reversed. By the beginning of August, all goods had arrived at Mozambique in order to be exported in the forthcoming monsoon.[9]

Because of their position as inland traders, the prazeros depended on coastal middlemen to supply them with the imported commodities and to purchase their ivory and gold. These transactions generally took place at Sena or Tete rather than in Quelimane. Until 1755, the government controlled *Junta do Comércio*, represented in Sena by the *Fazenda Real*, served as the principal supplier and purchaser. These royal servants retained a legal monopoly on all the principal cloths imported into the Zambesi and were the only authorized purchasers of ivory designated for export.[10] In practice, they used their role as official regulatory and credit agents to manipulate prices and, on occasion, actively competed with the prazeros. As a rule, the factors offered low quality cloth at inflated prices and purchased the ivory at deflated rates.[11] In

order to compete with Yao traders, who bought their products at northern duty-free ports, many prazeros purchased contraband goods.[12]
Those who were either unwilling or unable to obtain smuggled cloth
found that the volume of the trade which they controlled was severely
limited.[13]

By the 1750s, Lisbon recognized the counterproductive nature of its
mercantile policy, which encouraged smuggling and led to a shift in
the direction of trade outside the Portuguese controlled customs zone.
As a result, the government abolished the factorial system and in its
place introduced a policy of free trade, coupled with a 41.5 percent
export tax on all goods leaving Mozambique Island.[14] Although this
new legislation still left the prazeros in a disadvantageous competitive
position, most were able to absorb this tax or to pass it on without
jeopardizing their commercial relations.

One of the important outcomes of the shift to free trade was the
need to establish a new distribution system capable of providing a constant supply of imported goods to the Zambesi entrepôts. The Goan
merchants, who dominated both the Mozambique Island–India trade
and the northern network from the island to the Yao-Macua region,
quickly capitalized on this situation. Within a few years their commercial acumen and large capital reserves enabled them to emerge as the
principal importers.[15] The larger Indian firms established trading
houses in Quelimane and Sena. Firms that decided not to open permanent storehouses at either major center or at the subordinate inland
markets hired itinerant traders and local merchants to serve as their
agents to negotiate with the prazeros. In most cases, they were also
Goans, often related to the senior members of these firms.

Through cooperation and effective control of the flow of products
into the Zambesi, the Goan importers maintained artificially inflated
prices. Items which sold for two or three centavos on Mozambique
Island cost the prazeros six times that amount.[16] Attempts to break this
monopoly proved unsuccessful since ultimately any independent merchant had to purchase his trading goods from one of the Goan importers, all of whom would charge him double the amount that their
local agents paid.[17] The strength of their position allowed the Goans
to enforce a trading schedule which required that all the goods arrived
at Mozambique Island before the monsoons. Failure to meet this dead-
line resulted in a 10 percent reduction in the price which the prazero
received.[18] The tendency to purchase all their trade items on credit
reinforced the prazeros' dependence on the Indian merchants.[19] The
Goans naturally sought to promote such a relationship and reap the

high interest rates. According to one observer, all but the richest prazeros spent their entire lives attempting to liquidate growing debts.[20]

The shift to a free trade economy did not radically alter the commercial role of the prazeros. They continued to organize and dispatch trading expeditions into the vast interior. In this capacity, they, along with
the Yao, Bisa, Ovimbundu, and Chokwe, were among the more successful long-distance traders of South Central Africa. The size of their expeditions varied substantially, depending on the distance and potential
wealth of the trading area visited. Caravans ranged from ten men to
several hundred. Each commercial venture was directed by a misambadzi, who traditionally had served the chiefs and affluent members
of the indigenous society. The prazero selected the misambadzi from
among his slave officials, although a particularly successful colono
could be appointed to this prestigious and profitable position. Because
the success of a venture depended upon the skills and reliability of the
misambadzi, it was not uncommon for a prazero who lacked confidence
in his trading agent to rent one at a substantial price from a neighboring estate owner.[21] In addition to the misambadzi, the trading party
consisted of a number of achikunda and a group of colonos satisfying
their required services to the prazero. The colonos and some achikunda
acted as porters, while several squads of slave soldiers guarded the
caravan.

The caravans and smaller parties travelled to specific areas of the
interior which the misambadzi had selected. The principal sites were
either fixed markets, such as Manica, or the villages of inland peoples
known to have relatively large supplies of gold or ivory. Once the party
left the prazo, the misambadzi enjoyed complete responsibility for the
success of the caravan. He resolved all questions which affected the
safety of the expedition, including strategic selection of the camp sites,
the deployment of the achikunda, and the negotiations with the neighboring chiefs whose lands it traversed. He retained this role throughout
the entire journey, which could last as long as eighteen months.[22]

When the traders arrived at the designated site, or some intermediary village reputed to have goods for sale, the misambadzi directed the
caravan to the compound of the land chief or principal headman. There
he personally negotiated with the authorities for permission to establish a temporary market.[23] This agreement included payment for the
right to use the land, for protection, and for the service of notifying the
local population of their presence. After receiving a designated market
area, the misambadzi ordered his subordinates to establish a camp and
lay out the wares for display. Manchilla, a variety of Indian cloths, colored beads, arms, brass, alcoholic beverages, and salt constituted the

principal trading items. In exchange the caravan received gold and ivory and a small quantity of wax, precious metals, and slaves.[24] Scattered statistics indicate that gold and ivory alone comprised 80 or 90 percent of the total value of exports.[25]

Africans from the surrounding areas came to the chief's village to inspect the goods which the strangers had brought. After discussing the general value of the trade items with the local authorities, they entered serious negotiations with the misambadzi. In those areas where the royal family retained a monopoly on the principal trade goods, the misambadzi dealt directly with their agents.[26]

The actual trading process was often arduous and complex; favorable results depended upon the skills of the misambadzi. Members of the local population brought out the goods they desired to sell and placed them on a pile. The misambadzi then examined them thoroughly and made an initial offer by placing what he considered to be less than an equivalent value of cloth and imported goods in an adjacent pile. The prospective buyer, as expected, showed little interest in this exchange, whereupon the misambadzi added additional amounts, making certain, however, that the exchange rate remained well below the coastal market value. These negotiations could last for several days before a mutually satisfactory price was agreed upon. The misambadzi then presented the local seller with an additional gift as a sign of friendship and to encourage future commercial relations.[27] The bartering was repeated until all the local products had been purchased. The caravans then proceeded to another trading area. When all the cloths had been exchanged, the misambadzi directed the trading party back to the prazo. There the prazero supervised the cleaning, sorting, and weighing of the products which he sold to the Goan merchants.

The caravans also had important secondary economic functions. When travelling through elephant country, the misambadzi dispatched groups of achikunda on hunting expeditions. The members of the caravan consumed the meat from the elephant or traded it for grain with the local villagers. They transported the tusks back to the prazo. In addition, the caravans often paused on their return to the prazos to collect valuable forest products, especially wax and honey, which were in demand at the coast.[28]

Three commercial networks formed the greater Zambesi trading zone. Each remained autonomous though linked to one of the major inland entrepôts of Sena, Tete, and Zumbo. Before the nineteenth century, the Sena-Manica trade axis probably constituted the most important commercial zone. It linked the southern Zambesi town with a number of localized trading areas in the kingdom of Barue and along the route to the major fair at Manica. The entire journey took between fourteen and twenty-one days without any major stops. Caravans, however, often paused at Prazo Sungue, an intermediary market. Located on the northern frontier of the Barue Kingdom, it attracted a constant stream of traders who brought ivory, gold, and wax which they exchanged for the usual imported items and manchilla. From Prazo Sungue, the expeditions stopped at several Barue villages as well as the market at Aruangua on the Barue-Manica border. This trading site, located near Macombe's capital, had been established to divert trade from neighboring Manica.

Before entering the kingdom of Manica, where the fair was located, the misambadzi forwarded to Chikanga the required taxes. This generally consisted of assorted gifts worth twenty *cruzados* of gold, and a piece of prime cloth for his senior wife. The traders also annually sent tribute to his capital.[29] The taxes and gifts served as payment for the right to cross his lands in safety and to trade at the fair. The Rozvi king, Changamira, who was recognized as Chikanga's overlord, also received annual payments.[30]

The fair at Manica stood southwest of Sena on the northern frontier of the kingdom. A treaty with Chikanga allowed the Portuguese government to appoint a *capitão-mór* whose responsibilities included resolving litigations between the various negotiating parties and punishing crimes which occurred within the confines of the fair. In practice, most capitães-móres used this authority to their own advantage and it was not uncommon for them to manipulate prices in order to achieve a preferential buying or selling position. In addition to the capitão-mór a detachment of soldiers resided within the fair.[31] They reinforced the authority of the capitão-mór and protected the fair from invasion. A group of nonprazero traders also lived permanently at Manica as part of a small inland Portuguese settlement.

Although the fair remained open the entire year, the trade probably had a seasonal character. The bulk of the exchanges seem to have occurred during the winter months, May through July, in coordination with the Indian Ocean monsoon and local harvest schedules. Considering Manica's central geographic location, the great demand for cloth and the lack of other accessible markets, it is likely that traders from as far away as present-day Matabeleland regularly visited the fair. Scattered references to Africans travelling great distances to trade at Manica support this hypothesis.[32]

The misambadzi and the indigenous traders transacted their business within the confines of the fair. The latter brought wax, crystal, cotton, ivory, and precious metals, which they exchanged for arms, beads, cloths, and liquor. Of the products originating in the interior, gold constituted the single most important commodity. In peak years annual purchases were estimated at several thousand ounces, making Manica the single most important trading area in the greater Zambesian network.[33] The prohibition against establishing bares in Manica suggests that the royal family may have exerted some form of monopoly over gold production within the kingdom. If this was the case, Chikanga failed completely to enforce this regulation since clever misambadzi purchased small amounts of gold outside the fair from local inhabitants.[34]

In addition to the principal route to Manica, prazeros in the Sena area also sent misambadzi north of the Zambesi into the lands of Manganja. Before the nineteenth century, this remained a secondary trading area providing a limited amount of ivory, agricultural produce, and slaves.[35]

The trade routes originating in Tete were more diffuse than those from Sena. Small trading parties obtained ivory, wax, and gold from the neighboring Tawara peoples and elephant tusks from the Tonga, the Barue, and peoples living in Manica. Other caravans moved northward to the homelands of the southern Chewa where they traded at the villages of the land chiefs and important village headmen. As early as the seventeenth century, this area had become the most important source of ivory and gold north of the Zambesi River. In addition, the misambadzi purchased gold, iron hoes, cotton, and cereals, which were exported to Sena and to Mozambique Island. These grains proved to be particularly significant during droughts which the prazos suffered periodically.[36]

Towards the end of the eighteenth century, the Tete prazeros expanded the scope of their Malawi trade network to include the Southern Lunda of Kazembe. Previously, Bisa middlemen had periodically brought small amounts of copper, ivory, and other surplus goods to Zumbo and Tete from the Lunda kingdom. The Zambesi entrepôts, however, had remained a secondary market area with the vast bulk of the trade carried on the Lunda–Yao–Mozambique Island axis.[37]

From Kazembe's perspective his total dependence on the Yao presented serious problems. By virtue of their control of the coastal trade area, it remained impossible to deal directly with Mozambique Island, Mossuril, or even Kilwa. Although Kazembe sent some slaves to the Angolan coast, geographic factors precluded the export of bulk items west to the Atlantic.[38] As a result, Kazembe sought new outlets which would enable him to bypass the Yao monopoly.[39] One possibility was to establish direct commercial relations with the Portuguese whose misambadzi traded in neighboring Malawi chieftaincies. The earliest recorded contact between the Lunda chief and the Portuguese occurred in 1793. In that year, a group of Bisa subjects of Kazembe arrived at the home of Gonçalo Caetano Pereira, a prosperous trader and bare owner. The messengers informed him that Kazembe desired to open his lands to Portuguese traders and their misambadzi. A second group of Bisa arrived in Tete in 1795 with a valuable shipment of ivory as an incentive to stimulate trade. To insure the safety of the misambadzi, Kazembe decreed that any Bisa or Lunda chief who interfered with the caravans coming from Tete would be severely chastised.[40]

From the last decade of the eighteenth century, when Gonçalo Caetano Pereira made the first trip to Kazembe's capital, until at least 1829, commercial relations existed between the Tete prazeros and the Southern Lunda. From the sketchy documentation, it appears that the bank of the Luangwa River on the Malawi-Bisa frontier served as the principal trading point. At this market the misambadzi purchased ivory, copper, and a small number of slaves.[41]

Despite Kazembe's initial interest, there is no evidence that the prazeros ever attracted a substantial portion of the Southern Lunda trade, although it may have been a significant percentage of local Zambesi trade.[42] At least three factors explain why the trade never achieved its potential. First, the prazeros inability to compete with the Yao, who obtained their products in duty-free ports at substantially cheaper prices, placed them at an obvious disadvantage.[43] Furthermore, the Tete caravans traveled through a number of hostile chieftaincies which periodically taxed, harassed, and robbed them. Sustained Bemba attacks on the Bisa in the beginning of the nineteenth century exacerbated these dangers and temporarily disrupted all trade with Tete.[44] By the time commerce was reestablished, the prazeros had become immersed in the slave trade, and Kazembe preferred to continue exporting his captives to the Angolan markets.[45]

The kingdom of Abutua, in present-day Rhodesia, marked the southern limits of the prazeros' trading sphere. Misambadzi-led caravans purchased gold and ivory, and smaller amounts of copper and medicinal roots in the Rozvi kingdom. At its highpoint in the middle of the eighteenth century, Abutua temporarily surpassed Manica as the prime supplier of gold and was reputed to have supplied more than all the other trading areas combined.[46] The northern entrepôt of Zumbo served as the principal staging area for these expeditions. The imported trade goods and manchilla were gathered in Tete and transported overland to Chicoa where they were placed on canoes and forwarded to Zumbo. They were then sorted and distributed to the misambadzi. Because of the long distance and the difficult journey, no fixed rhythm characterized this trade. Caravans leaving Zumbo in October and expected back the following March or April often remained in the interior for as long as eighteen months.

Changamira, the Rozvi king, carefully regulated the commerce within his kingdom. He retained a monopoly over the rich gold trade and perhaps over the less significant ivory commerce as well. To insure his economic and political preeminence, he barred all Europeans from entering his territory.[47] As a result the misambadzi directed and negotiated all commercial transactions under the auspices of a royal agent.[48] It seems clear from the scattered documents that Changamira controlled the entire mineral output within his land. In a royal pronouncement he declared the mining areas closed to the misambadzi and ordered that any subject who assisted the misambadzi be killed. Similarly, no miner could extract gold except with the express approval of Changamira or his agents. They then forwarded the ore to selected trading centers where the actual bargaining between the royal agents and the misambadzi took place.[49]

Because of its central inland location, Zumbo developed into an important staging area for commerce with various interior peoples who otherwise would have fallen outside the sphere of the Zambesi trading system. Misambadzi, for example, periodically traveled north to the lands of "Orange," probably Ulenje in present-day Zambia, to purchase ivory and copper.[50] Zumbo also served as a secondary market for the Bisa middlemen. Although commercial relations remained sporadic, the caravans that did arrive brought valuable supplies of copper, ivory, and even a small number of slaves from the Lunda and other interior peoples.[51] This trade continued periodically long after all Lunda connections with Tete had ceased, and as late as the 1860s Livingstone reported that Bisa traders still sold ivory at Zumbo.[52]

A more permanent trade relationship existed with the western Nsenga who lived just north of the fair at Zumbo. As skilled elephant hunters, the Nsenga provided the merchants of Zumbo with a valuable supply of ivory. They also sold a number of slaves which the prazeros used on their estates. This early connection became more important in the nineteenth century when the prazeros became intimately involved in the trans-Atlantic slave trade.[53]

Commercial relations throughout the greater Zambesi region proved very lucrative for the prazeros. Profits of 200–300 percent often were realized.[54] Even if these estimates represent gross figures, the relatively high markups seems more than adequate to cover normal operating costs, spoilage, and theft, and to insure a comfortable margin of profit. Perhaps the best nonnumerical index of the profitability lies in the fact that for two centuries the cloth-gold-ivory trade constituted the dominant economic activity of the Zambesi prazeros and of the other Portuguese and Indians living in the area.[55]

COMPETITION AND OTHER TRADING DIFFICULTIES

Despite the high rate of return, intense competition and political instability within the surrounding chieftaincies limited the scope of the prazeros' commercial networks, the volume of their trade and, consequently, their absolute profits. By the end of the eighteenth century, these factors threatened the economic position of many prazeros.

Because of their ideal geographic position and their trading acumen, the Yao represented the principal source of competition. The opportunity to purchase high quality goods at duty-free ports reinforced their preferential position.[56] They also benefitted from an efficient distribution system which enabled them to ship goods overland at a much lower cost than that which the prazeros incurred.[57] Their early domination of the Malawi-Mozambique trade route, which dated back to the middle of the seventeenth century, was perhaps the most significant advantage they enjoyed. The Yao had become firmly entrenched in this region while the Portuguese focused their attention on the Karanga gold area.[58] Once the Yao established their preeminence as middlemen, it proved impossible for the prazeros to dislodge them. Throughout the eighteenth and the nineteenth centuries, the prazeros made their only major inroads in the southern Malawi chieftaincies, like Biwi, which were adjacent to Tete and at the inland bares.[59] Even in these areas, however, Chewa informants recall that their ancestors preferred to sell ivory and other items to the Yao because they received more and better cloth from them than from the misambadzi.[60] The Yao were also able to protect their favored trade position with the Southern Lunda despite the initial desires of both Kazembe and the Portuguese to establish commercial relations.

In the second half of the eighteenth century the Yao caravans began to traverse the Zambesi River, moving into an area which historically had been the core of the prazeros' trading sphere. By 1750 Yao traders had extended their trade network to include the area adjacent to Zumbo.[61] Their most significant penetration, and perhaps the greatest testimony to their commercial organization, came in the following decades when they entered the distant lands of Changamira. According to one despondent governor, they began to dominate the entire Abutua area by 1770.[62]

The entrance of the Goan middlemen into direct trade relations with the surrounding Karanga peoples reinforced the economic pressures on the prazeros. Although a few Indian merchants had been active in the period before 1750, their importance in this sphere remained small.[63] After the abolition of the factorial system, the Goans expanded their involvement in all areas of commerce and challenged the prazeros' preeminent trading position in areas south of the Zambesi. By virtue of their commercial links with the principal trading houses on Mozambique Island, the inland Goan merchants had access to an open supply of trading goods. Moreover, their preferential buying and credit position enabled them to cut prices by 50 percent and more.[64] Many prazeros deflated their prices in order to remain competitive; others found that it no longer remained profitable to continue. The competition at Manica reached such proportions that the Governor banned all Indian traders from the fair.[65]

Apart from these competitive pressures, the organization and nature of the prazeros' trade network presented a number of recurring problems. Most obvious was their total dependence on the misambadzi. Not only did they rely on the agent to negotiate all trade agreements, but also they had no recourse if the misambadzi, who, after all, was a slave, fled to the interior with the entire caravan. Other misambadzi, who remained loyal, reputedly altered the prices which they claimed to have paid for certain items and added the remainder to their personal trade goods which they sold independently.[66]

This type of expansive commercial venture suffered from an inherently vulnerable position. Neither the garrisons at Zumbo or Manica nor the achikunda guarding the caravans possessed the military capacity to ward off a major enemy thrust. The whole system remained predicated on the assumption that the local indigenous authorities benefitted either directly or indirectly from the commerce and had, therefore, a vested interest in insuring its perpetuation. Apart from occasional robberies and harassment, this system functioned reasonably well as long as good relations were maintained and the respective sovereigns could protect the caravans. The history of the Sena-Manica trade network reflects this problem. Throughout the eighteenth century, the misambadzi traded freely along this axis. The only reported disruption before 1780 occurred as a result of a civil war around 1757.[67] Commerce was resumed in the succeeding years without any detrimental effects on the trading system as a whole. While occasional attacks by dissident Manica or Barue chiefs served to underline the fragility of the system, they did not substantially reduce the volume of trade. In the latter two decades of the century, however, a series of civil wars and the accession of one or perhaps several successive rulers who were hostile to the Portuguese severely restricted commerce within this trading zone. The incidence of raids on the misambadzi increased sharply, and the market areas were periodically harassed. One anonymous observer noted that the frequency of robberies reduced trade with Manica to a bare minimum.[68] The only available recourse, an appeal to Changamira, theoretical overlord of Manica, failed to produce the desired results.[69]

Recurring succession struggles in Barue and the refusal of Macombe and his competitors to allow the misambadzi to cross their lands compounded the instability along the trade routes in the first part of the nineteenth century.[70] The Manica fair was subsequently moved north across the frontier to Aruangoa in an abortive attempt to revitalize the commerce.

Unfortunately for the prazeros, these structural difficulties built into the principal trading systems became most pronounced at approximately the same time. The inability of Changamira to guarantee the safety of the expeditions in the outlying areas, the continual robberies by the royal soldiers of the Muenemutapa, and the attacks on Zumbo halted all trade at that northern entrepôt by the beginning of the nineteenth century.[71] The Bisa-Bemba wars from 1806 to 1810 stunted the potential growth of the Lunda-Tete trade axis. When the routes were reopened new economic conditions and continued competition from the Yao limited the volume of commerce. By the beginning of the nineteenth century the once expansive trade network had been reduced to those marginal areas adjacent to Sena and Tete, primarily north of the Zambesi, and the total value of trade which the prazeros commanded had declined to a mere fraction of what it had once been.[72]

THE GROWTH OF THE SLAVE TRADE

The growth of the Zambesi slave trade at the beginning of the nineteenth century alleviated, at least temporarily, the economic dislocation which threatened many prazeros. It, in turn, produced new strains and contradictions within the prazo system and was a principal factor in its ultimate demise.

A small number of slaves had sporadically been exported from the

Zambesi. Slaves were sold as early as 1645 when the Dutch conquests in Angola forced the Portuguese to establish slave markets in Mozambique in order to meet Brazilian manpower needs.[73] During the succeeding century, exports continued on a relatively small scale. In the period 1750–60, Mozambique annually exported approximately 1,000 slaves. Since Inhambane, Sofala, and Querimba Island supplied 800, the Zambesi could have provided no more than 200 captives. A 1762 report which listed as 300 the average total annual export of slaves from the Zambesi to Mozambique Island corroborates this approximate figure.[74]

T A B L E 5   *Slaves Exported*
from Mozambique to the French Islands

Year	Portuguese Ships	Foreign Ships
1781	315	—
1782	1045	—
1783	1765	—
1784	2313	—
1785	2332	—
1786	2847	—
1787	3665	4548
1788	5506	5510
1789	2687	6987
1790	656	6697

Source: A.H.U., Moç., Cx. 33: "Mappa da Importância das fazendas, marfim, ouro, escravos, e patacoas (1781–90)" (unsigned), September, 1796.

In the last decades of the century, the number of slaves sent from Mozambique to the French Islands increased substantially (see Table 5). These slaves came primarily from the northern Mozambican trade routes, with regions farther south hardly affected.[75] The development of the Zambesi into an important slave exporting zone was inextricably linked to Brazil's economic prosperity. The resurgence of sugar production in northeastern Brazil and the subsequent establishment of the coffee plantations in the Parahíba Valley created new demands for cheap labor. At the first sign of renewed prosperity, enterprising Brazilian slavers established firms on Mozambique Island where they could purchase slaves at sufficiently inexpensive prices to offset both the increased transportation and food costs and the higher mortality rate of slaves transported back to Brazil.[76] Other Brazilian merchants allied themselves with the older Indian families who were actively involved in the slave trade to the French Islands. The existing trade networks in northern Mozambique, however, failed to meet the growing demands of both areas. This was probably due in part to the shift of Yao trade routes north to Kilwa.[77] To combat this shortage, foreign entrepreneurs shifted their attention to previously marginal slave trading areas, such as the Zambesi. The prazeros saw the opportunity for economic diversification and renewed wealth. In 1797, Governor Lacerda claimed that the Zambesi was already the principal source of slaves exported to Mozambique Island.[78] Although probably exaggerated, this clearly suggests the nature of the prazeros' response and the growing significance of the slave trade for the Zambesi economy.

An abundant supply of inexpensive slaves in the Zambesi motivated several Brazilian merchants to open trading houses in Quelimane, although this violated customs regulations.[79] Other dealers brazenly sailed into Quelimane harbor, bribed the local officials, purchased the slaves, and embarked for Brazil.[80] The government's inability to prevent these illegal transactions and the growing loss of revenue necessitated a modification of the export laws. As early as 1807, specific French and Brazilian merchants received authorization to trade in Quelimane, provided that they paid the prescribed customs duties. Four years later, all subordinate ports were officially opened to Brazilian vessels. This served as a strong stimulus to trade and reinforced the commercial links with Brazil. During the following decade, Quelimane challenged Mozambique Island as the principal slave market in Portuguese East Africa.[81]

The prazeros' previous experience in long-distance commerce, the trading acumen of the misambadzi, and the accessibility of potentially rich markets north of the Zambesi facilitated their entrance into the slave trade. Although the misambadzi continued to purchase available ivory and gold, they placed the highest priority on the acquisition of slaves. This shift in the nature of the commerce is reflected in the decline in the volume of gold and ivory and the corresponding increase in the slave export (see Table 6).[82]

The general trading pattern remained unchanged, despite the emphasis upon slaves. Caravans carrying cloth, beads, and imported goods traveled to the inland areas known to have large numbers of slaves available for sale. The misambadzi remained responsible for the safety of the expedition and the negotiations with the indigenous land chief or headman in whose area they intended to trade. Members of the local population brought the slaves before the misambadzi, who carefully checked them for physical defects and assessed their value. It often took several days before a mutually satisfactory price was reached. On occasion, a slave's claim that he could not legally be sold

TABLE 6 *Products Exported from Quelimane in 1806 and 1821*

| | 1806 | | 1821 | |
	Volume	Value in Reis Forte	Volume	Value in Reis Forte
Gold in Maticaes [a]	6,786	16:000$000	2,585	5:170$000
Ivory in Arrobas [b]	4,375	84:000$000	1,538	7:342$400
Slaves	1,484	30:720$000	5,040	151:200$000
Wheat in Alquiere [c]	6,142	9:827$000	325	4:325$000
Rice in Alquiere	14,121	17:920$000	1,695	2:712$000
Others	—	16:000$000	—	5:984$000
Total Value of Exports		174:467$000		176:733$400

Sources: Academia das Ciências de Lisboa, Ms. 648 Azul: António Vilas Boas Truão, "Estatística de Capitania dos Rios de Senna do Anno de 1806," 16 July 1807; Ajuda, 52–X–2, No. 3: José Francisco Alves Barbosa, "Analise estatística," 30 December 1821.

[a] 96 grains of gold each.

[b] A dry measure equal to 15 kilograms.

[c] A dry measure of widely varying dimensions, usually 13 liters in Mozambique.

created additional delays in the negotiations, which were not resumed until the local authorities had resolved the case. In addition to the purchase price, the misambadzi presented two symbolic gifts indicating that he now owned the blood of the slave and that the transaction had ended cordially.[83]

The newly acquired slaves were placed in chains or bound with leather and bamboo. On the journey back to the prazo, the achikunda guarded against attempted escapes and raids by the surrounding peoples. After the captive arrived at the estate, the prazero either sold him to an inland merchant or shipped him directly to the slave markets at Quelimane. There the slaves were washed, oiled, and divided into three groups. The first, known as *pesca*, consisted of men and women between eighteen and twenty-five years of age without any major physical defects; they commanded the highest price at the market. The *pote d'agua*, healthy slaves between the ages of fourteen and eighteen, sold for only slightly less than that of the pesca. The remaining slaves were deemed less desirable and cost an appropriate amount.[84]

The trade in slaves provided a high profit for both the prazeros and their coastal trading partners. Although precise statistical data are unavailable, it is possible to estimate the traders' profits at various periods in the nineteenth century (see Table 7). It should be noted that these data do not take into account such factors as the age, sex, health, and skills of the slaves or the local market conditions. Male carpenters, for example, commanded a price three times as high in Quelimane as an unskilled child, while slaves purchased in highly competitive areas, like Kazembe's territory, cost more than those acquired in the northern sertão adjacent to Sena and Tete.[85]

T A B L E 7   *Buying and Selling Prices of Zambesian Slaves*

	1800–10 ca.	*1820–36 ca.*	*1850–60 ca.*
Price in Interior	$2	2–3 Sp. $	11–16 shillings
Price at Quelimane	$15–$25	20–30 Sp. $	3–6 £
Gross Profits	$13–$23	17–28 Sp. $	44–109 shillings
Percentage Markup (App.)	650–1150%	600–1400%	250–1000%

Sources: W. F. W. Owen, "Letter from Captain W. F. W. Owen to J. W. Crocker, 9 Oct. 1823, in *Records of South-East Africa*, ed. G. M. Theal (Capetown, 1903), 9:33; F. Texugo, *Letter on the Slave Trade Still Being Carried On Along the Eastern Coast of Africa* (London, 1839), pp. 14–15; J. P. R. Wallis, ed., *The Zambesi Expedition of David Livingstone 1858–1863*, 2 vols. (London, 1956), 1:34.

Despite their imprecision, these statistics clearly indicate the possible range of profits at any one point in time. The actual profits which the prazeros realized were contingent upon both the Quelimane market price and their ability to establish direct trade relations with the coast. If, as in some cases, they circumvented the Indian middlemen, their profits were substantially greater than those of prazeros compelled to sell directly to the Goans. Even in the latter situation, profits rarely fell below 200 percent.[86] The attractiveness of this trade and the enthusiasm of the prazeros is evident in the reminiscences of a government official and former estate holder: "The *prazeros* conscious of the financial benefits that others had derived, and motivated by the lucrative profits in this commercial sphere, abandoned everything else and focused solely on the slave trade."[87]

To satisfy the spiraling demands from Brazil, the prazeros focused on the southern Chewa chieftaincies and, to a lesser degree on the Nsenga and Manganja. There are a number of interrelated demographic, historical, and political factors which help explain the availability of slaves and their accessibility to the prazeros.[88] Perhaps the most important was the disparity between the population density of the peoples living immediately north and south of the Zambesi. Despite the absence of statistical data, numerous informants all agreed that the highland areas to the north were much more heavily populated than the insalubrious southern lowlands. These demographic imbalances led to distinctly different, yet complementary, population pressures which fostered the growth of the indigenous slave trade. The underpopulated Tawara, Tonga, and Sena historically purchased akaporo from the Chewa, Nsenga, and Manganja to meet their manpower needs and to strengthen their lineage system. As late as the middle of the nineteenth century, one observer noted that although domestic slavery existed in the southern region the labor shortages precluded any commerce in slaves. The Nsenga, Manganja, and especially the Chewa used these trading connections to rid themselves of undesirables, acquire cloth and other highly valued items, and alleviate whatever demographic pressure may have existed. All sold enemy soldiers, thieves, witches, and adulterers to the peoples south of the Zambesi.[89] This pattern continued throughout the eighteenth and nineteenth centuries. The scattered data from this period indicate that the Chewa, Nsenga, and Manganja constituted the prime suppliers of slaves used on the prazos.[90] The limited amount of gold which they could offer and the initial lack of Portuguese interest in their ivory probably reinforced this tendency since the northern peoples needed another commodity to exchange for coveted European goods.

The unstable political and military conditions among the northern matrilineal peoples also increased their propensity to export slaves. This phenomenon is best documented in the case of the Chewa. The decline of Undi in the eighteenth century resulted in a general power vacuum, continued instability, and a proliferation of intermambo and intermfumu wars. This, in turn, provided a large captive population. According to Chewa elders, the women and children were often integrated into the victorious chieftaincy while the men were commonly sold to the misambadzi and Yao, who competed for them.[91] Scattered evidence suggests that Lundu's decline in Manganja, and the intensive competition between Nsenga chiefs produced a pattern similar to that which occurred among the Chewa.[92]

The prazeros attempted to increase the scope of their northern trade by purchasing slaves from the Lunda of Kazembe. With the exception of a small number which the Bisa middlemen brought during the early part of the nineteenth century, the Lunda never exhibited any interest and continued to send their slaves overland to the Angolan coast. Hence the prazeros had no alternative but to rely upon the intermittent contacts with Bisa traders and Yao caravans for slaves from the more distant northern zones.[93]

In order to maximize the favorable market conditions at Quelimane, the prazeros began a policy of slave raiding. Often these attacks masqueraded as recapture of slaves or colonos who had fled from the prazos to neighboring chieftaincies.[94] The prime targets were the relatively defenseless Nsenga, Chewa, and Manganja chieftaincies.[95] A late-nineteenth-century traveler noted that the decreased population in the Nsenga homeland was due entirely to slave raids and the subsequent migrations to areas which were safe from the Portuguese and their achikunda.[96]

Military and political considerations prevented the prazeros from employing similar tactics against the peoples living south of the Zambesi. The most vulnerable Sena, Tonga, and Tawara chieftaincies had already been incorporated into the prazo system. The more powerful Karanga states, such as Quiteve, Barue, and the reduced kingdom of the Muenemutapa, were sufficiently powerful, despite civil wars and succession struggles, to repel most attacks. In fact, by the beginning of the nineteenth century, the initiative had shifted to those kingdoms in their struggle with the prazeros.[97]

The colonos constituted the other principal source of slaves. As early as 1791 Africans residing on the prazos were exported without regard to their free status.[98] The prazeros ignored official decrees prohibiting such actions and, as the demand for slaves increased, it became accepted practice to arbitrarily enslave colonos.[99] Many shortsighted prazeros later began to export their achikunda, despite the obvious political and military implications. These abuses became one of the critical factors which undermined the prazo system.

The growth of the slave trade is reflected in the export statistics from Quelimane (see Table 8). These data represent the minimum number of slaves since most of the statistics relate only to the trade with Brazil. In fact, the only years for which they are complete are 1806 and 1820, and even these do not take into account the substantial contraband trade which operated in the Zambesi.[100]

Although Brazil was clearly the most important purchaser, small numbers of slaves were also exported to the French Islands, to India and, toward the end of this period, to Cuba.[101] The estimates of several Portuguese officials, British naval officers, and travelers who were involved in various ways with the trade suggest the possible range of error of these statistics. One Portuguese official noted that, in 1820, fourteen ships purchased approximately 7,000 slaves in Quelimane and that in the next five years, exports averaged between 4,000 and 6,000.[102] Captain Owen, who was stationed off the coast of Quelimane, concurred with the 1821 figure, but concluded that sales jumped sharply in the following two years to between 10,000 and 15,000.[103] The significance of the slave boom is reflected in the proportionate value of com-

TABLE 8   *Slaves Exported from Quelimane, 1764–1836*

Year	Slaves Exported
1764	108[a]
1768	158[a]
1794	467[a]
1796	602[a]
1806	1,484[b]
1814	1,859[c]
1815	995[c]
1816	3,381[c]
1817	2,680[c]
1818	1,117[c]
1819	5,023[c]
1820	5,040[b]
1821	3,110[d]
1822	4,398[e]
1823	2,559[f]
1824	3,768[d]
1825	4,055[d]
1826	—
1827	3,184[g]
1828	4,833[h]
1829	4,658[d]
1830	4,099[i]
1831	—
1832	5,601[d]

Sources: A.H.U., Moç., Cx. 11: António Jozé Rois, 13 August 1764; A.H.U., Moç., Cx. 13: "Registo da Carga que Leva deste Porto a Charrua Real Nossa Snra de Nazare para a Villa Capital de Mossambique neste monção Piqueno anno de 1768," 2 March 1768; A.H.U., Moç., Cx. 13: "Registo da Carga que Leva deste Porto, a Charrua Real Nossa Snra das Merces, para a Villa Capital de Mossqe nesta Piqueno anno de 1768," António Jozé Rodriques, Escrivão da Fazenda Real e Feitoria de Quelimane, 2 March 1768; A.H.U., Moç., Cx. 28: ?Britto, 8 March 1794; A.H.U., Moç., Cx. 28 (unsigned), August 1794; A.H.U. Moç., Cx. 30: "Mapa da Carga da Palla Minerva do que he commandante o Capitão Tenente do nome Jozé Henrique da Cruz Freitas, vinda de Quillimane para Mossambique, onde chegou a . . . do mez de Agosto de 1794" (unsigned); A.H.U., Moç., Cx. 30: "Livro de Cargo da Palla Nossa Senhora dos Remedios que principou a Caligar aos de Praça na villa de Quillimane"; A.H.U., Moç., Cx. 33: Andre Avelino de Souza, Quelimane, 9 March 1796; A.H.U., Moç., Cx. 33: Andre Avelino de Souza, Quelimane, 4 August 1796; A.H.U., Moç., Cx. 33: Andre Avelino de Souza, 5 August 1796; A.H.U., Moç., Cx. 33: Andre Avelino de Souza, Quelimane, 8 April 1796; A.H.U., Moç., Cx. 33: lists of small shipments leaving on 14 February, 9 June, 21 July, and 3 August 1796; Academia das Ciências de Lisboa, Ms. 648 Azul: António Vilas Boas Truão, "Estatística de Capitania dos Rios de Senna do Anno de 1806," 16 July 1807; Joaquim Mendes Vasconcelos e Cirne, *Memória Sobre e Província de Moçambique* (Lisbon, 1890); Ajuda, 52–X–2, No. 3: José Francisco Alves Barbosa, "Analyse estatística," 30 December 1821; A.H.U., Moç., Maço 5: João Bonifácio Alves da Silva to Sabastião Xavier Botelho; Public Records Office [cited hereafter as P.R.O.], FO 84/17: Hayne to Earl of Clanwilliam, Rio de Janeiro, 15 May 1822 (enclosure); P.R.O., FO 84/17: Hayne to Earl of Clanwilliam, 21 August 1822 (enclosure); P.R.O., FO 84/24: H. Chamberlain to George Canning, Rio de Janeiro, 25 January 1823 (enclosure); P.R.O., FO 84/24: H. Chamberlain to George Canning, Rio de Janeiro, 15 August 1823 (en-

modities exported in 1806 and 1821 (see Table 6). These data are particularly suggestive since the earlier period was one of transition from ivory and gold to slaves.

While the absolute value of exports remained virtually unchanged, the entire nature of the trade had been radically altered. In 1806, gold and ivory comprised 57 percent of the total value of exports. Although the value of slaves had increased substantially from the estimated 5 percent in 1762,[104] it represented only 17 percent in 1806. By 1821 the legal sale of slaves alone constituted 85 percent of the trade, while gold and ivory were reduced to a mere 7 percent.[105] In short, the Zambesi economy had become monocultural.

THE CONTRABAND TRADE

The 1836 decree abolishing the slave trade affected neither the volume nor the general organization of the trade; it merely became necessary for the prazero to institute certain modifications on the coast in order to bypass the British blockade. In 1837, for example, at least 8,105 slaves entered Brazil and, in the following year, the number had increased by more than 600.[106] Slave trading at Quelimane markets was booming: "It appears, that any number [of slaves] may be obtained and shipped from Quelimane itself at a few hours notice, and that the Governors have been in the habit of receiving fixed bribes from the slave dealers, whose launches are always ready to start the moment a ship makes her private signal."[107] Among those reputed to have been intimately involved in the contraband trade were Governors

closure); P.R.O., FO 84/31: H. Chamberlain to George Canning, Rio de Janeiro, 5 January 18/24 (enclosure), and 31 March 1824 (enclosure); P.R.O., FO 84/42: H. Chamberlain to George Canning, Rio de Janeiro, 4 January 1825 (enclosure); P.R.O., FO 84/55: H. Chamberlain to George Canning, Rio de Janeiro, 4 January 1826 (enclosure); P.R.O., FO 84/71: A. McCarthy to John Bidwell, Rio de Janeiro, 10 November 1827 (enclosure); P.R.O., FO 84/84: A. J. Heatherly to John Bidwell, Rio de Janeiro, 15 January 1828 (enclosure); P.R.O., FO 84/84: A. McCarthy to John Bidwell, Rio de Janeiro, 26 April 1828 (enclosure), and 9 August 1828 (enclosure); P.R.O., FO 84/95; A. McCarthy to John Bidwell, Rio de Janeiro, 26 February 1829 (enclosure), and 30 April 1829 (enclosure); P.R.O., FO 84/95: A. McCarthy to Earl of Aberdeen, Rio de Janeiro, 11 July 1829 (enclosure); P.R.O., FO 84/112: William Pennell to Earl of Aberdeen, Rio de Janeiro, 25 January 1830 (enclosure), and 15 July 1830 (enclosure); P.R.O., FO 84/112: Charles G. Weiss to Earl of Aberdeen, Bahia, 6 February 1830 (enclosure); P.R.O., FO 84/112: John Parkinson to Earl of Aberdeen, Pernambuco, 13 February 1830 (enclosure); P.R.O., FO 84/112: William Pennell to Earl of Aberdeen, Rio de Janeiro, 8 January 1831 (enclosure).

[a] Based on the records of individual ships leaving Quelimane.
[b] Complete annual statistics for all exports from Quelimane.
[c] Complete exports only to Brazil.
[d] Complete exports only to Rio de Janeiro.
[e] Complete exports to Rio and Maranha.
[f] Complete exports to Rio and Bahia.
[g] Exports to Rio, January to July.
[h] Exports to Rio, January to 31 March, October to 31 December.
[i] Exports to Rio, January to 31 June.

Cirne, Botelho, Alves da Silva, and d'Abreu de Lima.[108] On occasion, Portuguese officials actively obstructed the British anti-slave patrols, to the dismay of the government in Lisbon. These activities ranged from refusing to provide certain facilities for the British to forging documents.[109]

Despite the relative ease of obtaining slaves at Quelimane, the continual harassment and increased confiscations by the British navy necessitated the decentralization of the slave market. After 1840, most transactions took place at subordinate centers located at the mouth of the small channels and creeks which dotted the coast and the delta of the Zambesi. These sites had previously served as the principal outlets for other contraband trade. Because many remained on or adjacent to coastal estates, prazeros played an increasingly important role as middlemen.[110]

The slaves continued to be purchased at the usual inland sites and sent in caravans under the protection of the achikunda to designated coastal areas where they remained in baracoons until the Brazilian and Cuban slavers arrived. The ships remained off the coast, signaling their presence through the use of lanterns. The slavers then loaded the prearranged number of captives on launches and shipped them out to sea.[111] The difficulties and frustrations of curbing this smuggling were reflected in a correspondence between a Portuguese administrator and the captain of the English brig *Curte*:

It is not necessary for me to remind you that the number of easily accessible ports both north and south of Quelimane has facilitated the contraband trade. These ports are neither properly guarded by fortifications nor policed by troops, with the result that slavers have no difficulty making their purchases without the knowledge of the authorities since all the inhabitants have a vested interest in the commerce and do all they can to conceal it.[112]

In 1850 the trade continued to flourish. Despite official assurances that the traffic was under control, the available evidence overwhelmingly suggests that it remained the principal economic activity for a number of powerful prazeros who had established their hegemony over the entire Zambesi area. The only significant difference was that the major overseas slave markets were shifting from Brazil to the newer plantation areas in Cuba and to neighboring Reunion under the guise of the *engagé*, or forced-labor system.[113]

7

The External Relations of the Prazos

1750-1850

The impotency of the Portuguese government and the lack of an indigenous state system in the Zambesi allowed each prazo to function as an autonomous entity. To insure their independence and strengthen their relative power, the estateholders entered a series of shifting alliances. Despite the wide range of individual options, the prazeros as a collectivity seem to have followed a general pattern in their relationship with the Portuguese government, other estateholders, the independent chieftaincies, and the larger surrounding African states. Although treated independently for the purpose of analysis, these external policies and actions were designed concurrently to increase the power, wealth, status, and, above all, the autonomy of the estateholders.

PRAZERO-GOVERNMENT RELATIONS

In terms of legal theory, the prazero's role was clearly defined and highly structured. Underlying the vast amount of legislation prior to the initial abolition of the system in 1832 were three fundamental principles. First, that the prazos belonged to the crown. The lessees, therefore, were obliged to pay taxes, provide periodic services, and obey all the laws promulgated in Lisbon as well as the dictates of the local officials. Second, that anyone failing to satisfy these minimal requirements could and would be expelled from the crown estates.

Third, that the prazos served as the principal mechanism for the establishment of a permanent European racial and cultural community in the Zambesi. The last stipulation provided the philosophical basis for the legislation restricting ownership of the estates to European women. The first two, however, had greater relevance since they clearly established the superordinate-subordinate relationship which theoretically governed all interaction between the Lisbon government and the prazeros.

After the separation of Mozambique from India in 1752, the state promulgated a series of laws designed to reassert its authority in the Zambesi. Although a comprehensive analysis of this legislation falls beyond the scope of this study, a few of the more important laws are cited to illustrate the principal concerns of the government. The initial statutes in 1752 and 1755 dealt primarily with the need to prevent interracial unions and reaffirmed Lisbon's right to confiscate all land owned by donas who had not married Portuguese.[1] A 1753 statute was more central to the prazero-crown relationship, since it aimed at limiting the growing power and autonomy of the estateholders by declaring it illegal for any individual to possess more than one prazo and authorizing the governor of Mozambique to use force if necessary to insure compliance. Moreover, the governor was empowered to refuse to renew the *cartas de aforamento* of any person who owned more than a single prazo.[2] In theory, this decree had the added virtue of making additional estates available to new immigrants who would otherwise have remained landless.

Seven years later, the king issued a sweeping series of laws designed to supplement the earlier legislation and to solidify the state's authority in the Zambesi. Among the most important stipulations were that the size of the estate be limited to three leagues in length and one in width, that the recipient be required to pay an annual quitrent, or foro, that the lessee provide public services which state functionaries demanded, and that no grant be confirmed until the end of a four-year period.[3] If enforced, the impact of this legislation would have been substantial. By limiting the amount of land a prazero could hold, it restricted his potential power and wealth; and by clearly defining the recipient's responsibilities, the state established objective criteria for refusing to confirm the initial grant at the end of the four-year "trial period." In the succeeding decades, the government passed additional laws which ranged from the reaffirmation of the "one man — one prazo" principle to the nationalization of the newly acquired lands north of the Zambesi.[4]

The crown's legal prerogatives were reaffirmed in the aforemento, or lease, which every prazero was required to sign. Abstractly, this bound him to fulfill certain requirements which paralleled the more general legislation promulgated by the state. In the second half of the eighteenth century, the standard aforamento contained stipulations limiting tenure to three generations to be transmitted through the female line, and required the leasee to fulfill certain obligations. These included paying an annual foro, satisfying all services which local officials required, cultivating a specific area of new land, and forwarding all the gold, silver, and minerals found on one's estate. A family which met these requirements could apply to have its aforamento renewed upon its termination.

The only prazeros who were exempt from these responsibilities were the owners of *terras fatiotas*. They, or members of their families, had personally acquired the land from its indigenous African owners. As a result, the crown could only claim a vague, rather abstract suzerainty over the lands, and the prazeros were expected merely to acknowledge their loyalty to the king and to pay a minimal rent. The estate, however, belonged to them and their descendants, and it did not have to be transmitted through the female line. In actual practice, the legal differences between owners of terras fatiotas and *terras da coroa* remained blurred, since neither set of obligations was systematically enforced.[5]

Local political and military factors tended to neutralize the laws and contractual obligations which Lisbon sought to implement. The absence of an efficient administrative system necessary to transmit, institute, and enforce these regulations constituted a major impediment. In theory, the legislative, judicial, and executive functions were clearly defined. The highest state official was the *Governador Geral*, who resided on Mozambique Island. In the Zambesi area, the principal functionary was the *Tenente Geral dos Rios*, who also carried the title of governor. Apart from his general executive responsibilities, he supervised the distribution of prazos. Assisting him were the *Capitão Mór dos Rios*, the *Capitão Juiz*, the *Feitor dos Foros e Quintos Reais*, and a group of lesser officials stationed at Quelimane, Sena, and Tete. The feitors, or fiscal officials, received the foros and *dizimos* (rents), and were expected to make certain that the prazeros fulfilled the other stipulations of their contract.[6]

In practice, a group of generally incompetent men not particularly interested in enforcing the imperial legislation filled these positions. Their poor quality was due, in part, to Mozambique's unimportant position in the Portuguese empire. As a result, those assigned to this backwater area were often second-rate officials unworthy of a more important post. Locally recruited Portuguese, lacking any administrative skills, enlarged their ranks. According to Governador Geral Pereira do Lago, important bureaucrats, including the feitor of Quelimane, could not read, others were drunkards, and the Capitão Môr of Manica was a worthless relative of a former Governor.[7] Seventy years later, Governor Botelho noted that the judicial officials, members of the town council, and tax collectors were all inept.[8]

Corruption at every level of government reinforced this mismanagement and inefficiency. In the upper echelons, functionaries commonly treated their positions as a simple business venture. The substantial amounts they had to pay to gain their appointments engendered this economic spirit. Through special dispensations, selective grants, and other favors given to the prazero community, the officials could recoup their initial investment and amass a small fortune within a relatively short period of time. Several Zambesi residents told Governor Lacerda that "if you do not bring back 40,000 to 50,000 *cruzados* in the first year you do not have any good sense."[9] Minor functionaries, on the other hand, whose wage scale was depressed, accepted and even sought bribes to supplement their incomes. The prazeros, therefore, were able to exert their influence and gain assistance through selective gifts. In return, they received aid in securing additional estates, reductions in their assessed foros and dizimos and, most important, assurances that they would not be harassed for failure to satisfy the stipulations of their aforamentos.[10]

The familial links between high government officials and the principal prazeros enabled many to remain outside the law while simultaneously receiving numerous benefits. Similarly, it was common for important prazeros to purchase offices at all levels of government despite the inherent conflict of interests. Thus, in the period 1752–65 six out of eight capitães-môres of Quelimane held prazos during their years in office or shortly thereafter.[11]

Even under the most favorable political conditions, military considerations precluded any effective action against most estateholders. During the entire period prior to 1850, the Portuguese government was as impotent militarily as it was politically. Throughout the eighteenth century and first half of the nineteenth, the number of soldiers regularly stationed in the Zambesi usually ranged from 100 to 300. According to state officials, this was less than one-third of the estimated minimum required to provide even a modicum of defense and stability. Most were poorly armed, poorly trained, and poorly organized.[12]

This ragged force proved incapable not only of challenging the autonomy of the prazeros, but also of defending the Zambesi against external invasions. The civilian and military officials, therefore, depended on the goodwill and residual loyalty of the prazeros for assistance during a crisis. When the estateholders collectively agreed to supply a detachment of achikunda they did so only because it served their vested interest. In a 1761 memorandum, Governor Montaury candidly acknowledged the state's complete dependence on the prazeros.[13]

Despite the legal pronouncements from Lisbon, this inefficiency and impotency allowed most prazeros to remain outside the sphere of effective governmental control. This autonomy does not suggest, however, that the prazeros' relationship with the crown was essentially hostile or that there were no loyal estateholders. In most cases, their geographic isolation and the poor transportation and communications system precluded sustained interaction of any sort.

The prazeros manifested their independence in a number of ways, including their general disregard for the stipulations of the aforamento. They refused to plant the requisite acreage, forward the gold on their lands to the Fazenda Real, or provide most of the services which local officials demanded. Most important, many rejected the state's claim to the annual dizimos and foros. One early nineteenth-century prazero became so outraged that "on being called up for his arrears, he threatened not only the Governor of the place but also the authorities at Moçambique with his slaves, in number of about a thousand."[14] Other estateholders were delinquent for ten or fifteen years before they agreed to pay a portion of their debt. During the four-and-a-half-year period between July 1789 and December 1793, the average taxes collected were only one-eighth of the 1803 figure. Since there is no reason to believe that there was substantial increase in the number of estates by the latter date, the figures suggest the wide variance in the annual response of the estateholders.[15]

The prazeros' assertion of their autonomy stretched well beyond their failure to fulfill part of the contractual relationship. Indeed, a number of prazeros explicitly denied the validity and relevance of their aforamentos, and, by extension, the government's claim to be the ultimate owner of the land. These included estateholders who never bothered to obtain aforamentos, those who failed to have their grants approved at the end of four years, and those whose deeds had long since expired.[16]

Proposed punitive action ordered from Lisbon or Mozambique Island was rarely implemented. The government's relationship with the powerful owner of Prazo Luabo, Bernardo Caetano Botelho, is a case in point. As part of a crackdown planned against disobedient estate-owners, Governor Pedro Saldanha de Albuquerque ordered that under no circumstances should Botelho's grant be renewed. Furthermore, he suggested that an expedition be sent to dislodge Botelho from his lands. Local officials, aware of the state's unfavorable military position, cautioned against such a hasty act. They argued that not only would it be very difficult to penetrate the well-fortified estate, but also if they succeeded in arresting Botelho, his achikunda would invariably attack Sena, Quelimane, or any other site where he would be jailed. The subject does not seem to have been broached again.[17]

Armed confrontations were limited to the few instances in which the state attempted to reassert its theoretical authority over the prazeros. These actions proved most effective against first generation estateholders who had not had the time or the opportunity to consolidate their power and to establish a working relationship with the mambo and afumu. Similar tactics against the principal prazo families rarely succeeded. The achikunda and colonos of Manoel Gonçalves Gil of Prazo Massangano, for example, inflicted heavy casualties on the government troops when they tried to conquer his lands. He was ultimately killed, but not before his exploits had been transformed into a cause celebre within the prazero community.[18] Apart from such major battles, scattered incidents and robberies involving local functionaries occasionally occurred, but these do not seem to have had an anti-government character.[19]

An uneasy modus vivendi generally existed between the state and the prazeros. The inherent tensions and conflict in their relationship is graphically depicted in an official assessment that among any "group of twenty *prazeros* each one has nineteen enemies, however all are the enemy of the Governor."[20] Hostilities remained at a minimum because local civilian and military officials refused to challenge the independence of the prazeros as they did in the period after 1850. Apart from those cases in which the government interceded in inter-prazo disputes, and a few instances in which it did remove recalcitrant estateholders, the state abdicated its political and judicial powers.[21] In return, the estateholders made no attempt to undercut the last vestiges of government which operated in the Zambesi and paid lip service and periodic taxes to Lisbon.

On occasion, an individual or a group of prazeros even found that it was in their vested interest to temporarily ally themselves with the government. This occurred most frequently in times of crisis when their position seemed jeopardized. More specifically, they forged such agreements to combat an external invasion or to put down colono or slave uprisings.[22] Prazeros also sought the assistance of the government when involved in an interprazo war. Such an alliance, for example, accelerated the defeat of Manoel Gonçalves Gil, who terrorized both estateholders and local officials.[23]

At no point prior to 1832 did these temporary alliances and the limited intervention enable Lisbon meaningfully to bolster and consolidate its authority in the Zambesi. Thus when the Liberals came to power in Portugal, one of their major legislative acts was to abolish the entire prazo system as a means of reasserting governmental authority. As in the case of the earlier pronouncements, the practical implications were minimal, and the prazos continued to function in various forms until the beginning of the twentieth century.

INTERPRAZERO RELATIONS

The absence of effective government power had important ramifications on the general pattern of interprazo relationships and on the system of alliances and mechanisms of control which developed in the Zambesi. On the one hand, it meant that the state was incapable of either offering most prazeros a modicum of protection or preventing them from pursuing an independent course consistent with their perceived interests. This weakness, in turn, made it imperative for each prazero to possess a strong army and to enter various alliances with neighboring estateholders in order to improve his relative position. Without these, it was impossible to survive in an environment where force constituted the accepted method for resolving disputes.

The basis of the prazeros' power was the achikunda slave army. On most estates, a section or at least several squads were deployed at strategic locations on the frontiers. Smaller groups patrolled the area surrounding the prazos in order to provide early warning of an impending attack. The prazeros stationed the bulk of the achikunda in the area near his residence, which served as the inner core of defense. On some prazos, such as Massangano, Massingire, and Makanga, this inner area actually consisted of a rock fort lined with cannons. In the nineteenth century, this became the general pattern of defense, known as the *aringa* system.[24]

The colonos served primarily as a defensive reserve. At the first news of an imminent invasion, the mambo and afumu summoned all the male members of the chieftaincy and ordered them to prepare for battle. According to my informants, a number of disparate factors, including the desire to protect their homelands and fear of punishment, motivated them to assist a prazero.[25] There are several documented cases, however, in which the colonos took advantage of a prazero's preoccupation to rebel against him and, in some instances, even joined the invaders.[26]

The achikunda also provided the essential manpower for most offensive operations. During major battles the chuanga and the indigenous authorities might recruit colonos to aid the slave army. In most cases, however, their role was limited to certain types of logistic assistance. These ranged from serving as spies and guides to supplying the slaves with additional foodstuffs. Their reluctance to fight dissipated when colonos or achikunda from neighboring estates violated their traditional land, water, or hunting rights, and thereby challenged the religious, economic, and political underpinning of the chieftaincy.[27]

The estateholders reinforced their individual power and strengthened their relative position by forging a number of alliances within the prazero community. These can be divided into two major groupings: primary or permanent alliances, characterized by a fixed set of obligations and designed primarily to bolster the member's position in relation to competing prazero segments; and secondary or temporary affiliations organized in response to a particular crisis. The two systems did not remain mutually exclusive, and membership in one did not preclude involvement in the other. Moreover, competitors at the primary level often united against a common enemy which threatened their collective positions as prazeros.[28]

Sanguinal or conjugal ties constituted the basis of most primary alliances. It was very common for one family to acquire a number of prazos which it then parcelled out to junior kinsmen. Internal competition among relatives generally remained latent and most families functioned as homogeneous power groups with clearly defined interests and goals. Descendants of Sisnando Bayão, Manoel Gomes Nobre, and Gil Bernardo Coelho de Campos were among major early prazeros who successfully employed this tactic. In the nineteenth century, Bonga and the Ferrão family built their large personal empires, in part, through a series of interlocking estates.[29]

In most cases, the extended prazero family by itself proved neither politically nor militarily viable. In order to broaden their network of alliances, many estateholders arranged marital unions with other prazeros. In the seventeenth century, such links united the families of Sisnando Bayão, António Lobo da Silva, Manoel de Paes de Abreu, and João da Costa, enabling them to dominate almost the entire district of Sena. A similar pattern emerged in the middle of the following century as a result of the marriage of D. Catharina de Faria Leytão, most powerful prazero in Quelimane, and Bernardo Caetano de Sá Botelho, owner of the Cheringoma-Gorongoza complex. To the north, the wedding of Dionízio de Mello de Castro with the daughter of Manoel Gomes Nobre provided the basis of one of the more important alliances in the Tete area. Such tactics were by no means limited to the prazero elite; a number of smaller estateholders entered such relationships to bolster their marginal position.[30]

These primary alliances often included a number of less important prazeros unrelated to the principal families. These minor estateholders eagerly sought to affiliate, since they clearly benefitted from the protection, power, and prestige of such an association. In the middle of the seventeenth century, for example, most of the Sena prazeros coalesced around António Lobo da Silva and, in the succeeding century, such major estateholders as D. Inez Correia Cardozo, Manoel Gonçalves Gil, and Bernardo Caetano de Sá Botelho had large followings within the prazero community.[31]

Apart from these fixed relationships, the prazero community, or a localized segment of it, united in response to various external threats. During the numerous incursions of the Muenemutapa's army and the nineteenth-century Barue and Nguni invasions, most of the affected prazeros, regardless of their past affiliations, joined in an attempt to repel the attackers. Similarly, a colono or slave revolt often led to a coordinated military response from neighboring prazeros who feared that it would spread to their estates. Although these temporary unions were designed primarily to repel threats from the Africans, broadly based affiliations emerged to combat the expansive tendencies of one or a number of prazeros whose actions threatened to drastically alter the balance of power.[32]

The proliferation of alliances was the logical outcome of an isolated, yet fiercely competitive prazero community. During the entire history of the institution, individuals or groups of estateholders sought to extend their authority beyond the frontiers of their estates. This invariably led to conflicts with other prazeros, who not only resented such incursions, but held similar aspirations. Periodic raids, sustained battles, and prolonged wars continued to be an integral and recurring theme in interprazo relationships throughout the eighteenth and most of the nineteenth centuries.[33] This generalized rivalry for wealth, power, and prestige was reduced to very specific areas of competition, of which the most intense were over land, manpower, and trade.

Boundary disputes emerged as a particularly common cause of discord within the Zambesi. Poorly defined frontiers which separated neighboring estates exacerbated local tensions. Furthermore, the tendencies of villages and chieftaincies to slide into and out of prazo relationships meant that these boundaries remained imprecise. Aggressive prazeros capitalized on this fluid situation to claim, conquer, and annex adjacent areas which belonged to less powerful estateholders.[34] In one instance, no sooner had the owner of Prazo Matundue died than a neighboring prazero incorporated large portions of the frontier zone into his estate. When the deceased's widow made no attempt to resist, he proceeded to take over most of the remaining lands.[35]

Aggressive prazeros did not always initiate these confrontations. There are several documented cases of amambo who precipitated such actions when colonos from neighboring prazos infringed upon their customary land and water claims. The colonos of Prazo Inhamazi, for example, conquered and destroyed Prazo Sonne because of a disagreement over fishing privileges.[36] Similarly, boundary disputes and the violation of hunting rights provided the impetus for a series of confrontations between the colonos of Prazo Massangano and Prazo Maja.[37] This particular war was not in the interest of either of the estateholders, clearly suggesting that the indigenous authorities still retained more than a modicum of independence.

The competition among estateholders for colonos and slaves engendered a number of interprazo conflicts. Achuanga secretly recruited amambo and afumu from neighboring estates by offering them a variety of inducements. If the negotiations were successfully concluded and the mizimu approved, the members of the chieftaincy would migrate en masse to their new homes. These population movements provided the host prazero with numerous benefits and therefore created a constant cause of friction between competing estateholders. Because of their military value, however, most prazeros placed a higher priority on recruiting slaves. Many prazeros, their achuanga, and akazambo encouraged neighboring achikunda to seek asylum on their estates and as an added incentive offered them their freedom. Others rejected this type of subterfuge in favor of direct action. They sent achikunda on forays to adjacent estates to attack outlying colono villages and enslave the captives. Most of the captured males were subsequently integrated into the slave army.[38]

Intensive competition between estateholders transcended the legally acceptable range of business tactics. It was common practice, for example, to buy off the misambadzi of a competitor. The successful prazero not only benefitted from the trading skills of his new employee, but also gained the valuable goods which the misambadzi carried. Violence became an integral part of the trading process; robberies and raids were commonly perpetuated by one prazero and his agents on the caravans of another. This reinforced tensions increasing the number of confrontations both within the Zambesi and in the surrounding sertão.[39]

The use of force as a means of acquiring wealth was not limited to the commercial sphere. Military power constituted a key component in the search for and the acquisition of choice inland bares. News of a rich gold strike invariably led to armed incursions between envious prazeros anxious to gain control of the site.[40] The extensive list of casualties incurred during an eighteenth-century battle for control of the bare of Raphael — 2000 Africans and 80 Portuguese dead — reflects the intensity of such struggles.[41]

Economic and political competition reinforced the social conflicts within the prazero community. Intense rivalry for spouses, sexual improprieties, historical animosities, and intrafamily quarrels constituted the principal causes of contention.[42] Perhaps the most famous quarrel involved D. Inez Correia Cardozo, powerful owner of Prazo Luabo, and her husband of six months, António Joze Telles de Menezes. For a variety of reasons, she desired to divorce Menezes in order to marry her latest lover, who was a high Portuguese official. When her husband refused, she sent a large achikunda force which burned his lands and forced him to seek refuge in the interior. The conflict split the prazero community and the governor general of Mozambique ordered her to desist from such actions. She responded by invading a number of estates, attacking chieftaincies friendly to her husband and threatening local officials. The matter was ultimately resolved, but only after a great deal of bloodshed and turmoil.[43]

The conflict and dissension which fragmented the prazero community had far-reaching implications for the viability of the entire system. Clearly, these internal disputes placed additional pressure on a structurally unstable institution, and were directly responsible for the political demise of a number of prazeros. These actions, moreover, indirectly limited the prazeros' capacity to defend their estates against the continual threats and incursions by the surrounding African polities. Distrust and disharmony ran so deep that joint military operations designed to recapture strategic areas had to be cancelled on several occasions because competing prazeros refused to cooperate with each other.[44]

PRAZERO RELATIONS WITH THE SURROUNDING ZAMBESI POLITIES

Just as relationships within the prazero community remained fluid, their interaction with the independent chieftaincies and surrounding states seems to have been far more complex than the simple imperialism often attributed to it.[45] The critical factor which defined the re-

lationships both within the Zambesi and in the adjacent areas was the
absence of any one dominant power: neither the prazeros nor the surrounding African polities possessed enough force to establish their
hegemony over anything but the core of their respective domains. The
large fringe areas, which included the outlying chieftaincies and the
frontier prazos, developed into zones of confrontation. There, prazeros
and local amambo and afumu, usually operating independently of
any central authority, competed for power and prestige. There was,
nevertheless, another dimension to this relationship. When it was in
their interest, the estateholders anxiously forged an alliance with the
neighboring chiefs, and even became involved in court crises and succession struggles within the larger states. In this respect, the Zambesi
can be seen as a self-defined, although geographically imprecise, political system. The inclusion of the surrounding Manganja, Chewa, Tawara, Tonga, Sena, and Barue chieftaincies in the network of alliances
simply increased the number of possible combinations of polities that
could be considered as allies or enemies at any one time.

Military considerations remained an important factor in determining
the relationship between the prazeros and specific African peoples.
Although they no longer retained a monopoly on firearms, the prazeros
still enjoyed a relative advantage, which they attempted to maximize
with some success. As the result of a recent military expedition, wrote
Governor Alvim in 1769:

the princes and chiefs, near and far, remain obsessed with fear of our arms,
not knowing against whom they will be used. Biwi came to me asking mercy,
affirming that he did not want war but peace and good harmony with the
State. . . . In the same way, the rebellious prince Ganibazi came to me
suing for peace, saying that he did not want to have a war with the State.[46]

The effectiveness of the achikunda and the fear they inspired among
the adjacent populations reinforced the relative power advantage of
the prazeros. One contemporary observer, undoubtedly overstating the
case, estimated that 20 achikunda could conquer 1000 warriors armed
with the indigenous weapons.[47] The multiple alliances compounded
the superiority which many prazeros enjoyed individually. Throughout
the eighteenth century, the prazeros retained this limited advantage
in most of the fringe areas. In these, nevertheless, their ascendancy was
incomplete, and even the weaker Chewa chiefs scored several notable
victories.

The ostensible justification for the prazeros' imperial policy was the
need to eliminate potential threats and to punish neighboring chieftaincies considered disrespectful. The prazeros used such "insolent" acts

as the refusal to trade and the unwillingness to cede land as a rationale for conquest.[48] According to official reports, most of these accusations were contrived, and one governor general openly condemned these invasions and demanded the immediate return of the lands to their traditional African owners. His decrees, like most, fell on deaf ears.[49]

Apart from these fabrications, a number of real incentives underlay the prazeros' expansionist policy. In general, these can be reduced to four principal desires — land, mines, protection of trade, and slaves. It is interesting to note that these were also the principal causes of most interprazero confrontations.

The acquisition of new lands constituted the principal inducement for many offensive thrusts. Every successful operation against the Chewa, Manganja, Manica, and Barue chieftaincies led to the annexation of at least part of the conquered territory and the subsequent incorporation of the peoples living on them into the prazo system. As a result of the victories on the Manica-Barue frontier in the 1750s, twelve new estates were created, while thirteen prazos were carved out of the conquered land of the Chewa chiefs Biwi and Sazora at the beginning of the nineteenth century.[50] The new acquisitions increased both the relative and absolute wealth, power, and prestige of the recipients. The mutsonko and inhamucangamiza provided additional sources of revenue; the captured slaves and the colonos reinforced the military potential of the prazeros; and the number of estates they controlled influenced their status within prazero society.

Closely related to the practice of incorporation through conquest was the forced annexation of bares which the prazeros were unwilling or unable to purchase. The occupation of the bares did not lead to a cessation of the hostilities. The indigenous owners often attempted to reconquer them, and when this tactic failed, they shifted to a policy of harassment and periodic raids directed against both the mining camps and the caravans transporting supplies and trade goods to the bares. Such action merely reinforced tensions and increased the likelihood of punitive reprisals.[51]

Another point of friction, which invariably erupted into conflict, focused on the question of runaway slaves. The prazeros claimed that neighboring chieftaincies encouraged their slaves to flee and offered them asylum. They conveniently ignored the fact that many had been forcibly interned and were merely returning to their traditional homelands. In an effort to alleviate this manpower drain, the prazeros periodically attacked those chieftaincies whom they considered guilty. These raids were designed to dissuade similar actions, to reclaim fugitives, and to forcibly recruit additional slaves. They became more frequent with the growth of the external slave trade in the early nineteenth century.[52]

The prazero also applied military pressure in an attempt to insure the continuity of their trade networks. Action, on occasion, was taken against recalcitrant chieftaincies which refused to trade with the misambadzi. Such tactics were generally reserved for those who actively interfered with commerce. In the 1750s, for example, a group of prazeros inflicted a major defeat on Biwi when he refused to allow their agents to travel to the bares and trading centers at Mixonga.[53]

The majority of these military engagements occurred in the area north of the Zambesi. Intensive and repeated raids by the Sena prazeros ultimately led to the annexation and incorporation of a number of chieftaincies on the frontier of Manganja. In the Tete district, the prazeros invaded the Southern Chewa chieftaincies, especially Biwi, almost annually from 1755 until 1763. Although the frequency of these incursions diminished in the subsequent years, periodic conquests did occur, highlighted by two major encounters in 1804 and 1807. Nevertheless, toward the end of the eighteenth century, several Chewa chiefs adopted a more assertive policy toward the Tete prazeros. There are suggestions, moreover, that Biwi concluded secret alliances with dissident members of the royal family of the Muenemutapa to bolster his military position.[54] Other Chewa began to purchase guns which they used increasingly against the frontier estates.[55]

The number of offensive expeditions into the southern regions were much smaller. Apart from scattered battles with Barue and Manica warriors harassing trade, there seems to have been only one major operation designed to conquer new lands.[56] In fact in the southern region, especially on the frontiers of Chedima, the Africans represented a real challenge to the prazo system.

Because of the relative proximity of the outlying Tete prazos to the Muenemutapa's capital, internal feuds, civil wars, and succession struggles directly effected their stability. These eruptions often spilled onto the estates, much to the discomfort and displeasure of the prazeros. In the second half of the eighteenth century, this pattern occurred with some regularity and posed very serious problems for the Tete prazeros.[57] The extended conflicts which preceded the selection of the successor to Muenemutapa Punzogotte, for example, forced a number of prazeros to abandon their frontier estates. Some of these estateholders, in turn, attacked Chewa chieftaincies on the opposite bank of the Zambesi in order to recoup their losses.[58] Similarly, unsuccessful claimants as well as dethroned rulers and deposed chiefs sought sanctuary on crown estates, which invariably made the prazos prime targets for attack.[59]

In addition to these conflicts, unsuccessful pretenders often satisfied their lust for power at the expense of the outlying prazos. Prince Bangoma, son of the deceased Muenemutapa Punzogotte, conquered a number of estates in 1768 and appears to have temporarily incorporated them into his personal empire.[60] Periodic forays and sustained attacks by dissident members of the royal family motivated one governor to note despondently that many Tete prazos had been abandoned for more than forty years.[61] The position of the remaining prazeros became so desperate that some of the more powerful families began to buy protection from the surrounding chiefs and their warriors.[62]

These military pressures also affected the prazeros' northern trade network. Soldiers of the Muenemutapa and his territorial chiefs constantly attacked caravans carrying goods to Chicoa and north to Zumbo and harassed misambadzi returning from the lands of Changamira. The prazeros and local officials negotiated various treaties with the reigning Muenemutapa to insure free trade. But the once powerful king was either unwilling or unable to control the dissident territorial leaders and their warriors who continued their action unabated throughout the eighteenth and most of the nineteenth centuries.

On occasion, the Sena prazeros faced similar difficulties on the Barue frontier although the pressures seem to have been much less intense. The prazeros occasionally suffered from succession crises which inadvertently spilled over onto their estates. Several defeated claimants also sought sanctuary within the core area of the Zambesi. Although this angered the new Macombe, he rarely sent soldiers to recapture the fugitives. Rather, he attempted to extradite them with the compliance of the prazeros.[63] Harassments of caravans also remained less severe than in Chedima, although rebellious Barue amambo periodically attempted to disrupt trade.

In the final analysis, the differential policies and actions on the various frontiers reflected the political, military, and economic realities operative within the greater Zambesi region. The once powerful Malawi states remained badly fragmented and especially vulnerable in those areas adjacent to the prazos. The rich gold mines and the availability of slaves made them even more appealing. Conversely, although they may have enjoyed a relative power advantage over the outlying regions of Manica and Barue, the prazeros would have been hard pressed against the armies of either kingdom. In addition, the goodwill of Chikanga and Macombe remained essential for the continued operation of the important Manica-Sena trade nexus. To the north, the Tete prazeros had great difficulty containing the incursions and protecting their trade. The instability at the court of the Muenemutapa and the expansionist drives of various Karanga chiefs complicated these tasks.

Competition and military confrontations, however, constituted only one dimension of the complex relationships between the prazeros and the surrounding African polities. A complementary system of alliances uniting individuals or groups of prazeros with the neighboring peoples played a part in the history of the development of the Zambesi.[64]

Various prazeros and African leaders found it mutually beneficial to enter into long-term alliances. In their broadest outlines, the patterns paralleled those operative within the prazero community. The best documented are pacts between the major prazero families and surrounding kings and territorial chiefs. Among the most famous were those between Sisnando Bayão and the King of Quiteve, between Chamatowa and Undi, between the Bongas and the royal family of the Muenemutapa, and between Gouveia and Macombe.[65] Such alliances enabled the prazeros to increase their power against competing estateholders and neighboring chieftaincies and to reassert their effective independence from the crown.[66]

In addition to these fixed relationships, a number of prazeros forged unions with their African counterparts in response to specific threats and in exchange for assurances of future assistance. The instability and turmoil in Chedima, although detrimental to the prazo system as a whole, provided excellent opportunities for individual estateholders to extend their influence and eliminate threats of future invasion. Prazero involvement ranged from supplying arms to the direct military involvement of the achikunda. A 1769 decree prohibiting such activities suggests that they were, in fact, quite common.[67] To the south, the Sena prazeros occasionally aligned themselves with a friendly Manganja chief against his adversaries. Such was the case in 1829 when they assisted Davo against his rival Chidaco, who had previously caused substantial damage to several estates.[68]

Apart from such carefully planned agreements, there were instances when prazeros were drawn into temporary unions, often against their will. When, in 1750, Camota overthrew the Malawi chief Mutanica, the deposed leader fled with his followers to the Tete prazos. Camota reacted by attacking these estates, leaving the prazeros no alternative but to aid Mutanica.[69] On other occasions African chiefs used even more forceful methods of persuasion to gain the support of prazeros: during succession crises in Chedima, a number of aspirants received the assistance of the frontier prazeros after threatening to destroy their estates.[70]

Independent of the individual alliances, the Zambesi community had long-term informal agreements with the kings of Manica and Barue. Unlike the strategic military pacts described, these served primarily to maintain friendly relations and to insure favorable trading conditions.

Although there is no evidence that the broad agreement with Chikanga carried with it any explicit political or military responsibilities, both the prazero community and other inland Portuguese were invariably drawn into local political struggles. Several isolated events in the last half of the eighteenth century illustrate this point. Historically, the death of Chikanga marked a period of internal turmoil, as the various aspirants sought to establish their claims to the throne. The succession struggle from 1767 until 1770 was particularly fierce. Although none of the pretenders could demand Portuguese assistance during the crisis, the victor insisted that the Portuguese acknowledge his authority by sending a representative to his investiture. This increased his overall prestige and provided external legitimation to his claim. The prazeros also benefitted, since the new Chikanga guaranteed the continuity of the trade, and promised to cede several frontier areas reputed to have gold deposits.[71] Portuguese action, however, was not limited to an occasional court visit. In times of mounting opposition, various Manica kings used these alliances to extract military assistance. In 1796, when two princes, Marazua and Manaca, attempted to overthrow Chikanga, and in 1803, under similar circumstances, combined prazero-government forces aided the reigning king.[72]

The prazero community had a more clearly defined responsibility to Macombe. At the core was the historical practice of providing the *mazi-a-manga*, or holy water, used in the investiture of every new Barue king. One knowledgeable observer suggested that this ancient ceremony probably dated back to the seventeenth century when the Portuguese dominated Barue and priests regularly administered baptism at the coronations.[73] Although it is uncertain that the inland Portuguese systematically fulfilled this responsibility throughout the entire period, the available data clearly indicate that they did so in the last part of the eighteenth and first half of the nineteenth centuries. Delegations, including the most prominent prazeros and local officials, visited the capital of Macombe in 1795, 1811, 1819, 1823, 1830, 1844–45, and 1850.[74] Since there is no reason to believe that the Portuguese suddenly began to exhibit this interest, it seems safe to assume that such a practice existed in the earlier part of the period under examination, although it is not explicitly mentioned in any extant documents. Unlike Manica, where the occasional presence of a prazero added to the prestige of Chikanga, the presentation of the mazi-a-manga became an integral part of the investiture. According to contemporary observers, the new Macombe was not recognized until he had undergone the ritual baptismal which occurred at the end of the traditional ceremony.[75]

In these ways the prazero community became actively involved in court politics, intrigues, and subsequent crises. The recurring succession struggles merely exacerbated this tendency. Various claimants beseeched, bribed, and threatened the prazero community in order to gain the recognition as the rightful heir.[76] The rejected aspirants resorted to force as a means of pressuring the inland Portuguese and preventing their opponents from obtaining the mazi-a-manga. They invaded the prazos, robbed the caravans, and harassed the delegation bringing the holy water to Macombe's capital.[77] In order to prevent these abuses and restore a modicum of stability, the Sena estateholders often opted for one of the principal contenders. Their recognition bolstered his prestige, and the armed assistance which they often provided increased his military capabilities.[78]

Their commitment to a friendly contender did not terminate upon his accession. On several occasions, they sent combined achikunda armies to bolster the sagging position of their ally. In the 1750s, for example, Macombe crushed a major revolt by the powerful chief Linhembe with the assistance of a force from Sena. In repayment, he ceded the outlying provinces which were subsequently incorporated into the prazo system.[79] In the 1780s, Macombe again sought the aid of the prazeros and the government against two surrounding chiefs, Cuavan and Chincoma, who had threatened his position and had cut off trade.[80]

Their possession of the mazi-a-manga provided the prazero community with substantial leverage over the various pretenders and the ultimate victor. They were able to exert pressure in order to extract favors and assurances of future security. Furthermore, in at least one instance, they utilized their military might, and presumably the prestige of the mazi-a-manga, to help overthrow a Macombe considered to be unfriendly.[81] While it is difficult to determine how common this phenomenon was, it is clear that at least to a certain degree Macombe became dependent on the inland Portuguese, who retained the option of withdrawing recognition and refusing to acknowledge his designated heir.

This pattern of competition, confrontations, and alliances with the surrounding African polities continued at least throughout the eighteenth and first quarter of the nineteenth centuries. Nevertheless, it became clear that the prazeros were losing the momentum and were increasingly forced to adopt a defensive posture. An abortive frontal assault against the armies of the Muenemutapa in 1807 and the increased aggressiveness of the Chewa chiefs drastically reduced the prazeros' military power. This, coupled with the internal contradictions in the system stemming from the slave trade, marked the beginning of the decline of the Zambesi prazos.[82]

8

The General Decline of the Prazo System 1800-1850

During the first third of the nineteenth century the prazos suffered a dramatic decline. While it is often assumed that the Nguni[1] conquests precipitated this crisis, this was not the case; rather, a combination of new economic and political factors reinforced the contradictions inherent in the system.

THE STRUCTURAL WEAKNESSES REASSESSED

Historically, a series of structural discontinuities had jeopardized the stability of the prazos. These deficiencies existed primarily in the political and military spheres, areas which were critical for the well-being and perpetuation of the institution. At the core of the problem was the prazero's lack of traditional legitimacy. His position as a political chief or overlord remained poorly defined and often brought him into conflict with the mambo and other members of the royal family. Even when he was able to gain their approbation, his position was never institutionalized. As a result, any support could be withdrawn at the discretion of the traditional authorities, and could not be transmitted to future generations. In order to reinforce his position the prazero had to rely on achikunda, who were at best only marginally loyal.

In addition to these structural weaknesses, the low level of agricultural production, the high consumption requirements, and mutsonko and inhamucangamiza obligations meant that the Africans living on the prazos faced periodic food shortages and famines. Such situations invariably produced tensions and instability within the estates and were responsible for the downfall of a number of prazeros. External threats compounded this instability. This tendency became most pronounced on the frontier estates, which engaged in sporadic military confrontations with the surrounding African polities.

Given the structural weaknesses, the agricultural problems, and the fierce competition both among the prazeros and with the neighboring peoples, it is not surprising that most estates enjoyed only a short life span. Throughout the entire period an ongoing process of prazo formation and disintegration was occurring. Simultaneously, the African chieftaincies on the margins of the Zambesi moved into and out of prazo relationships. Thus, rather than a neat historical progression, the number of functioning prazos varied substantially from year to year. The system appeared, however, relatively stable, since the continued recruitment of new families into the prazero community approximated or surpassed the number forced to abandon their estates. The emergence of the decline factors in the early part of the nineteenth century reversed this historical pattern.

THE IMPACT OF THE SLAVE TRADE

The growth of the slave trade and, more specifically, the enslavement and export of colonos and achikunda, stands out as the single most important cause of the disintegration of the institution. The apparent correlation between the frequency of revolts and migrations from the prazos and the increase in slave exports supports such a hypothesis.[2]

Initially the prazeros sent their misambadzi and raiders north of the Zambesi in order to meet the needs of the Brazilian slavers. This traffic sufficed as long as demand remained relatively constant and slaves readily accessible. But between 1806 and 1820 legal exports increased by a factor of four, and it is likely that contraband trade increased proportionately. The supply of captives from the interior failed to keep pace. Motivated by the potential profits, the prazeros, as well as the newly emergent class of lessees and agents, transgressed their legal prerogatives and arbitrarily enslaved large numbers of colonos who lived on their estates.[3]

Despite the militant opposition of the colonos, the prazeros continued to perpetrate these abuses. Indeed, archival data suggest that the prazero community had almost universally adopted this practice by the 1820s.[4] The Nguni invasion in the 1830s, moreover, did not lead to a cessation of such actions. On the contrary, it seems to have served as a stimulant, since many estateholders viewed these attacks as signalling the last opportunity to cash in on the benefits of their aforamentos.

Although the prazeros focused their attention initially on the colonos, many achikunda and their families suffered a similar fate. This violated the historical stipulation that the slaves could not be sold and had obvious ramifications for the internal stability of the estates.[5]

The slave trade shattered the internal harmony of the prazos. By exporting the colonos and the slaves, the prazeros destroyed the delicate balance which had previously existed. In the past, a clearly defined series of roles, privileges, and obligations had determined the nature of the relationship between the various groups living on a prazo. The dependency of the prazero on the mambo and principal members of the royal family symbolized this fragile relationship. Because the prazero's position as political chief remained contingent upon the consent, cooperation, and, most important, recognition of the traditional authorities, he could not afford to alienate the indigenous leadership. Enslaving and exporting members of the local population clearly constituted a major violation of his role and undermined his position. Although some amambo attempted to drive the prazeros off their homelands, most chose to migrate to new homelands where they would be free from abuses.[6] One high official wrote in 1833 that: "The estates are abandoned as a result of the *prazeros* blind lust for profit, they transcended their rights and disregarded all legal procedure in committing the crime of selling their *colonos* as if they were their slaves and their property."[7]

In general, the achikunda opted for armed military action in response to the threat of exportation. The attacks, however, were not directed solely at their owners. They also participated in a wide range of armed actions designed both to insure their freedom and to increase their wealth and power. These activities included robbing the fields and stealing cattle which belonged to the colonos of various prazos, attacking misambadzi who passed through the areas they controlled, and burning the residence of their prazero, driving him from the land.[8] Its was fashionable in official circles to blame the sharp increase in the number of revolts on the meek Goan prazeros who failed to gain the respect of the achikunda. While this explanation is consistent with anti-Indian sentiment, it overlooks the underlying cause, which at least one functionary candidly acknowledged to be: "The inability of the *prazeros* to comprehend the ramifications of the slave trade."[9]

The indigenous authorities and their followers occasionally joined with the achikunda in a coordinated military action against their common oppressor. Four or five afumu on Prazo Cheringoma, for example, allied themselves with the slave leader Chidanua to conquer the estate and the adjacent area.[10] More commonly, however, individual colonos operating outside their traditional political and social units banded together with a number of achikunda to attack various estates. According to one prazero, all the estates from Gorongoza to the outskirts of Sena suffered heavily from such raids.[11]

In addition to the immediate effects, the internal upheavals had long-term repercussions. The alienation of large groups of achikunda undermined the military potential of the remaining estateholders. Most found it increasingly difficult to protect their lands from the marauding bands of unattached Africans and the warriors from the surrounding polities. Similarly, the constant migration of colonos reduced the defensive capacity of the prazeros and often increased the offensive capabilities of the surrounding chieftaincies who offered them asylum. Other amambo, who preferred to remain on their homelands, secretly negotiated with surrounding chieftaincies to assist them in driving the prazeros off the estates, as did various achikunda groups who united with invading forces. During the Barue wars of the 1820s, for example, this proved to be a decisive factor in the conquest of much of the Zambesi.[12]

THE GROWTH OF ABSENTEEISM

The shortsighted and self-destructive policy of enslaving the colonos and achikunda was closely related to the emergence of a class of absentee prazeros, agents, and lessees. Historically, most prazeros had resided on their estates and had had at least limited contact with the mambo and the larger colono population. As late as 1784, one official noted that most of the principal estateholders lived on their estates.[13] In the succeeding decades, this residential pattern altered radically.

Beginning in the last decade of the eighteenth century, a series of governors began to ignore the legally established criteria for distributing prazos. Instead of awarding them to the heirs of deceased prazeros or to estateless female inhabitants residing in the Zambesi, they sold prazos at public auctions. The wealthy merchants living on Mozambique Island and a few prosperous families who subsequently moved to Brazil emerged as the principal benefactors.[14] Over time, this group of absentee owners acquired an increasingly large number of estates. The high natural turnover of prazeros, the growing instability and turmoil in the Zambesi, and the sudden decision of the more established families to migrate to Brazil provided unprecedented opportunities to acquire or lease new estates. By the 1820s, this method of distribution had become institutionalized, and there were only a few estates which had not been obtained in this manner.[15]

The recipients usually leased these estates at a substantial profit to inhabitants residing in the Zambesi. In a number of such cases, however, the lessee simply ignored his contractual obligations and paid what he considered to be an appropriate amount. Other absentee owners, partially to avoid such difficulties, appointed agents, *administradores*, to supervise their estates.[16]

The development of a class of absentee owners and agents had far-reaching implications for the stability of the individual estates and, by extension, the perpetuation of the entire system. Both the agents and lessees shared a desire for quick profits to satisfy their employers or to recoup their initial investments. A high priority therefore was placed on short-term economic factors rather than on prolonged stability and security. The search for profit accentuated the exploitative aspects of the system. A growing number of slaves and colonos were exported to the coast; the mutsonko was arbitrarily increased, and a greater emphasis was placed on the inhamucangamiza or forced sale.[17]

In more fundamental terms, the introduction of a surrogate prazero precluded the establishment of a mutually satisfactory relationship or even a modus vivendi with the indigenous authorities. Most lessees, agents, and absentee owners either remained unaware of this historical relationship or chose to ignore it. According to Gamitto, who travelled through the Zambesi during this period, it was even common for these inexperienced newcomers to seek to remove arbitrarily uncooperative amambo and afumu.[18] Furthermore, a number of absentee owners believed that, by virtue of their aforamento, they automatically became entitled to the traditional mutsonko and tribute. The indigenous population rejected such assumptions.[19]

These presumptuous actions destroyed the historical relationship which had previously existed between the prazero and the mambo. The royal family refused to recognize the authority and jurisdiction of the lessees, absentee owners, or their agents. Thus, on most estates, the alien authorities failed to exert even a modicum of control without the use of achikunda, which many did not bother to recruit and others had alienated. This was true even on such important estates as Luabo and Gorongoza, where great prazero families had once governed unchallenged.[20] Most amambo merely reasserted their autonomy by migrating into the sertão, where they could once more function independently of any external forces.

DROUGHTS AND FAMINES

Natural factors added to the growing internal pressures challenging the stability of the prazos. Between 1823 and 1830, a prolonged drought, accompanied by a deluge of locusts, wrought havoc in the Zambesi and the adjacent areas.[21] On the prazos agricultural production, marginal at best, collapsed entirely. The effects on the Africans were particularly severe: "The horrible calamities which have for some years caused great droughts . . . have reduced the lands to complete desert and the free Africans and slaves to skeletons."[22]

The slave trade and the turmoil it created on the prazos aggravated the production problems. The most important and direct effect was the substantial population drain. Although it is difficult to assess the number of Africans who were exported to the coast from 1823 to 1830, an estimate of between 30,000 to 40,000 seems to be an acceptable minimum figure (see Chapter 6).

The tendency to export large numbers of younger men and women, who were most actively involved in agriculture, exacerbated the manpower shortage. As a result, both the percentage of land cultivated and total production declined substantially. This, in turn, placed an added responsibility on the remaining colonos, who not only had to provide for the elderly and the young, but had to pay the mutsonko, participate in the inhamucangamiza, and, in the coastal areas, supply the rice and grain used to feed the slaves being exported.[23]

For many, these additional burdens became unbearable and, as in the past, they migrated to new lands in the interior which presented better agricultural opportunities and where they would avoid the arbitrary taxes and requirements of the prazero. Those colonos and slaves who remained on the prazo fiercely competed with each other, with the bands of marauding achikunda, and with the prazero for the foodstuffs which were available. These conflicts reduced still further the level of production.[24]

INVASIONS

The drought also affected surrounding Barue, Quiteve, and Tonga chieftaincies, who began to invade the crown lands and pillage the fields in search for food. These incursions initially affected only the frontier estates, many of which had been abandoned. As the famines continued, however, enemy soldiers penetrated as far as the southern bank of the Zambesi River. In several instances these invasions provided the final blow to a wavering prazo.[25]

Apart from these raids, a number of surrounding chieftaincies took advantage of the general state of turmoil to settle old scores, to regain conquered lands, and to increase their power.[26] The Malawi chief Sazora, for example, conquered Prazos Chicore and Zenge; to the east, local chiefs such as Chimboa, Chidoza, and Gondozega asserted their hegemony over a number of estates in the Quelimane area.[27] In the Tete region those prazos which had not been abandoned remained subject to periodic attacks by the forces of the Muenemutapa as well as by those of dissident chiefs.[28] Of all the districts, Sena seems to have suffered most from Manganja, Tonga, and especially Barue attacks.[29]

Sustained Barue invasions occurred with great regularity during this period. The drought and a prolonged succession crisis explain this repeated violation of the prazos' territorial integrity. Internal battles spilled across the frontiers; a number of the combatants intentionally entered the crown lands in search of food, asylum, or competing pretenders. Others applied military pressure in order to convince the Portuguese to recognize them as legitimate heirs of Macombe and provide them with the mazi-a-manga. Although these attacks were probably no more severe than previous incursions, the impact was far greater. The decaying prazos were neither able to absorb the shock nor to adequately defend themselves.[30]

By 1830, the armies of Cagerina, Gondoga, Chideza, and other Barue chiefs had conquered at least twelve estates, including such powerful prazos as Cheringoma and Gorongoza. In fact, they loosely controlled most of the region from the frontiers of Cheringoma to the outskirts of Sena, and only the southern most prazos — Luabo, Ilha Timbua and Tapada de Manga — remained unaffected. In that year, a new king took the throne and most Barue troops withdrew from the Sena prazos.[31]

THE ZAMBESI UNTIL THE MIDDLE OF THE CENTURY

With the termination of the succession struggle, the cessation of the famines, and the consequent reduction in the level of hostilities, the Zambesi gained a measure of stability. Nevertheless, the prazo system had fallen into virtual decay. Most of the estates had been abandoned or functioned on only a marginal basis.[32] In the Sena area, only Ferrão,

Isodoro, and Santanna still retained effective control within their prazos.[33] Governor Cirne's poignant description of the Sena district in 1830 clearly suggests the extent of the disruption: "The disgraceful state of Sena is horrifying; all is reduced to bush and mountains of ruin; the inhabitants are all dispersed; the fort has almost completely fallen to the ground . . . and most of the great *prazos* have been destroyed."[34]

Within this general framework of decay, two important transitions had taken place. On the one hand, the small chieftaincies which had operated within the prazo system reasserted their complete independence. Many of these polities remained on their traditional lands, governed as in the past by the mambo, afumu, and other members of the royal family. Others migrated to northern areas which had been spared the full impact of the famines.

In addition, there emerged a number of nontraditional politico-military groups based on a union between achikunda and unattached colonos. Although there are only passing references to such groups, they bore a striking resemblance to the musitu, or fugitive slave communities, of the previous century. Unlike their predecessors, these groups operated freely within the Zambesi rather than on the fringes, and they do seem not to have had a fixed domicile. It is difficult to determine exactly what happened to all these marauding bands; some were subsequently absorbed into the newly emerging states of Massangano, Massingire, and the Nguni kingdom. It is probable that others migrated out of the immediate Zambesi region and established early chikunda settlements in present-day Malawi and Zambia.[35]

The Portuguese government attempted to take advantage of the relative stability in the period after 1830 to revitalize the prazo system. It offered a series of incentives to prospective estateholders, of which the most important was the waiving of the foro and dizimo requirement for an initial ten-year period.[36] Although this stimulated some interest, it was poorly conceived and tended to exacerbate the internal pressures by appealing to those interested in quick profits. As a result, the new prazeros failed to establish the proper relationship with the traditional authorities whose land they hoped to control. Furthermore, they continued to exploit and export the remaining colonos and achikunda, which produced the same types of dislocation as in the preceding decades.[37] Recurring droughts in the 1830s and periodic raids reinforced these tensions and undermined whatever authority the prazeros might have acquired. Thus despite the sharp increase in the number of aforamentos distributed in the 1830s, the government made little headway in its attempt to resuscitate the old system. In any case, the Nguni invasions precluded the possibility that the prazos would once again become the dominant institution in the Zambesi.

As a result of Shaka's victories in present-day Natal, a number of Nguni peoples fled into southern Mozambique and subsequently into the Zambesi region. At the head of two of these migrations were Soshangane, and Zwagendaba. Soshangane established his headquarters close to Delagoa Bay until 1828, when an attack by Shaka's warriors convinced him to move north, beyond the reach of the powerful Zulu king. He led his followers to the middle Sabi where he established his capital at Chaimite, consolidated his empire, and defeated his principal enemies, Zwagendaba and Nxaba.[38]

Soshangane then sent his warriors north to assert Nguni authority over the Zambesi region. As early as 1832, they attacked the fair at Manica and in the following year reached the outskirts of Sena. Although the prazeros and their followers prepared for an invasion, the Nguni warriors withdrew to the south. The pattern of attack, or imminent attack, and withdrawal became a recurring theme in their military and political relationships with the remnants of the prazero community. Apart from strategic considerations, these movements can probably be related to Nguni consumption requirements and local harvest schedules. In 1836, they again returned and established an expansive military front which stretched from Cheringoma to the Luenha River, just south of Tete. They succeeded in defeating a combined government-prazero force, and conquered a number of important prazos. By the end of the year the invaders had effectively surrounded Tete and controlled a number of outlying estates. In 1838 they again withdrew, even though Tete, Sena, and most of the prazos were totally defenseless. The remaining prazeros enjoyed only a short respite. In the following year, the Nguni returned and by 1840 they occupied twenty-eight of the forty-six legally functioning prazos.[39]

Despite Soshangane's military superiority, he chose not to annihilate select prazeros. Instead, he permitted them to live on their estates as long as they recognized him as the ultimate authority. As conquering overlord and owners of the lands, Soshangane and his successor Muzila collected a substantial annual tribute from each prazero.[40] Livingstone noted that the dona of Prazo Chupanga paid Soshangane's emissary $650 worth of cloth.[41] On occasion the Nguni king even appointed representatives to adjudicate the most serious litigations within the prazos and to punish the offenders.[42] Although many of the prazos were now loosely incorporated into the larger Nguni empire, they still suffered from periodic raids, and a number of young men and women were taken captive.[43]

Many small Zambesi chieftaincies, some of which had only recently asserted their independence, were also swept into Soshangane's kingdom. Although Soshangane made no attempt to culturally assimilate or integrate them into a larger Nguni state, they recognized the paramountcy of the Nguni chief. Indeed, local amambo and afumu swore allegiance to Soshangane and Muzila, and some even assisted them in their military pursuits.[44] The Zambesi chiefs also paid an annual tax, forwarded the elephant tusks, and obeyed the legal rulings of appointed Nguni officials.[45] From a political perspective, the Nguni represented yet another in a series of alien overlords who had historically dominated the Zambesi chieftaincies.

By the middle of the nineteenth century, only a small number of prazos continued to operate. An official report listed thirteen out of fifty-one estates in Tete as not invaded or abandoned. The number in Sena was even smaller; out of thirty-two prazos, seven were still occupied. Even these low figures represent only the possible upper limits of functioning prazos, since it is probable that at least some were merely legal abstractions with the estateholders unable to establish any effective control.[46]

9

The Growth of Supra-Prazo Polities and
Patterns of Resistance, 1850 to ca. 1900

The decline of the prazo system marked the end of a clearly defined period in the history of the Zambesi. Out of this fluid situation emerged new multi-ethnic political units which were larger and more complex than their historical antecedents. These polities dominated the Tete-Sena region and provided the principal indigenous opposition to Portuguese imperial aspiration until they were forcefully subdued during the scramble for Africa.

THE KINGDOM OF MAKANGA

The kingdom of Makanga constituted the oldest of these states. At the height of its power, it encompassed a substantial area stretching from the Zambesi River north as far as the Ruareze and Muchinge mountains (see Map 7). Composed primarily of Chewa chieftaincies, Makanga developed an ethnically heterogeneous character. Smaller groups of Nsenga, Manganja, and Ngoni lived within its frontiers. A number of Zambesi colonos and achikunda who had formerly been part of the prazo system also migrated to the region.[1]

Makanga's exact origin remains somewhat obscure. Contemporary accounts agree that a member of the Pereira family, either Chamatowa or his son Chicucuru, founded the kingdom by obtaining the rebellious southern province of Undi's empire and one of Undi's relatives in payment for assistance against enemies of the king. Chicucuru and his

124

achikunda followers then migrated south, established their political hegemony over the region, and built their royal capital at Massanza. This was accomplished with Undi's sanction and a discreet use of force.[2]

Having gained recognition as sovereign, Chamatowa and his successors attempted to legitimatize their positions and perpetuate the royal dynasty. Their direct links with Undi facilitated this process, and they tried to identify themselves with the Chewa king whenever possible. Thus, Chamatowa's heir apparent adopted the African title Chissaca-Maturi, which was one of Undi's principal praise names.[3] To strengthen their claim, Chamatowa's descendants negotiated marriage alliances with a number of the principal land chiefs who dominated Makanga. Thus Saka-Saka took the daughter of the powerful Chewa chief Safuri, and Chicucuru II married a maternal relative of Cadunguire, an important member of the royal council.[4]

The Pereiras reinforced their claims by adopting a number of rituals and symbols of kingship. Each new ruler of Makanga underwent extensive rites of investiture after a council of elders and afumu had selected him from among the eligible members of the royal family.[5] The rulers of Makanga lived in a vast royal village which, toward the end of the nineteenth century, was transferred from Massanza to Muchena.[6] At the capital Chicucuru and his principal advisers regularly held court, resolved disputes, gave ritual approval to the recently selected afumu, and made major political decisions.

In addition to these functions, the reigning sovereign periodically consulted the mizimu, either directly or through the various ancestor mediums. To be certain that the ancestors sanctioned his policies, for example, Saka-Saka conferred with the senior medium Chicucuru before negotiating a major peace treaty with the Portuguese in 1875.[7] The ruling family also retained their burial shrines and royal grave sites. These sites were considered sacrosanct, and the Chewa periodically visited them to beseech the spirits of the Pereiras for assistance in time of crisis.[8] This practice suggests that the Pereiras were considered the legitimate rulers of Makanga and their mizimu the guardians of the state.

It is unlikely that the adoption of these aspects of kingship was calculated to enhance their prestige and bolster their power. Instead it can be seen as part of a larger, unconscious process of acculturation in which the Pereiras adopted the indigenous life style, cosmology, value system, and social organization. As such, it tended to increase their legitimacy by blurring the differences between the alien overlords and their indigenous subjects.[9]

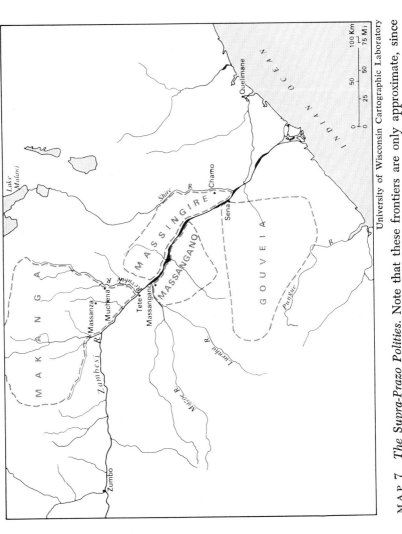

MAP 7 *The Supra-Prazo Polities.* Note that these frontiers are only approximate, since the boundaries were continually changing.

University of Wisconsin Cartographic Laboratory

As territorial chiefs, the Pereiras received the tribute, symbolic gifts, and mutsonko which had historically been paid to Undi. In order to reinforce their authority, they deployed slave regiments throughout Makanga. Although the primary function of the slave army was to protect the frontiers against external invasions, it was also used to collect taxes, transmit laws from Massanza, and, when necessary, to crush internal opposition.[10]

The Pereiras ruled Makanga until 1902. Despite numerous succession struggles, kingship remained within the family during the entire period. Because they governed with the approbation and assistance of the indigenous authorities, they faced limited internal opposition from the traditional chiefs. Such conflict as existed centered around the succession struggles which periodically divided the ruling house.[11]

T A B L E 9   *King List of Makanga*

1.	Chamatowa (Choutama, Shavatama, Dombo-Dombo)	?1800–?
2.	Chicucuru (Chikukulu) [son of Chamatowa]	?–1849
3.	Chissaca-Maturi [son of Chamatowa]	1849–1858
4.	Kanhenzi [son of Chissaca]	1858–?
5.	Chincomo (Chituza) [maternal nephew or son of Kanhenzi]	?–1870
6.	Chicuacha [maternal nephew of Chincomo]	1870–1874
7.	Saka-Saka (Kankuni) [son of Chissaca]	1874–1885
8.	Chicucuru II [son or maternal nephew of Chissaca]	1886–1889?
9.	Chigaga [maternal nephew of Chicucuru II]	?1889–1890?
10.	Chinsinga [son of Saka-Saka]	?1890–1902

Sources: Interviews with Malisseni Máuo, Simon Biwi, Chapavira Muiessa, Chiponda Cavumbula, and Leão Manuel Banqueiro Caetano Pereira; joint interviews with Calavina Couche and Zabuca Ngombe, and with Chetambara Chenungo and Wilson John; interviews with Chiponda Cavumbula and Leão Manuel Banqueiro Caetano Pereira; José Fernandes, Júnior, "Historia de Undi" (Paper, Makanga, n.d.); José Fernandes, Júnior, "Narração Do Distrito de Tete" (Paper, Makanga, 1955), pp. 104–9; *B.O.M.*, 1886, No. 29, pp. 362–63: "Viagem as Terras da Macanga, Apontamentos colhidos d'um relatório do padre Victor Courtois, vigário de Tete, 1885"; *B.O.M.*, 1887, No. 30, pp. 331–32: Augusto de Castilho, Portaria No. 306, 22 July 1887; *B.O.M.*, 1888, No. 12, p. 213: "Relatório do Commando Militar de Macanga do Anno de 1887"; A.H.U., Moç., Pasta 13: António Candido Pedro Gamitto to S.M.T., 31 December 1854; A.H.M., Fundo do Século XIX, Governo Geral, 2.37: C. J. da Silva to José Maria Pereira d'Almeida, 31 July 1858; A.H.M., Fundo do Século XIX, Governo Geral, Cx. 11: Carlos Pedro Barahona e Costa to Secretário do Governo Geral da Província, 22 June 1872; A.H.U., Moç., Pasta 30: Anselmo Joaquim Nunes de Andrade, 28 November 1875; A.H.U., Moç., Pasta 30: José Guedes de Menezes to Ministro e Secretário de Estado dos Negócios de Marinha e Ultramar, 21 January 1876; A.H.M., Fundo do Século XIX, Cx. 11: Luís Joaquim Vieira Braga to Secretário do Governo Geral, 6 November 1885.

Within Makanga, the historic role of the land chiefs remained virtually unchanged. The afumu retained their principal religious, social,
and political functions with regard to the members of the chieftaincy.
They invoked the mizimu, resolved most disputes, appointed all subordinates and were themselves elected in accordance with the traditional rules of descent. Only the most serious legal questions reached
the court of Chicucuru.[12]

The political functions of the land chiefs transcended the frontiers
of their own domain. The principal indigenous authorities and elders
periodically met with members of the royal family and important slave
chiefs to select the legitimate successor to the throne and to determine
policy. A new ruler could not be chosen without the approval of the
council, and his position was not legitimized until he had undergone
all the rites of investiture.[13] The Chewa chiefs played critical roles in
the succession crises which regularly wracked the royal family. When
Chigaga was charged with secretly plotting to kill Chicucuru II, he
defended himself in the royal council and ultimately submitted to
muabvi in order to prove his innocence.[14] The success of a particular
pretender also depended upon political and military support from such
powerful nfumu as Biwi. Conversely, no Makanga king could afford
to alienate the important indigenous authorities for fear of being overthrown. The demise of Kanhenzi demonstrates this point. According
to tradition, shortly after succeeding Chissaca-Maturi, he and his son
Cauta began to abuse their power. Most of the principal afumu, ap-
palled by these acts, gathered around Chincomo, Chicuacha, and
Saka-Saka and forced Kanhenzi to abdicate.[15]

The royal council also treated such questions as inter-afumu disputes, military actions against surrounding peoples, and relations with
the Portuguese. Before Saka-Saka could go to Tete and negotiate a
peace treaty with the Europeans he had to gain the support of the
elders. When a Portuguese official attempted to expedite matters, Saka-
Saka responded that he did not have the authority to make such a decision without first consulting his advisers.[16] The various peace treaties
with Lisbon all bear the signatures of the principal Chewa chiefs who
were instrumental in defining the content of these agreements.[17]

A large, well-trained military force enabled Chicucuru and his successors to maintain their independence from the Portuguese and to
expand the frontiers of their empire. An official report in 1845 estimated the standing achikunda army to be more than 4,000 soldiers,
excluding the Chewa reserves who could be mobilized on short
notice.[18] The recruitment of slaves and colonos who had formerly
lived on the Tete prazos constantly swelled the ranks of the army.

These unattached Africans migrated to Makanga to escape the Nguni, exploitative prazeros, and the recurring famines.[19]

The military success of Makanga was inextricably related to the widespread adoption of European weaponry. The initial victories against both the enemies of Undi and the recalcitrant Chewa afumu had demonstrated the value of European weapons.[20] To insure a constant supply of arms and powder, Makanga selectively traded ivory and slaves with those Tete and Quelimane merchants who would supply the necessary military equipment.[21] The scope and impact of the arms trade is reflected in an official Portuguese report transmitted from Tete in 1854: "Guns and powder have been sold freely in this district for a long time under the pretext of being used by hunters, so as to fool the Governor, while it is common knowledge that a large portion of these weapons are being traded in the interior; and as a result our enemies are well armed, and war on us with the very guns we have sold them."[22] Apart from light weapons, Makanga obtained a small number of cannons which lined the walls of their principal aringas or stockades.

An extensive commercial network supported Makanga's military strength. Makanga was ideally placed to dominate almost all the trade between the Zambesi commercial centers and the inland Malawi, Bisa, Nsenga, and Southern Lunda. Chicucuru and his successors exploited the geographic location to its fullest. Both misambadzi from Tete and African traders from the north were denied passage through their lands, insuring thereby that Makanga retained its profitable middleman position.[23] Chissaca-Maturi subsequently expanded the frontiers of Makanga's commercial empire to include areas south of the Zambesi in the region between Tete and Chicoa. Because Makanga monopolized the ivory and slave trade, the Zambesi merchants fulfilled their requests for arms and ammunition even though such trade violated Portuguese policy.

The foreign policy of Chicucuru and his successors centered on three fundamental objectives: the expansion of Makanga's frontiers, the perpetuation of its trade monopoly, and the retention of its independent status. Collectively they were designed to maintain Makanga's preeminent position north of the Zambesi.

Chicucuru's imperial policy presented the Portuguese government with a serious dilemma. In the past, the state had secured the friendship and apparent loyalty of the Pereiras by offering them prestigious titles, such as Capitão-Môr do Interior, which carried no real obligation to Lisbon. State officials, thereafter, thought of Makanga as informally belonging to the prazo system, although the Pereiras were not required to pay the usual taxes.[24] In short, as it had done in the past, Lisbon offered de jure recognition in exchange for a certain degree of loyalty and the general understanding that Makanga was part of her colonial empire.

Such a policy erroneously assumed that this understanding would be translated into concrete actions. The royal family refused to lift Makanga's blockade and to desist from attacking Tete merchants and their misambadzi. Chicucuru continued to assert his total independence and prerogatives as the leader of an autonomous polity.[25] However, this posture did not remain consistently anti-government. As long as Makanga's independence remained unchallenged, Chicucuru was willing to maintain cordial relations. When it was in Makanga's interest, as in the case of the wars against the Nguni, he even assisted the government.[26]

A detailed analysis of Makanga's external relations before the scramble falls outside the scope of this study. Nevertheless, it is important to highlight the central issues, both to illustrate the course of action pursued by Chicucuru's successors and to place the "partition" within its historical framework. All the rulers were committed to maintaining Makanga's independence, but they disagreed about the appropriate tactics. Chissaca-Maturi continued the expansionist policies of his father. He refused to acknowledge the authority of the Portuguese government, barred the misambadzi from entering his land, and extended the frontier of Makanga further west into Nsenga territory and east toward the Shire.[27] Lisbon revealed its concern by concluding a secret military treaty with the Muenemutapa which called for a coordinated attack on Makanga and by supplying dissident Makanga chiefs with arms to foment internal conflict.[28] When these measures failed, a prazero-government force of nearly two thousand soldiers attempted to conquer Makanga.[29] While unsuccessful, it did convince Chissaca-Maturi of the advisability of ending his overt anti-Portuguese activities.

With the death of Chissaca-Maturi, relations with the Portuguese government improved. Kanhenzi, Chincomo, Chicuacha, and Saka-Saka, the last in at least the initial part of his reign, adopted a more conciliatory attitude toward the state. As a gesture of friendship, they agreed to allow the misambadzi to trade in their kingdom and with the peoples to the north. This shift in policy came as a pleasant surprise to Portuguese officials, who privately admitted that they lacked the force effectively to challenge Makanga.[30]

A treaty which Saka-Saka and the principal afumu signed in 1875 constituted the closest that Makanga came to tacit recognition of the authority of the Portuguese government. Although the agreement stipulated that the Pereiras were Portuguese subjects and that Saka-Saka was to be recognized as capitão môr with certain obligations to the state, it also acknowledged the position of the royal family as the legitimate rulers of Makanga, its right to govern Makanga undisturbed, and the sanctity of the established selection process. From Saka-Saka's subsequent actions, this treaty seems to have been no more than a gesture, probably to repay the merchants for their assistance against dissident members of the royal family.[31]

The 1875 treaty did not alter Makanga's status, nor did it lead to a rapprochement. On the contrary, Saka-Saka adopted the most hostile and aggressive attitude toward the Portuguese since the reign of Chissaca-Maturi and violated the principles of the 1875 treaty. Like his grandfather, he reestablished the trade monopoly, and Makanga achikunda began to invade the Tete prazos for the first time in more than a decade. When Portuguese officials confronted him, he denied responsibility, claiming that dissident members of his empire were responsible.

Increased pressures from the Tete merchants and the British presence in the areas adjacent to the Zambesi moved Lisbon to adopt a more forceful policy toward Makanga.[32] Although there was a general consensus that the rebellious polity had to be conquered, military officials pointed out that they lacked the arms and manpower to fight simultaneously against both Makanga and the secessionist state Massangano. Because the latter was more strategically located and posed a greater threat to the Portuguese (see pp. 138–47), all efforts were directed against it, and Makanga's autonomous position went virtually unchallenged during the years immediately preceding the scramble.

In the light of Portuguese imperial aspirations, the leadership of Makanga probably realized the inevitability of a confrontation with Lisbon. The assassination of Saka-Saka in 1885 underscored this point. Although there was no evidence that the government was directly involved, his death at the hands of a European mobilized opinion against the Portuguese. The selection of Chicucuru II, rather than Chinsinga who was considered to be pro-Portuguese, signified the growing hostility. Portugal's renewed attempts to enforce the arms embargo and its demands that a Portuguese military command be established in Makanga removed whatever lingering doubts still existed. In what proved to be a tactical error, Chicucuru II reluctantly agreed to permit the state to maintain a small military base in Makanga, believing that it would forestall a major invasion.[33]

The Portuguese, thinking that they had peacefully gained control of Makanga, attempted to exert political authority. They demanded taxes, instituted laws, and invited Tete merchants to trade in the area. In order to reinforce their position, they entered a secret alliance with Chinsinga in the hope that he would overthrow Chicucuru II.[34] This subterfuge and the growing awareness of the Portuguese presence led a number of afumu and akazambo to challenge the inaction of Chicucuru II. His most outspoken critic was his maternal uncle, Cadunguire, who had previously engineered his succession victory against Chinsinga. Before the royal council, he publicly attacked his nephew's timidity: "declaring that he must stand ashamed, a chief who lacks the respect of the elders, who is governed rather than governs, none can exempt him from responsibility for all that has occurred."[35] Faced with mounting internal pressures and the increased demands of the Portuguese, Chicucuru II unequivocally reasserted Makanga's independence. He ordered his subjects to refuse to pay taxes, to attack foreign traders and hunters, and to harass the Portuguese military post. These hostilities culminated in a series of attacks on the Portuguese soldiers, forcing them to withdraw from Makanga.[36]

Simultaneously, Chicucuru II attempted to forge an alliance of disparate anti-Portuguese groups. Despite deep-rooted animosities, his principal ally was Mtontora, last of the rulers of Massangano. To this union, he added former supporters of Matequenha, dissident Makololo, bands of additional achikunda, and the followers of a powerful chief named Kazembe.[37] With the resurgence of Portuguese military power, Chicucuru's hastily formed alliance collapsed. Mtontora, anxious to reconquer Massangano, led his relatively small band of followers back across the Zambesi less than a year after they had arrived in Makanga. Other rebel groups fled to the north and west to areas which remained outside the sphere of Portuguese control. In the face of an impending attack Chicucuru II abandoned Makanga in 1889 in order to avoid a military disaster.[38]

The defeat of Chicucuru II marked the end of the initial phase of Makanga resistance. His successor, Chigaga, governed for only a short period before being overthrown by Chinsinga. The latter received substantial support from the Portuguese, for which he agreed to recognize the authority of the state and to renounce Makanga's independence.[39] In an attempt to integrate Makanga into the colonial system, the government appointed the Companhia da Zambézia to serve as the administrative and modernizing agent. Chinsinga and the royal family were compelled to sign a treaty with the company in which they reaffirmed their loyalty and obedience to Lisbon and, in effect, agreed to serve as paid employees.[40]

Although Chinsinga overtly accepted this subordinate status, he remained reluctant to renounce Makanga's independence. By covertly adopting an anti-Portuguese position, he regained the support of the principal land chiefs who had suspected his earlier links with the Europeans. The increased taxes, labor requirements, and reduced status of the chiefs, the appearance of alien elephant hunters, and the memory of Saka-Saka's assassination inflamed anti-Portuguese and anti-company feelings throughout Makanga. Chinsinga skillfully used the murder of his father as a rallying cry to unite most of the principal chiefs behind him. In 1899, he defiantly informed a state official that he would never recognize either the company or the government.[41] The failure of the company to establish any institutionalized control over Makanga enabled him to adopt such an autonomous position.[42]

Chinsinga's political aspirations apparently transcended Makanga. In at least one secret meeting with leading Tete mestizos and several unidentified chiefs he argued forcefully for a multi-ethnic confederation of African peoples which would forcibly drive the Portuguese out of the Zambesi. An eyewitness recalled Chinsinga's assertion that: "the Africans of all tribes must unite in good faith, in a coordinated attempt to acquire large supplies of arms and ammunition and when we have achieved this, we must expel all the Portuguese and make an alliance with the British who are sympathetic to the aspirations of the Africans."[43] Although the plan was well received and various participants encouraged him to lead such a movement, there is no evidence that it was translated into concrete actions outside of Makanga.

In the period after his 1899 declaration, Chinsinga met with his council on several occasions to coordinate various responses to the continuing Portuguese presence. One of the principal points of friction was the company's insistence that it had the right to all the ivory collected in Makanga. This policy ran directly counter to the traditional prerogative of presenting the "owner of the land" or sovereign with the tusk which fell closest to the ground. Chinsinga adamantly refused to obey a regulation which implicitly challenged his legitimacy. On several other occasions he vowed to crush the Portuguese.

Tensions reached a climax when the company ordered Chinsinga to send 300 men to work in Angonia. He refused. With the consent of afumu and akazambo, Chinsinga planned a surprise attack against the Europeans. The Portuguese had two secret agents at the council meeting, afumu Mafa and Chidzio, both of whom betrayed Chinsinga's plan. The government launched a preemptive attack which inflicted heavy losses on the Makanga forces. According to tradition, Chinsinga tried to flee to Blantyre, but was able to get only as far as the Revubue

River. There, he realized the futility of continuing his journey. He ordered his senior wife to sit on the bank of the river and, after drinking a poisonous potion, fell dead against her breast.[44] With the news of his death, the opposition rapidly disintegrated, and the Portuguese at last established effective control of Makanga.

MASSINGIRE

Not all of the emerging polities forged out of the decaying prazo system and the adjacent chieftaincies lasted as long as Makanga. To the southeast of Makanga, Mariano Vas Dos Anjos, better known by his African name of Matequenha, constructed a relatively short-lived state by uniting a number of Manganja chieftaincies and unattached Tonga, Sena, and achikunda who had migrated north from the prazos. At the height of its power Massingire included the territory bounded in a triangular shape by the Lupata Gorge, Murchison Cataracts, and the confluence of the Zambesi and Shire rivers (see Map 7).

The early history of Matequenha and his predecessors remains uncertain. It is likely that his family migrated from Goa, having settled in the Zambesi by the first quarter of the nineteenth century.[45] They probably acquired one or a number of prazos in this period, and were among the few families to capitalize on the turmoil and instability to improve their situation. They accomplished this primarily through their involvement in the slave trade, which enabled them to recruit and arm a large achikunda following. Their prestige and power increased subsequently as a result of a decisive victory over the Nguni in the 1840s.[46] In 1852, Galdim Fastino de Sousa, Matequenha's stepfather, conquered the southern frontiers of Manganja and in the following year he requested an aforamento for the lands which he had occupied.[47] The state was happy to comply, since it considered Manganja a crown possession based on conquests made a century earlier. State officials saw in Fastino de Sousa a loyal agent who had reasserted Portuguese control over this outlying area and merely sought to have his claims legitimized.

Fastino de Sousa died shortly after receiving the deed to Prazo Massingire, and his mestizo stepson Matequenha inherited the estate. He expanded the frontiers of Massingire, incorporating the lands of a number of Manganja chiefs. Smaller groups of dissident Chewa and "Anguru" peoples were also brought into the Massingire state.[48]

Although most Portuguese sources emphasized Matequenha's military exploits and treated Massingire as a simple conquest state, there is evidence that he tried, with some degree of success, to gain the ultimate allegiance of the southern Manganja. Matequenha married the daughter of at least one Manganja chief and acknowledged the ritual supremacy of the Mbona rain priests.[49] The scope of his support increased substantially after Massingire forces had repelled a Nguni invasion[50] and, despite some internal opposition, Manganja chiefs did select Matequenha's successor from his immediate family. This recognition, combined with the unyielding loyalty of the slave chiefs, insured the perpetuation of the royal family and the continuity of Massingire after Matequenha's death.[51]

Massingire's viability depended upon its military power and relative superiority vis-à-vis the surrounding African chieftaincies and the Portuguese government. The mainstay of the empire was the well-armed achikunda force. Matequenha, like the Pereiras, recruited numerous soldiers among smaller colonos and slaves who sought protection from the Nguni and from harsh prazeros. Through trade agreements with Portuguese slave dealers, he obtained a constant supply of modern arms and powder.[52] It is estimated that Massingire's forces included several thousand soldiers armed with muskets.[53] At its highpoint in 1862, state officials privately conceded that Massingire possessed the military capacity to conquer both Sena and Quelimane.[54]

The defense of Massingire centered around the aringa at Chamo, strategically located on an islet connected through a series of swamps to the eastern banks of the Shire River fifteen miles north of the confluence with the Zambesi. It was ideally positioned to control trade, prevent navigation, and repel overland attacks from Sena. The walls of the stockade consisted of double rows of stakes interspersed with brass guns, making is difficult to penetrate into the core of Chamo. A detachment of chikunda resided permanently at the aringa to guard against major attacks. A network of African and European spies gathered information about enemy troop deployments and provided advance notice of impending invasions. At the center of the European segment of this system were various family members, who not only transmitted secret data, but also recruited additional achikunda for Massingire.[55]

Matequenha's initial relations with the Portuguese government followed the same general pattern as that of Chicucuru's. When it was in his interest to cultivate ties with the Portuguese, Matequenha did so without hesitation. On one occasion, he sent a large chikunda force south of the Zambesi to help drive away the Nguni and, on another, he supplied 200 slave soldiers for a joint government-prazero force seeking to conquer Massangano.[56] Both the Nguni and Massangano posed very definite military and economic threats which had to be removed if Massingire was to survive.

Unlike his stepfather, Matequenha adopted an independent posture which often brought him into conflict with the Portuguese government. Massingire warriors robbed and burned crown estates, interfered with trade, and continued slave raiding despite official opposition. His most dramatic and defiant act was to attack the garrison at Sena. These actions challenged the tenuous Portuguese position and reduced the government prestige and influence which had already suffered at the hands of Makanga and Massangano.[57]

The government took advantage of a temporary peace with Massangano to attempt to reassert its authority over the southern part of Manganja. In 1857 an expedition, complete with artillery, attacked Chamo. Matequenha's achikunda and local Manganja soldiers repulsed the attack.[58] In the following year, a large force including regulars from the garrisons of Tete and Quelimane overpowered the defenders.[59] Simultaneously, Matequenha was jailed while visiting Quelimane. His followers fled inland, first to the Murrambala Mountains and then up the Shire, where they regrouped near Mount Mlanja. They continued to resist the Portuguese, and, when offered a general amnesty, Matequenha's lieutenant replied that they would never consider such an agreement unless their leader was released from prison.[60]

Matequenha remained a captive for three years, during which time the government made no attempt to impose any administrative control over Massingire.[61] Shortly after his release, Matequenha gathered his forces and renewed military activity against the Portuguese. Within several months, he had reestablished his authority over a substantial part of Massingire and had conquered new areas to the north, recruited additional slaves, and acquired a large supply of arms. Several small Portuguese expeditions failed to dislodge Matequenha, who expanded his holdings. On the strength of these victories he made the startling offer to cede half of his territory to Portugal if Lisbon would recognize and acknowledge his sovereignty over the remainder. This 1862 proposal constituted Matequenha's clearest expression of his long-term political aspirations. He died shortly thereafter, and there is no further mention of this detente in the documents.[62]

At about this time, several Manganja chiefs secretly signed peace treaties with the Portuguese government.[63] Despite these defections, most of the Manganja authorities and slave chiefs rallied around Matequenha's senior uncle as the logical heir. When the elder did not show any interest, the reign was passed on to Matequenha's son, who was then a young boy. Although never so forceful nor so prestigious as his father, Matequenha II together with select maternal relatives governed for almost twenty years with the approbation and support of the Manganja chiefs and the slave captains.[64]

After his investiture, Matequenha II agreed in principle to obey the Portuguese government. In practice, Massingire functioned as an autonomous political unit outside the sphere of Portuguese control. "There is no Portuguese jurisdiction here or pretense of it," commented one observer in 1879.[65] Moreover, when it was clear that Massingire could derive benefits from overt hostility, Matequenha II did not hesitate to act. In 1879, for example, he attacked and robbed several newly resurgent prazos north of Sena. Two years later, he died mysteriously after dissident elements within Massingire had turned him over to the Portuguese.[66]

Lisbon seized this opportunity to claim the lower Shire Valley as a means of preventing the British from moving south from Blantyre and of limiting the subversive activities of their Makololo ally Chipultura.[67] In 1882, the government sent a force under the auspices of its most powerful imperial agent, Gouveia, to dictate peace terms to the leaders of Massingire.[68] He compelled the rebels to renounce their independence, acknowledge their position as Portuguese subjects, and provide certain services. The Portuguese established a military command in Manganja to enforce these stipulations.[69]

As in the case of Makanga, a number of Manganja chiefs and slave leaders repudiated these agreements. Latent anti-Portuguese feelings emerged in 1884 when the commanding officer in Massingire interfered in the selection of Matequenha's successor and also prohibited the use of the poison ordeal to determine the party responsible for his death. The Portuguese arrested and imprisoned two important chiefs for their refusal to obey. They escaped and united their followers as well as other Manganja chiefs under the leadership of Marenga, formerly one of Matequenha's principal lieutenants. They revolted and massacred the small Portuguese garrison stationed in Manganja. Gouveia subsequently returned to Manganja at the head of an army of several thousand soldiers and crushed the dissident chiefs.[70] The spirit of rebellion persisted, however, and various Manganja chiefs formerly associated with Massingire directed uprisings in 1887 and 1896 before the Portuguese were able to establish effective control over Matequenha's former empire.

THE STATE OF MASSANGANO

At approximately the same time that Matequenha consolidated the Manganja polity of Massingire, Nhaude and his heirs were forming the Massangano state among the Tonga chiefdoms to the south. Initially centered around Prazo Massangano, the frontiers were subsequently expanded to include a triangular area stretching from the confluence of the rivers Luenha and Zambesi south to the Mazoe and east to Prazo Chiramba (see Map 7). From a strategic perspective, the emergence of Massangano as a political entity challenged the very basis of Portuguese administration and control within the core area of the Zambesi. As a result, the government made repeated efforts to conquer this secessionist state. In the period between 1850 and 1888, Lisbon sent numerous expeditions against Massangano.[71]

Of all the new Zambesi polities that emerged during this period, none was more integrally related to the disintegration of the prazo system than Massangano. In the aftermath of the famines and invasions of the 1820s Portugal attempted to regain a modicum of authority by redistributing a number of abandoned estates to loyal Portuguese subjects. One of the beneficiaries of this policy was the mestizo merchant and elephant hunter Joaquim da Cruz, who subsequently adopted the African praise name Nhaude — the terror. The grants for Prazos Massangano and Tipue were ostensibly given to reward valiant service against the Nguni. In reality, they probably reflected Nhaude's de facto control of these lands and a reluctance by the government to alienate him.[72]

Nhaude's ascension followed the same broad pattern as that of Chicucuru's. A number of Tonga amambo sought to reestablish their historic links with the prazo system in order to gain protection from the Nguni who were ravaging their lands.[73] In response to such requests, Nhaude gathered his soldiers, crossed the Luenha River and settled in the vicinity of the abandoned Massangano estate. He helped to organize the local Tonga and, with his well-armed slaves, repelled the invaders from the area adjacent to the Luenha.[74] The initial victory against the Nguni enhanced Nhaude's prestige, and several other Tonga amambo readily recognized him as sovereign in exchange for promises of future assistance. Nhaude conquered those Tonga chiefs who were unwilling to relinquish their independence.[75] He then sent his achikunda south to the Mazoe region where he established his authority.[76]

Once in power, Nhaude and his heirs strove to legitimize and institutionalize their authority as sovereigns. Marriage alliances with the royal family of the Muenemutapa and Macombe, both of whom had in the past governed large areas of Tonga-land, enhanced their prestige and facilitated this process.[77] Nhaude and his successors pursued a similar policy at the local level, marrying into the principal Tonga families.[78]

Like Chicucuru, Nhaude and his heirs adopted a number of the trappings associated with kingship. They underwent the traditional rites of investiture, gave ritual approval to the newly selected amambo and afumu, carried a royal walking stick, received African praise names, and were universally greeted by handclapping. They claimed special remedies from the mizimu, preserved royal burial sites, consulted frequently with the principal *mhondoro* mediums, and, in at least certain crises, personally invoked the ancestor spirits. The Tonga ritual of beseeching the deceased members of Nhaude's family before crossing the treacherous Lupata Gorge suggests that they had acquired recognition as the legitimate guardians of Massangano.[79]

The adoption of these Tonga rituals and practices indicated a larger acculturative process. Nhaude, Bonga, and their successors became progressively more Africanized in their life style, value system, and world view. They dressed in loin cloths, entered multiple marriages, believed in witchcraft, invoked the mizimu and consulted diviners. Taken together with the physical changes, this tendency blurred the differences between the alien rulers and their Tonga subjects, thus reinforcing the legitimacy of their claim.[80]

To insure the perpetuation of their authority, Nhaude and his heirs organized and directed a nontraditional administrative system similar to those used on the earlier prazos. The reigning sovereign governed the core area of the empire with the assistance of achuanga whom he assigned to oversee the principal villages. They transmitted orders from the capital, collected the mutsonko and ivory, and spied on the indigenous authorities. Strategically deployed achikunda assisted the achuanga, intimidated the population, and crushed any internal opposition. As the empire expanded, members of the royal family were appointed to rule various territorial units. This practice had the added advantage of removing potential rivals from the center of power.[81]

Despite the imposition of an alien administrative system, the Tonga amambo and afumu retained their rights, privileges, and responsibilities over all secular and religious matters affecting the members of their chieftaincy.[82] Apart from these local functions, the principal Tonga mambo sat on the royal council, which also included members of the royal family and important slave chiefs. This group met at the capital to resolve all important questions affecting Massangano. When the ruler passed away, the council selected his successors from among the members of the royal family. Similarly, the sovereign summoned them to examine such strategic matters as alliances, war policies, and treaties. According to Courtois, who was visiting Massangano at the time of an attempt on Chatara's life, the ruler sought counsel from his advisers regarding the fate of the culprit.[83]

The royal family also relied heavily on the religious mediums. In addition to their function as intermediaries with the mizimu, the senior lion spirits had great influence at the court, and at least one of their rank governed an important district. Others performed invaluable military functions. They helped mobilize the Tonga reserves, beseeched the ancestors before major battles, and secured remedies to insure success.[84]

Through the fifty-year history of Massangano, members of Nhaude's family dominated the principal positions of authority and legitimized their dynastic claims. They governed the major territorial units, directed the army, and were recognized as the rightful heirs to the throne. In every case, the successor was selected from among the male members of the royal patrilineage with preference given to the junior brothers and senior sons in accordance with the customary transmission pattern of the Tonga. Two informants reported that the successor also inherited all the deceased's wives with the exception of his natural mother[85] — a common phenomenon among the Tonga. Fierce competition within the royal family precluded either a long reign or a smooth transfer of power. Except for Bonga, who was acknowledged as the undisputed heir to Nhaude, court intrigue, revolts, and succession crises characterized the rule of the other members of the royal family.[86]

Despite these internal disputes and Massangano's precarious geographic position, Nhaude's heirs not only resisted the Portuguese but progressively expanded the frontiers of their empire. The powerful military machinery which the ruling family had assembled enabled them to impose their authority over the neighboring chieftaincies. Although their basic recruitment patterns, weaponry, information system, and offensive tactics paralleled those of Makanga and Massingire, a substantial difference existed in the scale of their operations. Equally important, the rulers were successful innovators who adopted and modified the aringa system to meet the particular defensive needs of Massangano.

At the core of Massangano's military power stood the achikunda. Throughout its entire history Massangano benefited from continual influx of recruits into its slave army. The abundant food supplies, which contrasted sharply with the general shortage in the Zambesi, attracted many former colonos and slaves. Others joined Massangano in order to gain protection from the Nguni, or a harsh prazero. Most of these strangers as well as the slaves captured in battle were employed in a military capacity. In addition to the standing army, the local Tonga, who were effective warriors, could be mobilized in times of national emergency. Massangano could, therefore, raise an army of anywhere from 10,000 to 15,000 soldiers, although most operations were not of this magnitude.[87]

TABLE 10   *King List of Massangano*

1.[a]	Nhaude	1849–1855
2.	Bonga (Muguarene, Chidagungaza)	1855–1879?
3.	Muchenga (Mirima, Chimuala)	?1879–1880?
4.	Nhamisinga (Xotaca)	?1880–1885?
5.	Chatara (Macombo)	1885–1887
6.	Mtontora	1887–1892?

Sources: José Fernandes, Júnior, "Narração Do Distrito de Tete" (Paper, Makanga, 1955), pp. 13–23; Joaquim d'Almeida da Cunha, *Estudo Àcêrca dos Usos e os Costumes dos Banianes, Bathias, Pares, Mouros Gentios e Indígenas* (Lourenço Marques, 1885), p. 88; Augusto de Castilho, *Relatório da Guerra da Zambézia em 1888* (Lisbon, 1891), pp. 39–41; A. P. Miranda, *Notícias Àcêrca do Bonga da Zambézia* (Lisbon, 1869), p. 6; A.H.U., Moç., Pasta 1, Segunda Repartição: Augustinho Coelho to Ministro e Secretário d'Estado dos Negócios da Marinha e Ultramar, 1 May 1884; A.H.U., Códice 1463, fol. 8: Joaquim d'Azévedo Alpoim to Vasco Guedes de Carvalho e Menezes, 8 July 1855; A.H.M., Fundo do Século XIX, Governo Geral, Cx. 11: Gov. do Distrito de Tete to Governo Geral, 30 August 1885; A.H.M., Fundo do Século XIX, Governo de Tete, Cx. 27: Luis Inácio to Gov. do Distrito de Tete, 7 March 1883; A.H.M., Fundo do Século XIX, Gov. do Distrito, Cx. 6: Luis Joaquim Vieira Braga to Gov. do Distrito de Tete, 20 August 1885.
    [a] Bereco did not rule.

The armies of Massangano were generally well equipped. One government official, writing in 1870, reported that more than two-thirds of the 14,000 man army carried guns.[88] The vast majority of the arms came from Tete and Sena merchants in exchange for ivory, slaves, and the right to use the middle Zambesi waterway which Massangano controlled. Like their counterparts in Makanga, they had no difficulty arranging these contacts.[89] When the government finally attempted to enforce an arms embargo, Massangano widened its trading network to include Quelimane merchants, and there are indications that arms and powder came from as far away as Lourenço Marques.[90] An unreliable, although invaluable, source of modern weapons were the Portuguese expeditions, which often retreated in such haste that they left behind their heavy guns and large supplies of small arms. "After each of our defeats," observed one commander, "the enemy acquired large caches of arms, munitions and other spoils of war."[91]

Massangano's arsenal was not limited to small arms and indigenous weapons. Lining the walls of the principal aringa at Massangano were twenty cannon of various sizes which had been taken in battle. These gun emplacements, located on the highlands overlooking the Zambesi, enabled Massangano to control all navigation of the river, and substantially increased its defensive capacity.[92] The presence of a small number of Portuguese soldiers who had deserted from the army increased the military capabilities and prestige of Massangano. Apart from the strategic information which they brought, several served as instructors and officers in the army. They introduced new types of drills, training, and tactics. The deserters were particularly valuable as artillery instructors; they provided rudimentary training for a corps of Massangano soldiers and members of the royal family.[93]

The presence of these Portuguese added to the general eclectic character of the army, which was designed to maximize morale and efficiency. Indigenous rituals, tactics, and weaponry were mixed with European technology, strategy, and symbols. Before going into battle, the soldiers gathered around the principal religious mediums who directed a war ceremony which culminated in the invocation to the mizimu. Similarly, the heads of their victims were often displayed on the walls of the aringa, both to inhibit their enemies and because this was believed to increase their power. The amambo and akazambo directed the actual military confrontations, but the royal family and a few Portuguese advisers often coordinated their movements. Members of the royal family also exhibited this dualism, employing charms, remedies, and European military dress to enhance their prestige.[94]

A well-developed spy system operating throughout the Zambesi provided Massangano with valuable political and military data. Individual chikunda were deployed beyond the frontiers of the empire to chart the activities of potential enemies and to serve as an advance warning system in the case of attack. Others infiltrated the local militia and promoted defections. Within the European community, members of Nhaude's family who were thought to be at odds with him secretly gathered strategic information, as did several merchants and soldiers who covertly worked for Massangano.[95] On several occasions, the data so collected enabled Massangano to avert a major defeat or score an impressive victory.[96]

At the core of the defense of the greater Massangano state stood a network of aringas located along the frontiers of the state. Although others had adopted this type of defensive structure, none used it so extensively nor so effectively as Bonga and his heirs. The initial and most sophisticated structures were located adjacent to the royal capital, overlooking the confluence of the Zambesi and Luenha rivers. This complex included a group of small rock fortresses in the lowlands on the southern margin of the Luenha which served as the outer perimeter of defense and a very large stockade built on an overlying cliff. Lining the walls of the principal stockade were a cluster of cannon which not only protected the immediate area below, including the capital, but also the adjacent rivers. An elite regiment of 200 achikunda manned the principal fortification, and several other units were billeted in the lowlands adjacent to Bonga's personal aringa. If necessary, hundreds of chikunda and Tonga warriors could be mobilized from various districts to bolster the defense of the capital.[97]

During their initial confrontations with the Portuguese, Nhaude and Bonga relied primarily upon their defensive position at Massangano and a series of well-executed ambushes.[98] In response to the changing conditions of the 1870s, Bonga's heirs built a vast nework of aringas which acted both as a first line of defense against enemy incursions and as military and administrative centers for the major territorial subdivisions. In all, they constructed a minimum of twenty aringas of various dimensions and forms. Together, they formed an imperfect rectangular configuration which bounded the entire empire. The aringas were not evenly dispersed along the entire frontier, but were generally clustered at critical junctures, reflecting the military realities with which Massangano had to cope.[99] The aringas served a number of other functions. Located on the frontiers, they were ideally situated for both rapid forays and major thrusts against enemy positions. They also formed a vast network of mobilization centers. On orders from Massangano, the Tonga amambo and their followers from throughout the district gathered at the principal aringa where they joined with the local achikunda to form a section of the larger Massangano army.

To reinforce Massangano's military position, the ruling family entered a series of short-term alliances. In the 1850s Massangano became the center of an anti-Makanga coalition of prazeros specifically organized to combat the raids of Chissaca-Maturi. Once this goal had been achieved, the union disintegrated and, in fact, most of the members subsequently united against Massangano. During this period several dissident Makanga chiefs negotiated temporary alliances with Massangano, as did a handful of rebellious prazeros who, like Bonga, endeavored to assert their autonomy from the Portuguese.[100]

Massangano's rulers received their principal source of assistance from a number of Tawara chiefs who recognized them as allies and legitimate, if distant, members of the royal family of the Muenemutapa. Their support ranged from preferential hunting agreements to direct military assistance.[101] This union culminated in a movement among Tawara chiefs, supported by the Muenemutapa, to recognize Bonga as the legitimate ruler of a larger Tonga-Tawara-Karanga state.[102]

Muenemutapa Kandie's willingness to renounce his sovereignty in favor of a union with Massangano cannot be taken out of the context of the changing political and military conditions in the Zambesi. Various African leaders realized that Portugal's long-term imperial aims included the annexation of their lands. This fear, coupled with the great success of Massangano in repelling the military incursions of the state, motivated an undetermined number of independent Sena, Tonga, and Manganja chiefs to align themselves with Massangano.[103]

Perhaps the most significant new alliances were concluded with Barue and Makanga. Previous relationships with Barue had been very uneven. At one time the reigning Macombe and Nhaude had had a cordial relationship, cemented with a marriage alliance between the two royal families. Nevertheless, Massangano did conquer lands which had formerly belonged to Barue, motivating Macombe to aid Lisbon in exchange for the return of his territory.[104] When the Portuguese half-caste Gouveia usurped the Barue throne, a number of legitimate heirs, including Macombe's son Canga, once more allied themselves with Massangano. Other disaffected members of the royal family who hoped, with the help of Massangano, to drive out Gouveia and his Portuguese allies, subsequently joined this alliance.[105] The agreement with Makanga, on the other hand, indicates the extent to which historical enemies would bury their differences in order to retain their independence.

Not surprisingly, the actual relationship between the Portuguese government and Massangano paralleled those which Lisbon had with the other secessionist states. Initially, the crown awarded Nhaude an aforamento and the title of *sargento-môr* as a reward for past services and subsequently attempted a similar ploy when Bonga replaced his deceased father.[106] In general, during Nhaude's reign, Lisbon did have relatively amicable relations with Massangano. The one major exception was a series of battles in 1853 and 1854 which government officials initiated.

Having suffered a serious setback in this campaign, Lisbon was particularly pleased when Bonga made friendly overtures and agreed to reestablish a modus vivendi. To show his good faith, Bonga agreed to pay the outstanding foros and dizimos, and return a number of stolen goods.[107] In subsequent years, he also aided the government against the Nguni and Matequenha, although it is clear that patriotic considerations were a secondary factor. In return he received a three-year tax exemption, modern weapons, deeds to Prazos Mabombe, Sangara, and Mathundo, and official titles.[108]

Bonga's cooperation did not jeopardize or even adversely effect Massangano's independent status. On the contrary, these actions strengthened its autonomous position. The arms Bonga acquired increased Massangano's offensive capabilities; the new prazos enhanced his power and prestige; and the military assistance resulted in the defeat of his enemies. The officials who deluded themselves into believing that Bonga was a loyal subject must have been shocked in 1863 when he adamantly refused to sign a treaty of vassalage.[109] In short, Bonga, like his counterparts north of the Zambesi, assisted the Portuguese against common enemies and professed occasional friendly gestures as long as these actions did not threaten Massangano's autonomy.

In 1867 the Portuguese government initiated a more militant policy designed to curtail the rebellious activities of Massangano. The strategic location of Massangano, Portugal's growing imperial desires, and renewed self-confidence in the aftermath of Matequenha's defeat, inspired this decision.

Between 1867 and 1875, several unsuccessful military expeditions were sent to restore Portuguese control over Massangano.[110] Despite their ample size and abundant supplies, the task forces encountered a series of recurring problems which prevented any major successes. These included a number of well-executed ambushes, enemy infiltration within the ranks of the army, poor leadership, improper displacement of troops and utilization of weapons, and a high level of demoralization and desertion among the militia.[111] Perhaps the most humiliating defeat which the Portuguese suffered occurred in the 1869 campaign, which only 107 of 1000 troops survived.[112]

These wars clearly indicated the precarious nature of the Portuguese position in the Zambesi. A short-term peace treaty, signed in 1867, proved totally ineffective. The agreement, furthermore, made no mention of Massangano's subordination to the state, but implicitly treated the former as an independent political unit. Through this omission, Massangano gained unequivocal de jure recognition, reinforced through subsequent military victories, as an autonomous polity. By his death in 1879, Bonga had forged a mighty empire and openly threatened to destroy the last vestiges of Portuguese power and authority in the Zambesi.[113]

During the succeeding eight years, his successors, Muchenga, Nhamesinga, and Chatara, governed without any new Portuguese attempts to infringe upon their autonomy. The realities of international politics and Lisbon's intense desire to retain her colonies, however, precluded any long-term modus vivendi. The British presence along the Shire and the emergence of Massangano as the center of anti-Portuguese activities reinforced these external pressures. The militant anti-Massangano position which a group of powerful prazeros held increased Massangano's vulnerability. Gouveia's army alone had inflicted heavy casualties on Massangano in 1883 and again in 1886, proving that Massangano was not invincible.[114]

The Berlin Conference of 1885, which laid the ground rules for the scramble, had made it clear that territorial claims were to be contingent upon effective control. The Portuguese therefore could no longer hope to gain international recognition on the basis of their historical presence and minimal authority in the Zambesi. Chatara's repeated refusal to renounce Massangano's independence precipitated a new series of confrontations. "Chatara, judging himself, with good reason to be an independent sovereign wrote to the Governor of Tete, affirming his friendship for the Portuguese nation, with whom he desires to live in peace, and suggested that in order to improve relations the Portuguese nominate a counsel to reside at Massangano." [115] In 1887, the Portuguese carried out a coordinated attack from four directions, designed to isolate the aringa at Massangano and to prevent the royal family from fleeing. The 7000 soldiers rapidly overwhelmed the frontier aringas and moved to encircle the royal capital. When news arrived at Massangano, Chatara and his followers fled into the interior, allowing the government to take possession of the capital.[116]

Despite this defeat the principal members of the royal family, several Tonga amambo, and the most important slave chiefs refused to recognize the authority of the Portuguese government. As their first act, the dissident leaders forced Chatara to abdicate and selected Mtontora who, in turn, pledged to continue the fight against the Europeans. Mtontora gathered his followers and in a startling maneuver recaptured Massangano. After rebuilding and refortifying the stockade and gaining new Barue and Manganja recruits, he began to attack Portuguese traders and garrisons. Simultaneously, he sent an ambassador to Tete in an attempt to negotiate a peace treaty based on mutual recognition. The Portuguese government promptly rejected it. The government, however, badly underestimated Mtontora's ability to reconstitute Massangano's military power, and the first expedition sent to dislodge Mtontora was badly mauled and large quantities of arms were captured.[117]

Massangano's resurgence was short-lived. Portugal could not allow an autonomous enclave to belie her claim to effective control of the valuable Zambesi region. A major force of almost 5000 men, armed with

European weapons and supported by artillery, was dispatched to liquidate the rebels. According to official accounts, Massangano's army fought bravely, tenaciously holding off the Portuguese for six months. But ultimately shortage of supplies and mounting casualties, estimated at 6000 dead, forced Mtontora to flee with his followers to Makanga.[118]

When the alliance with Makanga proved unsatisfactory, Mtontora led the remnants of his army back across the Zambesi, uniting with several Tonga amambo who had continued to resist the Portuguese. In 1892, it was reported that he had reconstructed several small aringa in the interior and was harassing traders passing through his lands.[119] In an attempt to extend the scope of his power Mtontora appealed to his former Barue ally, Canga, who had just helped to overthrow Gouveia.[120] The latter, involved in an internal struggle with several other claimants, was unable to provide significant assistance. Although Mtontora died shortly thereafter, his followers continued to resist the Portuguese on a limited scale until at least 1897 and probably into the twentieth century.[121]

GOUVEIA AND THE LAST OF THE GREAT SUPRA-PRAZO POLITIES

Despite the prolonged and intense resistance against the Portuguese, it would be a distortion to imply that all the prazeros and their followers reacted in a similar manner. On the contrary, both a group of new estateholders and a small number of older prazeros actively assisted the Portuguese government in all phases of the pacification process. The latter are particularly interesting since they seem to have a deeper political, cultural, and social affinity with the Bongas, Pereiras, and Matequenhas than with the Portuguese administrators with whom they chose to cooperate. In the period preceding the scramble they forged their own supra-prazo polities which remained outside the sphere of effective Portuguese control. When given the option of resistance or cooperation, they chose accommodation. Among the most important of these prazeros were the Ferrão family, Ignácio de Jesus Xavier, and António Manoel de Sousa, more commonly known as Gouveia.[122]

As in the case of the other empire builders, Gouveia's rapid ascendancy was closely linked to the disruption and instability within the Zambesi. He arrived in the area in the early 1850s, having migrated from India. Like Nhaude, Gouveia's initial interests were primarily in trading and ivory hunting. With the assistance of a small inheritance, he recruited and armed a large personal following of former slaves and colonos which he used in his various economic endeavors. By 1860 this force consisted of more than 800 men. During the preceding decade, he utilized the military power at his disposal to help conquer Massingire, to thwart several Nguni incursions, and to repel a major Nguni invasion. Informants recalled that several Sena and Tonga amambo who had formerly paid allegiance either to a prazero overlord or Macombe agreed to obey Gouveia in exchange for protection against the Nguni. Other recalcitrant chiefs had to be forcibly persuaded before they agreed to recognize his preeminence. As of 1865, he ruled over a belt of former prazos, extending from north of Sena to Gorongoza. The Portuguese government acknowledged his power and, to insure his continued loyalty, granted him aforamentos for the lands he already governed and offered him the prestigious position of capitão-môr of Manica.[123]

Gouveia consolidated his position in much the same way as the Pereiras, Bongas, and Matequenhas. He married into the families of principal amambo and afumu, offered them gifts as well as protection, made no attempt to abrogate their local power, and even adopted some of the trappings of kingship.[124] Like his contemporaries, he underwent extensive culture change which facilitated his political ascendancy.[125] Various achikunda regiments were dispatched to strategic military positions and royal villages throughout the empire to supervise the indigenous authorities, to collect the mutsonko and ivory, and to prevent internal disorder. Because of the size of the area, Gouveia appointed his principal mestizo lieutenant, Cambuemba, as territorial chief over the land west of Chemba.[126]

Having reinforced his internal position, Gouveia directed preemptive military expeditions against Massangano, Massingire, and the Nguni, all of whom posed a real or potential threat to his holdings.[127] In addition, he constructed a vast network of aringa stretching from Gorongoza to the outskirts of Sena. The principal stockades were fortified with cannons. This chain of stockades served as an effective deterrent against both the westward thrusts of the Nguni and the southern raids of Massangano.[128]

Ironically, Gouveia's most dramatic and significant success was not accomplished through force but by brilliantly engineering an alliance with Macombe Xipapata. Through a series of negotiations, veiled threats, and collusion with a number of Barue elders, Gouveia convinced Xipapata to present him with an ivory tusk filled with dirt as a signal of submission. These negotiations were concluded with an agreement that Gouveia be given Xipapata's daughter in marriage. The wedding took place at the royal court, according to Barue customs. At the time of Xipapata's death, Gouveia had two children from this marriage and, although their genealogical position prevented any legitimate claim to the throne, Gouveia persuaded the royal council to recognize his elder son as heir apparent, while he assumed the position of regent. This coup did not go unchallenged. A number of patrilineal members of the royal family unsuccessfully attempted to dislodge Gouveia, who emerged as de facto ruler of Barue.[129]

By 1881, Gouveia rivaled the rulers of Massangano and Makanga as the dominant power in the Zambesi. In his capacity of capitão-môr, he exerted informal control over Manica and part of Quiteve, ruled over Barue, and dominated most of the former prazos between Chemba and Gorongoza. According to one report, undoubtedly exaggerated, he could raise an army of 12,000 within a day.[130]

Gouveia's relationship with Lisbon in the period preceding the scramble was amicable. His policies with regard to Massangano, Massingire and the Nguni coincided with that of the state and as a result there developed a close working agreement between the two. This alliance did not imply acceptance of a subordinate status, and prominent officials courted Gouveia in the hope that he would remain loyal. He received honors, titles, and special privileges, including free education for his sons in Portugal. This latter ploy had the additional advantage of increasing Portuguese influence in Barue, since his eldest son had already been designated as the heir apparent.[131]

Despite his invaluable assistance, Portuguese officials privately exhibited growing concern about his power and de facto independence. The governor of Manica expressed the hope that Gouveia would willingly transfer Barue to the state for a reasonable sum.[132] Gouveia had no intention of making such a noble gesture and, in the clearest expression of his long-term goals, informed officials that he considered Barue and the Sena prazos to be his personal domain.[133] This posed a serious dilemma for Lisbon, which lacked the military force to depose him and yet was unwilling to allow an independent enclave to operate within its territory. The government's problem was solved when a successful uprising of dissident Barue chiefs resulted in Gouveia's death.[134] This rebellion not only reduced the potential power of Gouveia's descendants, but also meant that Barue was again independent, setting the stage for the 1902 Barue war.

After the revolt, Gouveia's daughter, his principal lieutenant, Cambuemba, and several Tonga, Sena, and Barue chiefs regrouped in the

Sena district and continued to control a large complex of former prazos. She reportedly urged her followers to drive out the Europeans from the Zambesi and periodically demanded tribute from the Companhia de Moçambique to insure the continued security of its plantations.[135] In 1896, the company unsuccessfully sent a force to conquer Gorongoza and other rebellious areas, but in the following year it managed to pacify the area. Several of Gouveia's principal followers subsequently aligned themselves with Macombe in the 1902 war in an attempt to reassert their autonomy.[136]

CONCLUSION

The destruction of Massingire, Massangano, Makanga, and Gouveia's empire marked the twilight of primary resistance in the Zambesi. To place the origin and nature of these resistance movements in their proper historical perspective, three points need to be emphasized. Although each possessed a unique quality they all had common historical antecedents dating back two centuries, exhibited similar characteristics, and shared the same long-term goals and aspirations as the numerous other African polities which forcibly opposed European penetration at the time of the scramble.

The actions of the Pereiras, Matequenhas, Bongas, Gouveia, and the numerous Zambesi peoples who rebelled cannot be separated from historical events and relationships which developed over three centuries. Despite the fiction of Portuguese control, it is quite clear that most prazos had functioned as independent political entities. While the estateholders often paid taxes and provided limited services, these actions were essentially gestures which did not compromise their sovereignty. When pressed, most were willing to defy Lisbon and to use force if necessary. The various chieftaincies incorporated into the prazo system retained a similar spirit of independence with relationship to both the estateholder and the government. The frequency of revolts, migrations, and prazo turnovers attests to the durability of the Zambesi chiefdoms. Given this pattern, it is not surprising that several of the more powerful prazeros and a substantial number of Zambesi chieftaincies forcibly resisted the Portuguese government when it tried to impose its rule over their homelands.

Despite obvious differences, the history of the Pereiras, Matequenhas, Bongas, and Gouveia contains a number of striking parallels:

All were awarded aforamentos which stipulated their subordinate relationship to the Portuguese government.

All forged their empires out of disparate peoples who had already been weakened as a result of invasions, the slave trade, and civil wars.

All sought and acquired at least a modicum of traditional legitimacy.

All underwent various degrees of acculturation which reinforced their political positions.

All relied heavily on the ivory and slave trade.

All adopted and effectively used European weaponry to defend their states and expand the frontiers.

All publicly acclaimed their states to be independent and, at least initially, attempted to gain recognition through peaceful negotiations with the Portuguese.

All entered intricate systems of alliances with neighboring prazeros and/or African polities which became more encompassing as Portuguese military pressure increased.

Portugal's claim that the legal basis of Massangano, Massingire, Makanga, and Gorongoza lay in the aforamentos obviously bore no relationship to the reality of the situation. In all four cases, the grants were probably awarded after the recipient had effectively established control over the land and were intended to insure their loyalty. As a result, this policy set definite parameters within which the state could move if it wished to maintain its fictional position.

The instability and fluidity within the Zambesi enabled Chicucuru, Nhaude, Matequenha, and Gouveia to create and extend the scope of their domains. This process of state formation had two basic dimensions — peaceful incorporation and conquest. A number of Zambesian chieftaincies and unattached colonos and achikunda sought to be integrated into these newly emergent states. Membership provided several advantages, including protection from external threats and internal rivals, an adequate food supply, and easier access to certain highly prized European goods. The new recruits increased the military capacity of these polities and facilitated the ongoing conquest of recalcitrant chieftaincies.

Having gained initial control, all were able to consolidate and perpetuate their rule in varying degrees through the legitimization of their positions in traditional terms. Chicucuru, Nhaude, Matequenha, Gouveia, and their heirs entered strategic marital alliances at various levels of the indigenous political hierarchy. These ranged from betrothals with female members of the royal families of Undi, the Muenemutapa, and Macombe to well-placed unions at the territorial and local level. They reinforced their political positions by adopting a number of the trappings of kingship. This pattern is best documented in the cases of the Bongas and Pereiras, who actually gained recognition as the ruling dynasties of Makanga and Massangano respectively.

All were conquest states which had effectively adopted European weaponry on an unprecedented scale. Although the prazos had relied heavily on military prowess, it is doubtful that they placed the same emphasis on imported arms. What eighteenth-century prazero could claim to possess 5000 guns or twenty cannon of any type or quality? This dependence on European weapons suggests the applicability of the concept of secondary empires which Curtin has recently suggested. With the advent of the industrial revolution, and especially after the Napoleonic wars, a large number of relatively modern yet inexpensive weapons were introduced into Africa. This phenomenon created a period of disequilibrium. Those people who secured a steady supply of imported arms enjoyed a distinct power advantage over their neighbors whom they were now able to subjugate. This, in turn, led to the proliferation of new conquest states, or secondary empires. These states were among the most successful during the period of the scramble, although all were ultimately conquered. The historical development of the supra-prazo polities follows the same broad outline as the secondary empires which developed throughout other parts of Africa.[137]

Despite their expansionist policies, Massangano, Massingire, and Makanga sought a modus vivendi with the Portuguese government based on the principle of mutual recognition. Gouveia chose instead to assist the state and maintain the façade of a loyal subject as long as it did not impinge upon the independence of his empire. As the pressures of the scramble increased, the leaders of Massangano, Makanga, and Massingire opted for armed resistance, while Gouveia took a calculated risk and agreed to assist the Portuguese.

Each of the rebellious states established alliances with neighboring peoples to repel the Portuguese. In the cases of Mtontora, Chicucuru II, and Chinsinga, there is evidence that they were thinking in terms of a wider Zambesi confederation. Once the Portuguese government had defeated these three rebels it felt strong enough to question Gouveia's sovereignty, at which point he declared his intention to rule as an independent potentate. With his death, the empire fell apart, although his daughter and Cambuemba tried unsuccessfully to reconstruct a viable political unit in the Sena-Gorongoza region.

In the final analysis, the resistance movements in the Zambesi should not be treated differently from those in other parts of Africa because of the mestizo leadership at the very top. Such an interpretation would deny the mass support of the local population, the critical political and military roles of the indigenous authorities, and the significant contribution of the religious leaders. Most significantly, resistance movements throughout Africa shared a common raison d'être — to drive out the Europeans and protect their homelands and way of life.

10

Conclusion: An Overview of Zambesian History

From a demographic perspective, the history of the Zambesi can be examined in terms of a series of migrations, which provided the basis for the ethnically heterogeneous Zambesian population. An analysis of the clan composition of the Sena, Tonga, Tawara, Chewa, and Manganja suggests a continual influx and absorption of alien peoples. The present-day chikunda undoubtedly personify this phenomenon.

These migrations into the Zambesi took a variety of forms. The Karanga, Nguni and, perhaps the Malawi fall into the general category of conquering warriors who imposed their will on subject peoples. Although spectacular, this pattern is the exception both in the Zambesi and in Africa generally. At the opposite extreme is the more localized movement of villages, kinship segments, or unattached individuals who sought new lands, additional food, protection, or the propitiation of the mizimu. This recurring process characterized most population diffusion within the Zambesi. Indeed, the frequency with which the colonos withdrew from the prazos attests to their mobile heritage. Apart from these two patterns of dispersion, the forced recruitment of the distant achikunda and the arrival of the alien Europeans suggest the multitude of variations between the two extremes. Like the Karanga, the Portuguese moved rapidly over long distances and even conquered some of the areas within the Zambesi. But because of their relatively small numbers they were forced to rely on the constant trickle of new immigrants from Portugal and Goa to maintain their marginal presence.

The Portuguese entered the Zambesi at a particularly auspicious time. The decline of the Muenemutapa and Kalonga and the inability of Undi, Lundu, Macombe, Chikanga, and the king of Quiteve to es-

154

tablish effective control over their outlying provinces created a power vacuum within the Zambesi. This situation allowed the aliens to capitalize on their limited technological advantages and to subjugate a number of Tonga, Sena, Manganja, and Chewa chieftaincies. The tensions and disputes inherent in such an unstable situation also provided an ideal opportunity for the inland mestizos, Goans, and Portuguese to become intimately involved in local African politics. By entering into preexisting disputes between local polities, between ruling chiefs and disenchanted members of the royal family, between the Zambesi amambo and the surrounding kings, and between the latter and their rebellious subjects, they were able to establish a modicum of political control over various areas in the Zambesi and its immediate confines. Through the selective use of force, and the presentation of highly valued gifts, other Portuguese citizens acquired recognition as overlords or political chiefs. This status accorded them prerogatives which had formerly belonged to the indigenous land chiefs.

Although this transference of authority was a recurring pattern, the growth of the prazo system should not be viewed in terms of a neat lineal progression, and the development of individual estates cannot be examined in terms of the parallel evolution of the system as a whole. While the institution functioned for more than 250 years, the longevity of a given prazo depended upon a number of internal factors, and the available data indicate that most estates had a relatively short life span. At any point in time, therefore, individual prazos were at various stages of development. As a result, the configuration of functioning prazos varied from year to year as did the boundaries of any one estate. Given the relatively high incidence of decay, it is not surprising that the combined pressures of the slave trade, absentee ownership, prolonged famines, and repeated invasions led to a general decline of the system during the first half of the nineteenth century.

Because the prazos were, above all else, a political institution, the nature of the relationship between the alien political chiefs and the indigenous authorities largely explains the instability. This relationship was conditioned by one overriding fact — the prazero's inability to acquire institutionalized legitimacy. As a result, he operated from a poorly defined position, which often brought him into conflict with the amambo and afumu whose cooperation and sanction he desperately needed to retain his authority. Even when he managed to gain the approbation of the royal family, it was of a personal rather than structural nature. Not only could it be arbitrarily withdrawn, it was rarely transmitted to future generations. In the annals of Zambesian history only a few men, such as Chicucuru and Bonga, successfully legitimized their positions both as political chiefs and as the acknowledged owners of the land.

Despite this major handicap and the dependence on a slave army, most prazeros, in the short run at least, established a relatively efficient political, administrative, and military system. They accomplished this by indirect rule through a nontraditional administrative system. The virtue of this mechanism was its adaptability to local political forms, since it did not necessitate either the removal of the ruling elite or the restructuring of the preexisting political system. It had the further advantage of having historical antecedents in the area which dated back to the Karanga and Malawian period.

Simultaneously, by entering a wide range and variety of shifting alliances many prazeros effectively reduced the possibilities of external invasions and increased their relative power within the highly competitive world of the Zambesi. Perhaps the classic manipulators were the Bongas. In response to particular external conditions, they forged alliances with the Portuguese government, pro-government prazeros, anti-government prazeros, the rulers of Makanga, and Barue, Tonga, Sena, and Manganja chieftaincies. On other occasions they found it expedient or necessary to attack most, if not all, of their allies.

One of the overriding themes in African history has been the impact of population diffusion on the nature and direction of change in the receiving areas. Operating at the highest level of generalization, the interaction of migrant groups and the preexisting population in Central and Southern Africa has generated four basic patterns. First, those instances in which the imposition of cultural and political forms of the migrants led to profound changes in the indigenous population. Second, those instances in which migrant groups introduced some new institutions and ideas, generally in the political sphere, but had only a limited cultural impact and tended themselves to be absorbed into the dominant local culture. Third, those instances in which the impact of the stranger group remained almost negligible and absorption of the strangers was rapid and complete. Fourth, those instances in which the fusion of the two groups resulted in the emergence of a new ethnic and cultural unit.

In this respect, the Zambesi region is simply a microcosm of Central Africa, and the four patterns of contact and change operated at both the macro and micro levels. Malawian, Sotho, Ndebele, and Lunda migrations are examples of the first pattern, while the Kololo and Malawian conquests of the Lozi and the Nsenga respectively and perhaps the Karanga expansion into Mozambique are examples of the second.

The complete incorporation of stranger groups and individuals into the dominant Sena, Tonga, and Tawara societies is a prevalent theme in Zambesian history, and the transformation of the achikunda into a clearly defined ethnic group has its parallel in other neighboring areas.

Allowing for such unique characteristics as place of origin, and the nature of the influx, the impact of the prazeros and their mestizo heirs falls within the bounds of the second pattern of change. Such a conclusion differs substantially from the standard portrayal of the overseas culture-bearers common to most Portuguese accounts. This does not suggest that the Portuguese and their descendants did not have a measurable impact on Zambesian history. Their political role as prazeros and directors of the nontraditional administrative system, their significant position in long-distance trade, their intimate involvement in local African politics, and the resistance of some of their members in the late nineteenth century all preclude such a judgment. Nevertheless, viewed in terms of the social and cultural history of the Zambesi their impact was relatively insignificant. The Sena, Tawara, Chewa, Tonga, and Manganja continued to practice shifting agriculture, to mine with hoes and pans, to be organized around village and localized lineage segments, to employ the historical rules of descent, to recognize and obey the mambo, and to propitiate the mizimu.

The prazeros preeminent political position notwithstanding, their presence led neither to the radical restructuring of the local social, political, and economic institutions nor to a parallel shift in the values and belief system. This is not to imply that the African societies were static but that changes occurred gradually and cannot be directly related to the presence of the inland Portuguese. The introduction of an alien slave system into the Zambesi and the development of a new basis of social organization within slave society constituted the major exceptions.

Rather than initiating radical change, the prazeros tended to be absorbed into the predominant local culture. Such a generalization, however, must be treated with the utmost care since the cultural variations between a family which resided in the Zambesi for six months and one which had lived there for six generations were obviously enormous. Similarly, a multitude of local factors, including relative isolation from European socializing agents and the nature of the relationship with maternal African relatives, affected the extent of acculturation. It is evident, nevertheless, that the prazero community underwent such profound changes in its value system, religious beliefs, social organization, communication patterns, and general life style as to warrant the generalization. In the extreme cases, such as the Bongas and Pereiras, this absorption was virtually complete and helps explain their prolonged resistance to the European imperialists.

Finally, the prazos must be viewed as a frontier institution. From the Portuguese perspective, the Zambesian estates demarcated the outer areas of European culture and political authority. From an internal perspective this frontier character derived from their location on the borders of the two major state systems and culture zones of South-Central Africa. Both the historical development and the structure of relationships on the prazos reflect the impact of the two sets of frontiers and the dominance of African society.

11

Postscript: A Note on the Transformation of the Prazos

This study has focused on the prazos as a precolonial institution. Despite the plethora of legislation calling for the abolition of the system in the nineteenth century,[1] Portugal made no attempt to initiate such action in the immediate post-pacification period. On the contrary, the government reorganized and redefined the prazos so that they would serve as the primary modernizing agents and principal administrative units during the first half of the colonial period.

The realization that the government lacked the necessary manpower and capital simultaneously to establish permanent military and political control over the Zambesi and to develop a viable economic base necessary to cover these administrative costs underlay this abrupt shift. The alternative selected was to restructure the prazos and award aforamentos only to responsible individuals and modern companies. Through these grants, Lisbon hoped to settle large numbers of Europeans in the interior and to develop the retarded agricultural sector. These expectations were based both on the relative economic success which a small number of Quelimane prazos had achieved in the period preceding the scramble and on the assumption that with the proper mix of capital and labor this could be duplicated throughout the entire Zambesi.[2]

Even before the final pacification, Lisbon had promulgated a series of laws designed to reestablish its control and foster agricultural production. These included an 1880 decree abolishing the old prazo system and an 1886 ordinance replacing the historic mutsonko with a standard "hut tax" of 800 reis per adult.[3] Since this early legislation proved ineffectual, the government appointed a Commission of Inquiry in 1888 to prepare a detailed plan for the reformation of the prazos. At the end of only three months, with research carried out solely in Portugal, the Committee submitted its proposals. It called for a twenty-year lease with a minimum rent based on half the taxes collected from the indigenous population. The tax rate was to be set at 800 reis per adult and 400 per child. In the case of the adults a minimum of half had to be paid in labor at a rate of 400 reis per week. It envisioned a system of inspectors to protect the Africans from any abuses. These changes were to be implemented only in the pacified zones; in the frontier areas, an arrendatario or preferably a military official would be appointed merely to keep the peace and to collect taxes.[4] The 1892 legislation which provided the basis of the new system incorporated these recommendations, along with a vagrancy clause. Although this decree and subsequent laws failed to produce the desired results, they did dramatically alter the structure and function of the prazos.

The new estateholders neither enjoyed nor apparently desired the independence and political prerogatives of their predecessors. As agents of the government they remained subject to a series of clearly defined rules which limited their authority and insured their subservience. Their principal functions included taking the census, resolving local disputes, supervising the clearing of roads, and increasing agricultural production.[5] Although a number of estateholders abused their power, there is no evidence that they sought any independent political position.[6] With the possible exception of a few estateholders in the Chicoa-Zumbo region, most prazeros continued to serve in this new capacity as long as they reaped the economic benefits.

The restructuring of the indigenous authority postions paralleled the role shift of the prazero. This transformation was apparently limited to Quelimane province, where the new prazos developed most rapidly. To facilitate census taking, tax collection, and labor recruitment, the government divided the prazos into a number of districts, or *circumscrições*, each of which was further subdivided to include one or a number of villages, depending on the indigenous residential patterns. A mukazambo, assisted at the local level by a *samacoa* (an appointed Portuguese official) and by a police force, governed each *circumscrição*. In theory, all were selected from among the indigenous chiefs. In actual practice, however, Portuguese officials often bypassed the indigenous rulers. Despite the appointment of nontraditional authorities and the elevation of minor chiefs to important positions, there is evidence that on at least some estates the local village headmen and land chiefs retained limited functions and that their followers continued to recognize their historical positions.[7]

In the Sena-Tete area, the amambo and afumu continued to govern as long as they cooperated with the prazero and the state. If they did not, more pliable members of the dominant lineage or prestigious village members replaced them. In either situation, a group of appointees, often strangers, supervised their activities and collected the taxes. These were generally known as chuanga and tsachikunda, which suggests that the positions were essentially carry-overs from the previous nontraditional administrative system. Whatever structural differences existed between the form of government on the Quelimane and Tete-Sena prazos, it is clear that the Africans who filled the positions of authority were merely salaried employees who could be demoted, replaced or transferred.[8]

The new prazos, unlike their historical antecedent, were designed to promote agricultural production and the export of cash crops. In order to achieve this goal, the state made a concerted effort to attract modern companies and insure an adequate supply of cheap labor through the implementation of a hut tax. Like most European powers, they believed some artificial incentive was needed to stimulate the Africans, whom they considered to be uneconomic men. The choicest tracts of lands were leased to several Portuguese, French, German and English companies. Almost all of the Zambesi from Chinde to Zumbo was divided up among these firms which, in turn, subleased many of the estates to individual prazeros.[9]

The companies and a few of the more innovative prazeros introduced some modern equipment, certain aspects of modern scientific farming, and a few new crops. They also trained a small class of African technicians to operate and repair the machinery. Through the hut tax regulations, they were able to mobilize a large labor force which they employed primarily during the planting and harvesting period. Within a short period, a number of sugar, coconut, and rubber plantations dotted the coastal zones, and smaller fields of coffee, sisal, tobacco, and cotton were also under cultivation.[10]

The colonos sold their surplus crops and gathered forest products, such as ivory, wax, and rubber, at fixed fairs situated on the prazos. In theory, these were to be free markets where the indigenous population could sell their products to any of a number of merchants, usually Goans, who had rented stalls at these trading centers. In actual practice, most prazeros, either through collusion or by driving the Goans out, were able to maintain a monopoly on all goods bought and sold within their estates. As a result, they were able to buy goods at deflated prices and sell them at several times their real market value. Force was employed to dissuade the Africans from trading outside the prazo and to prevent itinerant Indian merchants from trading on the estates.[11]

The manipulation of trade on the prazos was the most obvious of a series of abuses perpetrated against the indigenous population. As a number of twentieth-century Portuguese critics pointed out, the restructured system had an inherently exploitative character. "The institution will always have the same defects and abuses, and the current reforms have not altered the basic problem which is allowing the same individual to serve in the role of landowner-merchant and public official."[12] The relaxation and revocation of laws specifically designed to protect the Africans and the belief of important colonial officials that these abuses constituted an inevitable part of the "civilizing" and modernizing process enabled the companies and individual prazeros to exercise their power in such a way as to maximize profits.[13] Numerous reports in the Portuguese archives noted that many times the estate-holder or agents demanded excessive taxes, compelled the Africans to grow specific products, refused to pay the colonos the prescribed wages, and illegally exported members of the indigenous population to neighboring prazos.[14] The maltreatment included a variety of repressive acts and corporal punishment designed to inculcate fear in the local population.[15]

The Africans, many of whom had recently been "pacified," reacted as they had in the past. Some grouped around their village headmen and chiefs and defied the mukazambo, samacoa, and *sangira*. They refused to take part in the census, to pay the taxes, or to provide any labor services. Others migrated outside the prazos, often as far as Rhodesia and Malawi, where their descendants still reside.[16] A number of land chiefs and nontraditional leaders used these grievances as a means to mobilize their followers in one last struggle against the Portuguese. From Quelimane to Zumbo, uprisings of various sizes and durations occurred almost annually in the period from 1875 to 1900, and with less frequency until 1917.[17] In some cases, they formed part of larger resistance movements, involving such major African polities as Barue and Maganja da Costa.[18] Perhaps the most serious and sustained uprising within the confines of a single estate took place on Prazo Bororo. From 1892 to 1898, local chiefs independently resorted to force to emphasize their grievances. In 1898, they united around a principal amambo and declared they would never pay taxes or recognize the authority of the arrendatario.[19]

By 1915, the new prazos had failed to achieve even the most basic goals which the Commission of Inquiry had envisioned. One critic of the system calculated that less than one-fifth of 1 percent of all land in the Zambesi was under cultivation.[20] Even though this figure was based on total rather than arable area, and ignored local African production, it graphically indicated the misdirected nature of this scheme.

From its inception, the plan to reorganize the prazos had failed to take into account the geographic, economic, and social realities operative in the Zambesi. The soils, climate, and distance from the coast, for example, deterred any meaningful development in the Tete district. Similarly, the indigenous pattern of shifting agriculture remained incompatible with any type of fixed plantation economy. Apart from the shortcomings in design, there was no real economic incentive for the undercapitalized companies and individual prazeros to invest large sums of money in this backwater area as long as they could derive satisfactory profits from taxes, subleasing, exploitation of cheap labor, and manipulation of trade. In short, what emerged was a speculative, exploitative, and generally inefficient tribute system rather than a modern agricultural sector which could serve as a catalyst for change.

Despite the failure and the vociferous outcry against the abuses by a number of prominent colonial officials and intellectuals, no serious attempt to rationalize or humanize the institution emerged during the next fifteen years. Rather, the new prazos continued albeit in an abbreviated form, until the 1930s, when the Salazar government ordered their abolition as one more program to revitalize the economy of Portugal and her overseas colonies.

REFERENCE
MATTER

A Note on the Collection of Oral Data

Historians are rather conservative. Thus, it is not surprising that the profession as a whole has traditionally taken a dim view of oral data. This reaction ranges from contempt to a more healthy scepticism. Yet, in adopting this posture, traditionalists violate the cardinal rule of the craft that every possible source of evidence must be critically examined. In African historiography the failure to follow this maxim has led to a whole generation of Euro-centric accounts which do a disservice to both the continent and the profession. Fortunately, a dramatic reversal in this trend has occurred during the last decade. Spurred on by the pioneering work of Jan Vansina, a new generation of oral historians is attempting to redirect the thrust of African history. Because reservations about the validity of oral data still linger, it is useful to sketch the methodology employed in this study of the prazos.

Ideally, the historian should be fluent in the languages of the people whom he is studying. This is especially true in societies where the traditions are either fixed or controlled by formula. In such cases the intended and the symbolic levels are often more significant than the literal narration. The choice of words, sounds, metaphors, structure, and other literary devices provides invaluable insights into the culture and history. Unfortunately, neither my wife nor I had command of the diverse Shona and Malawian dialects spoken throughout the Zambesi. This was obviously a limiting factor. Nevertheless, the ramifications were not so profound as they might have been since no fixed traditions were found in this region.

Our complete dependence on interpreters made it imperative that we select them with the greatest care. Two problems complicated this process. The virtual absence of an educational infrastructure meant that there were very few Africans who were bilingual. In some remote areas it was impossible to find anyone totally fluent in Portuguese — a tragic testimony to Lisbon's assimilation policy. Even where qualified interpreters existed, overly cautious Portuguese administrators often insisted that we choose Africans working for the state so that they could report on our activities. Under the best circumstances we were able to select interpreters who not only possessed the necessary linguistic skills, but were born in the region and enjoyed the trust of the elders. It was also important to establish an informal friendly relationship with them to differentiate ourselves from the inland Portuguese community.* In a climate of oppression and fear they provided an invaluable entrée into an African community reticent to have any unnecessary relations with Europeans. Even under these optimal conditions, there were still a few elders who chose not to speak with us.

Historical and geographical considerations played an important role in determining what areas we selected to visit. Because the prazos were scattered along a five-hundred-mile stretch on both banks of the Zambesi River, it was physically impossible to visit more than a small number of former estates during one dry season. The inadequate road system complicated matters. From a list of prazos we carefully selected twelve estates which were relatively accessible. This sample was designed to include the homelands of each of the principal Zambesian peoples. In this way, we sought to determine if local cultural variations affected the structure and operation of the prazos. Most of the estates chosen had a relatively long life span and played an important role in Zambesian history. The advantages of studying such prazos were twofold: the indigenous population would be familiar with the organization of the prazos, and there existed a substantial body of archival material which could be used to corroborate the oral accounts. We also selected three less significant estates to provide a more balanced sample.

We tried to visit a minimum of two or three villages on each of the former prazos, interviewing several elders at each site. In every instance possible we conferred with the descendants of the royal family. We also sought out rain-callers, whose position presupposed a profound understanding of the past, elders reputed to be great repositories of tradition, and Africanized descendants of former prazeros. For those who did not fit into these categories, the only selection criteria we employed were that their ancestors had lived in the region for at least three generations and that they could answer some rather general historical questions which were posed prior to the interview.

The actual taped interview took two forms.† The most common was to question the Zambesian elders individually. Generally, we held the discussions near the compound of the royal family in the presence of a large number of village members. Throughout the interview the audience played a vital role. Not only did they correct specific facts, but they elaborated on many points which remained vague in the mind of the informant. This constant interaction added an invaluable dimension, and, whenever possible, we at-

---

* Out of concern for our interpreters, I choose not to be more specific about them or our relationship.

† A copy of this tape collection, along with my field notebook, will be deposited in the Archives of Traditional Music, Indiana University, Bloomington, Indiana.

tempted to get the exact exchange between the audience and the informant on tape.

Group interviews constituted the second approach. We employed this technique when an elder either was reticent to speak by himself or suggested that the presence of two or three of his compatriots would enhance the overall quality of the interview. On occasion an informant would invite a knowledgeable member of the audience to become a full participant in the formal interview. The constant dialogue between informants elaborated many obscure points and suggested new areas of questioning. The obvious shortcoming of this technique was their search for consensus. As a result, variations as well as subtle differences were lost or blurred.

While the general interview schedule included three broad types of questions, each oral testimony was a unique expression of the personality, interests, and knowledge of the informant. The initial queries dealt with the elder's family history. The responses not only provided valuable genealogical and ethnographic data, but helped to place him at ease. The formal interview began with several open-ended questions about the origin and historical development of his ethnic group. Considering the fragmented nature of the political system, it was not surprising that these questions failed to reveal any fixed traditions or formalized accounts. The bulk of the interview consisted of specific questions about African society and the workings of the prazo system. These ranged from the nature of kingship to the cultural conversion of the estateholders. Throughout the interview the interpreter provided capsulated summaries of each response which enabled me to pursue particular points and to formulate subsequent questions.

During the interview my wife listed every question in a field notebook. Notations were made next to those queries which the informant could not answer or misunderstood in order to facilitate the subsequent transcription and editing process. They remain, however, on a collection of original unedited tapes.

Before departing from the village, we generally spent about an hour replaying portions of the taped account. This served not only as a source of great entertainment, but proved to the elders that their exact testimony would remain intact for posterity. Concern about this matter reflected the profound historical sense of most of the informants. As a token of our appreciation, we presented them with a small gift. These were presents rather than payments, and only once were there any negotiations.

With a few outstanding informants, the interviews took several sessions to complete. In most cases the optimal time period was a two-hour sitting. After that both the informant and I began to tire. By returning on a subsequent day, we not only overcame the fatigue problem, but I had an opportunity to carefully study his testimony and to determine which areas I needed to probe still further. Often the informant utilized this interlude to work out parts of the narrative which had been unclear.

The next phase was to edit, transcribe, and translate the interviews. Generally, we began these interrelated processes immediately after completing the first session in any geographic area. In most cases it took between six and eight hours to produce an hour of finished tape. The end product consisted of two complementary sets of edited and annotated accounts — one in the local African language and the other translated into Portuguese.

Three considerations were paramount during this entire process. The first was to determine the exact wording and meaning of the questions which the interpreter had asked. Throughout our entire field experience we remained very conscious of our linguistic shortcomings and the possibility that questions might be modified or substantially altered in the process of translation. The problem became acute in a few cases where the interpreters spoke Portuguese very poorly. To control for this type of error, we asked the interpreter to translate his question from the original tape. We then compared this with the question I had originally proposed in Portuguese. If the two were reasonably close or if the modified query seemed suitable, the interpreter proceeded to translate the response. When misinterpretations occurred, both the question and response were deleted from the final texts. If the material had any historical validity, however, it was retained even though it was not pertinent to the question raised. This decision was consistent with the idea that we were creating an archive rather than simply collecting data for a single study.

In addition to translating and editing the collection, notes of explication were placed after every signficant proper noun as a type of oral footnote. These annotations served as a complementary historical document which located a person or event in time and space or elaborated upon points which an informant mentioned in passing.

Before accepting data from these interviews, I subjected them to intensive analysis to determine whether their vital political and social functions limited their historical utility. The Zambesi oral testimonies tended to validate the rule of specific families, to legitimize a mambo's position as owner of the land, and to justify the preeminence of one people over another. This was done by manipulating past events to make them conform to contemporary realities. Thus, the Tawara claimed to have conquered the indigenous Zambesian peoples as agents of the Muenemutapa, when the Muenemutapa probably conquered them. The Malawi accounts emphasized the absence of previous sedentary peoples in order to legitimate their ownership of the land. All Zambesian peoples acknowledged having domestic slaves, but each denied that any of their people ever entered into this low status position; and the descendants of achikunda have conveniently forgotten their origin because of the social stigma attached to the warrior slaves. There were also conflicting accounts of the prazero's ascension to power and his political relationship vis-à-vis the mambo. The presence of these questionable or contradictory accounts does not invalidate the entire testimony but rather demands that they, like written sources, be treated with the utmost care.

There are a number of checks which can be used simultaneously to help validate the oral testimonies. Some, such as public interviews or the use of multiple informants, are built into the collection process. Both internal mechanisms enhance the value of the interview and check certain types of misinformation. In this situation, however, individual insights and interpretations may be blurred or totally lost, and those assumptions which are accepted as historical truth by all the members of the chieftaincy cannot be exposed.

Individual oral testimonies were examined both independently and in conjunction with other texts for possible distortions. Such characteristic problems as etiological explanations and the imposition of ahistorical clichés, generally associated with fixed texts and formulated traditions, were absent.* Nevertheless, careful scrutiny of the interviews revealed two other forms of distortions. The introduction of questionable or specious data to legitimize both historical and contemporary relationships recurred with some frequency. This type of functional adaptation is common to oral traditions throughout Africa. In certain instances there was also a tendency to explain the origin of the chieftaincy in terms of the actual history of the ruling lineage.

A few archival documents and travel accounts which were written by observers with a good understanding of Zambesian society provided another check on the oral data. In a small number of cases the written material actually verified a specific event noted in the testimony. More often, they corroborated generalized political, social, and economic relationships which operated on the prazos. In a few instances linguistic, ethnographic, and archeological material served a similar function.

In addition to possible distortions, the oral data suffered from an absence of fixed chronology. Instead of precisely dating a phenomenon, the Zambesian elders used the reign of specific amambo or the lifetime of a deceased ancestor as their temporal indicator. The end product was a relative chronology bound to make most historians uncomfortable. The tendency to telescope the past compounded this problem. While most elders recalled both the founding ancestors and important events which had transpired during the last four generations, actions which occurred during the interlude were either forgotten or transposed to one of these time periods.

The extensive archival documentation enabled me to impose precise time parameters, especially for nineteenth-century Zambesian history. Often an informant would note that an event occurred during the life of a particular prazero. By determining the period of his residence, we were able both to approximately date events and to provide the genealogies with a fixed time dimension. The Nguni invasion served as a second temporal indicator. Most elders utilized these invasions as an historical landmark and discussed events in terms of their relative proximity to these attacks. While the Nguni incursions span a twenty-year period, they still provide a valuable temporal dimension. Finally, these corroborative sources indicate the relatively shallow time span of most of the oral data which generally does not antedate the nineteenth century.

* Both the mode of analysis and the terminology reflect the influence of Jan Vansina's brilliant work in this field.

An Historiographical Note on the Prazos

Scholarly interest in the prazos dates from the end of the last century. During the past eighty years three schools of thought have attempted to explain the origin and nature of the institution. According to Oliveira Martins and his disciples, large parts of Mozambique, including the Zambesi region, were divided into small Arabic sultanates. In each of these polities the indigenous African rulers were allowed to govern as long as they recognized the suzerainty of the sultan and gave him the prescribed taxes and services. When the Portuguese defeated the Arabs, they merely replaced them at the apex of this system.

At the beginning of this century the colonial administrator Ernesto Vilhena put forward the conquest-substitution thesis. Most historians who have studied the prazos accept it, at least in its broad outline. According to this version, "traditional" African society was divided into a series of chieftaincies governed at the highest level by a mambo who appointed members of his lineage to supervise local areas. These subordinate chiefs were known as afumu. In exchange for their positions, the local chiefs recognized the supremacy of the mambo and fulfilled a clearly defined set of obligations which included collecting and transmitting the traditional tax, or mutsonko, and providing certain services. Initially, inland Portuguese, aided by their slave armies, conquered and dislodged the afumu. Over time, they took advantage of the declining power of the mambo to usurp his position as well. Through this process the prazero acquired all the political prerogatives which had formerly belonged to the indigenous authorities. In the seventeenth century, the prazeros received legal sanction when the Portuguese crown recognized their position and issued them aforamentos, or land grants.

A number of Portuguese scholars, most notably Lobato, have examined the prazos from a more limited legal perspective. Within this framework, the prazos have been defined as a land grant, or aforamento, which the crown distributed to female inhabitants of the Zambesi or to prospective female

172

immigrants for a period of three generations. The legalists are particularly interested in those characteristics which differentiated the prazos as a legal entity from the *sesmarias* of Portugal, the donações of Madeira and Brazil, and the land system which developed in Goa. At the same time, they stress their common derivation from medieval Portuguese land law, especially the *Enfiteuses* and the *Leis das Sesmarias*. For the legalist, the prazos implicitly date from the first aforamento, but there is no agreement among historians as to when this phenomenon actually occurred. Lobato avoids this problem by suggesting that at an unspecified point in time the crown nationalized the entire Zambesi. Since most of the lands were already occupied, the king merely exerted his feudal rights and took title of the entire region. After this, the Portuguese landholders recognized the suzerainty of the crown and entered into a contractual relationship which became the legal basis of the prazo system.

Each of these interpretations contains a number of obvious weaknesses. The thesis of Arab origin is the least acceptable since none of the proponents of this position seriously studied the historical development of the prazos. They simply assumed an Arab origin and used it as a point of departure for a defense of or an attack on the decaying prazo system at the beginning of this century. In fact, there is little evidence that Muslim sultans or traders established political hegemony over substantial areas of the Zambesi. In most cases, the inland Arab traders concentrated exclusively on the lucrative commerce in gold and ivory with the surrounding Karanga states and the Malawian confederation.

The conquest-substitution thesis suffers, in part, from an uncritical acceptance of the writing of seventeenth-century observers like Barreto who overemphasized Portuguese military efforts and defined them in medieval European terms.

The holders of these lands have the same powers and jurisdiction as the Kaffir fumos from whom they were conquered . . . and therefore they are like the potentates of Germany, and can pronounce sentences in all cases, put to death, declare war, and impose tribute, in which great barbarities were committed, but they would not be duly respected by their vassals if they did not hold the same powers as the fumos whom they succeeded.[1]

Consequently, there has been a tendency to disregard or to treat only superficially other less obvious means by which prazeros acquired their political positions, such as marriage alliances or the prazeros' involvement in local African politics. These were especially significant in the eighteenth and nineteenth centuries when the prazeros no longer enjoyed an absolute power advantage.

The simple substitution of a Portuguese chief for an African chief, furthermore, is an oversimplification of a far more complex phenomenon. Its proponents have failed to examine the exact nature of the relationship between the prazeros and the indigenous land chiefs and have disregarded the social and religious factors which legitimized kingship.

A number of difficulties with the legalistic approach stem from its failure to differentiate between the prazos as a legal or theoretical abstraction and the prazos as a functioning system.

All three theories share two significant weaknesses, they ignore both the internal organization of the institution and the ways in which the prazos changed over time. By focusing solely on the continuity of the system they overlook the inherent instability of individual prazos and implicitly assume that their historical development paralleled that of the system as a whole. The recent writings of M. D. D. Newitt constitute a substantial break with the previous approaches. His treatment of the European community in the Zambesi is particularly insightful. Together with this study, it marks a new phase in the historiography of the prazos.

Notes

PREFACE

1 Alexandre Lobato, *Evolução Administrativa e Económica de Moçambique 1752–63* (Lisbon, 1957), p. 213.
2 Throughout this study I have substituted the term prazero for the legal titles *emphyteuta* and *arrendatário*, which actually appear in the archival documentation.
3 Chi-Sena and Chi-Tawara forms are used instead of the corrupted Portuguese forms found in the documents. Thus, the preferred plural forms of *mambo* and *mfumu* are *amambo* and *afumu*, respectively. See Emilio Alves, *Dicionário Português-Chisena e Chisena-Português* (Lisbon, 1930); and Padre Victor José Courtois, *Diccionário Cafre-Tetense-Portugues* (Coimbra, 1900).

CHAPTER 1: THE AFRICAN BACKGROUND

1 The term "Anões" is substituted for "bushmen" throughout this chapter since "bushmen" is considered to have pejorative connotations. Other local variants used to denote the "bushmen" are Anhapache and Akafula.
2 Interviews with Jasse Camalizene and Mozesse Domingos; Gustavo do Bivar Pinto Lopes, *Respostas Ao Questionário Ethnográfico* (Beira, 1928), p. 3; W. H. J. Rangeley, "The Earliest Inhabitants of Nyasaland," *Nyasaland Journal* 16 (1963): 39; José Fernandes, Júnior, "Narração Do Distrito de Tete" (Paper, Makanga, 1955), p. 3; M. G. Marwick, "History and Tradition in East Central Africa Through the Eyes of the Northern Cewa," *Journal of African History* 4 (1963): 379; Harry Langworthy, "A History of the Undi to 1890" (Ph.D. diss., Boston University, 1969), p. 130.
3 Interviews with Gaspar Cardoso and Conrado Msussa Boroma; Fernandes, Júnior, "Narração," p. 14.

4 Interviews with João Cristóstomo, Gaspar Cardoso, and João Alfai; Fernandes, Júnior, "Narração," pp. 2–3; Carlos Wiese, "Expedição Portugueza À Mpeseni," *Boletim Da Sociedade De Geografia De Lisboa* 10 (1891): 255.

This interpretation must be treated with care, however, since there is a tendency among the Tawara to identify themselves with the subsequent Karanga warriors. It is therefore possible that it was the army of the Muenemutapa which actually subjugated the Zimba and Pimbe. The presence of Zimba among the present-day Chewa is noted in a number of oral testimonies and lends some credence to Donald Abraham's hypothesis that the southern bank of the Zambesi constituted part of the Malawian kingdom before the Karanga conquest. Langworthy, "A History of the Undi," p. 191; interviews with Malisseni Máuo, Chiponda Cavumbula, and Conrado Msussa Boroma; D. P. Abraham, "The Early Political History of the Kingdom of Mwene Mutapa (850–1589)" in *Historians in Tropical Africa*, Proceedings of the Levehulme Inter-Collegiate History Conference (Salisbury, 1962), p. 64.

5 Interviews with Gaspar Cardoso, Conrado Msussa Boroma, Chale Lupia, Niquicicafe Presente, and Renço Cado; Hugh Tracey, *António Fernandes, Descobridor do Monomotapa, 1514–1515* (Lourenço Marques, 1940), p. 39; João dos Santos, "Ethiópia Oriental," in *Records of South-East Africa*, ed. G. M. Theal (Capetown, 1901), 7:263; António Bocarro, "Década da India," ibid. (Capetown, 1899) 3:372; Eric Axelson, ed., "Viagem que fez o Padre António Gomes . . . ," *Studia* 3 (1959): 186. Linguistic evidence suggests that the Tonga are historically related to the Barue. Abraham contends that they are culturally related to the matrilineal Plateau and Valley Tonga despite their patrilineality. Henry Alexandre Junod, "Notes on the Ethnological Situation in Portuguese East Africa, South of the Zambesi," *Bantu Studies* 10 (1937): 297–300; D. P. Abraham, "The Early Political History," p. 75.

6 Interviews with Chale Lupia, Niquicicafe Presente, and Simões Zindo. Among the other important Tonga clans are Tembo, Makate, Malungu, Chironga, and Chuambo.

7 Interviews with João Vicente, Chale Lupia, Niquicicafe Presente, and Renço Cado; joint interview with Tomás Chave and Oliveira Sinto. It is difficult to assess the actual time span because the Tonga tend to telescope their traditions. Thus, in the Chemba area several informants mentioned that their ancestors were the original settlers of the land. The first mambo was Maya, followed by Nchaua, Ntassa, and Nhantali, who ruled in the life time of the present chief, Tomás Chave.

8 Tracey, *António Fernandes*, pp. 39–40; Santos, "Ethiópia Oriental," p. 263; Bocarro, "Década," pp. 227, 233.

9 The most important Sena offshoots are the Cheringoma and Gorongoza who have taken the names of the areas in which they live.

10 Francisco de Aragão e Mello, *Memória e Documentos Acêrca dos Di-*

reitos de Portugal Aos Territórios de Machona e Nyasa (Lisbon, 1890), p. 57; Biblioteca Pública de Ajuda [cited hereafter as Ajuda], 51–VIII–40, fols. 212–15: Vasco Fernandes Homen to Luyo da Sylva, 15 February 1576; Eric Axelson, *Southeast Africa 1480–1530* (London, 1940), p. 270; interviews with Jasse Camalizene, Mozesse Domingos, Gonçalves Chibante, Botão Ganunga, and Gimo Tito.

11 Langworthy, "A History of the Undi," pp. 127–28.

12 D. W. Phillipson, "The Early Iron Age in Zambia — Regional Variants and Some Tentative Conclusions," *Journal of African History* 9 (1968): 191–211.

13 Langworthy, "A History of the Undi," pp. 130–32; Rangeley, "The Earliest Inhabitants of Nyasaland," p. 38.

14 R. A. Hamilton, "Oral Tradition: Central Africa," in *History and Archaeology in Africa*, ed. R. A. Hamilton (London, 1955), p. 21; Marwick, "History and Tradition," p. 378.

15 Interviews with Malisseni Máuo, Capachika Chúau, and Chiponda Cavumbula; Langworthy, "History of the Undi," p. 143.

16 Brian Fagan, *Southern Africa During the Iron Age* (New York, 1965), p. 123; K. R. Robinson, "The Archeology of the Rozwi," in *The Zambesi Past*, ed. E. Stokes and R. Brown (Manchester, 1966), pp. 3–27; Roger Summers, "The Southern Rhodesian Iron Age," *Journal of African History* 2 (1961): 7–8.

Throughout this study numerous, often unrelated, references are made to the kingdom of the Muenemutapa. The author expects to treat this subject in a more coherent manner as part of a larger social and political history of the Zambesi region.

17 A number of hypotheses have been advanced to explain the Karanga expansion. The most common focuses on the need for salt. According to one set of traditions, Karanga hunters tracking game on the frontiers of the Zambesi region noted the fertility of the land and its high salt content. A variant of this account states that Mtota dispatched his trusted servant Netonda (Nyakatonda) to examine the Dande-Chedima region. He returned not only with a block of salt but with news of the abundance of ivory and the relative weakness of the Tawara. Political disputes involving the principal segments of the royal family provide another possible cause of the northward movement. Of all the theories the least acceptable is Abraham's suggestion that Mtota was merely acting as an imperial agent for the Muslim traders who desired to expand the frontiers of their economic empire. Interview with Conrado Msussa Boroma; Abraham, "Early Political History," p. 63; D. P. Abraham, "Maramuca: An Exercise in the Combined Use of Portuguese Records and Oral Tradition," *Journal of African History* 2 (1961): 212–13.

18 Interviews with João Cristóstomo, Conrado Msussa Boroma, and João Alfai; Fernandes, Júnior, "Narração," pp. 3–4; Abraham, "Early Political History," p. 62.

19 According to scattered Nsenga, Barue, and Karanga traditions, Matope

chose his daughter Mureche to govern Barue. A Tawara account which noted that the rulers of Barue were the grandchildren of the Muenemutapa corroborates this point. Junior kinsmen, probably sons of the Muenemutapa, also conquered the vast areas east and west of Barue known as Quiteve, Sedanda, and Manica. *Boletim Oficial de Moçambique* [cited hereafter as *B.O.M.*], 1883, No. 21, p. 147: Albino Manoel Pacheco, "Uma Viágem de Tete ao Zumbo"; Abraham, "Early Political History," p. 82; interviews with Conrado Msussa Boroma, José da Costa Xavier; Santos, "Ethiópia Oriental," p. 275; Gerhard Liesegang, *Respostas Das Questões Sobre Os Cafres*, Occasional Paper no. 2, Centro de Estudos De Antropologia Cultural (Lisbon, 1966), p. 20; Arquivo Histórico Ultramarino, Moçambique, Caixa 17 [cited hereafter as A.H.U., Moç., Cx.]: "Descrição corográfica do Reino de Manica, seus costumes e leis" (unsigned, undated); Mello, *Memória e Documentos . . . Machona e Nyasa*, pp. 148–49.

20 A.H.U., Moç., Cx. 1: Dom Nuno Alferes Pereira, Ambrózio de Feitas da Camara, Francisco de Lucena, 16 March 1631; A.H.U., Moç., Cx. 17: "Descrição corográfica do Reino de Manica, seus costumes e leis" (unsigned, undated); Arquivo Nacional da Torre do Tombo [cited hereafter as A.N.T.T.], Ministério do Reino, Maço 604: António Pinto de Miranda, "Monarchia Africana," pp. 123–24 (undated); Frei António da Conceição, "Tratados Dos Rios de Cuama," in *O Cronista de Tissuary Periódico*, ed. J. H. da Cunha Rivara (Nova Goa, 1867), 2:45 (original manuscript in Ajuda 51–VI–29); Ajuda, 51–VIII–40, fols. 212–15: Vasco Homen to Luyo da Sylva, 2 February 1576; Dionízio de Mello e Castro, "Notícia do Império Marave e dos Rios de Sena, 20 de Janeiro de 1763," *Anais da Junta de Investigações do Ultramar* 9, tomo 1 (1954), pp. 133–35.

21 Interview with Conrado Msussa Boroma; Santos, "Ethiópia Oriental," p. 268; Fernandes, Júnior, "Narração," pp. 4–5; Francisco de Sousa, *Oriente Conquistado A Jesú Christo Pelos Padres Da Companhia De Jesús da Província De Goa*, 2 vols. (Lisbon, 1710), 1:834; personal communication with D. P. Abraham. According to Tawara traditions, the area of Chedima was divided among four territorial chiefs — Canhenbanhema, who lived at Nseguezi; Nsambo, who lived to the south; Magoe, who lived along the Zambesi; and Msussa, who lived in the west.

22 Interviews with Aleixo José, João Cristóstomo, and João Alfai.

23 Interviews with João Cristóstomo, Pedro Damião Chamualira, Conrado Msussa Boroma, José da Costa Xavier, and João Alfai.

24 Ajuda, 51–VIII–40, fols. 212–15: Vasco Fernandes Homen to Luyo da Sylva, 15 February 1576; Conceição, "Tratados," p. 66.

25 Interviews with Jasse Camalizene, Gimo Tito, Lole Nhanticole, and Sete Catondo.

26 For detailed information on the organization and power of the army see: Ajuda, 51–VIII–40, fols. 212–15: Vasco Fernandes Homen to Luyo

da Sylva, 15 February 1576; A.H.U., Moç., Cx. 30: "Descripção do Imperio Moanamotapa . . ." (undated, unsigned); A.N.T.T., Ministério do Reino, Maço 604: António Pinto de Miranda, "Monarchia Africana," pp. 123–24 (undated).

27 Bocarro, "Década," pp. 358–59; *B.O.M.*, 1883, No. 21, p. 205: Albino Manoel Pacheco, "Uma Viagem de Tete ao Zumbo"; Sousa, *Oriente Conquistado*, 1:843; Manuel De Faria e Sousa, "Ásia Portuguesa," in *Records of South-East Africa*, ed. G. M. Theal (Capetown, 1898), 1:24; D. P. Abraham, "The Role of Chaminuka and the Mhondoro Cults in Shona Political History," in *The Zambesian Past*, eds. E. Stokes and R. Brown (London, 1966), p. 38.

28 A.H.U., Moç., Cx. 30: "Descripção do Império Moanomotapa . . ." (unsigned, undated); A.N.T.T., Ministério do Reino, Maço 604: António Pinto de Miranda, "Monarchia Africana," pp. 120–22 (undated); Charles Ralph Boxer, ed., "A Dominican Account of Zambézia in 1744," *Boletim da Sociedade de Estudos de Moçambique* 29 (1960): 9; D. P. Abraham, "Maramuca," p. 214.

29 D. P. Abraham, "Ethno-History of the Empire of Mutapa — Problems and Methods," in *The Historian in Tropical Africa*, ed. Jan Vansina (London, 1964), p. 108; Conceição, "Tratados," pp. 105–6; A.H.U., Moç., Cx. 17: "Descrição corográfica do Reino da Manica, seus costumes e leis" (unsigned, undated); Castro, "Notícias do Império Marave," p. 133.

30 Santos, "Ethiópia Oriental," p. 237; Mello, *Memória e Documentos . . . Machona e Nyasa*, pp. 99–100.

31 Bocarro, "Década," p. 373; Mello, *Memória e Documentos . . . Machona e Nyasa*, pp. 99–100.

32 A.N.T.T., Ministério do Reino, Maço 604: António Pinto de Miranda, "Monarchia Africana," pp. 111–12 (undated); Santos, "Ethiópia Oriental," p. 273; Bocarro, "Década," p. 373.

33 Interviews with Jasse Camalizene, Gimo Tito, Lole Nhanticole, and Sete Catondo; A.H.U., Moç., Cx. 17: José Álvares Pereira to Gov. dos Rios de Sena, 8 March 1780; Manuel Barretto, "Informação do Estado e Conquista dos Rios de Cuama, 1667," in *Records of South-East Africa*, ed. G. M. Theal (Capetown, 1899), 3:486–87; Santos, "Ethiópia Oriental," p. 217; Tracey, *António Fernandes*, pp. 20–22.

34 A.H.U., Moç., Cx. 17: "Descrição corográfica do Reino da Manica, seus costumes e leis" (unsigned, undated); Conceição, "Tratados," p. 64; Santos, "Ethiópia Oriental," pp. 217, 273; Bocarro, "Década," p. 373.

35 Barretto, "Informação," pp. 486–87; Conceição, "Tratados," pp. 44–45.

36 Langworthy, "A History of the Undi," p. 112. The only noticeable exceptions are the accounts which tend to idealize the Malawian past through the identification with Egypt, Timbucktu, or some other medieval African center. Such a version is found in A. Y. Mazula, "História dos Nianjas," *Portugal em África* 19 (1962): 162–63. A Portuguese report written in the eighteenth century noted that Kalonga was the

offspring of a union between an unknown Malawian chief and the daughter of the Muenemutapa (Castro, "Notícias," p. 139).

37 José Fernandes, Júnior, "História de Undi" (Paper, Makanga, n.d.), pp. 8–11; Mazula, "História dos Nianjas," pp. 162–63; Langworthy, "A History of the Undi," pp. 121–22. Because of telescoping in traditions, it is impossible to determine the period which elapsed between their departure from Katanga and their arrival, which can be dated from Portuguese sources as pre-1614.

38 Fernandes, Júnior, "História de Undi," pp. 11–12; Mazula, "História dos Nianjas," pp. 165–66; Conceição, "Tratados," p. 42; Langworthy, "A History of the Undi," pp. 147–48.

39 Barreto, "Informação," p. 480; Mello, *Memória e Documentos . . . Machona e Nyasa*, p. 125; Conceição, "Tratados," p. 42.

40 Axelson, ed., "Viagem," p. 184.

41 D. P. Abraham, "Tasks in the Field of Early History," in *Conference on the History of the Central African Peoples*, Proceedings of the 17th Conference of the Rhodes-Livingstone Institute (Lusaka, 1963), p. 3. This is also implied in Barretto, "Informação," p. 480.

42 Abraham, "Tasks," p. 13.

43 Barreto, "Informação," pp. 470–71, 480.

44 Quoted in Alpers, "The Mutapa and Malawian Political System to the Time of the Ngoni Invasions," in *Aspects of Central African History*, ed. T. O. Ranger (London, 1968), p. 24.

45 Langworthy, "A History of the Undi," pp. 173–78.

46 Manganja is often cited in Portuguese sources as Bororo.

47 Axelson, ed., "Viagem," p. 181; Barretto, "Informação," p. 476; Conceição, "Tratados," p. 42; Manoel Godinho, *Relação Do Novo Caminho que fez por Terra e Mar Vindo da Índia para Portugal no Anno de 1633* (Lisbon, 1842), p. 200.

48 Alpers, "The Mutapa and Malawi Political Systems," p. 21. Barretto noted that Malawian chiefs controlled the area as far north as the coastline opposite Mozambique Island, but he did not specifically identify them (Barretto, "Informação," p. 470). The traditions that Mazula recalled suggest that this area was given to a Malawian chief other than Lundu (Mazula, "História dos Nianjas," pp. 236–37).

49 A.H.U., Moç., Maço 38: Pedro José Pereira, "Proposta que se fez aos moradores de Sena para darem seu voto p. escritos aos pontos seguintes," 27 August 1753; A.H.U., Códice 1314, fol. 34: D. Manoel António de Almeida to Francisco de Mello de Castro, 9 July 1757; A.H.U., Moç., Cx. 5: Pedro José Pereira, 1 December 1756; A.N.T.T., Ministério do Reino, Maço 604: António Pinto de Miranda, "Monarchia Africana," p. 79 (undated).

Another possible explanation for Lundu's decline could be his conflict with Mbona, the great Manganja rainmaker. The dispute occurred sometime before 1800 and ended with Mbona's murder. After his burial the Manganja began to worship him as the rain god and a

Mbona cult was organized and directed by earthly mediums who could have used their links with the supernatural to undermine Lundu's religious and ritual authority. (A. W. R. Duly, "The Lower Shire: Notes on Land Tenure and Individual Rights," *Nyasaland Journal* 1 [1948]: 11–14; W. H. J. Rangeley, "Mbona — The Rain Maker," ibid. 6 [1952]: 8–27.) Father Mathew Schoffeleers is in the process of conducting a major study of the Mbona which undoubtedly will shed light on this problem.

50 Fernandes, Júnior, "História de Undi," pp. 11–12; Langworthy, "A History of the Undi," p. 184; Mazula, "História dos Nianjas," p. 165; Bocarro, "Década," pp. 402–3. There are conflicting traditions about Undi's departure. According to the generally accepted version, Undi was bypassed in favor of a junior relative upon the death of the reigning Kalonga. Undi sought the assistance of the raincaller Makewana and beseeched her to destroy his rival. Instead, she presented him with some hoes and seed and suggested that he and his followers migrate to distant lands. An alternate account emphasizes the close relationship of Kalonga and Undi and Kalonga's wish to have his loyal subject govern the important western region. This would serve to legitimize Undi's position and probably was a reconstruction after the fact.

51 In order to retain a constant orthography throughout and to minimize confusion, the southern Zambesi term *mfumu* is used to signify a Chewa land chief rather than the actual Chewa term *nfumu*.

52 See Jan Vansina, *Kingdoms of the Savanna* (Madison, 1966) for a detailed description of the political organization of various Lunda states, and Ian Cunnison, *The Luapula Peoples of Northern Rhodesia* (Manchester, 1959), for a similar study of Kazembe. Primary accounts of the court structure of the Muenemutapa are found in A.N.T.T., Ministério do Reino, Maço 604: António Pinto de Miranda, "Monarchia Africana" (undated); and A.H.U., Moç., Cx. 30: "Descripção do Império do Moanomotapa" (unsigned, undated).

53 Fernandes, Júnior, "História de Undi," p. 16; Langworthy, "A History of the Undi," pp. 35–44. For a detailed nineteenth-century account, see A. C. P. Gamitto, *King Kazembe*, trans. Ian Cunnison, 2 vols. (Lisbon, 1960).

54 Fernandes, Júnior, "História de Undi," p. 16; Langworthy, "A History of the Undi," p. 72; interviews with Capachika Chúau and Chiponda Cavumbula.

55 Langworthy, "A History of the Undi," p. 250.

56 A.H.U., Códice 1310: Francisco de Mello de Castro to David Marques Pereira, 2 April 1755; A.H.U., Moç., Cx. 5: Pedro José Pereira, 1 December 1756; A.H.U., Códice 1314, fol. 135: D. Manoel António de Almeida to Francisco de Mello de Castro, 9 July 1757; joint interviews with Calavina Couche and Zabuca Ngombe and with Chetambara Chenungo and Wilson John.

57 This subject has been treated at great length in the writings of both Eric Axelson and Alexandre Lobato. Their principal works are listed in the bibliography.

CHAPTER 2: THE PROCESS OF PRAZO FORMATION

1 The term *chikunda* (pl. *achikunda*) signifies vanquisher in Chi-Tawara and Chi-Nyungwe and is derived from the verb *kukunda*, which means to vanquish.

2 E. Axelson, ed., "Viagem que fez o Padre António Gomes . . . ," *Studia* 3 (1959): 203; Manuel Barretto, "Informação do Estado e Conquista dos Rios de Cuama, 1667," in *Records of South-East Africa*, ed. G. M. Theal (Capetown, 1899), 3:475. For a short summary in English see Eric Axelson, *The Portuguese in South-East Africa 1600–1700* (Johannesburg, 1962), pp. 40–42. See Chapter 4 for an analysis of the various slave systems on the prazos.

3 Ajuda, 51–VI–24, No. 67, fol. 290: "Tres Papeis feitos pellos Mouros em França sobre os Rios de Cuama e sobre Índia" (unsigned), 1677.

4 A.H.U., Moç., Cx. 2 (unsigned, undated).

5 A.H.U., Moç., Cx. 22: António Manoel de Mello de Castro, "Relação de Algumas Armas," 11 June 1785. Although it was written in 1785 there is no reason to believe that the Africans were using different types of weapons during the previous century. In fact, his report is supported by the more general description of African arms given by a number of earlier observers, such as João de Santos.

6 Some historians have placed great significance on the Portuguese possession of guns. See Axelson, *The Portuguese in South-East Africa*, p. 34.

7 Barretto, "Informação," p. 507; Alexandre Lobato, *Evolução Administrativa E Económica De Moçambique 1752–63* (Lisbon, 1957), pp. 191–92; A.H.U., Moç., Cx. 2: Francisco Mateus, Conde Val de Reis, et al., 9 January 1681; A.H.U., Moç., Cx. 3: Conde D. Luíz de Menezes to the King, 4 November 1730.

8 Barretto, "Informação," p. 473. Two principal exceptions were Prazos Cheringoma and Luabo.

9 A.H.U., Moç., Cx. 2 (undated and unsigned).

10 A.H.U., Moç., Cx. 3: Conde D. Luíz de Menezes to the King, 4 November 1730.

11 Prazeros like Dona Ignez Pessoa de Almeida Castelo Branco of Prazo Cheringoma could put 6,000 men into the field. One anonymous early eighteenth-century document mentions a prazero who had a slave army of 15,000 (A.H.U., Moç., Cx. 2 [unsigned, undated]).

12 A.H.U., Moç., Maço 7: Francisco Henriques Ferrão, "Mapa da População da Vila de Senna," 12 November 1826.

13 A.H.U., Moç., Cx. 17: António Manoel de Mello de Castro to Jozé de Vasconcellos Almeida, 18 June 1780.

14 In the seventeenth century it was quite common for the inland Portuguese who were searching for gold to buy land. It was less frequent in the following century (A.H.U., Moç., Cx. 2: Conde de Val de Reis, Francisco Mateus, Feliciano Dourado, Carlos Gueses, 8 February 1684; A.H.U., Moç., Cx. 2: Gaspar de Souza e Lacerda, 3 July 1682).

15 A.H.U., Moç., Cx. 2: Gaspar de Souza e Lacerda, 3 July 1682.

16 Arquivo Histórico de Moçambique [cited hereafter as A.H.M.], Fundo do Século XVIII: Ignácio de Mello Alvim, 12 July 1769.

17 M. D. D. Newitt, "The Portuguese on the Zambesi: An Historical Interpretation of the Prazo System," *Journal of African History* 10 (1969): 71; Barretto, "Informação," p. 465.

18 A.H.U., Moç., Cx. 20 (unsigned), 11 and 16 July 1783; A.N.T.T., Documentos Remettidos da India, Livro Arquivo da Torre do Tombo, Lx, fol. 230, cited in Francisco de Aragão e Mello, *Memória e Documentos Ácêrca dos Direitos de Portugal Aos Territórios de Machona e Nyasa* (Lisbon, 1890), p. 122; Charles Boxer, "Sisnando Dias Bayão: Conquistador do Mae d'Ouro," *Primeiro Congresso da História da Expansão Portuguesa no Mundo* 3 (1938): 107–9; A.H.U., Moç., Cx. 14: Petition written by Ricardo José de Lima for Dona Ignez Pessoa d'Almeida Castello Branco, with supporting statements from various inhabitants in Sena.

19 Courtois' allusion to civil war is corroborated by oral testimonies and other contemporary accounts.

20 *B.O.M.*, 1886, No. 29, p. 361: "Viagem as Terras da Macanga, Apontamentos colhidos d'um relatório do padre Victor José Courtois, vigário de Tete, 1885." A similar account was written by Augusto de Castilho (ibid., 1887, No. 306). One suspects, however, that he was greatly influenced by Courtois' report.

21 José Fernandes, Júnior, "História de Undi," (Paper, Makanga, n.d.), p. 17.

22 Ibid; interview with Chiponda Cavumbula.

23 Interviews with Conrado Msussa Boroma, Alberto Vicente de Cruz, and Leão Manuel Banqueiro Caetano Pereira.

24 Joint interviews with Calavina Couche and Zabuca Ngombe, and with Chetambara Chenungo and Wilson John.

25 Interview with Simon Biwi.

26 A.H.U., Moç., Cx. 1: Dom Nuno Alferes Pereira, Ambrózio de Feitas da Camara, Francisco de Lucena, 16 March 1631.

27 A.H.U., Códice 1462, fol. 50: Custódio José da Silva to José Maria Pereira de Almeida, 1 September 1860.

28 A.H.U., Moç., Cx. 31: unsigned document probably written for Macombe, the King of Barue, 2 February 1795. Another example is that of Muenemutapa Chissampharu who is reputed to have fled to Prazo Bena after going blind (interview with Conrado Msussa Boroma).

29 Gamitto noted that the Africans living on the margins of the Zambezi were without guns and were, therefore, vulnerable to invasion and enslavement (A.H.U., Moç., Pasta 13: António Candido Pedroso Gamitto to S.M.T., 31 December 1854); interviews with Jasse Camalizene, António Vaz, and Renço Cado, and joint interview with Gente Renço and Quembo Pangacha.

30 A.H.M., Fundo do Século XIX, Quelimane, Governo do Distrito, Cx. 1: Venâncio Raposo de Amarel, 28 January 1849.

31 Interviews with Jasse Camalizene, Renço Cado, and António Vaz; A.H.U. Moç., Documentos, Annexos, e as Plantas: Francisco de Mello de Castro to Marquês de Tavora, 10 August 1750.

32 Interview with Mortar Nhacalizi.

33 Interview with Leão Manuel Banqueiro Caetano Pereira. Salt continued to be in great demand throughout the nineteenth century. One observer commented that its value remained second only to gold (*B.O.M.*, 1883, No. 29, p. 206: Albino Manoel Pacheco, "Uma Viagem de Tete ao Zumbo").

34 Francisco José de Lacerda e Almeida, *Travessia da África* (Lisbon, 1936), p. 130.

35 The data on which these compilations are based come from the following sources: A.N.T.T., Ministério do Reino, Maço 604: António Pinto de Miranda, "Memória Sobre a Costa da África," pp. 91–97 (undated); A.H.U., Moç., Cx. 18: José Vasconcellos Colleço, 3 December 1782; Dionízio de Mello e Castro, "Notícia do Império Marave e dos Rios de Sena, 20 de Janeiro de 1763," *Anais da Junta de Investigações do Ultramar* 9, tomo 1 (1954): pp. 144–45.

36 A.H.U., Moç., Cx. 62: Francisco Henriques Ferrão, "Relação dos Prazos de Real Corôa e do Real Fisco do Districto desta Vila e quem posse pela maneira abaixo declarado," 5 February 1818.

CHAPTER 3: POLITICAL ORGANIZATION
OF THE PRAZOS

1 For examples of such cases see: A.H.U., Moç., Maço 4: José Luís Rodrigues to João da Costa Xavier, 22 August 1828; A.H.M., Fundo do Século XVIII: João Felipe de Carvalho to Francisco Guedes de Carvalho e Menezes da Costa, 9 October 1800; interview with Joaquim Anseni Saíca.

2 This is not to imply that the system as a whole was static, but rather that its general character and principal authority roles continued over time as chieftaincies moved in and out of prazo relationships. Because of the lack of published primary data dealing specifically with this fringe area, the following discussion is based primarily on oral data I collected among the Sena, Tonga, and Tawara living on the margins of the Zambesi and the southern Chewa residing in Casula and Chiuta.

In the Portuguese archival documents and ethnographic studies, the African political terms are often used interchangeably and with little regard for the actual positions they represent. Thus, mambo, *nhacuaua*, and mfumu are all used to describe the independent Zambesi chiefs. For the purpose of this study the land chief will be known as mambo and the village headman as mfumu, which is consistent with the way these positions were defined by my informants in Mozambique. The only exceptions are among the southern Chewa, where the land chief had the title of mfumu, and in Cheringoma, where he was known as nhacuaua.

3 Joint interview with Chetambara Chenungo and Wilson John; interview with Simon Biwi; José Fernandes, Júnior, "História de Undi" (Paper, Makanga, n.d.), p. 9.

4 Interviews with Gaspar Cardoso, José António de Abreu, José da Costa Xavier, Marco Coutinho, and Niquicicafe Presente.

5 Interviews with Gonçalves Chibante, Botão Ganunga, and Renço Cado.

6 Since the two-level structure constituted the dominant form, the discussion is limited to it. It must also be reemphasized that the Chewa mfumu and the southern Zambesi mambo shared similar political and religious functions as land chiefs (interviews with João Cristóstomo, Gaspar Cardoso, Chale Lupia, Gimo Tito, and Renço Cado; joint interviews with Gente Renço and Quembo Pangacha, with Calavina Couche and Zabuca Ngombe, and with Chetambara Chenungo and Wilson John).

7 Interviews with Pedro Damião Chamualira, Khaliche António Camundi, Sete Marqueza, António Gavião, Chale Lupia, Gaspar Cardoso, José da Costa Xavier, and Gimo Tito; joint interviews with Chale Penga, Tomás Chambe, and Jamusse Guede, with Calavina Couche and Zabuca Ngombe, and with Gente Renço and Quembo Pangacha.

8 Interview with José da Costa Xavier.

9 A.N.T.T., Ministério de Reino, Maço 604: António Pinto de Miranda, "Monarchia Africana," pp. 122–24 (undated); interviews with Gaspar Cardoso, Dauce Angolete Gogodo, Malisseni Máuo, and Capachika Chúau.

10 In the case of witchcraft accusations, the mambo personally administered a lethal solution to the accused witch; if the individual vomited the potion, it was viewed as proof of his innocence.

11 Interviews with Luís Gonzaga Cebola, José da Costa Xavier, Marco Coutinho, Jasse Camalizene, and Renço Cado; Manóel Monteiro Lopes, "Usage and Customs of the Natives of Sena," *Journal of the African Society* 6 (1907): 354.

12 In Makanga, for example, when a person was found guilty of murder, his maternal uncle or another member of the matrilineage was required to give the lineage of the deceased a male or female slave (Fernandes, Júnior, "História de Undi," pp. 9–13).

13 Ibid.; interviews with Zacarias Ferrão, Andisseni Tesoura; joint inter-

view with Chetambara Chenungo and Wilson John; António Candido Pedroso Gamitto, *King Kazembe*, trans. Ian Cunnison, 2 vols. (Lisbon, 1960), 1:11, 148.

14 Fernandes, Júnior, "História de Undi," pp. 10–13.

15 Interviews with Gaspar Cardoso, José António de Abreu, Marco Coutinho, Gonçalves Chibante, Botão Ganunga, Renço Cado, and Simon Biwi.

16 Gustavo do Bivar Pinto Lopes, *Respostas ao Questionário Ethnográfico* (Beira, 1928), p. 54; interviews with Gaspar Cardoso, José António de Abreu, Marco Coutinho, Gonçalves Chibante, Botão Ganunga, Renço Cado, and Simon Biwi.

17 Joaquim d'Almeida da Cunha, *Estudo Acêrca dos Usos e os Costumes dos Banianes, Bathias, Pares, Mouros, Gentios e Indígenas* (Lourenço Marques, 1885), p. 92. This practice persisted as late as 1880 among groups living outside the prazos.

18 Interviews with José da Costa Xavier, Marco Coutinho, Chale Lupia, Niquicicafe Presente, Jasse Camalizene, João Pomba, Simon Biwi, and Capachika Chúau; joint interview with Tomás Chave and Oliveira Sinto; Lopes, "Uses and Customs," p. 355; António Candido Pedroso Gamitto, "Prasos Da Corôa Em Rios De Sena," *Archivo Pittoresco* 1 (1857–58): 62.

19 Interviews with Gaspar Cardoso, José António de Abreu, José da Costa Xavier, João Alfai, Sete Marqueza, Renço Cado, Simões Zindo, Malisseni Máuo, Capachika Chúau; joint interviews with Calavina Couche and Zabuca Ngombe, and with Chetambara Chenungo and Wilson John.

20 Interviews with Jasse Camalizene, Renço Cado, and Simões Zindo.

21 Interview with João Vicente, and Chale Lupia; joint interview with Chetambara Chenungo and Wilson John.

According to tradition, in the early fall and during periods of famine and drought, Tonga and Tawara amambo called together all the inhabitants of the chieftaincy and ordered them to prepare a great feast, known among the Tawara as *nsembe*. The local population gathered sorghum, beer, chickens, and goats and placed them all in front of a designated tree or high rock which was considered a holy place. The people began to clap their hands and dance while the mambo invoked the mizimu. When he raised his royal staff from one side to another, it began to rain.

The southern Chewa performed a similar ritual at a shrine hut, or *kucisi*, which was dedicated to the spirits of the previous chiefs. While the mfumu organized and directed the ceremony, his role in the actual invocation seems to have varied from one Chewa group to another. Among the Chewa living in the area of Casula and Chiuta, the mfumu commonly beseeched the ancestors, while in other areas an official rain-caller was summoned. All the members of the chieftaincy brought offerings to the kucisi and simultaneously invoked the spirits of their ancestors.

22 Gamitto, "Prasos da Corôa," p. 62; Cunha, *Estudo Acêrca dos Usos,* p. 92; Lopes, *Repostas ao Questionário,* p. 57; interviews with Guiraza Passo, Bruto Sabão, Quembo Passalampapi, and Carlota Checanhanza.

23 Gamitto, *King Kazembe,* 1:181; interview with João Alfai.

24 Interviews with Gaspar Cardoso, José António de Abreu, José da Costa Xavier, Mortar Nhacalazi; joint interview with Gente Renço and Quembo Pangacha; A.H.M., Fundo do Século XIX, Governo do Distrito de Quelimane, Prazos, Caixa 2–47 (2): João de Souza to Izidro Manoel de Carrezado, 3 September 1836.

25 Neither primary data nor oral traditions support the contention that: "In prazo society the fumo was the *prazo* holder's deputy among the colonos. He was clearly an appointee of the *prazo* holder who could remove or replace him at will" (M. D. D. Newitt, "The Portuguese on the Zambesi from the Seventeenth to the Nineteenth Centuries," *Race* 9 [1968]: 483).

26 Gamitto is one of the few pre-1850 observers who stated that the prazero did have the power to appoint and dismiss afumu and mambo. His observations were made during the 1820s and 1830s when the entire system was in decay and the traditional relationships had been altered. It was not until the 1880s that the prazero or the government systematically appointed and dismissed afumu and mambo (*King Kazembe* 2:183–85).

Among my informants there was universal agreement that the prazero did not have the right to commit such an act (interviews with Gimo Tito, Renço Cado; joint interviews with Gente Renço and Quembo Pangacha, and with Chale Penga, Tomás Chambe, and Jamusse Guede).

27 Among the patrilineal Tonga, Sena, and Tawara, the mfumu's brother or the eldest son of his senior wife was chosen, while among the matrilineal Chewa it was the senior nephew of the deceased.

28 Interviews with António Gavião, Chale Lupia, Gimo Tito, Mortar Nhacalazi, and Dauce Angolete Gogodo.

29 Interviews with António Gavião, Niquicicafe Presente, Domingo Kunga, and Chale Lupia; joint interview with Chetambara Chenungo and Wilson John; Cunha, *Estudo Acêrca dos Usos,* p. 92.

30 A.H.M., Fundo do Século XVIII: João Felipe de Carvalho to Francisco Guedes de Carvalho e Menezes da Costa, 9 October 1800.

31 Gamitto, "Prasos da Corôa," p. 62.

32 Interviews with Gaspar Cardoso, José da Costa Xavier, and Jasse Camalizene.

33 Interviews with Pedro Damião Chamualira, Chale Lupia, Dauce Angolete Gogodo, and Andisseni Tesoura; joint interview with Chetambara Chenungo and Wilson John.

34 The Bongas of Prazo Massangano continually propitiated the mizimu and sought their assistance in times of crises. Interviews with Chale

Lupia and Niquicicafe Presente; José Fernandes, Júnior, "Narração do Distrito do Tete" (Paper, Makanga, 1955), p. 30.

35 See Francisco José de Lacerda e Almeida, *Travessia Da África* (Lisbon, 1938), p. 14.

36 Interviews with Gaspar Cardoso and António Vas.

37 Gamitto, "Prasos Da Corôa," p. 62; Newitt presents a good example of what he believes to be a rite of investiture but unfortunately does not give the original source (Newitt, "The Portuguese on the Zambesi from the Seventeenth to the Nineteenth Centuries," p. 492).

38 The famous nineteenth-century prazeros Gambete, Ferrão, Bonga, and Chicucuru all had African wives.

39 João dos Santos, "Ethiópia Oriental," in *Records of South-East Africa*, ed. G. M. Theal (Capetown, 1901), 7:215.

40 Personal communication with Harry Langworthy, 30 October 1968; A.H.U., Moç., Pasta 10: Domingos Fortunato de Valle to Ministro e Secretário d'Estado dos Negócios da Marinha e Ultramar, 8 February 1850.

41 N. J. Brendon, "Chiuzungu," *NADA* 36 (1959): 19.

42 Lacerda e Almeida, *Travessia*, p. 236.

43 Interviews with José António de Abreu, Chale Lupia, Renço Cado, Lole Nhanticole, and Chiponda Cavumbula; joint interview with Calavina Couche and Zabuca Ngombe; Gamitto, "Prasos Da Corôa," p. 63; Sr. Ferão, "Account of Portuguese Possessions Within the Captaincy of the Rios de Sena," in *Records of South-East Africa*, ed. G. M. Theal (Capetown, 1901), 7:376.

44 Academia das Ciências de Lisboa, MS. 648 Azul: António Norberto de Barbosa de Villas Boas Truão, "Estatística de Capitania dos Rios de Senna do Anno de 1806," 16 July 1807. This is corroborated by interviews with Pedro Damião Chamualira, João Vicente, Niquicicafe Presente, Tomás Chave and Oliveira Sinto, and Capachika Chúau.

45 A.H.U., Moç., Cx. 52: Fr. Jozé Machado do Aguia, ca. 1783.

46 A.H.U., Moç., Cx. 17: António Manoel de Mello de Castro to Martinho de Mello e Castro, 17 May 1780.

47 A.H.U., Moç., Cx. 13: Balthazar Manoel Pereira de Lago, 20 July 1769.

48 On Prazo Segundo Tipue the fixed mutsonko was 1,287 bushels of sorghum and 67 manchillas. Below are the amounts collected in the period 1779–83, listed in A.H.U., Moç., Cx. 53: Fr. Jozé Machado do Aguia, ca. 1783.

	Manchilla	Panjas of sorghum
1779	32	460
1780	28	158
1781	45	270
1782	10	64
1783	79	450

49 Gamitto, "Prasos Da Corôa," p. 62; interviews with Botão Ganunga and João Pomba; joint interview with Gente Renço and Quembo Pangacha.

50 Interviews with Botão Ganunga and João Pomba; joint interview with Gente Renço and Quembo Pangacha.
51 A.H.U., Moç., Cx. 34: Francisco José Lacerda e Almeida to the King, 22 March 1798.
52 According to informants in Chemba, Gambete believed in witchcraft and regularly administered muabvi, the poison ordeal, to the colonos on his estate.
53 Interviews with Chale Lupia and Chiponda Cavumbula.
54 Among the neighboring Chewa the chuanga's role was similar to his namesakes' on the prazos (Gamitto, *King Kazembe*, 1:42).
55 Gamitto, "Prasos Da Corôa," p. 62; A.H.M., Fundo do Século XIX, Governo Geral, Cx. 11: Gov. do Distrito de Tete to Sec. Geral do Governo, 30 August 1885; interviews with Luís Gonzaga Cebola, João Alfai, João Vicente, Simões Zindo, and Andisseni Tesoura.
56 Interviews with Conrado Msussa Boroma, Chale Lupia, Gimo Tito, Renço Cado, Andisseni Tesoura, and Chiponda Cavumbula.
57 Ajuda, 52-X-2, No. 3: José Francisco Barbosa to Cortes Geraes e Extraordinárias e Constituintes da Nação Portugueza, "Analyse estatística, Topográfica e Política da Capitania de Rios de Senna," 30 December 1821; Gamitto, *King Kazembe*, 2:186.
58 Lacerda e Almeida, *Travessia*, p. 123; Gamitto, "Prasos Da Corôa," p. 62.
59 See A.N.T.T., Ministério do Reino, Maço 604: António Pinto de Miranda, "Memória sobre a Costa de África," pp. 43–53 (undated).
60 Interviews with José António de Abreu, Chale Lupia, António Vas, and Dauce Angolete Gogodo; joint interviews with Gente Renço and Quembo Pangacha, and with Chale Penga, Tomás Chave, and Jamusse Guede; A.H.U., Moç., Cx. 3: Fr. Fernando Jesús, M.A., 13 April 1752.
61 A.N.T.T., Ministério do Reino, Maço 604: António Pinto de Miranda, "Memória sobre a Costa de África," p. 55 (undated).
62 A.H.U., Moç., Cx. 3: Fr. Fernando Jesús, M.A., 13 April 1752.
63 Interview with Chale Lupia; joint interview with Chetambara Chenungo and Wilson John.
64 Fernandes, Júnior, "Narração," p. 22; António Candido Pedroso Gamitto, "Escravatura da África Oriental," *Archivo Pittoresco* 2 (1859): 399; A.N.T.T., Ministério do Reino, Maço 604: António Pinto de Miranda, "Memória sobre a Costa de África," pp. 55–57 (undated).
65 Interviews with José da Costa Xavier, Niquicicafe Presente, Renço Cado, Lole Nhanticole, João Pombe, and Alface Pangacha; joint interviews with Gente Renço and Quembo Pangacha, with Chale Penga, Tomás Chave, and Jamusse Guede, and with Calavina Couche and Zabuca Ngombe; Henry Rowley, *The Story of the Universities Mission to Central Africa* (London, 1867), p. 46; A.H.M., Fundo do Século XVIII João Felipe de Carvalho to Francisco Guedes de Carvalho e Menezes da Costa, 9 October 1800.
66 *B.O.M.*, 1830, No. 3, p. 13: José Manoel Correia Monteiro to Manoel

Joaquim de Vasconcellos Cirne, 13 June 1830. This information is supported by an interview with Chiponda Cavumbula.

67 Joint interviews with Chetambara Chenungo and Wilson John, and with Calavina Couche and Zabuca Ngombe; interviews with Chiponda Cavumbula, Malisseni Máuo, and Simon Biwi.

68 Interview with Leão Manuel Banqueiro Caetano Pereira; A.H.U., Moç., Pasta 29: Anselmo Joaquim Nunes de Andrade, 28 November 1875.

69 Interviews with Renço Cado and António Vas.

70 João Baptista de Montaury, "Moçambique, Ilhas Querimbas, Rios de Sena, Villa de Tete, Villa de Zumbo, Manica, Villa de Luabo, Inhambane," in *Relações de Moçambique Setecentista*, ed. António Alberto de Andrade (Lisbon, 1955), p. 365.

71 A.H.U., Códice 1439, #2051 (unsigned), 30 October 1832. The year that Bayão presented the gift to the crown was either 1672 or 1673.

    In addition to Cheringoma Dona Ines owned prazos Gorongoza, Bumba, Agora Santa, Tungue, Maringue de Inhambu, and Maringue Bumbu (A.H.U., Moç., Cx. 20 [unsigned], 11 and 16 July 1783).

72 A.H.U., Moç., Cx. 34: Francisco José de Lacerda e Almeida to the Queen, 22 March 1798.

73 A.H.U., Moç., Cx. 27: D. Diogo de Souza to João de Souza e Brito, 2 December 1794; A.H.U., Moç., Cx. 34: Francisco José de Lacerda e Almeida to the Queen, 22 March 1798; A.H.U., Moç., Cx. 31: Custódio de Av. Bragança, 13 March 1797; A.H.U., Moç., Cx. 27: D. Diogo de Souza to João Felipe de Carvalho, Gov. dos Rios, 28 May 1803.

74 A.H.U., Moç., Cx. 31: Manuel Ribeira da Costa, 7 January 1795.

75 A.H.U., Moç., Cx. 42: João Felipe de Carvalho to the Gov. dos Rios, 28 May 1803; A.H.U., Moç., Cx. 27: D. Diogo de Souza to João de Souza Brito, 21 May 1794; Lacerda e Almeida, *Travessia*, p. 86; A.H.U., Códice 1464, fol. 45: Joaquim d'Azévedo Alpoim to Vasco Guedes de Carvalho e Menezes, 5 January 1856; João de Azévedo Coutinho, *Manuel António de Sousa: Um Capitão-môr da Zambézia* (Lisbon, 1936), p. 7.

76 A.H.U., Códice 1469, fol. 105: Izidro Manoel de Carrazedo, 18 February 1835.

77 A.H.U., Códice 1758, fol. 156: Custódio José da Silva to Jozé Maria Pereira d'Almeida, 24 July 1859.

78 Ibid.

79 A.H.U., Moç., Cx. 31: Manuel Ribeira da Costa, 7 January 1795; A.H.U., Moç., Cx. 31: Custódio de Av. Bragança, 13 March 1797.

80 A.H.U., Moç., Cx. 42: Jozé Diniz Menezes, 20 July 1803.

81 A.H.U., Códice 1464, fol. 45: Joaquim d'Azévedo Alpoim to Vasco Guedes de Carvalho e Menezes, 5 January 1856.

82 A.H.M., Fûndo do Século XVIII: José Caetano da Mota, 12 January 1768.

83 A.H.U., Moç., Cx. 33: Diogo da Costa Xavier et al., ca. 1796. Mas-

sangano was particularly important because it was located at the confluence of the Zambesi and Luenha rivers and therefore controlled all trade up the Zambesi.

84 A.H.M., Fundo do Século XVIII: Inácio de Mello Alvim, 12 July 1769.

85 A.H.U., Moç., Cx. 9: Marco António de Azévedo Coutinho de Montaury, 13 July 1762.

86 A.H.U., Moç., Cx. 17: António Manoel de Mello de Castro to Jozé de Vasconcellos Almeida, 18 June 1780; António Norberto de Barbosa de Villas Boas Truão, *Estatísticas da Capitania dos Rios de Sena no Anno de 1806* (Lisbon, 1889), p. 160.

87 A.H.U., Moç., Cx. 17: "Côpia do Paragrafo da Carta do Governador dos Rios de Sena António Manoel de Mello de Castro em Resposta ao Gov. e Cap. M. General de Mossambique na datta de 14 de Fevereiro de 1781."

88 Gamitto, "Prasos Da Corôa," p. 62. A.H.U., Moç., Cx. 34: Francisco José de Lacerda e Almeida, 22 March 1798; A.H.U., Moç., Cx. 17: António de Mello de Castro to Jozé de Vasconcellos Almeida, 18 June 1780.

89 A.H.U., Moç., Cx. 3: Fr. Fernando Jesús, M.A., 13 April 1752.

90 A.H.U., Moç., Cx. 17: António Manoel de Mello de Castro to Jozé de Vasconcellos Almeida, 18 June 1780.

91 A.H.U., Códice 1756, fol. 57: Joaquim d'Azévedo Alpoim to Vasco Guedes de Carvalho e Menezes, 27 April 1854.

92 The standard work on the *quilombos* is Ernesto Ennes, *As Guerras nos Palmares* (São Paulo, 1938).

93 Francisco Raimundo Moraes Pereira, "Account Of A Journey Made Overland From Quelimane to Angoche," trans. and ed., M. D. D. Newitt, *Central African Historical Association*, Occasional Paper no. 14 (Salisbury, 1965), p. 27.

94 Jan Vansina, "A Comparison of African Kingdoms," *Africa* 32 (1962): 333.

95 For a discussion of Kazembe's incorporation of the Bwilile and Shila peoples see: Ian Cunnison, *The Luapula Peoples of Northern Rhodesia* (Manchester, 1959), pp. 180–84.

CHAPTER 4: COMPOSITION OF PRAZO SOCIETY

1 The Portuguese archives are characterized by a virtual absence of ethnographic material dating from the eighteenth and nineteenth centuries. Those references which do exist emphasize the Africans' material culture, agricultural patterns, and religious forms. There is no extant documentation which examines the system of descent or the residential and marital patterns of the Zambesian peoples. This lacuna complicates any reconstruction of the social organization of the colonos. Such documentation would have provided a valuable time dimension for the oral data

and would have avoided any possible difficulties of the "ethnographic present" which conceivably could have biased the oral testimonies. (See Jan Vansina, "Anthropologists and the Third Dimension," *Africa* 39 [1969]: 62–68.) Family genealogies, collected in some interviews, however, tend to minimize the possible distortions in the oral data.

Despite the weaknesses of the written documents, they do provide suggestive data which, in the absence of solid material, become significant. There is a substantial body of information which examines the social organization of the peoples living in the kingdoms of the Muenemutapa and Quiteve. Since they are related to the southern Zambesian peoples, the material provides a comparative time dimension. More importantly the documentation corroborates the oral testimonies. One account (A.H.U., Moç., Cx. 30: "Descripção do Império do Moanamotapa daquem do Río Zambeze" [undated, unsigned]) moreover, noted that the patterns of social organization among the Karanga followers of the Muenemutapa were similar to those of the peoples of the Zambesi. Material collected by Lopes ("Usages and Customs of the Natives of Sena," *Journal of the African Society* 6 [1907]: 350–65) at the end of the nineteenth century, when the Portuguese impact was still minimal, also supports the oral data.

The absence of both written and oral material suggesting any structural transformations among the Zambesi peoples reinforces the conclusion that the changes which occurred during the period under examination were relatively insignificant and did not alter the fabric of the society.

2 Interviews with João Cristóstomo and Sete Marqueza.

3 Interviews with Pedro Damião Chamualira, Luciano Camilo, Khaliche António Camundi, Jasse Camalizene, and Renço Cado.

4 Among the Tawara the tendency was to limit the selection to full brothers of the deceased while half-brothers filled this role among the Tonga and Sena colonos (interviews with João Alfai, João Cristóstomo, António Gavião, Chale Lupia, Lole Nhanticole, and Alface Pangacha).

5 Interviews with João Cristóstomo, Pedro Damião Chamualira, Sete Marqueza, João Vicente, Domingo Kunga, Chale Lupia, Jasse Camalizene, Renço Cado, Lole Nhanticole, and José António.

6 Interviews with João Christóstomo, Pedro Damião Chamualira, Luciano Camilo, and Sete Marqueza.

7 Interviews with José António and Alface Pangacha; Lopes, "Usage and Customs of the Natives of Sena," p. 362.

8 Ibid.

9 Interviews with Luciano Camilo, Sete Marqueza, Chale Lupia, José António, and Alface Pangacha.

10 Interviews with João Cristóstomo, Luciano Camilo, Sete Marqueza, Chale Lupia, Mozesse Domingos, Renço Cado, José António, and Alface Pangacha.

11 Lopes, "Usage and Customs of the Natives of Sena," p. 361; Gustavo

do Bivar Pinto, *Respóstas ao Questionário Ethnográfico* (Beira, 1928), p. 43; interviews with João Cristóstomo, Andisseni Tesoura, Chale Lupia, Pedro Damião Chamualira, and Domingo Kunga.

12 Interviews with Pedro Damião Chamualira, Gaspar Cardoso, Domingo Kunga, Chale Lupia, Lole Nhanticole, Tomás Zimbaue, José António, and Alface Pangacha.

13 Interviews with João Cristóstomo, Sete Marqueza, Domingo Kunga, Chale Lupia, Jasse Camalizene, Zacarias Ferrão, and Andisseni Tesoura.

14 This information is based on: joint interviews with Chetambara Chenungo and Wilson John, and with Calavina Couche and Zabuca Ngombe; interviews with Chaparira Muiessa, Simon Biwi, and Capachika Chúau.

15 The major ethnographic study of Makanga is A. Rita-Ferreira, *Os Cheuas Da Macanga* (Lourenço Marques, 1966). For an examination of other Chewa groups see the very interesting articles of J. P. Bruwer, which are listed in the bibliography.

16 See Chapter 5 for a list of European products introduced. In addition to the artifacts, certain Portuguese words were often borrowed. See Robert H. Baker, "Portuguese Words in Chimanyika," *NADA* 24 (1947): 62–64.

17 A.H.U., Moç., Cx. 64: "Mappa dos Casamentos, Baptizados e Mortúrios e números dos Christaons da Frequeza da Villa de Tete principiando a 1° de Junho 1821 e findo ao fim de Maio 1821 [*sic*]," 22 May 1822 (unsigned).

18 Interviews with João Cristóstomo, Tomás Zimbaue, and José António; joint interviews with Aleixo Jasere and José Gunda, with Chale Penga, Tomás Chambe, and Jamusse Guede, and with Calavina Couche and Zabuca Ngombe; A.H.M., Códice 2–448, F.D.9, fol. 29: João de Sousa Nunes de Andrade to António Alves de Azévedo Campos (undated).

19 Interviews with Gimo Tito, Lole Nhanticole, José António, and Dauce Angolete Gogodo; joint interviews with Aleixo Jasere and José Gunda, with Tomás Chave and Oliveira Sinto, and with Calavina Couche and Zabuca Ngombe.

20 Interviews with Aleixo José and João Cristóstomo; joint interview with Calavina Couche and Zabuca Ngombe.

21 Interviews with Gimo Tito, João Cristóstomo, José da Costa Xavier, Dauce Angolete Gogodo, and Andisseni Tesoura; joint interviews with Tomás Chave and Oliveira Sinto, and with Aleixo Jasere and José Gunda.

22 Interview with José António; joint interviews with Tomás Chave and Oliveira Sinto, and with Gente Renço and Quembo Pangacha.

23 Interviews with Marco Countinho, Sete Marqueza, and Chiponda Cavumbula; joint interview with Calavina Couche and Zabuca Ngombe; Joaquim d'Almeida da Cunha, *Estudo Ácêrca dos Usos e os Costumes*

dos Banianes, Bathias, Pares, Mouros, Gentios e Indígenas (Lourenço Marques, 1885), p. 96.

24 A.N.T.T., Ministério do Reino, Maço 604: António Pinto de Miranda, "Memória sobre a Costa de África," p. 58 (undated); António Candido Pedroso Gamitto, "Escravatura na África Oriental," *Archivo Pittoresco* 2 (1859): 370.

25 Interviews with Gaspar Cardoso, José António de Abreu, Sete Marqueza, João Pomba, José António, and Andisseni Tesoura; joint interview with Gente Renço and Quembo Pangacha; A.N.T.T., Ministério do Reino, Maço 604: António Pinto de Miranda, "Memória sobre a Costa de África," p. 58 (undated); Gamitto, "Escravatura," p. 370.

26 José Fernandes, Júnior, "Narração do Distrito de Tete" (Paper, Makanga, 1955), p. 6; interview with Capachika Chúau; joint interview with António Anselmo Almeida and Inácio Petrinho.

27 Fernandes, Júnior, "Narração," p. 6.

28 A.N.T.T., Ministério do Reino, Maço 604: António Pinto de Miranda, "Memória sobre a Costa de África," p. 58 (undated).

29 Interviews with Aleixo José, Pedro Damião Chamualira, José da Costa Xavier, João Pomba, and Dauce Angolete Gogodo; joint interview with Calavina Couche and Zabuca Ngombe.

30 Interviews with Mortar Nhacalizi, Gimo Tito, José António, Andisseni Tesoura, and Alface Pangacha; joint interview with Aleixo Jasere and José Gunda, and with Calavina Couche and Zabuca Ngombe.

31 Interviews with Jasse Camalizene, Mortar Nhacalizi, Dauce Angolete Gogodo, and José António; joint interview with Aleixo Jasere and José Gunda. This pattern is also common among the Tawara where dependents were generally expected to marry within their rank.

32 Interviews with José da Costa Xavier, Jasse Camalizene, and Dauce Angolete Gogodo.

33 Interviews with Sete Marqueza, Jasse Camalizene, Mortar Nhacalizi, João Pomba, Dauce Angolete Gogodo, Gimo Tito, and José da Costa Xavier; joint interview with Gente Renço and Quembo Pangacha.

34 Interviews with Mortar Nhacalizi, João Pomba, and Dauce Angolete Gogodo; joint interviews with Tomás Chave and Oliveira Sinto, and with Gente Renço and Quembo Pangacha.

35 Interviews with Lole Nhanticole and Tomás Zimbaue.

36 Interviews with Aleixo José, Gaspar Cardoso, José António de Abreu, José da Costa Xavier, and Sete Marqueza.

37 Joint interviews with Tomás Chave and Oliviera Sinto, with Aleixo Jasere and José Gunda, with Calavina Couche and Zabuca Ngombe, and with António Anselmo Almeida and Inácio Petrinho; interviews with Dauce Angolete Gogodo, Alface Pangacha, and Avaringa Avarinho.

38 Interviews with Gaspar Cardoso, Sete Marqueza, and Jasse Camalizene.

39 Interviews with Mortar Nhacalazi and Lole Nhanticole.

40 A.H.U., Códice 1755, fol. 150: Custódio Jozé António Texeira to Cypriano de Noronha, 31 May 1847; A.N.T.T., Ministério do Reino,

Maço 604: António Pinto de Miranda, "Memória sobre a Costa de África," pp. 50–57 (undated); Gamitto, "Escravatura," p. 399; Francisco José de Lacerda e Almeida, *Travessia Da África* (Lisbon, 1938), pp. 116–17; interviews with José António de Abreu, José da Costa Xavier, Jasse Camalizene, João Pomba, and Dauce Angolete Gogodo; joint interview with Calavina Couche and Zabuca Ngombe.

41 Gamitto, "Escravatura," p. 299.

42 Interview with Dauce Angolete Gogodo; Lt. R.N. Barnard, *Three Years Cruise in the Mozambique Channel* (London, 1848), p. 143; Gamitto, "Escravatura," p. 398.

43 Gamitto, "Escravatura," p. 362.

44 A.H.U., Códice 1469, fol. 7: António Mariano da Cunha, 10 March 1833; Fernandes, Júnior, "Narração," p. 3; interviews with Marco Coutinho and Alface Pangacha.

45 A.H.M., Fundo do Século XVIII: José Francisco Oliveira, "Lista dos Escravos . . . em Leilão Publica," 29 January 1769.

46 A.H.U., Códice 1451, fol. 111: Joaquim d'Azévedo Alpoim to Galdinho José Nunes, 9 January 1855; interview with Chale Lupia; joint interview with Calavina Couche and Zabuca Ngombe.

47 Interviews with Mozesse Domingos and Simon Biwi. One nineteenth-century observer wrote: "As a rule the Portuguese do not go into the interior, attack the villages, and bring away the inhabitants as captives . . . but generally they send their agents, natives whom they designated and trained to the purposes to which they put them in order to purchase slaves" (Henry Rowley, *The Story of the Universities Mission to Central Africa* [London, 1867], p. 47).

48 A.H.U., Moç., Cx. 3: Fernando Jesús, M.A., 13 April 1752.

49 A.H.U., Moç., Cx. 13: Manoel Pereira da Conceição (undated).

50 A.N.T.T., Ministério do Reino, Maço 604: "Mappas do Rendimento da Terra Cheringoma" (unsigned, undated).

51 A.H.U., Códice 1469, fol. 7: António Mariano da Cunha, 10 March 1833.

52 A.H.M., Códice 2–1167, fols. 1–58: "Registo dos Libertos do Districto E da Villa de Tete," Livro I, 1856. For a detailed discussion of the Malawian preponderance, see Chapter 7.

53 Interviews with Conrado Msussa Boroma and Simon Biwi. For a detailed examination of the slave raiding, see Chapters 6 and 7.

54 A.H.U., Moç., Cx. 15: Jerónimo Pereira (undated).

55 A.N.T.T., Ministério do Reino, Maço 604: António Pinto de Miranda, "Memória sobre a Costa de África," pp. 56–58 (undated); Gamitto, "Escravatura," p. 398.

56 Interviews with António Gavião, Chale Lupia, and José da Costa Xavier; joint interview with Calavina Couche and Zabuca Ngombe; A.H.U., Códice 1755, fol. 150: Custódio Jozé António Texeira to Cypriano de Noronha, 31 May 1847.

57 Oral data provides no evidence to support the claim that: "For a full tribal society within the *prazos,* however, it was necessary for the *colonos* and the slaves to lose their identities and to submerge their institutions and functions in *prazo* society" (M. D. D. Newitt, "The Portuguese on the Zambesi: An Historical Interpretation of the Prazo System," *Journal of African History* 10 [1969]: 78).

58 Bronislaw Stefaniszyn and Hilary de Santana, "The Rise of the Chikunda Condotteiri," *Northern Rhodesia Journal* 4 (1960): 362.

59 Rowley, *Universities Mission,* p. 66.

60 Interviews with João Pomba and Chiponda Cavumbula; joint interviews with Calavina Couche and Zabuca Ngombe, and with Chetambara Chenungo and Wilson John.

61 Interviews with João Vicente and Chale Lupia; joint interview with Chetambara Chenungo and Wilson John; Lacerda e Almeida, *Travessia,* p. 130; Gamitto, "Escravatura," pp. 399–400.

62 A.H.U., Moç., Cx. 64: "Mappa dos Casamentos . . . ao fim de Maio" (unsigned), 22 May 1822.

63 J. P. R. Wallis, ed., *The Zambesi Expedition of David Livingstone 1858–1863,* 2 vols. (London, 1956), 2:306.

64 Personal communication with D. Abraham, Salisbury, 7 July 1968. This information is based on material in the Goan archives which Mr. Abraham has carefully examined.

65 Manuel Barretto, "Informação do Estado e Conquista dos Rios de Cuama, 1667," in *Records of South-East Africa,* ed. G. M. Theal (Capetown, 1899), 3:470–80.

66 See ibid. for the principal families.

67 A.H.U., Moç., Cx. 12: Balthazar Manoel Pereyra do Lago, 17 August 1766; A.H.U., Moç., Cx. 19: Balthazar Manoel Pereyra do Lago to the Queen, 30 August 1775.

68 A.H.U., Moç., Códice 1314, fol. 82: Pedro de Saldanha de Albuquerque to António Caetano de Campos, 16 April 1759; A.H.U., Moç., Cx. 9; Marco António de Azévedo de Montaury, 18 June 1752.

69 A.H.U., Moç., Cx. 34: Francisco José de Lacerda e Almeida to the King, 22 March 1798; A.H.U., Moç., Cx. 12: Balthazar Manoel Pereyra do Lago, 17 August 1766.

70 The three Governors were Marco António de Azévedo de Montaury, Inácio de Melo Alvim, and Manoel de Almeida.

71 A.H.U., Moç., Cx. 34: Francisco José de Lacerda e Almeida to the King, 22 March 1798.

72 António Candido Pedroso Gamitto, *King Kazembe,* trans. Ian Cunnison, 2 vols. (Lisbon, 1960), 1:113.

73 A.N.T.T., Ministério do Reino, Maço 604: António Pinto de Miranda, "Memória sobre a Costa de África," pp. 35–36 (undated); Gamitto, "Escravaturã," p. 50.

74 Several marginal prazeros were also involved in marriage alliances to strengthen their relative positions in Zambesian society. See, for ex-

ample, A.H.U., Moç., Cx. 35: Cópia duma carta de António da Cruz e Almeida (undated).

75 These estimates are based on compilations of prazo lists found in the caixas of the A.H.U. for this period.

76 A.H.U., Moç., Cx. 53: E.R.M., 1810. There appears to be a substantial increase in petitions for aforamentos in the A.H.U. caixas between 1785 and 1820.

77 Jerónimo José Nogueira de Andrade, "Descrição do Estado em que ficava os Negócios da Capitania de Moçambique nos fins de Novembro do anno de 1789," *Arquivo das Colónias* (Lisbon, 1887) 1:119.

78 Interviews with Gaspar Cardoso, José António de Abreu, and José da Costa Xavier.

79 Biblioteca Nacional de Lisboa, Fundo Geral [cited hereafter as B.N.L., F.G.]: Inácio Caetano Xavier, "Notícias dos Dominíos Portuguezes Actuaes na Costa de África," fol. 3, 21 May 1762; A.H.U., Moç., Cx. 13: Inácio de Mello Alvim to the Queen, 8 February 1768; Lacerda e Almeida, *Travessia*, p. 83.

80 Ajuda, 52–X–2, No. 3: José Francisco Alves Barbosa, "Analyse estatística," 30 December 1821.

81 Interviews with José António de Abreu, António Vas, and Zacarias Ferrão.

82 A.H.U., Moç., Cx. 68: "Cópia de 18° S do Offício de 7 de Abril de 1755 dirigido pello Exmo Sr. Diogo de Mendonça Corte Real ao Governador e Capitão General deste Estado."

83 João de Azévedo Coutinho, *Manuel António de Sousa: Um Capitão-mór da Zambézia* (Lisbon, 1936), pp. 56–57.

84 Joaquim Mendes Vasconcelos e Cirne, *Memória Sobre a Província de Moçambique* (Lisbon, 1890), p. 28.

85 Ibid.

86 A.H.U., Moç., Cx. 6: Fr. João de Nossa Senhora, Administrador Episcopal, 8 August 1758.

87 Interviews with João Vicente, Domingo Kunga, Alberto Vicente da Cruz, António Vas, Dauce Angolete Gogodo, and Leão Manuel Banqueiro Caetano Pereira; joint interview with Tomás Chave and Oliveira Sinto; A.H.U., Moç., Cx. 31: Jozé Pedro Dinillo, 21 May 1796.

88 Cunha, *Estudo Àcêrca dos Usos e Costumes*, pp. 93–98.

89 Lacerda e Almeida, *Travessia*, p. 115.

90 Gamitto, *King Kazembe*, 1:35.

91 Interviews with João Vicente, Domingo Kunga, Alberto Vicente da Cruz, Zacarias Ferrão, and Leão Manuel Banqueiro Caetano Pereira; joint interview with Tomás Chave and Oliveira Sinto.

92 A.H.U., Moç., Cx. 29: Jozé João d'Araujo Aranha e Oliveira (undated); A.H.U., Moç., Maço 16: José Manoel Correia Monteiro to Manoel Joaquim Mendes de Vasconcelos e Cirne, 20 November 1803; A.H.U., Códice 1306; Izidoro de Almeida Souza e Sá to António Noberto de Barbosa Truão, 20 November 1803.

93 A.H.U., Códice 1306: Izidoro de Almeida Souza e Sá to António Noberto de Barbosa Truão, 20 November 1803.
94 Lacerda e Almeida, *Travessia*, pp. 114–15.
95 Gamitto, *King Kazembe*, 1:35.
96 Ajuda, 52–X–2, No. 3: José Francisco Alves Barbosa, "Analyse estatística," 30 December 1821.
97 Fr. João de Pilar and Manoel António Ribeiro, "Edital da Inquisição de Goa," in *O Chronista de Tissaury*, ed. Joaquim Helidoro da Cunha Rivara (Nova Goa, 1867), p. 274.
98 Wagley's study indicates that a similar phenomenon occurred in the Amazon (Charles Wagley, *Amazon Town: A Study of Man in the Tropics* [New York, 1964], p. 255).
99 These can be located both in the A.H.U. and the A.H.M. Since the Mozambican archive tends to be the repository of more local documents, they are found there in greater abundance.
100 Interviews with Domingo Kunga, Chale Lupia, João Pomba, and Chapavira Muiessa; joint interviews with Tomás Chave and Oliveira Sinto, with Aleixo Jasere and José Gunda, and with Chetambara Chenungo and Wilson John.
101 Lacerda e Almeida, *Travessia*, p. 113.
102 Interviews with Chale Lupia, Mortar Nhacalizi, Renço Cado, João Pomba, Lole Nhanticole, and Simon Biwi; joint interviews with Tomás Chave and Oliveira Sinto, with Calavina Couche and Zabuca Ngombe, and with Chetambara Chenungo and Wilson John.
103 Gamitto, *King Kazembe*, 1:35.

CHAPTER 5: ECONOMICS: PRODUCTION

1 A.H.U., Moç., Cx. 17: António Manoel de Mello de Castro to Jozé Vasconcellos Almeida, 18 June 1780.
2 A.H.U., Moç., Cx. 12: Balthazar Manoel Pereyra do Lago, 17 August 1776.
3 A.H.U., Códice 1358, fol. 80: António Manoel de Mello de Castro to Agostinho de Mello e Almeida, 3 December 1787; A.H.U., Moç., Cx. 14 (unsigned, undated); Francisco José de Lacerda e Almeida, *Travessia Da África* (Lisbon, 1938), p. 118; António Candido Pedroso Gamitto, "Prasos Da Corôa Em Rios De Sena," *Archivo Pittoresco* 1 (1857–58): 63; interviews with Pedro Damião Chamualira, Sete Marqueza, Jasse Camalizene, Renço Cado, António Vas, and Zacarias Ferrão; joint interviews with Gente Renço and Quembo Pangacha, and with Chale Penga, Tomás Chave, and Jamusse Guede.
4 António Candido Pedroso Gamitto, *King Kazembe*, trans. Ian Cunnison, 2 vols. (Lisbon, 1960), 1:31.
5 A.N.T.T., Ministério do Reino, Maço 604: António Pinto de Miranda,

"Memória sobre a Costa de África," p. 22 (undated); Gamitto, "Prasos Da Corôa," p. 63; interview with Gaspar Cardoso.

6 Interview with Luíz Gonzaga Cebola.

7 A.H.M., Códice 443–2, F.E. 7, fol. 56: José Gomes Barbosa to Joaquim de Azévedo Alxaim, 30 July 1855.

8 A.H.U., Moç., Cx. 19: António Manoel de Mello de Castro to Martinho de Mello e Castro, 7 May 1783.

9 A.H.U., Moç., Cx. 52: Fr. Jozé Machado do Aguia, ca. 1783.

10 Francisco de Mello de Castro, *Descrição dos Rios de Senna, Anno de 1750* (Lisbon, 1861), p. 21.

11 See, for example: A.H.M., Códice 2–443, F.E. 7, fol. 56: José Gomes Barbosa to Joaquim de Azévedo Alxaim, 30 July 1855; Gamitto, "Prasos Da Corôa," p. 66.

12 Interviews with Gaspar Cardoso, Guiraza Passo, Bruto Sabão, Quembo Passalampapi, João Vicente, Renço Cado, and Simões Zindo; Gamitto, "Prasos Da Corôa," p. 66.

13 Gamitto, "Prasos Da Corôa," p. 66.

14 Lacerda e Almeida, *Travessia*, p. 130; A.H.U., Códice 1315, fol. 292: Francisco Henriques Ferrão to Sebastião Xavier (undated). A major famine also occurred in the late 1750s (A.H.U., Moç., Cx. 10: Dionízio de Mello e Castro to Pedro de Saldanha de Albuquerque, 20 January 1763).

15 Richard Thorton, "Notes on the Zambesi and the Shire," *Journal of the Royal Geographic Society* 34 (1864): 196.

16 A.H.M., Códice 2–443, F.E. 7, fol. 56: José Gomes Barbosa to Joaquim de Azévedo Alxaim, 30 July 1855; Gamitto, "Prasos Da Corôa," p. 66; Thorton, "Notes on the Zambesi and the Shire," p. 196; interview with Gaspar Cardoso.

17 Ibid.

18 Gamitto, "Prasos Da Corôa," p. 66.

19 A.H.U., Códice 1473, fols. 7–8: Izidro Manoel de Carrazedo, 24 January 1835; A.N.T.T., Ministério do Reino, Maço 604: "Memórias da Costa de África Oriental e algumas reflexões úteis para estabelecer melhor e fazer mais florente o su comércio," fol. 17 (unsigned), 21 May 1762; Academia das Ciências de Lisboa, Ms. 648 Azul: António Norberto de Barbosa de Villas Boas Truão, "Estatísticas da Capitania dos Rios de Sena no Anno de 1806," 16 July 1807; Ajuda, 52–X–2, no. 3: José Francisco Alves Barbosa, "Analyse estatística," 30 December 1821.

20 Sebastião Xavier Botelho, *Memória Estatística sobre Os Domínios Portuguezes na África Oriental* (Lisbon, 1835), pp. 286–87.

21 Ibid.

22 Ajuda, 52–X–2, no. 3: José Francisco Alves Barbosa, "Analyse estatística," 30 December 1821.

23 João Pedro Baptista and José Amaro, "Journey of the Pombeiros from Angola to the Rios de Sena, in *The Lands of Cazembe: Lacerda's Journey to Cazembe in 1798*, trans. Richard Burton (London, 1873),

p. 238; A.H.U., Moç., Cx. 23: Mateus Ignácio de Almeida to Martinho de Mello e Castro, 3 December 1786.

24 Castro, *Rios de Senna*, p. 14; Manuel Galvão da Silva, "Diário ou Relação das Viagens Filosóficas, nos Terras da Jurisdição de Tete e em algumas dos Maraves," in *Anais De Junta De Investigações Do Ultramar*, 9, tomo 1 (Lisbon, 1954), pp. 317–19; A.N.T.T., Ministério do Reino, Maço 604: Luís António de Figuerido, "Notícias do Continente de Moçambique e abbreviada relação do seu Commércio," 1 December 1788; A.H.U., Moç., Cx. 23: Mateus Ignácio de Almeida to Martinho de Mello e Castro, 3 December 1786.

25 A.N.T.T., Ministério do Reino, Maço 604: António Pinto de Miranda, "Memória sobre a Costa de África," p. 79 (undated); Silva, "Diário ou Relação," pp. 311–16; Gamitto, *King Kazembe*, 1:42; A.N.T.T., Ministério do Reino, Maço 604: Ignácio Caetano Xavier, "Relação do Estado presente de Moçambique, Sena, Sofala, Inhambane, e todo Continente de África Oriental," 26 December 1758.

26 See Chapter 6 for the respective trade agreements with the Karanga-related kings.

27 Castro, *Rios de Senna*, p. 114.

28 A.N.T.T., Ministério do Reino, Maço 604: António Pinto de Miranda, "Memória sobre a Costa de África," pp. 79–80 (undated); Gamitto, *King Kazembe*, 1:58; A.H.U., Moç., Documentos, Annexos, e As Plantas: Francisco de Mello de Castro to Marquês de Tavora, 10 August 1750.

29 Charles Ralph Boxer, ed., "A Dominican Account of Zambésia in 1744," *Boletim da Sociedade de Estudos de Moçambique* 29 (1960): 5–6. The competition for the bares is treated in greater detail in Chapter 7.

30 A.H.U., Moç., Cx. 22: António Manoel de Mello de Castro to Martinho de Mello e Castro, 15 June 1785; Silva, "Diário ou Relação," p. 315; Ajuda, 52–X–2, no. 7 (unsigned, undated); Gamitto, *King Kazembe*, 1:42.

31 João dos Santos, "Ethiópia Oriental," in *Records of South-East Africa*, ed. G. M. Theal (Capetown, 1901), 7:218–19.

32 Silva, "Diário ou Relação," p. 316; Gamitto, *King Kazembe*, 1:55; A.N.T.T., Ministério do Reino, Maço 604: "Memórias da Costa de África . . . ," fols. 5–6, 21 May 1762 (unsigned).

33 Gamitto, *King Kazembe*, 1:58; A.N.T.T., Ministério de Reino, Maço 604: "Memórias da Costa de África . . . ," fols. 5–6, 21 May 1762 (unsigned); David Livingstone, *Missionary Travels and Research in South Africa* (London, 1857), p. 630.

CHAPTER 6: ECONOMICS: DISTRIBUTION

1 During the eighteenth century there were two major trade networks, the one discussed here and a northern nexus linking Mozambique Island with the Yao and Macua homelands and stretching into the in-

terior as far inland as the Southern Lunda and to southern Tanzania. For more on this subject see Edward Alpers, "The Role of the Yao in the Development of Trade in East Central Africa" (Ph.D. diss., London School of Oriental and African Studies, 1966).

2 Interviews with Pedro Damião Chamualira, Gaspar Cardoso, and Marco Coutinho; joint interview with Tomás Chave and Oliveira Sinto; A.H.U., Moç., Cx. 19: António Manoel de Mello de Castro to Martinho de Mello e Castro, 7 May 1783.

3 Francisco José de Lacerda e Almeida, *Travessia Da África* (Lisbon, 1938), p. 123; António Candido Pedroso Gamitto, *King Kazembe*, trans. Ian Cunnison, 2 vols. (Lisbon, 1960), 2:123; A.H.U., Moç., Cx. 19: António Manoel de Mello de Castro to Martinho de Mello e Castro, 7 May 1783.

4 António Candido Pedroso Gamitto, "Prasos da Corôa em Rios de Sena," *Archivo Pittoresco* 1 (1857–58): 62; Lacerda e Almeida, *Travessia*, p. 123; Francisco de Mello de Castro, *Descripção dos Rios de Senna, Anno de 1750* (Lisbon, 1861), p. 109; A.H.U., Moç., Documentos, Annexos, e as Plantas: Francisco de Mello de Castro to Marquês de Tavora, 10 August 1750.

5 António Norberto de Barbosa de Villas Boas Truão, "Extracto do Plano para um Regimento ou Nova Constituição Económica e Política da Capitania de Rios de Senna," *Annais do Conselho Ultramárino, Parte não oficial* (Lisbon, 1857), p. 412; Ajuda, 52–X–2, No. 3: José Francisco Alves Barbosa, "Analise estatística," 30 December 1821; A.H.U., Moç., Cx. 28: Luís de Sousa Ferrez de Moura, 2 August 1794.

6 A.H.U., Moç., Documentos, Annexos, e as Plantas: Francisco de Mello de Castro to Marquês de Tavora, 10 August 1750.

7 A.H.U., Moç., Cx. 19: António Manoel de Mello de Castro to Martinho de Mello e Castro, 7 May 1783; Ajuda, 52–X–2, No. 3: José Francisco Alves Barbosa, "Analise estatística," 30 December 1821; A.H.U., Moç., Documentos, Annexos, e as Plantas: Francisco de Mello de Castro to Marquês de Tavora, 10 August 1750.

8 Ibid. This aspect of the interior trade has been virtually ignored.

9 A.H.U., Códice 1310, fol. 69: Francisco de Mello de Castro to David Marques Pereira; Mabel Jackson Haight, *European Powers and South-East Africa* (London, 1967), pp. 82–83.

10 A.H.U., Moç., Cx. 4: Francisco de Mello de Castro, 10 November 1754; A.H.U., Moç., Cx. 5: Francisco de Mello de Castro, 17 June 1757; A.H.U., Moç., Cx. 4: Francisco Raymundo de Moraes Pereira, 15 August 1753; Alexandre Lobato, *Evolução Administrativa e Económica De Moçambique 1752–63* (Lisbon, 1957), p. 251. Lobato presents a short but interesting history of the Junta de Comércio and its predecessors.

11 A.N.T.T., Ministério do Reino, Maço 603: Antonio Jozé de Mello, "Proposta sobre o estabelecimento de Senna, Sofalla, e Inhambane, Cabo dos Correntes e Ilhas de Querimba" (undated); A.H.U., Moç., Cx. 4: Francisco de Mello de Castro, 10 November 1754.

12 A.H.U., Códice 1328, fol. 148: João Peryra da Silva Barba to Marco António de Azévedo Coutinho de Montaury, 25 April 1764.

13 A.H.U., Moç., Cx. 4: António de Brito Ferreira, 8 November 1754, supported by previously cited reports of Francisco de Mello de Castro.

14 Luís António de Figuerido, "Notícia do Continente de Mocambique e abreviada relação do seu comércio," *Anais de Junta da Investigacoes do Ultramar* 9, tomo 1 (1954), pp. 251–67; A.H.U., Moç., Cx. 33: Francisco António Tavares de Sigueira, Juiz d'Alfándega de Moss. to D. Diogo de Souza, 28 September 1796. The 41.5 percent import tax was periodically reduced, reaching a low point of 10 percent in 1796.

15 Biblioteca Nacional de Lisboa, Fundo Geral [cited hereafter as B.N.L., F.G.] 826: "Notícias dos Domínios Portugueses Actuaes na Costa da África," fol. 13 (unsigned), 21 May 1762.

16 Ajuda, 52–X–2, No. 3: José Francisco Alves Barbosa, "Analyse estatística," 30 December 1821; A.H.U., Moç., Códice 1473, fol. 50: Izidro Manoel Carrazido to Commandante de Quillimane, 31 July 1835.

17 Ajuda, 52–X–2, No. 3: José Francisco Alves Barbosa, "Analyse estatística," 30 December 1821.

18 Ibid.

19 A.H.U., Moç., Códice 1368, fol. 230: Francisco Guedes de Carvalho e Menezes da Costa to Jerónimo Pereira (undated); Lacerda e Almeida, *Travessia*, p. 109.

20 Ajuda, 52–X–2, No. 3: José Francisco Alves Barbosa, "Analyse estatística," 30 December 1821.

21 B.N.L., F.G. 826: "Notícias dos Domínios Portugueses Actuaes na Costa da África," fols. 22–23 (unsigned), 21 May 1762; interviews with Gaspar Cardoso and Dauce Angolete Gogodo.

22 António Candido Pedroso Gamitto, "Escravatura na África Oriental," *Archivo Pittoresco* 2 (1859): 370.

23 Ibid.

24 Castro, *Senna*, pp. 8–37; interview with Gaspar Cardoso; joint interview with Chetambara Chenungo and Wilson John.

25 A.N.T.T., Ministério do Reino, Maço 604: "Memórias da Costa de África," fol. 17 (unsigned), 21 March 1762.

26 Ajuda, 51–VI–24–29: Frei António Conceição, "Tratados Dos Rios De Cuama," 12 December 1696; interviews with Simon Biwi and Capachika Chúau.

27 A.H.U., Moç., Cx. 21: António Manoel de Mello de Castro to Martinho de Mello e Castro, 15 June 1785; Gamitto, *King Kazembe*, 2:27; interview with Gaspar Cardoso.

One variant of this pattern, used especially in bartering for gold, was for the seller to dig two holes in the ground and place gold in the first. The musambadzi was then expected to fill the second with the appropriate trade items. As in all exchanges, this was preceded by long negotiations (Alexander Hamilton, *A New General Account of the East Indies* [London, 1727], p. 55).

28 A.H.U., Moç., Documentos, Annexos, e as Plantas: Francisco de Mello de Castro to Marquês de Tavora, 10 August 1750.

29 A.H.U., Moç., Cx. 22: João de Almeida, 22 June 1784.

30 A.H.U., Moç., Cx. 22: António Manoel de Mello de Castro to Martinho de Mello e Castro, 15 June 1785.

31 The number of soldiers varied annually, depending on how many new appointments had been made and on the desertion rate. There never seems to have been more than fifty, and the total was often closer to fifteen men. A.H.U., Moç., Cx. 46: Manuel Martiniz Palmas, 21 May 1805; A.H.U., Códice 1318, fol. 139: Alvira de Regulamento, e Soldado para o Capitão Môr da Manica, 20 February 1771.

32 A.H.U., Moç., Cx. 73: José Francisco Alves Barbosa to King (undated).

33 Castro, *Senna*, p. 109.

34 B.N.L., F.G. 826: "Notícias dos Domínios Portugueses Actuaes na Costa da África," fol. 12 (anonymous), 21 May 1762; Figuerido, "Notícia do Continente," p. 261.

35 A.H.U., Moç., Pasta 10: António Gamitto, "Memória sobre uma systema para as Colónias Portuguezas," 2 January 1850.

36 Manuel Barretto, "Informação do Estado e Conquista dos Rios de Cuama, 1667," in *Records of South-East Africa*, ed. G. M. Theal (Capetown, 1899), 3:481; Ajuda, 52–X–2, No. 3: José Francisco Alves Barbosa, "Analise estatística," 30 December 1821; Lacerda e Almeida, *Travessia*, p. 184; Gamitto, *King Kazembe*, 1:80; interviews with José António de Abreu, José da Costa Xavier, and Simon Biwi; joint interview with Chetambara Chenungo and Wilson John.

37 Within the Southern Lunda empire Kazembe retained a royal trade monopoly over all ivory, and perhaps over copper, slaves, and wax. See: Lacerda e Almeida, *Travessia*, p. 392; B.N.L., Pombalina 721, fol. 305: Francisco José de Lacerda e Almeida to D. Rodrigues de Souza Coutinho, 21 March 1798; A.H.U., Moç., Cx. 35: Francisco João Pinto to Gov. dos Rios de Sena (undated).

38 B.N.L., Pombalina 721, fols. 303–5: Francisco José de Lacerda e Almeida to D. Rodrigues de Souza Coutinho, 21 March 1798.

39 Lacerda e Almeida, *Travessia*, p. 387.

40 João Pedro Baptista and José Amaro, "Journey of the Pombeiros from Angola to the Rios de Senna," in *The Lands of Cazembe; Lacerda's Journey to Cazembe in 1798*, trans. Richard Burton (London, 1873), p. 231.

41 A.H.U., Códice 1315, fol. 403: Francisco Henriques Ferrão to Paulo Jozé Miguel de Brito, 5 April 1829.

42 A.H.U., Moç., Maço 9: Joaquim Mendes Vasconcelos e Cirne to Sebastião Xavier Botelho (undated).

43 Gamitto, *King Kazembe*, 2:87.

44 Ibid., 1:55.

45 A.H.U., Códice 1315, fol. 403: Francisco Henriques Ferrão to Paulo Jozé Miguel de Brito, 5 April 1829; A.H.U., Moç., Maço 17: Jozé António

de Almeida (undated); A.H.U., Códice 1703, fol. 22: João Pedro Xavier da Silva Botelho to José Francisco Alves Barbosa, 2 August 1832.

46 Castro, *Senna*, p. 113; Ajuda, 52–X–2, No. 7 (untitled, unsigned, undated).

47 A.H.U., Moç., Cx. 4: Francisco de Mello de Castro, 22 November 1753; Figuerido, "Notícia do Continente," pp. 259–60.

48 A.H.U., Moç., Cx. 42: Manoel Francisco Rozário, 21 December 1802; A.H.U., Moç., Cx. 21: António Caetano de Souza, 20 June 1784; A.H.U., Moç., Cx. 16: "Instrucção do Commandante João de Almeida sobre a Embaixada ao Rey Xangamira pa o reestablecimento do Comércio da Abutua" (undated); A.H.M., Fundo do Século XVIII: Gil Bernardo Coelho de Campos to Capitão Geral, 10 June 1768.

49 B.N.L., F.G. 826, fols. 20–21: Inácio Caetano Xavier, "Notícias dos Domínios Portugueses na Costa de África Oriental," 26 December 1758.

50 A.H.U., Moç., Cx. 3: Fr. Joaquim de Rita (undated); A.H.U., Moç., Cx. 42: Manoel Francisco Rozário, 1803; Sebastião Xavier Botelho, *Memória Estatística sobre Os Domínios Portuguezes na África Oriental* (Lisbon, 1835), p. 304.

51 A.H.U., Códice 1315, fol. 403: Francisco Henriques Ferrão to Paulo Jozé Miguel de Brito, 5 April 1829.

52 J. P. R. Wallis, ed., *The Zambesi Expedition of David Livingstone*, 2 vols. (London, 1956), 1:141.

53 A.H.U., Moç., Cx. 16: António Manoel de Mello de Castro to José Vasconcellos de Almeida, 17 July 1780; Carlos Wiese, "Expedição Portugueza À Mpeseni (1889)," *Boletim Da Sociedade De Geografia de Lisboa* 10 (1891): 247; interview with Conrado Msussa Boroma.

54 Francisco Monclaros, "Account of the Expedition Under Francisco Barretto," in *Records of South-East Africa*, ed. G. M. Theal (Capetown, 1899), 3:234; A.H.U., Moç., Cx. 3: Duarte Salter de Mendoça, 7 December 1751; A.H.U., Moç., Cx. 4: António de Brito Ferreira, 8 November 1754.

55 Ajuda, 52–X–2, No. 3: José Francisco Alves Barbosa, "Analise estatística," 30 December 1821.

56 A.H.U., Moç., Cx. 4: Francisco de Mello de Castro, 20 November 1753; A.H.U., Códice 1338, fols. 71–72: Balthazar Manoel Pereira de Lago, August, 1773; Alpers, "The Role of the Yao," pp. 138–39.

57 A.H.U., Moç., Cx. 4: Francisco de Mello de Castro, 20 November 1753; A.H.U., Moç., Cx. 9: Moradores de Senna, 15 July 1762; A.H.U., Códice 1338, fols. 71–72: Balthazar Manoel Pereira de Lago, 16 August 1773.

58 Alpers, "The Role of the Yao," pp. 261–63, 275.

59 A.H.U., Moç., Cx. 4: Francisco de Mello de Castro, 20 November 1753.

60 Interviews with Simon Biwi and Chiponda Cavumbula; joint interviews with Calavina Couche and Zabuca Ngombe, and with Chetambara Chenungo and Wilson John.

61 A.H.U., Moç., Cx. 12: Balthazar Manoel Pereira do Lago and Francisco Xavier de Mendonça Furtado, 15 August 1766; A.H.U., Códice 1338, fols. 71–72: Balthazar Manoel Pereira do Lago, 16 August 1773.

62 Balthazar Manoel Pereira do Lago, March 11, 1766, document published in Fritz Hoppe, *Portugiesisch-Ostrafrika in der Zeit des Marques de Pombal (1750–1777)* (Berlin, 1965), p. 238.

63 A.N.T.T., Ministério do Reino, Maço 603: Francisco de Mello de Castro, 28 December 1753.

64 A.H.U., Moç., Cx. 6: António Manoel de Mello de Castro to Martinho de Mello e Castro, 6 June 1783.

65 A.H.U., Moç., Cx. 16: António Manoel de Mello de Castro, 22 March 1782; A.H.U., Moç., Cx. 21: António Jozé de Moraes Durão, 6 June 1783.

66 A.N.T.T., Ministério do Reino, Maço 604: Diogo Guerreis de Aboime, 27 August 1779.

67 T. E. Bowdich, *An Account of the Discoveries in the Interior of Angola and Mozambique* (London, 1824), p. 105.

68 A.H.U., Moç., Cx. 30 (unsigned), 8 July 1795.

69 A.H.U., Moç., Cx. 30: João de Sousa e Brito to Diogo de Souza, 8 July 1795; A.H.U., Moç., Cx. 42: Manoel Francisco Rozário, 1803; A.H.U., Moç., Cx. 31: Jozé Pedro Dinillo, 21 May 1796; A.H.U., Moç., Cx. 42: 15 December 1803 (name illegible).

70 For a discussion of the recurring succession crises see Chapter 7.

71 A.H.U., Moç., Cx. 42: Manoel Francisco Rozário, 1803; A.H.U., Moç., Cx. 17: Caetano Manoel Correa, Feliciano Jozé da Silva Lisboa, Gracomo Bodano, Alexandre da Costa de Santa Maria, Francisco Xavier de Menezes, Diogo Rodrigues (undated); A.H.U., Moç., Cx. 32: João de Souza e Brito, 2 March 1796.

72 A.H.U., Códice 1358, fol. 29: António Manoel de Mello e Castro to Caetano Manoel Correa, 4 May 1786.

73 George McCall Theal, *The Portuguese in South Africa* (Capetown, 1896), p. 252; José Justino Texeira Botelho, *História Militar E Política Dos Portugueses Em Moçambique*, 2 vols. (Lisbon, 1936), 1:329–31.

74 A.N.T.T., Ministério do Reino, Maço 604: "Memórias da Costa de África Oriental," fol. 17 (unsigned), 21 March 1762; B.N.L., F.G. 826: Inácio Caetano Pereira, "Notícias dos Domínios Portugueses na Costa de África Oriental," fol. 52–54, 26 December 1758. A document written four years later estimated that almost 2,000 slaves were being exported annually to Mozambique Island. It mentions, however, that the vast majority came from the Yao-Macua area. There is, therefore, no reason to believe that the sudden increase in slave exports to Mozambique came from the Zambesi. A.H.U., Moç., Cx. 12: Pereira do Lago and Francisco Xavier de Mendonça Furtado, 15 August 1766.

75 As late as 1773 one observer noted that the prazeros and inland merchants traded cloth and beads in exchange for gold, ivory, and a few slaves" (Figueirdo, "Notícia do Continente," p. 258).

76 A.H.U., Códice 1358, fol. 120: António Manoel de Mello de Castro.
77 This shift is one of the very interesting points that Alpers has detailed in his "The Role of the Yao."
78 A.H.U., Moç., Cx. 34: Francisco José de Lacerda e Almeida to Matheus Jozé Vianna, 1797.
79 Antonio Norberto de Barbosa de Villas Boas Truão, "Extracto do Plano para um Regimento ou Nova Constitução Económica e Política da Capitania de Rios de Senna," *Annais do Conselho Ultramarino, Parte não Oficial* (Lisbon, 1857), p. 408.
80 A.H.U., Moç., Maço 33: "Requerimento por Lt. Colonel Zeferno José Pinto de Magalhões (attached to a *Bando* written on 24 October 1825 by Sebastião Xavier Botelho); A.H.U., Moç., Maço 33: Manoel José Maria da Costa e Sá to Inácio da Costa Quitela, 10 December 1826.
　　There were, in fact, attempts to smuggle out slaves prior to 1800. As early as 1787 the *Nossa Senhora da Piedade* was shipwrecked off the coast of Quelimane with slaves destined for the Americas. A.H.U., Códice 1358: António Manoel de Mello de Castro to Jozé Alvares Pereira, 7 May 1787.
81 Gamitto, "Escravatura," p. 398; Torres F. Texugo, *Letter on the Slave Trade* (London, 1839), p. 34.
82 A.H.U., Códice 1358, fol. 130: António Manoel de Mello de Castro (undated).
83 *Muropa* and *rusambo* were the two symbolic gifts; the former consisted of a small number of beads which were paid for the blood of the slaves, while the latter served as a receipt and formally marked the end of the transaction (Gamitto, "Escravatura," p. 370; Gamitto, *King Kazembe*, 1:56).
84 Gamitto, "Escravatura," p. 398; Henry Salt, *A Voyage to Abyssinia and Travels into the Interior of that Country* (London, 1814), p. 33; J. P. R. Wallis, ed., *The Zambesi Journal of James Stewart 1862–1863* (London, 1952), p. 172.
85 Truão, "Extracto do Plano," p. 408; Salt, *A Voyage*, p. 33; A.H.U., Moç., Maço 4: João Bonifácio da Silva to Sebastião Xavier Botelho, 14 December 1828.
86 Henry Rowley, *The Story of the Universities Mission to Central Africa* (London, 1867), p. 50.
87 Gamitto, "Escravatura," p. 399.
88 Interviews with João Cristóstomo, Gaspar Cardoso, Conrado Msussa Boroma, and Chiponda Cavumbula; A.H.U., Moç., Cx. 70: José Francisco Alves Barbosa to Conde de Arcos, 30 August 1821; A.H.U., Moç., Maço 38: Nicolão Pascoal da Cruz, ca. 1810; Gamitto, *King Kazembe*, 2:86; A.H.U., Moç., Cx. 69: Paulo Jozé Diniz to Gov., 21 May 1821; Lacerda e Almeida, *Travessia*, p. 101; *B.O.M.*, 1833, No. 9, p. 205: Albino Manoel Pacheco, "Uma Viagem de Tete ao Zumbo." The ethnic composition of slaves freed in the middle of the nineteenth century con-

firms the preponderance of peoples of Chewa, Nsenga, and Manganja origin (see Chapter 4).

89 Interviews with João Cristóstomo, Gaspar Cardoso, Conrado Msussa Boroma, Lole Nhanticole, Gimo Tito, Dauce Angolete Gogodo, Zacarias Ferrão, and Chiponda Cavumbula; joint interviews with Tomás Chave and Oliveira Sinto, with Calavina Couche and Zabuca Ngombe; Pacheco, "Viagem," p. 205; A. W. R. Duly, "The Lower Shire: Notes on Land Tenure and Individual Rights," *Nyasaland Journal* 1 (1948): 14.

90 Barretto, "Informação," pp. 48–81; Eric Axelson, ed., "Viagem que fez o Padre Antonio Gomes . . . ," *Studia* 3 (1959): 203; Lacerda e Almeida, *Travessia*, p. 101.

91 Interviews with Conrado Msussa Boroma, Chiponda Cavumbula, and Simon Biwi; joint interviews with Calavina Couche and Zabuca Ngombe and with Chetambara Chenungo and Wilson John.

92 Joaquim d'Almeida da Cunha, *Estudo Ácêrca dos Usos e os Costumes dos Banianes, Bathias, Pares, Mouros, Gentios e Indígenas* (Lourenço Marques, 1885), p. 84; Weise, "Expedição," p. 248.

93 B.N.L., Pombalina 721, fol. 303: Francisco José de Lacerda e Almeida to D. Rodrigues da Souza Coutinho, 21 March 1798; B.N.L., Pombalina 721, fol. 698: Sebastião de Moraes e Almeida, 10 March 1798; Wallis, ed., *Zambesi Expedition of Livingstone*, 1:141; A.H.U., Códice 1758, fols. 154–55: Custódio José de Silva to José Maria Pereira de Almeida, 10 July 1859.

94 A.H.U., Moç., Maço 4: Sebastião Xavier Botelho, 2 October 1828. The prazeros not only participated in slave raids but inflamed wars between competing chieftaincies in order to get additional slaves (A.H.U., Moç., Maço 33: Manoel José Maria da Costa e Sá to Inácio da Costa Quintela, 10 December 1826).

95 I. Schapera, ed., *Livingstone's African Journal 1853–1856* (Berkeley and Los Angeles, 1963), p. 461; Wallis, ed., *Zambesi Expedition of Livingstone*, 2:349.

96 Wiese, "Expedição," p. 248.

97 See Chapter 7 for an examination of the impact of the slave trade on the prazos.

98 A.H.U., Códice 1358, fol. 113: António Manoel de Mello de Castro to Cristovão de Azévedo e Vasconcellos, 29 January 1781; A.H.U., Moç., Maço 33: Manoel José Maria da Costa e Sá to Inácio da Costa Quintela, 10 December 1826; A.H.U., Códice 1477, fol. 132: Rodrigues Luciano de Abreu de Lima to Gov. de Quilimane e Rios de Senna, 8 October 1846.

99 See the following for personal testimonies from colonos: A.H.U., Códice 1350: Izidro de Almeida Souza e Sá to António Norberto Barbosa Truão, 24 October 1803; A.H.U., Códice 1458: Goldinho Jozé Nunes to Custódio Floriam Vaz, 6 June 1850; A.H.U., Códice 1450: Tomás Jozé Peres to Anselmo Henriques Ferrão (undated). Also consult

A.H.U., Moç., Maço 33: Manoel José Maria da Costa e Sá to Inácio da Costa Quintela, 10 December 1826, for a general statement on this abuse.

100 A.H.U., Códice 1489, fol. 87: original report from Feitor de Quelimane to the Gov. dos Rios de Sena, 6 February 1808.

101 A.H.U., Moç., Cx. 62: Joaquim da Silva Guidero, 1818; Texugo, *Letter on the Slave Trade*, p. 34; Gamitto, "Escravatura," p. 399; A.H.U., Moç., Maço 6: João Bonifaço Alves da Silva to Sebastião Xavier Botelho, 14 June 1828.

102 A.H.U., Moç., Maço 33: Requerimento by Lt. Colonel Zefereno Jozé Pinto de Magalhões (attached to a Bando written by Sebastião Xavier Botelho, 24 October 1825); W. F. W. Owen, *Narrative of Voyages to Explore the Shores of Africa, Arabia, and Madagascar* (London, 1833), p. 293; W. F. W. Owen, "Letter from Captain W. F. W. Owen to J. W. Crocker, 9 October, 1823," in *Records of South-East Africa*, ed. G. M. Theal (Capetown, 1903), 9:32–33.

103 Owen, "Owen to Crocker," pp. 32–33.

104 A.N.T.T., Ministério do Reino, Maço 64: "Memórias da Costa de África Oriental," fol. 17 (unsigned), 21 March 1762.

105 Ajuda, 52–X–2, No. 3: José Francisco Alves Barbosa, "Analyse estatística," 30 December 1821; Academia das Ciências de Lisboa, MS. 648 Azul: António Norberto de Barbosa de Villas Boas Truão, "Estatística de Capitania dos Rios de Senna do Anno de 1806," 16 July 1807.

106 These figures are based on import statistics collected in Brazil by the British consuls; they are deposited in PRO, FO 84. A copy is available at the University of Wisconsin.

107 Lt. R. N. Barnard, *Three Years Cruise in the Mozambique Channel* (London, 1848), p. 37.

108 A.H.U., Moç., Maço 18: Membros da Cámara de Quelimane, 6 July 1830; A.H.U., Moç., Maço 14: Joaquim Mendes de Vasconcelos e Cirne to Conde de Basto, 13 October 1830; A.H.U., Moç., Maço 16: Paulo Jozé Miguel de Brito to Conde de Basto, 13 September 1830; A.H.U., Moç., Maço 18: Paulo José Miguel de Brito to Manoel Joaquim Mendes de Vasconcelos e Cirne, 15 June 1830; A.H.U., Moç., Pasta 9: Jozé António de Fazia, 12 November 1847; A.H.U., Moç., Pasta 22: Caetano de Sousa e Vasconcellos to Ministro e Secretário d'Estado dos Negócios da Marinha e Ultramar, 17 May 1864.

109 A.H.U., Moç., Pasta 10: G. G. Seymour to Conde Tojal, 6 March 1851; Texugo, *Letter on the Slave Trade*, p. 34; A.H.U., Moç., Maço 14: Joaquim Mendes de Vasconcelos e Cirne to Conde de Basto, 13 October 1830; Gamitto, "Escravatura," p. 399.

110 A.H.U., Códice 1458, fol. 110: Lourenço de Andrade to Juiz Ordinário de Senna, 21 September 1850.

111 Barnard, *Three Years*, p. 37; A.H.U., Moç., Pasta 9: Jozé António de Fazia, 12 November 1847.

112 A.H.U., Códice 1450, fol. 116: João Souza Machado to Thomas C. Rose (commander of the *Curte*), 11 April 1841.

113 A.H.U., Moç., Pasta 13: António Candido Pedroso Gamitto to S.M.T., 31 December 1854.
   Although theoretically free, most of the Africans exported to Réunion from the Zambesi were, in fact, slaves captured in wars and raids (A.H.M., Códice 2–666–2M.H., fol. 53: C. J. da Silva to José Cristanto Dias, 19 May 1859; Wallis, ed., *Zambesi Journey of David Livingstone*, 2:346.)

CHAPTER 7: EXTERNAL RELATIONS OF THE PRAZOS

1 A.H.U., Moç., Cx. 68: "Cópia de 18° S. da Instrucçao Régia de Abril de 1752, dirigido pello Exmo Sr. Diogo de Mendonça, Corte Real e Ministro Secretário d'Estado, ao Governador e Capitão General que foi deste Estado Francisco de Mello e Castro"; A.H.U., Moç., Cx. 68: "Cópia de 18° S. do Offício de 7 de Abril de 1752 dirigido pello Exmo Sr. Diogo de Mendonça, Corte Real, ao Governador e Capitão General deste Estado."

2 A.H.U., Moç., Cx. 68: Cópia da Provizão do Concelho Ultramarino, 29 March 1783.

3 A.H.U., Moç., Cx. 55: El Rey ao Concelheiro do Conselho Ultramarino, 3 April 1760.

4 A.H.U., Moç., Cx. 68: Cópia da Provizão do Conselho Ultramarino, 29 March 1783; A.H.U., Moç., Cx. 75: Barão da Villa da Praia, "Projeto sobre o modo mais prompto, e favorável aos Officiais Militares, que servem nas Colónias Portuguezas, de obterem as suas Patentes, e aos agraciados com Prazos, ou Sesmarias de poderem conseguir os Títulos legais para a sua fruição, aprovado pelo Conselho Ultramarino na Sessão de 14 de Dezembro de 1825."

5 A.H.U., Moç., Cx. 17: António Manoel de Mello de Castro to Jozé de Vasconcellos Almeida, 18 June 1780.

6 Alexandre Lobato, *Colonização Senhorial da Zambésia* (Lisbon, 1962), pp. 39–42.

7 A.H.U., Moç., Cx. 5: David Marques Pereira, 10 June 1756.

8 A.H.U., Moç., Maço 1: Sebastião Xavier Botelho, 10 August 1826.

9 Francisco José de Lacerda e Almeida, *Travessia Da África* (Lisbon, 1938), p. 112.

10 Ajuda, 52–X–2, No. 3: José Francisco Alves Barbosa, "Analise estatística," 30 December 1821; Lacerda e Almeida, *Travessia*, p. 104; A.H.U., Moç., Cx. 34: Dr. Francisco José de Lacerda e Almeida to the Queen, 22 March 1798; A.H.U., Moç., Maço 24: Sebastião Xavier Botelho to Joaquim Jozé Monteiro Torres, 30 December 1835.

11 M. D. D. Newitt, "The Zambesi *Prazos* in the Eighteenth Century"

(Ph.D. diss., University of London, 1967), p. 178. A similar pattern occurred in Sena and Tete.

12 A.H.U., Moç., Cx. 35: Doutor Francisco José de Lacerda e Almeida, "Mappa Geral da Guarnição desta Praça e Artilharia della Senna" (undated); A.H.U., Moç., Cx. 37: Luís Pinto de Souza, 25 October 1796; A.H.U., Moç., Maço 30: "Mapa Geral de Força do Regimento de Milícia da Villa de Senna," 14 December 1833; A.H.U., Moç., Cx. 29: Cristovão de Azévedo, "Mappa Geral da Troppa que Guarnecem as fortelezas e prezídios dos Rios de Senna," 11 July 1793; A.H.U., Moç., Cx. 10: Dionízio de Mello e Castro to Pedro de Saldanha de Albuquerque, 20 January 1763; Ajuda, 52–X–2, No. 3: José Francisco Alves Barbosa, "Analyse estatística," 30 December 1821; A.H.U., Moç., Cx. 38: Luís Pinto de Souza, 27 October 1796; A.H.U., Moç., Cx. 31: Manoel Baptista Coutinho, 1795; A.H.U., Moç., Maço 9: unsigned to Conde de Basto, 9 December 1825; A.H.U., Códice 1470, fol. 147: Izidro Manoel de Carrazedo, 19 March 1836.

13 A.H.U., Moç., Cx. 9: Marco António de Azévedo Coutinho de Montaury to Pedro de Saldanha de Albuquerque, 15 July 1761.

14 F. Torres Texugo, *Letter on the Slave Trade Still Being Carried on Along the Eastern Coast of Africa* (London, 1839), p. 65.

15 A.H.U., Moç., Cx. 12: Francisco de Brum, 12 February 1767; A.H.U., Moç., Cx. 33: "Balanço Geral do Cofre da Fazenda Real Administrado pela Junta da Fazenda Real de Capitanía de Moss^e," 10 January 1795; A.H.U., Moç., Cx. 41: Vicente José da Santa Negrão, "Balanço Geral do Estado da Junta da Fazenda Real da Capitania de Mossambique, Janeiro–Decembro 1802."

16 A.H.U., Moç., Cx. 21: António Manoel de Mello de Castro, 7 July 1784; A.H.U., Moç., Cx. 40 (unsigned and undated); A.H.U., Moç., Cx. 58: Alvares Caetano d'Abreu e Menezes, 12 November 1814.

17 A.H.U., Moç., Cx. 9: "Extracto das Cartas do Governador e Cappitão Geral de Moss^e e Algumas do Dezembregador Jozé Dias de Valles vendo na nos [?] da Índia questa na B^a," 23 December 1761; A.H.U., Moç., Cx. 9: Marco António de Azévedo Coutinho de Montaury to Pedro de Saldanha de Albuquerque, 15 July 1761.

18 A.N.T.T., Ministério do Reino, Maço 603: Francisco de Mello de Castro, 28 December 1753; A.H.U., Moç., Cx. 4: Francisco de Mello de Castro, 20 November 1753.

19 A.H.U., Moç., Cx. 6: David Marques Pereira, 30 August 1758; A.H.U., Códice 1469, fol. 11: António Mariano da Cunha to Luís Rodrigues, 22 March 1833.

20 A.N.T.T., Ministério do Reino, Maço 604: Inácio Caetano Xavier to Gov. Gen., 26 December 1758.

21 A.H.U., Moç., Cx. 31: João Fernandes do Rozário, 16 August 1795; A.H.U., Moç., Cx. 20: Pedro de Saldanha de Albuquerque to António Manoel de Mello de Castro, 30 September 1783.

22 A.H.U., Códice 1489, fol. 78: Jozé Cançado to Francisco Nicolão Bar-

reto, 1 September 1768; A.H.U., Moç., Maço 7: Francisco Henriques Ferrão, 1 August 1829; A.H.U., Moç., Cx. 59: Marco Caetano d'Abreu e Menezes to Manoel Joaquim Mendes de Vasconcellos, 6 July 1816.

23 A.H.U., Moç., Cx. 4: Francisco de Mello de Castro, 20 November 1753.

24 António Candido Pedroso Gamitto, "Prasos Da Corôa Em Rios De Sena," *Archivo Pittoresco* 1 (1857–58): 62.

25 Interviews with Domingo Kunga, Chale Lupia, Jasse Camalizene, and João Pomba; A.H.M., Fundo do Século XIX, Governo Geral, Cx. 2.37: Manoel d'Abreu Madeira to Rodrigo Luciano d'Abreu, 15 April 1845; Francisco de Mello de Castro, *Descripção dos Rios de Senna, Anno de 1750* (Lisbon, 1861), p. 12.

26 See, for example, A.H.M., Fundo do Século XVIII: José Caetano da Mota, 12 January 1768.

27 A.H.U., Moç., Pasta 14: Vasco Guedes de Carvalho e Menezes to Ministro e Secretário do Estado dos Negócios da Marinha e Ultramar, 28 March 1856; A.H.U., Moç., Cx. 16: António Manoel de Mello de Castro to Jozé de Vasconcellos de Almeida, 17 July 1780; A.H.U., Códice 1473, fol. 104: Izidro Manoel de Carrazedo to Jozé Manuel Correia Monteiro, 15 April 1836; A.H.M., Códice 2–440, F.D.9, fol. 95: Marcos A. R. de Cardenas to Commandante de Tete, 5 August 1849; A.H.M., Fundo do Século XIX, Governo Geral, Cx. 2.37: Fernandes Alves da Valle to João da Souza Machado, 23 May 1858; A.H.U., Códice 1358, fol. 91: António Manoel de Mello de Castro to Agostinho de Mello e Almeida, 4 November 1788; A.H.U., Códice 1469: António Mariano da Cunha to Gov. Gen., 16 April 1833.

28 See Chapter 8 for a discussion of this phenomenon.

29 Zacarias, Anselmo, and Henriques Ferrão were able to link several small Sena prazos into one large power bloc in the nineteenth century.

30 Manuel Barretto, "Informação do Estado e Conquista dos Rios de Cuama, 1667," *Records of South-East Africa*, ed. G. M. Theal (Capetown, 1899), 3:476; A.H.U., Códice 1314, fol. 28: Pedro de Saldanha de Albuquerque to António Caetano de Campos, 16 April 1759; A.N.T.T., Ministério do Reino, Maço 604: António Pinto de Miranda, "Memória Sobre a Costa de África," p. 50 (undated); A.H.U., Moç., Cx. 35: Cópia duma carta de António da Cruz e Almeida (undated).

31 Barretto, "Informação," p. 476; A.H.U., Códice 1314, fol. 55: David Marques Pereira to Manuel António de Almeida, 16 April 1758.

32 A.H.U., Moç., Cx. 33: Diogo da Costa Xavier (undated); A.H.U., Moç., Maço 10: Francisco Henriques Ferrão to Sebastião Xavier Botelho (undated).

33 A.H.U., Moç., Cx. 5 (unsigned, undated [folder marked No. 60]).

34 A.H.U., Códice 1358, fol. 85: António Manoel de Mello de Castro, 29 May 1788; A.H.U., Moç., Cx. 17: Jozé Martinho Pereira, 9 July 1780; interviews with José António de Abreu and José da Costa Xavier.

35 A.H.U., Moç., Cx. 17: Jozé Martinho Pereira, 9 July 1780.

36 A.H.U., Moç., Cx. 17: Jozé Braz de Campo to the Gov., 22 February 1781.

37 A.H.U., Moç., Cx. 25: Correa Moutinho de Mattos to Gov. Gen. de Moç., 21 November 1787; Padre Victor José Courtois, *Notes Chronologiques sur les Anciennes Missions Catholiques au Zambesi* (Lisbon, 1889), p. 47.

38 A.H.U., Moç., Maço 35 (unsigned and undated); A.H.U., Moç., Cx. 24: Jozé João d'Araujo Aranho e Oliveira (undated); A.H.U., Moç., Cx. 33: Jozé Pedro de Diniz, March 1796; Lacerda e Almeida, *Travessia*, p. 106.

39 A.H.U., Moç., Cx. 33: Jozé Pedro de Diniz, March 1796; Ignácio Caetano Xavier, "Relação do Estado presente de Moçambique, Sena, Sofala, Inhambane e todo o Continente de África Oriental, 26 Dec. 1758," *Anais da Junta de Investigações do Ultramar* 9, tomo 1 (1954), pp. 195–96.

40 Xavier, "Relação," pp. 195–96.

41 Ibid.

42 A.H.M., Fundo do Século XVIII: Dionízio de Mello e Castro *et al.*, "Representação dos Moradores de Tete contra o Capitão e Juiz de Villa de Tete, José Carlos Coelho de Campos" (undated); A.H.U., Moç., Cx. 14: Dionízo de Mello e Castro *et al.* (undated).

43 For a detailed account of this conflict see: A.H.U., Moç., Cx. 6: Francisco de Mello de Castro, 23 March 1758; A.H.U., Códice 1310, fols. 96–98: Francisco de Mello de Castro to David Marques Pereira, 2 April 1755; A.H.U., Moç., Cx. 5: José Pereira, 1 December 1756; A.H.U., Moç., Cx. 5: David Marques Pereira, "Interrogatórios para o Capitão e Juiz da Provoação de Senna — Jozé Coelho Loureiro perguntar por elles na rezidência do General q foy dos Rios de Senna," 1 December 1756.

44 A.H.U., Moç., Cx. 13: Ignácio de Mello Alvim, 11 February 1768; Lacerda e Almeida, *Travessia*, p. 133.

45 See, for example, Mabel Jackson Haight, *European Powers and South-East Africa* (London, 1967), p. 74.

46 A.H.M., Fundo do Século XVIII: Ignácio de Mello Alvim, 3 February 1769.

47 A.H.U., Moç., Cx. 3 (unsigned, undated).

48 A.H.U., Códice 1314, fol. 35: Manoel António de Almeida to Francisco de Mello de Castro, 9 July 1757; A.H.U., Moç., Cx. 5: Pedro Jozé Pereira, Francisco de Souza, Bernardo Caetano de Sá Botelho *et al.*, 20 July 1756; A.H.U., Moç., Cx. 6: Francisco de Mello de Castro, 11 August 1758; A.H.U., Moç., Cx. 5: António Martins (undated); A.H.U., Moç., Cx. 3: "Memória do que tenho obrão do nestes Rios no Serviço de S. Magestade que Deos Guarde" (unsigned, undated).

49 A.H.U., Códice 1310, fols. 98–99: Francisco de Mello de Castro to David Marques Pereira, 8 April 1785; A.H.U., Códice 1314, fol. 36: Francisco de Mello de Castro to Manoel António de Almeida, 7 September 1757.

50 A.H.U., Moç., Cx. 9: Mello Caetano Ruíz, 15 July 1762; A.H.U., Códice 1314, fol. 55: David Marques Pereira to Manoel António de Almeida, 16 April 1755; T. E. Bowdich, *An Account of the Discoveries
in the Interior of Angola and Mozambique* (London, 1824), p. 111;
A.H.U., Moç., Cx. 9 (unsigned, undated); A.H.U., Códice 1314, fol.
36: Francisco de Mello de Castro to Manoel António de Almeida,
11 August 1758.

51 A.N.T.T., Ministério do Reino Maço 604: Luís António Figuerido,
"Nóticias do Continente," 1 December 1788; A.H.U., Moç., Cx. 6:
Francisco de Mello de Castro, 11 August 1758; A.H.U., Moç., Cx. 10:
Dionízio de Mello e Castro to Pedro de Saldanha de Albuquerque,
20 January 1763; A.H.U., Moç., Cx. 4: Francisco de Mello de Cas-
tro, 30 December 1753.

52 A.H.U., Moç., Cx. 61: Francisco de Mello de Castro, 11 August 1758.

53 A.H.U., Moç., Cx. 5: João Mascarenhas (undated); A.H.U., Moç., Cx.
3: "Memória do que tenho obrão de nestes Rios no serviço de S. Ma-
gestade que Deos Guarde" (undated, unsigned); A.H.U., Moç., Cx. 8:
Manoel de Caetano, 5 March 1760; A.H.M., Fundo do Século XVIII:
Miguel José Pereira to Balthazar Manoel Pereira do Lago (undated);
A.H.U., Moç., Cx. 8: Manoel de Caetano, 5 March 1760.

54 A.H.M., Fundo do Século XVIII: Manuel Gomes Nobre to Capitão
General de Tete, 9 July 1769.

55 A.H.M., Fundo do Século XVIII: Jerónimo Pereira, 10 January 1800;
A.H.U., Moç., Cx. 28: António Jozé Texeira Siges (undated).

56 A.H.U., Moç., Cx. 9: Mello Caetano Ruíz, 15 July 1762.

57 A.H.U., Códice 1336, fol. 37: Balthazar Manoel Pereyra de Lago to
Ignácio de Mello Alves, 5 April 1769; A.H.U., Moç., Cx. 12: João
Moreira Pereira, 28 January 1766; A.H.U., Moç., Cx. 3: Duarte Salter
de Mendoça, 7 December 1751; A.H.U., Códice 1358, fol. 158: Dom
Diogo de Souza to João de Souza e Brito, 2 May 1795; A.H.U., Moç.,
Cx. 28: João de Souza e Brito, 7 October 1794.

58 A.H.U., Moç., Cx. 10: António da Sylva Pinto (undated).

59 Interview with Conrado Msussa Boroma; A.H.U., Moç., Cx. 10: António da Sylva Pinto, 9 May 1763.

60 A.H.U., Moç., Cx. 13: Ignácio de Mello Alvim, 8 February 1768.

61 A.H.U., Moç., Cx. 17: António Manoel de Mello de Castro to Jozé de
Vasconcellos Almeida, 18 June 1780.

62 A.H.U., Moç., Cx. 13: Balthazar Manoel Pereyra de Lago, 8 August
1769.

63 A.H.U., Moç., Cx. 31 (unsigned [written for Macombe]), 2 February
1795.

64 Because of the paucity of sources and the general assumptions about
the aggressive nature of the prazeros, historians have commonly over-
looked these treaties.

65 See Chapters 2 and 9 for detailed analyses of these relationships.

66 The history of the Bongas is such a case. As a result of the marital union
between his grandfather Bereco and a maternal relative of the Muene-

mutapa, Bonga was able to legitimize his position and gain valuable support among his Tawara relatives in confrontations with the Portuguese government, neighboring prazeros, and the Barue and Nguni raiders (interview with Conrado Msussa Boroma; A.H.U., Moç., Pasta 10: António Gamitto to S.M.T., 30 December 1854; Augusto de Castilho, *Relatório da Guerra da Zambésia em 1888* [Lisbon, 1891], pp. 30–31; A.H.M., Códice 2–449, F.E. 9, fols. 48–49: D. J. Oliveira to Gov. de Quelimane e Rios de Sena, 21 October 1853).

67 A.H.U., Moç., Cx. 13: Ignácio de Mello Alvim, 8 February 1768.

68 A.H.U., Moç., Maço 7: Francisco Henriques Ferrão *et al.*, 15 September 1829.

69 A.H.U., Moç., Cx. 9: Marco António de Azévedo Coutinho de Montaury to Pedro de Saldanha de Albuquerque, 15 July 1761.

70 A.H.U., Moç., Cx. 3: Duarte Salter de Mendoça, 7 December 1751.

71 A.N.T.T., Ministério de Reino, Maço 604: Luís António Figuerido, "Notícias do Continente," 1 December 1788.

72 A.H.U., Moç., Cx. 31: Francisco Henriques Ferrão, 1796; José Justino Texeira Botelho, *História Militar e Política Dos Portugueses Em Moçambique*, 2 vols. (Lisbon, 1934), 1:525–26.

73 A.H.U., Códice 1480, fol. 9: Fernando Carlos da Costa to Galdinho Facestino de Sousa, 9 May 1844; A.H.U., Moç., Cx. 65: Vicente Fiscira de Souza *et al.* (undated); A.H.U., Moç., Cx. 65: António Jozé de Almeida to José Francisco Alves Barbosa (undated); António Candido Pedroso Gamitto, "Successão e Acclamação dos Reis de Barué," *Archivo Pittoresco* 1 (1857–58): 28.

74 A.H.U., Moç., Cx. 31 (unsigned letter [written for Macombe]), 2 February 1795; A.H.U., Moç., Cx. 30 (unsigned), 11 April 1794; A.H.U., Moç., Cx. 65: António Jozé de Almeida to José Francisco Alves Barbosa (undated); A.H.U., Códice 1480, fol. 2: Fernando Carlos da Costa to Anselmo Henriques Ferrão, 5 January 1844; A.H.U., Códice 1480, fol. 9: Fernando Carlos da Costa to Galdinho Facestino da Sousa, 9 May 1844; Gamitto, "Successão," p. 28.

75 A.H.U., Códice 1480, fol. 2: Fernando Carlos da Costa to Anselmo Henriques Ferrão, 5 January 1844; A.H.U., Códice 1480, fol. 9: Fernando Carlos da Costa to Galdinho Facestino da Sousa, 9 May 1844; Gamitto, "Successão," p. 28.

76 A.H.U., Moç., Cx. 31 (unsigned letter [written for Macombe]), 2 February 1795; A.H.U., Moç., Cx. 30 (unsigned), 11 April 1794; A.H.U., Moç., Cx. 65: António Jozé de Almeida to José Francisco Alves Barbosa (undated); A.H.U., Códice 1480, fol. 2: Fernando Carlos da Costa to Anselmo Henriques Ferrão, 5 January 1844; A.H.U., Códice 1480, fol. 9: Fernando Carlos da Costa to Galdinho Facestino da Sousa, 9 May 1844; Gamitto, "Successão," p. 28; A.H.U., Moç., Cx. 65: Vicente Fiscira de Sousa *et al.* (undated).

77 A.H.U., Moç., Cx. 31 (unsigned letter [written for Macombe]), 2 February 1795; A.H.U., Moç., Cx. 72: António de Avarijo to Jozé Francisco

Alves Barbosa, 25 October 1822; A.H.U., Moç., Cx. 65: Vicente Fiscira de Sousa *et al.* (undated).

78 A.H.U., Moç., Pasta 10: António Candido Pedroso Gamitto to S.M.T., 30 December 1854.

79 A.H.U., Moç., Cx. 3: José Francisco de Oliveira, 11 April 1752.

80 A.H.U., Moç., Cx. 18: João de Almeida *et al.* (undated).

81 A.H.M., Fundo do Século XVIII: Miguel José Pereira Gião, 8 July 1768.

82 The decline is treated in Chapter 8.

CHAPTER 8: DECLINE OF THE PRAZO SYSTEM

1 Nguni are a group of linguistically related peoples who lived primarily in South Africa. As a result of Shaka's ascension, a number of Nguni offshoots migrated north. One group, under the leadership of Soshangane, played a dominant role in Zambesian history during the middle third of the nineteenth century. They are treated in the latter part of this chapter.

2 Although there are no statistical data, an analysis of the archival documentation clearly indicates a sharp increase in the number of revolts and migrations in the post-1815 period. This pattern parallels the substantial increase in slave exports.

3 A.H.U., Moç., Maço 33: Manoel José Maria da Costa e Sá to Inácio da Costa Quintela, 10 December 1826; A.H.U., Moç., Maço 18: Manoel da Silva Gonçalves to Manoel Joaquim Mendes de Vasconcelos e Cirne, 1830; A.H.U., Códice 1469, fol. 7: António Mariano da Cunha, 10 March 1833; A.H.U., Moç., Cx. 77: José Alves Candida de Mendonça to Procurador da Fazenda, 20 March 1824; A.H.U., Moç., Maço 8: Sebastião Xavier Botelho to Francisco Henriques Ferrão, March, 1829.

4 A.H.U., Moç., Maço 33: Manoel José Maria da Costa e Sá to Inácio da Costa Quintela, 10 December 1826.

5 A.H.U., Códice 1469, fol. 105: Izidro Manoel de Carrazedo, 18 February 1835; A.H.U., Moç., Maço 8: José Luís Rodrigues to Francisco Henriques Ferrão, 22 September 1829.

6 A.H.U., Códice 1469, fol. 7: Izidro Manoel de Carrazedo, 10 March 1833; A.H.U., Moç., Maço 7: Francisco Henriques Ferrão, 3 December 1829.

7 A.H.U., Códice 1469, fol. 7: Izidro Manoel de Carrazedo, 10 March 1833.

8 A.H.U., Códice 1755, fol. 89: Manoel d'Abreu Madeira to Jozé Francisco de Borja Xavier Soares, 28 March 1846; A.H.U., Moç., Cx. 69: João do Rozário Tavares, 22 December 1821; A.H.U., Moç., Maço 2: João Bonifácio Alves da Silva to Francisco Henriques Ferrão, 10 January 1827; A.H.U., Moç., Maço 10: Manoel Joaquim Mendes de Vasconcelos e Cirne to Conde de Brito, 7 December 1829.

9 A.H.U., Códice 1452: J. B. A. da Silva, 14 May 1825.
10 A.H.U., Códice 1315, fol. 424: Francisco Henriques Ferrão to Joaquim Mendes de Vasconcelos e Cirne, 23 April 1829.
11 A.H.U., Moç., Maço 7: Francisco Henriques Ferrão to Joaquim Mendes de Vasconcelos e Cirne, 23 November 1829.
12 A.H.U., Códice 1315, fol. 208: Francisco Henriques Ferrão to Sebastião Xavier Botelho, 10 January 1828; A.H.U., Códice 1469, fol. 7: António Mariano da Cunha, 10 March 1833; A.H.U., Moç., Maço 14: Joaquim Mendes de Vasconcelos e Cirne to Paulo Jozé Miguel de Brito, 29 September 1830.
13 A.H.U., Moç., Cx. 21: António Manoel de Mello de Castro, 7 July 1784.
14 Ajuda, 52–X–2, No. 3: José Francisco Alves Barbosa, "Analyse estatística," 30 December 1821; A.H.U., Moç., Maço 5: João Bonifácio da Silva to António Manuel de Noronha, 29 September 1828; A.H.U., Moç., Maço 1: Sebastião Xavier Botelho (undated); A.H.M., Fundo do Século XIX, Governo Geral, Cx. 2.37: Manoel Joaquim Mendes de Vasconcelos e Cirne to Paulo Jozé Miguel de Brito (undated); António Candido Pedroso Gamitto, *King Kazembe*, trans. Ian Cunnison, 2 vols. (Lisbon, 1960), 2:185; A.H.U., Moç., Cx. 56: Francisco Carlos da Costa Lacé, 1812; A.H.U., Moç., Maço 12: João Bonifácio Alves da Silva to António Manuel de Noronha, 29 September 1828.
15 Ajuda, 52–X–2, No. 3: José Francisco Alves Barbosa, "Analyse estatística," 30 December 1821; Gamitto, *King Kazembe*, 2:185.
16 Ajuda, 52–X–2, No. 3: José Francisco Alves Barbosa, "Analyse estatística," 30 December 1821; A.H.U., Moç., Maço 5: João Bonifácio Alves da Silva to António Manuel de Noronha, 29 September 1828; A.H.U., Códice 1315, fol. 392: Francisco Henriques Ferrão to Fortunato Piriano da Silva, 4 April 1829.
17 A.H.M., Fundo do Século XIX, Governo Geral, Cx. 2.37: Manoel Joaquim Mendes de Vasconcelos e Cirne to Paulo Jozé Miguel de Brito, 26 March 1830.
18 António Candido Pedroso Gamitto, "Prasos Da Corôa Em Rios De Sena," *Archivo Pittoresco* 1 (1857–58): 62.
19 A.H.U., Códice 1469, fol. 7: António Mariano da Cunha, 10 March 1833; Joaquim Mendes Vasconcelos e Cirne, *Memória Sobre a Província de Moçambique* (Lisbon, 1890), p. 26.
20 Academia das Ciências, MS. 648 Azul: António Norberto de Villas Truão, "Estatística de Capitania dos Rios de Senna do Anno 1806," 16 July 1807.
21 A.H.U., Moç., Maço 2: João Bonifácio Alves da Silva to Francisco Henriques Ferrão, 10 January 1827; A.H.U., Moç., Maço 3: Francisco Henriques Ferrão to Sebastião Xavier Botelho, 29 October 1828; A.H.U., Moç., Maço 7: Severino da Almeida to José Dinis Afonso, 23 February 1829; A.H.U., Códice 1315, fol. 410: Francisco Henriques Ferrão to Sebastião Xavier Botelho, 2 October 1828.

22 A.H.U., Moç., Maço 3: Francisco Henriques Ferrão to Sebastião Xavier Botelho, 29 October 1828.

23 A.H.U., Moç., Maço 4: José António de Oliveira to Leite de Barros, 9 September 1829; Sebastião Xavier Botelho, *Memória Estatística sobre Os Domínios Portuguezes na África Oriental* (Lisbon, 1835), p. 263; F. Torres Texugo, *Letter on the Slave Trade Still Being Carried on Along the East Coast of Africa* (London, 1839), p. 48; A.H.U., Códice 1469, fol. 7: António Mariano da Cunha, 10 March 1833.

24 A.H.U., Moç., Maço 7: Francisco Henriques Ferrão to Joaquim Mendes de Vasconcelos e Cirne, 23 October 1829.

25 A.H.U., Moç., Maço 7: Francisco Henriques Ferrão to Joaquim Mendes de Vasconcelos e Cirne, 23 October 1829; A.H.U., Moç., Maço 15: Caetano Bendito Lobo and Francisco Pereira Coutinho de Vilhena, 1830.

26 A.H.U., Moç., Maço 8: António Mariano da Cunha to Francisco Henriques Ferrão, 10 September 1829.

27 Ibid.

28 A.H.U., Códice 1703, fol. 61: Andres Victorino de Souza *et al.* (undated).

29 A.H.U., Moç., Maço 15: Manoel Joaquim Mendes de Vasconcelos e Cirne to Paulo Jozé Miguel de Brito, 14 July 1830.

30 A.H.U., Moç., Maço 14: Manoel Joaquim de Vasconcelos e Cirne to Conde de Basto, 28 July 1830; A.H.U., Moç., Maço 19: José Dinis Afonso to Gov. Geral, 2 April 1830; A.H.U., Moç., Maço 14: Manoel Joaquim Mendes de Vasconcelos e Cirne to Conde de Basto, 28 July 1830.

31 A.H.U., Códice 1315, fol. 37: Francisco Henriques Ferrão to Commandante de Tete, 10 December 1829; A.H.U., Moç., Maço 7: Francisco Henriques Ferrão to António Mariano da Cunha, 20 August 1829; A.H.U., Moç., Maço 8: Jozé Luís Rodrigues to Francisco Henriques Ferrão, 22 April 1829.

32 A.H.U., Códice 1422, fols. 1–2: Paulo J. M. de Brito to Manoel Joaquim Mendes de Vasconcelos e Cirne, 24 September 1829; A.H.U., Moç., Maço 2: Manoel Joaquim Mendes de Vasconcelos e Cirne to Conde de Basto, 28 June 1830; A.H.U., Moç., Maço 19: Manoel Joaquim Mendes de Vasconcelos e Cirne to Paulo Jozé Miguel de Brito, 18 July 1830.

33 A.H.U., Moç., Pasta 1: Augusto Pires Gonçalves to Joaquim d'Azévedo Alpoim, 20 September 1834.

34 A.H.U., Moç., Maço 25: Joaquim Mendes de Vasconcelos e Cirne to Paulo Jozé Miguel de Brito, 6 March 1830.

35 For their absorption into the empires of Massingire, Massangano, and Makanga see Chapter 9.

36 A.H.U., Códice 1468: Joaquim Mendes de Vasconcelos e Cirne to Paulo Jozé Miguel de Brito, 24 April 1830.

37 A.H.U., Códice 1458, fol. 40: Custódio Jozé António to Commandante de Tete, 10 February 1847.

38 J. D. Omer-Cooper, *The Zulu Aftermath: A Nineteenth Century Revolution in Bantu Africa* (Evanston, 1966), pp. 58–59. For an interesting account of the Nguni invasion of Mozambique see, Gerhard Liesegang, *Beiträge zur Geschichte des Reiches der Gaza Ngoni im südlichen Moçambique, 1820–1895* (Cologne, 1969).

39 A.H.U., Códice 1463, fol. 97: Joaquim d'Azévedo Alpoim to Vasco Guedes de Carvalho e Menezes, 19 August 1856; A.H.U., Códice 1469, fols. 79–80; António Mariano da Cunha to Gov. Geral de Moç., 6 April 1833; A.H.U., Códice 1469, fol. 96: António Mariano da Cunha to Gov. Geral de Moç., 21 March 1834; A.H.U., Moç., Pasta 1: Izidro Manoel de Carrazedo, 17 October 1834; A.H.U., Códice 1473, fol. 81: Izidro Manoel de Carrazedo to Camilo Vas dos Anjos, 26 January 1836; A.H.U., Códice 1473, fol. 160: Izidro Manoel de Carrazedo to Manuel Correia Monteiro, 20 December 1836; A.H.U., Códice 1457, fol. 31: Manuel Abreu de Madeira to Tito Augusto d'Araujo Sicard, 20 May 1845.

40 A.H.M., Fundo do Século XIX, Governo Geral, Cx. 2.37: Manuel Abreu de Madeira to Rodrigo Luciano de Abreu de Lima, 24 July 1845; A.H.U., Códice 1760, fols. 167–69: Delfim José de Oliveira to Secretário do Governo Geral, 3 December 1866; A.H.M., Fundo do Século XIX, Governo Geral, Cx. 2.37: Custódio Jozé António Texeira to Governador Geral da Província de Moçambique, 24 August 1847; A.H.U., Códice 1454, fol. 196: Adelino Coelho da Cruz to Secretário Geral, 19 April 1875.

41 J. P. R. Wallis, ed., *The Zambesi Expedition of David Livingstone, 1858–1863*, 2 vols. (London, 1952), 1:34.

42 A.H.M., Fundo do Século XIX, Governo Geral, Cx. 2.37: D. J. da Silva to Jozé Pereira d'Almeida, 27 November 1858.

43 Interviews with Conrado Msussa Boroma, Domingo Kunga, and Jozé António; A.H.M., Fundo do Século XIX, Governo Geral, Cx. 2.37: C. J. da Silva to Jozé Pereira d'Almeida, 27 November 1858; A.H.U., Códice 1760, fol. 133: Delfim José de Oliveira, "Relatório do Governo do distrito de Quelimane," 25 January 1855; A.H.U., Códice 1755, fol. 18: Fernando Carlos da Costa to Jozé António da Silveira, 6 September 1844; A.H.U., Códice 1463, fol. 97: Joaquim d'Azévedo Alpoim to Vasco Guedes de Carvalho e Menezes, 19 August 1856.

44 A.H.M., Códice 2–439, F.E. 5, fol. 144; T. A. d'Araujo Sicard to Custódio Jozé António Texeira; A.H.M., Fundo do Século XIX, Governo Geral, Cx. 2.37: C. J. da Silva to Jozé Maria Pereira d'Almeida, 2 August 1859.

45 A.H.U., Moç., Pasta 31: Francisco Maria d'Azévedo to Ministro e Secretário d'Estado dos Negócios da Marinha e Ultramar, 6 September 1878; A.H.M., Fundo do Século XIX, Governo Geral, Cx. 2.37: C. J. da Silva to Jozé Pereira d'Almeida (undated).

46 Sousa Ribeiro, ed., *Regimen dos Prazos da Corôa, 1832–1906* (Lourenço Marques, 1907), p. 33.

CHAPTER 9: GROWTH OF SUPRA-PRAZO POLITIES

1 *B.O.M.*, 1888, No. 12, p. 214: Augusto Fonseca de Mesquita e Solla, Comando Militar de Macanga, "Relatório do anno de 1887," 31 December 1887; *B.O.M.*, 1886, No. 29, p. 361: "Viagem as Terras de Macanga, Apontamentos colhidos d'um relatório do padre Victor José Courtois, vigário de Tete, 1885"; *B.O.M.*, 1887, No. 30, p. 331; Augusto de Castilho, Portaria No. 306, 22 July 1887.

2 The exact process of state formation has never been satisfactorily worked out. Through oral traditions and archival material, however, it is possible to determine the broad outlines of early Makanga history as well as to reconstruct a very tentative chronology of the royal family and its immediate antecedents.

The first of the Pereiras to enter Chewa country was Gonçalo Caetano Pereira. He settled north of the Zambesi during the second half of the eighteenth century and rapidly emerged as a prosperous mine owner and trader. With the assistance of a growing achikunda force he probably enjoyed some type of informal control over the local Chewa chieftaincies, although there is no evidence that a structured political relationship developed. He was still alive in the 1790s and two of his progeny, Manoel Caetano Pereira and Cypriano Caetano Pereira played a prominent role in early Portuguese relations with the Bisa and the Lunda of Kazembe. The latter accompanied Lacerda on his famous expedition to the Lunda court.

The most famous of Gonçalo's heirs was Pedro Caetano Pereira. It was he who founded the kingdom of Makanga. Both Courtois and Foà, who collected histories from Makanga elders in the late nineteenth century, dated Pedro's ascension from the end of the eighteenth or the beginning of the nineteenth century. Their informants indicated that Chamatowa (Pedro's African appellation) was able to gain formal recognition as territorial chief both through selective force and by providing military assistance to threatened Chewa afumu. Castilho, who may have been heavily influenced by the writings of Courtois, presents a similar account. The local Chewa historian Chimpazi, however, transmitted a very different version. According to him, the first ruler of Makanga was a member of the Pereira family known as Chicucuru. He received the southern provinces of Undi's empire and one of Undi's maternal relatives in return for assistance against internal opponents. Chicucuru and his achikunda then migrated south and established political hegemony over Makanga. Although oral accounts which we collected in Makanga differed in detail, most concurred with Chimpazi's interpretation, and all agreed that Chicucuru was the founder of Makanga.

The possibility that Chicucuru and Chamatowa were the same individual is one way to explain the apparent contradictions in the two accounts. Both a vague reference by Chimpazi to "Chicucuru or Chatama" and independent references to each as the father of Chissaca-

Maturi, a subsequent king of Makanga, reinforce this hypothesis. This argument also assumes that the Portuguese references Choutama and Shavatama are inverted forms of Chamatowa. The evidence against this interpretation, however, is quite strong. Courtois, who was an excellent observer and who had close links with members of the Makanga royal family, clearly stated that Chicucuru was the son of Chamatowa. Foà independently collected a similar account. While Castillo's supporting version remains suspect, the fact that neither Leão Caetano Pereira, the oldest living descendent of the Makanga royal family, nor any other elders that we interviewed could identify the name Chamatowa casts serious doubt on the validity of the double appellation argument.

A much stronger possibility is that the accounts of both Courtois and Chimpazi are correct and actually reinforce each other. The key to understanding the two sets of traditions is that they treat the consolidation of different parts of the Makanga state. This occurred in several phases and involved both Chamatowa and his son Chicucuru. From Lacerda's account, it is clear that the territory which the former controlled was well to the north of the Casula-Muchena area, which was the center of Makanga under Chicucuru and where we conducted our interviews. It is most likely, therefore, that, after his father's death, Chicucuru expanded the frontiers of the empire to include the entire southern region to the Zambesi River. Since Chamatowa never governed the riverine area, it is not surprising that he remains unknown to the Chewa elders of today who date the founding of Makanga from the arrival of his son, Chicucuru. Similarly, because the Portuguese had only limited commercial relations with Chamatowa, they probably were unaware of his formal political position. This situation changed, however, when Chicucuru gained effective control over the nearby areas of Casula, Chiuta, and Muchena, since his presence posed a very definite threat to Tete and the neighboring prazos. The only difficulty is determining with which member of the Pereira family Undi concluded the various agreements and marital alliance. It is possible that Chicucuru claimed ownership of the southern Chewa lands and links with the royal family based on the relationship between his father and Undi. This, however, is a moot point. The important facts are that Chicucuru did have the sanction of the Chewa king, and that he was able to take advantage of the unstable conditions to carve out a large state with a new capital at Massanza.

For information on the origin of Makanga see Chapter 2 and: A.H.U., Moç., Cx. 8: Manoel de Caetano, 5 March 1760; B.N.L., Pombalina 721, fol. 300: Francisco José de Lacerda e Almeida to D. Rodrigues Cutinho, 21 March 1798; Walter Montagu Kerr, *The Far Interior*, 2 vols. (London, 1886), 2:46–47, 65–66; A.H.U., Moç., Maço 38: Nicolão Pascoal da Cruz, 1810 ca; *B.O.M.*, 1886, No. 29, p. 361: "Viagem as Terras de Macanga, Apontamentos colhidos d'um relatório do padre Victor José Courtois, vigário de Tete, 1885"; Edouard Foà, *Do Cap au*

Lac Nyassa (Paris, 1901), pp. 265–67; interviews with Simon Biwi, Capachika Chúau, Chapavira Muiessa, Chiponda Cavumbula, Leão Manuel Banqueiro Caetano Pereira, and Conrado Msussa Boroma; joint interviews with Calavina Couche and Zabuca Ngombe, and with Chetambara Chenungo and Wilson John.

3 Personal communication with Harry Langsworthy.

4 José Fernandes, Júnior, "Narração do Distrito de Tete" (Paper, Makanga, 1955), p. 105; A.H.M., Fundo do Século XIX, Tete, Governo do Distrito, Cx. 11: Augusto Fonseca de Mesquita e Solla to Gov. de Tete, 26 June 1888.

5 A.H.M., Fundo do Século XIX, Governo do Quelimane, Cx. 7: Anselmo Joaquim Nunes de Andrade to João de Souza Machado, 12 April 1858; A.H.U., Moç., Pasta 30: Anselmo Joaquim Nunes de Andrade, 28 November 1875.

6 A.H.U., Moç., Pasta 30: Anselmo Joaquim Nunes de Andrade, 28 November 1875.

7 Ibid.; *B.O.M.*, 1886, No. 29, pp. 360–61: "Viagem as Terras de Macanga, Apontamentos colhidos d'um relatório do padre Victor José Courtois, vigário de Tete, 1885"; *B.O.M.*, 1861, No. 3, p. 13: José Manoel Correia Monteiro to Manoel Joaquim Mendes de Vasconcelos e Cirne, 13 June 1830; interview with Chiponda Cavumbula; joint interview with Calavina Couche and Zabuca Ngombe.

8 A.H.U., Moç., Pasta 30: Anselmo Joaquim Nunes de Andrade, 28 November 1875; *B.O.M.*, 1886, No. 29, p. 361: "Viagem as Terras de Macanga, Apontamentos colhidos d'um relátorio do padre Victor José Courtois, vigário de Tete, 1885"; M. D. D. Newitt, "The Portuguese on the Zambesi: An Historical Interpretation of the Prazo System," *Journal of African History* 10 (1969): 82.

9 Interview with Chiponda Cavumbula; joint interviews with Calavina Couche and Zabuca Ngombe, and with Chetambara Chenungo and Wilson John.

10 Interviews with Malisseni Máuo, Simon Biwi, Capachika Chúau, Chiponda Cavumbula, and Leão Manuel Banqueiro Caetano Pereira; joint interviews with Calavina Couche and Zabuca Ngombe, and with Chetambara Chenungo and Wilson John.

11 The transference of power was marked by violent upheavals and wars in every instance with the single exception of the death of Chicucuru and the succession of Chissaca-Maturi. A monograph dealing, in part, with the internal history of Makanga will be finished shortly. For more information on the nature of these succession crises see: A.H.U., Moç., Pasta 13: António Candido Pedroso Gamitto to S.M.T., 31 December 1854; A.H.M., Fundo do Século XIX, Governo do Distrito de Quelimane, Cx. 7: João de Souza Nunes d'Andrade to Governador de Quel. e Rios de Sena (undated); A.H.U., Moç., Pasta 30: Anselmo Joaquim Nunes de Andrade, 28 November 1875; interview with Leão Manuel Banqueiro Caetano Pereira; A.H.M., Fundo do Século XIX, Governo do

Distrito, Cx. 11: Augusto Fonseca de Mesquita e Solla to Gov. do Distrito de Tete, 15 April 1888; *B.O.M.*, 1888, No. 12, p. 213: "Relatório do Commando Militar de Macanga," 31 December 1887; Fernandes, Júnior, "Narração," pp. 105, 110.

12 Interview with Capachika Chúau; joint interviews with Calavina Couche and Zabuca Ngombe, and with Chetambara Chenungo and Wilson John.

13 Interview with Leão Manuel Banqueiro Caetano Pereira; Fernandes, Júnior, "Narração," p. 105; A.H.U., Moç., Pasta 30: Anselmo Joaquim Nunes de Andrade, 28 November 1875; *B.O.M.*, 1888, No. 12, p. 214: "Relatório do Commando Militar de Macanga," 31 December 1887.

14 A.H.M., Fundo do Século XIX, Governo do Quelimane, Cx. 7: João de Souza Nunes d'Andrade to João de Souza Machado, 12 April 1858.

15 *B.O.M.*, 1888, No. 12, p. 214: "Relatório do Commando Militar de Macanga," 31 December 1887; A.H.U., Moç., Pasta 30: Anselmo Joaquim Nunes de Andrade, 28 November 1875; Fernandes, Júnior, "Narração," p. 105; *B.O.M.*, 1887, No. 30, pp. 331–32: Augusto de Castilho, Relatório No. 306; *B.O.M.*, 1886, No. 29, p. 361: "Viagem as Terras de Macanga, Apontamentos colhidos d'um relatório do padre Victor José Courtois, vigário de Tete, 1885."

16 A.H.U., Moç., Pasta 30: Anselmo Joaquim Nunes de Andrade, 28 November 1875; A.H.M., Códice 2–439, F.E. 5, fol. 69: João de Sousa Nunes de Andrade to Tito Augusto d'Araujo Sicard, 5 July 1845.

17 For a copy of the 1875 treaty see *Termos de Vassalagem Nos Territórios de Machona, Zambézia e Nyasa 1858 a 1889* (Lisbon, 1890).

18 A.H.M., Códice 2–439, F.E. 5, fol. 69: João de Sousa Nunes de Andrade to Tito Augusto d'Araujo Sicard, 5 July 1845; interview with Chiponda Cavumbula.

19 A.H.M., Códice 2–449, F.E. 9, fol. 50: D. J. de Oliveira to Governador de Quelimane e os Rios de Sena (undated).

20 A.H.M., Códice 2–439, F.E. 5, fol. 69: João de Sousa Nunes de Andrade to Tito Augusto d'Araujo Sicard, 5 July 1845.

21 A.H.M., Códice 2–439, F.E. 5, fol. 17: João de Sousa Nunes de Andrade to Fernando Carlos de Costa, 29 November 1844; A.H.U., Códice 1756, fol. 149: Joaquim d'Azévedo Alpoim to Vasco Guedes de Carvalho e Menezes, 2 April 1854.

22 A.H.U., Códice 1756, fol. 149: Joaquim d'Azévedo Alpoim to Vasco Guedes de Carvalho e Menezes, 2 April 1854.

23 A.H.M., Códice 2–440, F.D. 9, fol. 64: M.A.R. de Cardenas to António Alves, 16 April 1849; A.H.U., Moç., Pasta 13: Galdinho José Nunes to Governador dos Rios de Sena e Tete, 18 January 1854.

24 Both Chicucuru's father and older brother were given the honorific title of capitão-môr of the interior. *B.O.M.*, 1861, No. 3: Jozé Manoel Correia Monteiro to Manoel Joaquim Mendes de Vasconcelos e Cirne, 13 June 1830; A.H.U., Códice 1477, fols. 163–65: João de Souza Machado, 11 August 1843.

25 A.H.U., Códice 1477, fols. 163–65: João de Souza Machado, 11 August 1843.

26 A.H.M., Códice 2–439, F.E. 5, fol. 15: João de Souza Nunes de Andrade to Fernando Carlos da Costa, 18 November 1844.

27 Carlos Wiese, "Expedição Portugueza À Mpeseni (1889)," *Boletim Da Sociedade De Geografia de Lisboa* 10 (1891): 336; A.H.U., Moç., Pasta 13: António Candido Pedroso Gamitto to S.M.T., 31 December 1854; *B.O.M.*, 1883, No. 18, p. 125: Albino Manoel Pacheco, "Uma Viagem de Tete ao Zumbo"; J. P. R. Wallis, ed., *The Zambesi Expedition of David Livingstone, 1858–1863*, 2 vols. (London, 1956), 1:93.

28 A.H.U., Moç., Pasta 10: Domingos Fortunato do Valle to Ministro e Secrétario d'Estado dos Negócios da Marinha e Ultramar, 8 February 1850; A.H.M., Códice 2–44, F.D. 9, fol. 84: Marcos A.R. de Cardenas to Anselmo Gomes Xavier (undated).

29 A.H.U., Moç., Pasta 10: Domingos Fortunato do Valle to Ministro e Secretário d'Estado dos Negócios da Marinha e Ultramar, 8 February 1850.

30 Fernandes, Júnior, "Narração," p. 105; A.H.U., Moç., Pasta 14: Vasco Guedes de Carvalho e Menezes to Ministro e Secretário do Estado dos Negócios da Marinha e Ultramar, 28 March 1856.

31 A.H.M., Fundo do Século XIX, Governo Geral, Cx. 11: Sec. do Governador do Distrito de Tete to Secretário Geral, 25 November 1886; A.H.M., Fundo do Século XIX, Governo Geral, Cx. 11: Luís Joaquim Braga to Capitão-môr da Macanga, 5 October 1883; A.H.M., Fundo do Século XIX, Governo Geral, Cx. 11: Augusto Cesar de Oliveira Gomes to Secretário Geral, 1 December 1886; A.H.M., Fundo do Século XIX, Governo Geral, Cx. 11: Luiz Francisco de Brito Collaço, 22 October 1883; A.H.M., Fundo de Século XIX, Governo Geral, Cx. 11: Inácio de Jesús Xavier to Gov. do Distrito de Tete (undated).

32 *B.O.M.*, 1886, No. 29, p. 560: "Viagem as Terras de Macanga, Apontamentos colhidos d'um relátorio do padre Victor José Courtois, vigário de Tete, 1885."

33 A.H.M., Fundo do Século XIX, Governo Geral, Cx. 11: Sec. do Gov. do Distrito de Tete to Sec. Geral, 25 November 1886; Fernandes, Júnior, "Narração," pp. 109–110; A.H.M., Fundo do Século XIX, Governo Geral, Cx. 11: Henrique Frederico d'Andrade to Governador de Tete (undated); A.H.M., Fundo do Século XIX, Quelimane, Prazos da Corôa, Cx. 5 (3): Luís António de Brito, 18 December 1899; Foà, *Du Cap Au Lac Nyassa*, pp. 267–69.

34 A.H.M., Fundo do Século XIX, Tete, Governo do Distrito, Cx. 11: Augusto Fonseca de Mesquita e Solla to Gov. do Distrito de Tete, 15 April 1888.

35 Ibid.

36 A.H.M., Fundo do Século XIX, Governo do Distrito, Tete, Cx. 11: Augusto Fonseca de Mesquita e Solla to Gov. do Distrito de Tete, 15 April 1888; Fernandes, Júnior, "Narração," p. 39; Foà, *Do Cap au*

Lac Nyassa, p. 267; Eric Axelson, *Portugal and the Scramble for Africa* (Johannesburg, 1967), p. 145.

37 A.H.M., Fundo do Século XIX, Governo Geral, Cx. 11: Nicolão Pontes de Ataide e Azévedo to Secretário do Governo Geral da Província de Moçambique, July 1869; A.H.M., Fundo do Século XIX, Governo Geral, Cx. 11: Desederio Dias Guilhermo to Governador Geral da Província de Moçambique, 8 August 1871; Fernandes, Júnior, "Narração," pp. 109–110; A.H.M., Fundo do Século XIX, Cx. 11, Tete, Governo do Distrito: Augusto Fonseca de Mesquita e Solla to Gov. do Distrito de Tete, 1 May 1888; A.H.M., Fundo do Século XIX, Governo Geral, Cx. 11: Alfredo Júlio d'Alpoim Leite Peixoto to Conselheiro Governador d'esta Província, 1 September 1890.

38 A.H.M., Fundo do Século XIX, Governo Geral, Cx. 11: Alfredo Júlio d'Alpoim Leite Peixoto to Secretário Geral da Província, 1 September 1890.

39 Fernandes, Júnior, "Narração," p. 110; joint interview with Calavina Couche and Zabuca Ngombe; interviews with Chiponda Cavumbula and Leão Manuel Banqueiro Caetano Pereira.

40 Fernandes, Júnior, "Narração," pp. 39–57.

41 Ibid., pp. 47–48.

42 A.H.M., Fundo do Século XIX, Quelimane, Prazos da Corôa, Cx. 5 (3): Luís António de Brito, 18 September 1899.

43 Fernandes, Júnior, "Narração," p. 50.

44 Interview with Alberto Vicente da Cruz.

45 Newitt dates the arrival of the Vas dos Anjos family from 1820. M. D. D. Newitt, "The Portuguese on the Zambesi from the Seventeenth to the Nineteenth Centuries," *Race* 9 (1968): 490.

46 A.H.M., Códice 2–1530, G.G. 13, fol. 29: Joaquim d'Azévedo Alpoim to Izidro Correa Pereira (undated).

47 A.H.U., Códice 1463, fol. 106: Joaquim d'Azévedo Alpoim to Vasco Guedes de Carvalho e Menezes, 23 September 1856; A.H.M., Fundo do Século XIX, Governo Geral, Cx. 2.37: João de Souza Machado to Secretário do Governo Geral da Província, 20 February 1858; A.H.U., Códice 1758, fol. 56: Custódio José da Silva to José Maria Pereira de Almeida, 22 June 1858.

48 A. W. R. Duly, "The Lower Shire: Notes on Land Tenure and Individual Rights," *Nyasaland Journal* 1 (1948): 13–15; A.H.U., Códice 1760, fol. 12: Tito Augusto d'Araujo Sicard to Francisco de Salles Machado, 26 March 1863; interviews with Andisseni Tesoura and Avaringa Avarinho; joint interview with António Anselmo Almeida and Inácio Petrinho.

It should be noted that, like the term Chikunda, Anguru did not signify a clearly defined ethnic group but was used by the Portuguese to describe a whole series of people living north of the Zambesi and south of the Shire. Mr. Alpers has informed the author that Malawi-speaking peoples use the term to refer to groups living east of them.

49 A.H.M., Fundo do Século XIX, Governo Geral, Cx. 20: Custódio de Sal to Galdinho José Nunes; W. H. J., Rangeley, "Mbona — The Rain Maker," *Nyasaland Journal* 6 (1953): 25.

50 A.H.U., Códice 1463, fol. 120: Joaquim d'Azévedo Alpoim to Vasco Guedes de Carvalho e Menezes, 19 December 1856; A.H.U., Códice 1463, fol. 115: Joaquim d'Azévedo Alpoim to Vasco Guedes de Carvalho e Menezes, 10 November 1856.

51 A.H.U., Moç., Pasta 21: Fernando Alves de Valle to Custódio José da Silva, 29 January 1863.

52 Interviews with Gimo Tito, Andisseni Tesoura, Avaringa Avarinho; joint interview with António Anselmo Almeida and Inácio Petrinho; A.H.M., Códice 2–1530, G.B. 12, fol. 113: Jozé de Souza Machado to Commandante Militar de Tete, 3 November 1857; David and Charles Livingstone, *Livingstone's Narrative of an Expedition to the Zambesi and Its Tributaries* (New York, 1866), pp. 24–27. One result was the migration of a substantial number of Manganja south to Mopeia, where they were integrated into the Podzo, the dominant ethnic group.

53 A.H.M., Fundo do Século XIX, Quelimane, Governo do Distrito, Cx. 5: Frederico Augusto to Gov. dos Rios de Sena (undated); A.H.M., Fundo do Século XIX, Governo Geral, Cx. 2.37: Fernando Alves de Valle to Jozé da Souza Machado; A.H.M., Fundo do Século XIX, Governo Geral, Cx. 2.37: C. J. da Silva to José Maria Pereira d'Almeida, 15 March 1859; A.H.M., Códice 2–1530, G.B. 12, fol. 158 (signature and date torn off); Wallis, ed., *Zambesi Expedition of Livingstone*, 1:284; A.H.M., Fundo do Século XIX, Governo Geral, Cx. 2.37: João de Souza Machado to Gov. Geral da Província, 23 February 1858.

54 A.H.U., Moç., Pasta 19: João Tavares de Almeida to Ministro e Secretário de Estado dos Negócios da Marinha e Ultramar, 20 September 1862.

55 A.H.M., Fundo do Século XIX, Governo Geral, Cx. 2.37: João de Souza Machado to Secretário do Governo Geral da Província, 27 March 1858; A.H.U., Códice 1758, fol. 39: João de Souza Machado to Gov. Geral da Província, 12 May 1858; A.H.U., Códice 1758, fol. 34: João de Souza Machado to Gov. Geral da Província, 27 March 1858; A.H.M., Fundo do Século XIX, Governo Geral, Cx. 20: Luís Joaquim Vieira Braga to Secretário do Governo de Quelimane, 30 August 1874.

56 A.H.M., Códice 2–1530, G.B. 12, fol. 29: Joaquim d'Azévedo Alpoim to Izidro Correa Pereira; A.H.U., Códice 1463, fol. 115: Joaquim d'Azévedo Alpoim to Vasco Guedes de Carvalho e Menezes, 10 November 1856; A.H.U., Códice 1451, fol. 95: Joaquim d'Azévedo Alpoim to António Jozé da Cruz Coimbra, 9 November 1854.

57 A.H.M., Fundo de Século XIX, Governo Geral, Cx. 2.37: Francisco Maria d'Azévedo to João de Souza Machado, 23 January 1858; A.H.U., Códice 1463, fol. 106: Joaquim d'Azévedo Alpoim to Vasco Guedes de Carvalho e Menezes, 23 September 1856; A.H.M., Fundo do Século XIX, Governo Geral, Cx. 2.37: Sebastião Manoel Correa to João de Souza

Machado, 5 February 1858; A.H.U., Códice 1758, fol. 45: Custódio José da Silva to Governador Geral da Província, 10 May 1859; José Justino Texeira Botelho, *História Militar e Política dos Portugueses Em Moçambique*, 2 vols. (Lisbon, 1934), 2:193.

58 A.H.M., Fundo do Século XIX, Governo Geral, Cx. 2.37: Miguel Agostinho de Gouveia to João de Souza Machado, 8 February 1858; Botelho, *História Militar*, 2:193.

59 A.H.M., Fundo do Século XIX, Governo Geral, Cx. 20: Custódio José da Silva to Galdinho José Nunes, 5 November 1861; Livingstones, *Expedition to the Zambesi*, pp. 26–28.

60 Wallis, ed., *Zambesi Expedition of David Livingstone*, 1:117.

61 A.H.U., Códice 1462, fol. 131: Galdinho José Nunes to Secretário do Governo Geral da Província, 8 April 1861; A.H.U., Moç., Pasta 19: João Tavares de Almeida to Ministro e Secrétario de Estado dos Negócios da Marinha e Ultramar, 23 January 1862; A.H.M., Fundo do Século XIX, Governo Geral, Cx. 20: Custódio José da Silva to Galdinho José Nunes, 5 November 1861.

62 A.H.M., Fundo do Século XIX, Quelimane, Governo do Distrito, Cx. 5: Fernando Alves de Valle to Custódio José da Silva, 1 January 1863.

63 A.H.U., Moç., Pasta 21: Tito Augusto d'Araujo Sicard to Custódio José da Silva, 24 January 1863; A.H.U., Moç., Pasta 21: Custódio José da Silva to Francisco de Salles Machado, 3 February 1863; A.H.U., Moç., Pasta 21: Fernando Alves de Valle to Custódio José da Silva, 29 January 1863.

64 A.H.U., Moç., Pasta 21: Fernando Alves de Valle to Custódio José da Silva, 29 January 1863; A.H.U., Códice 1456, fol. 78: José d'Almeida d'Avila to Secretário do Governo Geral, 12 September 1882.

65 A.H.M., Fundo do Século XIX, Governo Geral, Cx. 20: António Maria Cardozo to Secretário Geral do Governo Geral, 1 June 1879.

66 A.H.M., Fundo do Século XIX, Governo Geral, Cx. 20: José d'Almeida d'Avila to Secretário Geral do Governo, 12 December 1881; A.H.U., Moç., Pasta 1, Primeira Repartição: Visconde de Paço d'Arco to Ministro e Secretário d'Estado dos Negócios da Marinha e Ultramar, 30 January 1882.

67 *Termos de Vassalagem*, pp. 23–29.

68 A.H.U., Moç., Pasta 1, Primeira Repartição: Visconde de Paço d'Arco to Secretário d'Estado dos Negocios da Marinha e Ultramar, 30 January 1882.

69 A.H.U., Códice 1464, fol. 226: José Augusto Pimenta de Miranda to Commandante Militar de Sena, 31 September 1885.

70 A.H.U., Moç., Pasta 2, Primeira Repartição: António Abranches to Ministro e Secretário d'Estado dos Negócios da Marinha e Ultramar, 10 January 1887; A.H.M., Fundo do Século XIX, Quelimane, Governo do Distrito, Cx. 46 (1): Pereira e Dulio to Gov. do Distrito da Zambézia, 16 April 1896.

71 Boundaries based on information from: A.H.M., Fundo do Século XIX,

Quelimane, Governo do Distrito, Cx. 5: Manoel António de Souza to Commandante Militar da Villa de Sena, 6 January 1877; A.H.M., Fundo do Século XIX, Governo Geral, Cx. 11: Secretário do Governador do Distrito de Tete to Sec. Geral, 27 November 1855; *B.O.M.*, 1888, No. 1, pp. 9–10: Joaquim Carlos Paiva d'Andrada to Conselheiro Governador da Província de Moçambique, Relatório, 27 October 1887; Botelho, *História Militar*, 2:251.

72 A.H.U., Códice 1477: Domingos Fortunato de Valle to Gov. de Quelimane e os Rios de Sena, 27 June 1849.

73 Interviews with Conrado Msussa Boroma, Domingo Kunga, António Gavião, and Chale Lupia; Fernandes, Júnior, "Narração," p. 8; A.H.U., Códice 1477, fol. 144: Domingos Fortunato de Valle to Gov. de Quelimane e os Rios de Sena, 9 May 1849.

74 Interviews with Domingo Kunga, Chale Lupia, and António Gavião; A.H.U., Códice 1477: Domingos Fortunato de Valle to Gov. de Quelimane e os Rios de Sena, 27 June 1849; A.H.M., Fundo do Século XIX, Governo Geral, Cx. 2.37: C. J. da Silva to Jozé Pereira d'Almeida, 27 November 1858.

75 Interviews with Conrado Msussa Boromo, João Vicente, Domingo Kunga, António Gavião, Chale Lupia, and Niquicicafe Presente; Fernandes, Júnior, "Narração," p. 8.

76 Interviews with António Gavião and Alberto Vicente da Cruz; Fernandes, Júnior, "Narração," p. 8.

77 Several independent sources noted that Bereco (see Table 10) married a member of the Muenemutapa's family (interviews with Conrado Msussa Boroma and Alberto Vicente da Cruz; Augusto do Castilho, *Relatório da Guerra da Zambézia em 1888* [Lisbon, 1891], pp. 30–31; A. P. Miranda, *Notícia Âcêrca do Bonga da Zambézia* [Lisbon, 1869], p. 6; A.H.U., Moç., Pasta 10: António Candido Pedroso Gamitto to S.M.T., 30 December 1854). There is also evidence that Bonga's family (see Table 10) entered into a marriage alliance with the Barue royal family (Fernandes, Júnior, "Narração," p. 23; interview with Conrado Msussa Boroma).

78 Interview with Alberto Vicente da Cruz.

79 Interviews with Domingo Kunga, António Gavião, Niquicicafe Presente, and Chale Lupia; Fernandes, Júnior, "Narração"; *B.O.M.*, 1888, No. 1, p. 10: Joaquim Carlos Paiva d'Andrada to Conselheiro Governador da província de Moçambique, Relatório, 27 October 1887.

80 Interviews with João Vicente, Domingo Kunga, António Gavião, Chale Lupia, and Alberto Vicente da Cruz; Miranda, *Notícias Âcêrca do Bonga*, p. 14; A.H.M., Fundo do Século XIX, Governo de Quelimane, Cx. 7: João Gomes Barbosa to Joaquim d'Azévedo Alpoim, 16 June 1855; A.H.U., Moç., Pasta 13: António Candido Pedroso Gamitto to S.M.T., 30 December 1854; Castilho, *Relatório da Guerra*, p. 35; Delfim José de Oliveira, *A Província de Moçambique e o Bonga* (Coimbra, 1879), p. 14.

81 Interviews with João Vicente, Domingo Kunga, António Gavião, Chale Lupia, Niquicicafe Presente, Chacundunga Mavico, and Alberto Vicente da Cruz; A.H.M., Fundo do Século XIX, Tete, Governo do Distrito, Cx. 127: Jozé Luís to Gov. do Distrito de Tete, 15 July 1885; *B.O.M.*, 1888, No. 1, pp. 15–16: Joaquim Carlos Paiva d'Andrada, to Conselheiro Governador da Província de Moçambique, Relatório, 27 October 1887.

82 Interviews with João Vicente, Domingo Kunga, António Gavião, Chale Lupia, and Niquicicafe Presente.

83 A.H.M., Fundo do Século XIX, Tete, Governo do Distrito, Cx. 11: João Marques Serra to Secretário do Governador de Tete, 18 August 1888; A.H.M., Fundo do Século XIX, Quelimane, Governo do Distrito, Cx. 35 (1): Jozé Maria Fontes de Bragança to Gov. do Distrito de Quelimane, 21 April 1875; A.H.M., Fundo do Século XIX, Governo Geral, Cx. 11: Gov. to Secretário Geral, 23 June 1887; *B.O.M.*, 1888, No. 1, p. 10: Joaquim Carlos Paiva d'Andrada to Conselheiro Governador da Província de Moçambique, "Relatório" 27 October 1887.

84 *B.O.M.*, 1886, No. 29, pp. 253–54: "Viagem as Terras de Macanga, Apontamentos colhidos d'um relatório do padre Victor José Courtois, vigário de Tete, 1885"; *B.O.M.*, 1888, No. 1, pp. 9–10: Joaquim Carlos Paiva d'Andrada to Conselheiro Governador da Província de Moçambique, Relatório 27 October 1887; Castilho, *Relatório da Guerra*, p. 59.

85 Interviews with Domingo Kunga and Alberto Vicente da Cruz.

86 For detailed accounts of specific succession crises see: Castilho, *Relatório da Guerra*, p. 59; Fernandes, Júnior, "Narração," pp. 13–17.

87 A.H.U., Códice 1453, fol. 89: Germano Augusto da Silva to Secretário do Governo Geral, 10 April 1869; A.H.M., Fundo do Século XIX, Governo Geral, Cx. 2.37: C. J. da Silva to Jozé Pereira d'Almeida, 27 November 1858; A.H.U., Códice 1453, fol. 89: Germano Augusto da Silva to Secretário do Governo Geral, 10 April 1869; Oliveira, *A Província de Moçambique*, p. 9; David Livingstone, *Missionary Travels and Research in South Africa* (London, 1857), p. 559; Miranda, *Notícias Àcêrca do Bonga*, pp. 15–16; Wallis, ed., *Zambesi Expedition of David Livingstone*, 2:284–85; interviews with João Vicente, Domingo Kunga, and Chale Lupia.

88 A.H.M., Fundo do Século XIX, Governo Geral, Cx. 11: José Maria de Queiroz Abranches to Chefe de Repartição Militar da Província de Moçambique, 18 February 1870.

89 Interviews with João Vicente, Domingo Kunga, and Alberto Vicente da Cruz; A.H.M., Fundo do Século XIX, Governo Geral, Cx. 20: António de Carvalho Sancho to Secretário Geral, 11 August 1886; A.H.M., Fundo do Século XIX, Governo Geral, Cx. 11: João da Silva *et al.* (undated); Wallis, ed., *Zambesi Expedition of Livingstone*, 1:161; A.H.U., Códice 1451, fol. 3: Jerónimo Romeiro to João de Jezús Miranda, 8 April 1854; A.H.M., Fundo do Século XIX, Governo Geral, Cx. 20: Joaquim Jozé Ferreira to Gov. de Quelimane, 15 March 1886.

90 A.H.M., Fundo do Século XIX, Governo Geral, Cx. 11: João da Silva *et al.* (undated); A.H.M., Fundo do Século XIX, Governo Geral, Cx. 20: António de Carvalho Sancho to Secretário Geral, 11 August 1886.

91 Castilho, *Relatório da Guerra*, p. 8; A.H.U., Moç., Pasta 13: António Candido Pedroso Gamitto to S.M.T., 30 December 1854.

92 A.H.M., Fundo do Século XIX, Governo Geral, Cx. 11: Augusto Cesar de Oliveira Gomes to Secretário Geral, 26 May 1887; A.H.U., Moç., Pasta 13: António Candido Pedroso Gamitto to S.M.T., 30 December 1854; Wallis, ed., *Zambesi Expedition of David Livingstone*, 1:161; E. D. Tabler, ed., *The Zambesi Papers of Richard Thorton*, 2 vols. (London, 1963), 1:70.

93 A.H.M., Fundo do Século XIX, Governo Geral, Cx. 11: João António Rodrigues to Secretário do Governador Geral da Província, 27 November 1868; A.H.M., Fundo do Século XIX, Governo Geral, Cx. 11: copied inserts in a letter from Carlos Pedro Barahona e Costa Major to Secretário do Governo Geral da Província, 23 August 1874; A.H.M., Fundo do Século XIX, Governo Geral, Cx. 11: Augusto Cesar de Oliveira Gomes to Secretário Geral, 26 May 1887; José Joaquim Ferreira, *Recordações Da Expedição da Zambézia em 1869* (Lisbon, 1891), p. 46.

94 Castilho, *Relatório da Guerra*, p. 36.

95 A.H.M., Fundo do Século XIX, Governo Geral, Cx. 20: Germano Augusto da Silva to Secretário do Governo Geral, 10 April 1869; Castilho, *Relatório da Guerra*, p. 35; A.H.M., Fundo do Século XIX, Governo Geral, Cx. 11: José Joaquim da Cunha to Secretário do Governo do Distrito de Tete, 31 March 1844.

96 Castilho, *Relatório da Guerra*, p. 35; Fernandes, Júnior, "Narração," pp. 11–12; Felipe Gastão de Almeida de Eça, *História Das Guerras No Zambeze*, 2 vols. (Lisbon, 1953–54), 1:102–118.

97 Interview with Alberto Vicente da Cruz; A.H.M., Fundo do Século XIX, Governo Geral, Cx. 11: Theodório Francisco Diaz to Governo do Distrito de Tete (undated); Tabler, ed., *Papers of Thorton*, 1:70.

98 A.H.M., Fundo do Século XIX, Governo Geral, Cx. 20: José Fontes de Bragança, 20 May 1872; A.H.U., Códice 1454, fol. 140: Adelino Abel Coelho da Cruz to Secretário Geral, 29 September 1874.

99 The principal aringas were located on the banks of the four major rivers — Luenha, Mazoe, Muira, and Zambesi — and on an overland stretch extending from the confluence of the Nhacacombe and Muira rivers across the Luenha to the Mazoe (A.H.M., Fundo do Século XIX, Governo Geral, Cx. 11: Gov. do Distrito de Tete to Secretário Geral do Governo, 30 August 1885; A.H.M., Fundo do Século XIX, Governo Geral, Cx. 11: Augusto Cesar de Oliveira Gomes to Secretário Geral, 26 May 1887; B.O.M., 1888, No. 1, pp. 10–11: Joaquim Carlos Paiva d'Andrada to Conselheiro Governador da Província de Moçambique, "Relatório," 27 October 1887; A.H.M., Fundo do Século XIX, Queli-

mane, Governo do Distrito: Manoel António de Souza to Commandante Militar da Villa de Senna, 6 January 1877).

100 A.H.U., Moç., Pasta 13: António Candido Pedroso Gamitto to S.M.T., 30 December 1854; A.H.M., Códice 442, F.E. 9, fols. 88–90: to Gov. do Distrito (unsigned, undated); A.H.U., Moç., Pasta 14: Vasco Guedes de Carvalho e Menezes to Ministro e Secretário de Estado dos Negócios da Marinha e Ultramar, 28 March 1856.

101 Interviews with Conrado Msussa Boroma and Alberto Vicente da Cruz; A.H.M., Códice 2–442, F.E. 9, fols. 48–49; D. J. Oliveira to Gov. de Quelimane e os Rios de Sena (undated); A.H.U., Moç., Pasta 14: Vasco Guedes de Carvalho e Menezes to Ministro e Secretário de Estado dos Negócios da Marinha e Ultramar, 28 March 1856; A.H.M., Fundo do Século XIX, Governo Geral, Cx. 20: José d'Almeida d'Avila to Secretário Geral do Governo Geral (undated); A.H.U., Códice 1456, fol. 56 (unsigned), 14 September 1881; Joaquim Carlos Paiva de Andrada, "Campanhas da Zambézia," *Boletim da Sociedade de Geografia de Lisboa* 7 (1887): 727–28; Botelho, *História Militar*, 2:189–90; Axelson, *Portugal and the Scramble*, p. 139.

102 Andrada, "Campanhas da Zambézia," pp. 727–28.

103 A.H.M., Fundo do Século XIX, Quelimane, Governo do Distrito, Cx. 13: Sebastião dos Anjos de Lima e Souza to Gov. do Distrito, 16 September 1892; Axelson, *Portugal and the Scramble*, p. 139; A.H.U., Moç., Pasta 4, Primeira Repartição: Augusto de Castilho to Ministro e Secretário d'Estado dos Negócios da Marinha e Ultramar, 7 July 1888; A.H.M., Fundo do Século XIX, Governo Geral, Cx. 11: Carlos Pedro Barahona e Costa to Secretário do Governo Geral da Província, 4 September 1874; A.H.M., Fundo do Século XIX, Cx. 127, Tete, Governo do Distrito: Jozé Luíz to Gov. do Distrito de Tete, 17 July 1885.

104 Interviews with Conrado Msussa Boroma, João Vicente, Chale Lupia, and Niquicicafe Presente.

105 *B.O.M.*, 1888, No. 1, pp. 9–10: Joaquim Carlos Paiva d'Andrada to Conselheiro Governador da Província de Moçambique, "Relatório," 27 October 1887; A.H.U., Moç., Pasta 4, Primeira Repartição: Augusto de Castilho to Ministro e Secretário d'Estado dos Negócios da Marinha e Ultramar, 7 July 1888; A.H.M., Fundo do Século XIX, Governo Geral, Cx. 11: João Feijão Teixeira to Gov. do Distrito de Tete, 27 December 1891; Axelson, *Portugal and the Scramble*, p. 141.

106 A.H.U., Moç., Pasta 19: António Vicente da Cruz, 14 June 1862, enclosed in a letter from João Tavares de Almeida to Ministro e Secretário de Estado dos Negócios da Marinha e Ultramar, 22 July 1862; Livingstones, *Narrative of an Expedition to the Zambesi*, p. 43.

107 A.H.U., Códice 1463, fols. 77–78: Joaquim d'Azévedo Alpoim to Vasco Guedes de Carvalho e Menezes, 1 April 1856.

108 A.H.M., Fundo do Século XIX, Governo Geral, Cx. 2.37: C. J. da Silva to Jozé Pereira d'Almeida, 27 November 1858; A.H.M., Fundo do Século

XIX, Governo Geral, Cx. 11: António d'Almeida to Secretário Geral Interno, 16 August 1863.

109 Eça, *História das Guerras*, 2:72.

110 For a detailed description see Botelho, *História Militar*, vol. 2.

111 A.H.U., Moç., Pasta 28: "Extracto da Correspondência do Governador de Moçambique o Conselheiro José Rodrigues Coelho do Amaral, desde a sua chegada a aquella Província em 24 Augusto de 1870 até ao seu fallecimento em 10 Dezembro 1873," 25 March 1874; A.H.M., Fundo do Século XIX, Governo Geral, Cx. 11: Theodório Francisco Dias to Gov., 12 February 1874; Fernandes, Júnior, "Narração," pp. 11–12; Pinheiro Chagas, *As Colónias Portuguesas no Século XIX* (Lisbon, 1890), pp. 167–69; Oliveira, *A Província de Moçambique*, pp. 15, 22; Eça, *História das Guerras*, vol. 2; Botelho, *História Militar*, vol. 2; Castilho, *Relatório da Guerra*; Ferreira, *Recordações da Expedição*.

112 M. D. D. Newitt and P. S. Garlake, "The Aringa at Massangano," *Journal of African History* 8 (1967): 142.

113 A.H.M., Fundo do Século XIX, Governo Geral, Cx. 20: José Joaquim Maria Cabral to Secretário do Governo Geral, 28 September 1868; Eça, *História das Guerras*, 2:311; Botelho, *História Militar*, 2:212. Some confusion remains as to the date of Bonga's death; according to official records he died on September 27, 1879.

114 A.H.M., Fundo do Século XIX, Governo Geral, Cx. 11: Luíz Inácio e João Martins to Gov. do Distrito de Tete, 7 March 1833 (copy included in a letter from José Augusto Pimenta de Miranda to Secretário Geral do Governo Geral da Província, 21 March 1883); A.H.M., Fundo do Século XIX, Governo Geral, Cx. 11: José Augusto Pimenta de Miranda to Commandante Militar da Villa de Sena, 2 March 1883 (copy enclosed in a letter from José Augusto Pimenta de Miranda to Secretário Geral do Governo Geral, 2 March 1883); A.H.M., Fundo do Século XIX, Governo de Tete, Cx. 127: Jozé Luíz to Governador do Distrito de Tete (undated); B.O.M., 1888, No. 1, p. 10: Joaquim Carlos Paiva d'Andrada to Conselheiro Governador da Província de Moçambique, "Relatório," 27 October 1888.

115 Castilho, *Relatório da Guerra*, p. 37.

116 A.H.M., Fundo do Século XIX, Quelimane, Governo do Distrito, Cx 5: Francisco Maria de Machado to Gov. de Quelimane, 23 September 1887; A.H.M., Fundo do Século XIX, Governo Geral, Cx. 11: Augusto Cesar de Oliveira Gomes to Secretário Geral, 5 October 1887; B.O.M., 1887, No. 42, p. 476: Francisco António Dulio Ribeiro *et al.*, 16 September 1887, "Auto da entrega da aringa do Bonga em Massangano ao governador do distrito de Tete"; B.O.M., 1888, No. 1, pp. 10–11: Joaquim Carlos Paiva d'Andrada to Conselheiro Governador da Província de Moçambique, "Relatório," 27 October 1887. For a complete account of the confrontation see Castilho, *Relatório da Guerra*.

117 A.H.M., Fundo do Século XIX, Governo Geral, Cx. 20: Gonçalo Duarte to Secretário do Governo Geral, 28 June 1888; Axelson, *Portugal and*

the Scramble, p. 143; A.H.M., Fundo do Século XIX, Tete, Governo do Distrito, Cx. 124: Farquino Sérgio d'Aguia Mendes (undated); A.H.M. Fundo do Século XIX, Governo Geral, Cx. 11: Augusto Cesar de Oliveira Gomes to Conselheiro Governador Geral da Província, 21 September 1888; A.H.M., Fundo do Século XIX, Quelimane, Governo do Distrito, Cx. 13: Sebastião dos Anjos de Lima e Souza to Gov. do Distrito de Quelimane, 28 August 1892; A.H.M., Fundo do Século XIX, Governo Geral, Cx. 11: Augusto Cesar de Oliveira Gomes to Chefe da Repartição Militar, 9 August 1888.

118 Botelho, *História Militar,* p. 242; A.H.M., Fundo do Século XIX, Governo Geral, Cx. 20: Gonçalo Duarte to Governador Geral, 24 June 1888.

119 A.H.M., Fundo do Século XIX, Quelimane, Governo do Distrito, Cx. 13: Sebastião dos Anjos de Lima e Souza to Gov. do Distrito, 16 September 1892.

120 Ibid.

121 Ibid.

122 The principal members of the Ferrão family were Anselmo and Henriques. They were the dominant prazero family in the Sena district prior to the arrival of Gouveia. Inácio de Jesús Xavier was also a mestizo prazero who was appointed capitão-môr of Chicoa and conquered much of the area north of Tete for Lisbon. His African appellation was Cariza-Mimba.

123 João de Azévedo Coutinho, *Manuel António de Sousa: Um Capitão-môr da Zambézia* (Lisbon, 1936), p. 12; Tabler, ed., *Zambesi Papers of Thorton,* 2:269–70; Fernandes, Júnior, "Narração," pp. 24–25; A.H.U., Códice 1760, fol. 57: Guilherme Frederico de Portugal e Vasconsellos to Secretário do Governo Geral, 18 August 1864; interviews with Gimo Tito and João Pomba.

Among the prazos which he legally controlled were Chemba, Sonne, Tambara, Gorongoza, and Inarupundo. In addition he exerted indirect influence over a number of chieftaincies in the Sena-Gorongoza zone which had formerly been part of the prazo system (A.H.U., Códice 1462, fol. 51: Custódio José da Silva to José Maria Pereira de Almeida, 1 September 1860; A.H.U., Moç., Pasta 26: Tomáz de Aquino to Gov. do Distrito de Quelimane, 1 September 1868; A.H.U., Códice 1460, fol. 16: A. M. da Silva Valente to Commandante Militar de Sena, 12 February 1877; Tabler, ed., *Zambesi Papers of Thornton,* 1:191; Coutinho, *Manuel António de Sousa,* p. 12; R. C. F. Maugham, *Zambezia* (London, 1910), p. 139.

124 Interviews with Gimo Tito, Renço Cado, Lole Nhanticole, João Pomba, and D. Anna Mascalenha Costa.

125 Ibid.

126 Interviews with Gimo Tito and João Pomba; Coutinho, *Manuel António de Sousa,* p. 13.

127 Coutinho, *Manuel António de Sousa,* pp. 15–16; A.H.U., Códice 1458, fol. 60: Manoel d'Almeida Coelho to Commandante Militar de Sena,

17 March 1875; A.H.U., Códice 1455, fol. 85: M. V. Guedes Bacellar to Secretário Geral, 12 October 1876; A.H.U., Moç., Pasta 30: José Guedes de Carvalho e Menezes to Ministro e Secretário de Estado dos Negócios da Marinha e Ultramar, 29 October 1876; A.H.U., Códice 1460, fol. 59: António Maria da Silva Valente to Commandante Militar de Sena, 17 October 1877; A.H.U., Códice 1464, fol. 123: João José d'Almeida Pirão to Capitão-môr de Manica e Quiteve, 28 August 1884.

128 Coutinho, *Manuel António de Sousa*, p. 12.

129 Interview with Joaquim Anseni Saíca; A.H.U., Moç., Pasta 1, Primeira Repartição: Visconde de Paço d'Arco to Ministro e Secretário d'Estado dos Negócios da Marinha e Ultramar, 3 December 1881; Maugham, *Zambezia*, pp. 140–41; Coutinho, *Manuel António de Sousa*, p. 12.

130 A.H.U., Moç., Pasta 1, Primeira Repartição: Visconde de Paço d'Arco to Ministro e Secretário d'Estado dos Negócios da Marinha e Ultramar, 3 December 1881.

131 Ibid.

132 A.H.U., Moç., Pasta 2, Primeira Repartição: Augusto de Castilho, "Instruções para o Snr. Governador do Distrito de Manica Carlos Maria de Souza Fereira Simões, Major de Cavalaria," 17 March 1887.

133 Ibid.

134 Maugham, *Zambezia*, pp. 242–43; Coutinho, *Manuel António de Sousa*, p. 29.

135 Interview with António Vas; Joaquim Mousinho de Albuquerque, *Moçambique 1896–1898* (Lisbon, 1913), p. 152.

136 M. D. D. Newitt, "The Portuguese on the Zambesi," p. 85.

137 Personal communication from Professor Philip D. Curtin, 3 January 1970. Among the best known were the states forged by Rabeh, Samori, Msiri, and Menelik.

POSTSCRIPT: TRANSFORMATION OF THE PRAZOS

1 *Decretos* and *portarias* were passed in 1832, 1838, 1841, 1854, and 1880 either abolishing the prazos or declaring that no new aforamentos should be issued.

2 *B.O.M.*, 1888, No. 42, p. 630: "Relatório de Quelimane referido ao anno económico de 1887–1888," João Manoel Guerreiro d'Amorim, 15 September 1888.

The best example of the small group of new prazeros in the prescramble period is João António Correa Pereira. He was born in Portugal in 1840 and migrated to Mozambique in 1853 where he spent a good portion of his early adulthood in the Zambesi interior. In 1873 he received an aforamento for Prazo Mahindo located in Quelimane. Within ten years Prazo Mahindo had been transformed into a modern agricultural company complete with the newest imported equipment. The principal products grown were coconut, cotton, cereals, and sugar cane.

See A.H.M., Fundo do Século XIX, Governo Geral, Cx. 2: Governador de Quelimane to Secretário Geral do Governo, 4 February 1886; and João Correa Pereira, *João Correa: Colono Zambeziano* (Porto, 1952).

3 Sousa Ribeiro, ed., *Regimen dos Prazos Da Coroâ, 1832–1906* (Lourenço Marques, 1907), pp. 32–39.

4 Ibid., pp. 211–24.

5 A.H.M., Fundo Do Século XIX, Quelimane, Prazos da Coroâ, Cx. 5 (2): Gorjão de Moura, "Inspecção dos Prazos da Coroâ, Relátorio," April 1894.

6 A.H.M., Fundo do Século XIX, Quelimane, Governo do Distrito, Cx. 43: António Maria de Souza Ennes (undated).

7 A.H.M., Fundo do Século XIX, Quelimane, Governo do Distrito, Cx. 45: Eugénio Pimentas d'Albuquerque, 10 March 1877; A.H.M., Fundo do Século XIX, Quelimane, Governo do Distrito, Cx. 45: Jozé Albuquerque to Gov. de Quelimane, 18 April 1877; A.H.M., Fundo do Século XIX, Quelimane, Prazos da Coroâ, Cx. 6 (5G): José Bernardo d'Albuquerque, "Mappa demonstrativa dos distritos de que sa compôe o praso . . . com designação dos nomes dos . . . Moçambos, Samaçoas e Sangiras," 4 June 1877; A.H.M., Fundo do Século XIX, Quelimane, Governo do Distrito, Cx. 45: Joaquim Xavier da Cunha to Gov. do Distrito de Quelimane, 20 April 1887; A.H.M., Fundo do Século XIX, Quelimane, Governo do Distrito, Cx. 46 (6): Joaquim Augusto Maija to Governador deste distrito, 28 March 1878; A.H.M., Fundo do Século XIX, Quelimane, Prazos da Coroâ, Cx. 6 (28): "Projecto de regulamento para a administração do praso Angoase," (unsigned) 9 November 1886; A.H.M., Fundo do Século XIX, Quelimane, Governo do Distrito, Cx. 45 (2): Raphael de Mello Amaral to Secretário do Governo do Distrito de Quelimane, 23 November 1887; A.H.M., Fundo do Século XIX, Quelimane, Governo do Distrito, Cx. 45: Thadeu Jozé da Silva to Governador do Distrito, 19 April 1890; A.H.M., Fundo do Século XIX, Quelimane, Governo do Distrito, Cx. 45: José da Silva Pimenta to Inspector Geral dos Prazos, 28 January 1893; A.H.M., Fundo do Século XIX, Quelimane, Governo do Distrito, Cx. 45: José da Silva Pimenta to Inspector Geral dos Prazos, 20 January 1893; A.H.M., Fundo do Século XIX, Quelimane, Governo do Distrito, Cx. 45: Manoel Joaquim António de Sousa, 17 October 1896; A.H.M., Fundo do Século XIX, Quelimane, Governo do Distrito, Cx. 44 (2): Romão de Jesús Maria to Gov. do Distrito da Zambézia, 8 June 1896; A.H.M., Fundo do Século XIX, Quelimane, Governo do Distrito, Cx. 45: António Maria de Souza Ennes (undated).

8 A.H.M., Fundo do Século XIX, Quelimane, Prazos da Coroâ, Cx. 6 (28): "Projecto de regulamento para a administração do praso Angoase," 9 November 1886; A.H.M., Fundo do Século XIX, Tete, Governo do Distrito, Cx. 107: Eustáchio da Costa to Gov. do Distrito de Tete, 6 September 1892; A.H.M., Fundo do Século XIX, Quelimane, Governo do Distrito, Cx. 15: Sebastião dos Anjos de Lima e Souza, "Relação dos

grandes do praso Massingire que em 5 de corrente receberam saquate," 30 September 1893; A.H.M., Fundo do Século XIX, Quelimane, Governo do Distrito, Cx. 45: Leandro António de Rego to Governador do Distrito, 29 January 1897; M. Henry Seyrig, *Rapport Sur La Situation Actuelle et L'Avenir Possible du Prazo de Gorongoza* (Lisbon, 1897), p. 15.

9 Albano Augusto de Portugal Durão, "Considerações sobre a Zambézia," *Congresso Colonial Nacional* (Lisbon, 1903), p. 9; A.H.U., Códice 1415, fol. 164: António Maria Cardosa to Secretário do Gov. Geral, 18 February 1879.

The principal Portuguese companies were Companhia de Moçambique and Companhia da Zambézia. The major foreign firms were Sena Sugar (English), Companhia de Bororo (German) and Societé du Madal (French).

10 A.H.M., Fundo do Século XIX, Quelimane, Governo do Distrito, Cx. 43 (2): Raphael de Mello Amaral to Inspector Geral dos Prazos da Corôa, 7 December 1893; A.H.M., Fundo do Século XIX, Quelimane, Prazos da Corôa, Cx. 5 (2): Gorjão de Moura, "Inspecção Geral dos Prazos da Corôa, Relatório," April 1894; Durão, "Considerações sobre a Zambézia," p. 9; Correa Pereira, *João Correa*, pp. 14–17; Ernesto Jardim de Vilhena, *O Regime do Prazos da Zambézia* (Lisbon, 1916), pp. 9–10.

11 A.H.M., Fundo do Século XIX, Quelimane, Governo do Distrito, Cx. 45: Jozé da Silva Pimenta to Inspector Geral dos Prazos, 14 March 1893; A.H.M., Fundo do Século XIX, Quelimane, Governo do Distrito, Cx. 45: Jozé da Silva Pimenta to Gov. do Distrito de Quelimane, 22 June 1893; A.H.M., Fundo do Século XIX, Governo do Distrito, Quelimane, Cx. 45: Leandro António de Rego, 1897; A.H.U., Códice 1454, fols. 12–13: José Maria de Magalhaes to Secretário Geral, 20 February 1872; B.O.M., 1880, No. 42, p. 633: João Manoel Guerreiro d'Amorin, "Relátorio do Distrito de Quelimane referido ao anno económico de 1887–1888," 15 September 1888; J. Mousinho de Albuquerque, *Moçambique 1896–98* (Lisbon, 1913), pp. 121–22; Vilhena, *Regimen dos Prazos*, p. 29; A.H.M., Fundo do Século XIX, Quelimane, Prazos da Corôa, Cx. 5 (1): Henrique Cezar da Costa, "Relatório do Anno de 1895" (undated); Seyrig, *Rapport*, p. 12.

12 Ernesto Vilhena, *Questões Coloniaes* (Lisbon, 1910), p. 539.

13 Ruy Ennes Ulrich, *Economia Colonial* (Coimbra, 1910), pp. 382–89; Vilhena, *Regimen dos Prazos*, pp. 10–11; A. Freire de Andrade, *Relatório Sobre Moçambique* (Lourenço Marques, 1907), p. 165; R. J. Hammond, *Portugal and Africa 1815–1910* (Stanford, 1966), p. 162.

In his classic defense of the prazos Albuquerque wrote: "Os abusos dos arrendatários nem têem a importância que muitos lhe querem dar, num constituem só por si um argumento contra o arrendamento dos prazos. Do momento em que uma raça extranha conquista e domina um paíz já povoado por uma raça tão inferior como a negra, é bem natural que haja um ou outro abuso, porque nem todos os indivíduos sabem cohibir-se na defeza dos seus interesses (Albuquerque, *Moçambique 1896–1898*, p. 122).

"The abuses which the renters committed neither carry the importance which many ascribe to them, nor constitute a valid argument aginst renting the prazos. From the moment that an alien race conquers and dominates a country populated by a race as inferior as the negro, it is inevitable that some abuses will occur . . . ." He concluded that this was a necessary price if Mozambique was to modernize.

14 *B.O.M.*, 1886, No. 45, p. 549: Manoel Rodrigues Pereira de Carvalho, 15 October 1866, "Relatório de uma viagem á Zambézia interior"; A.H.M., Fundo do Século XX, Pacote 151, Pasta 698: Alfredo Augusto da Silva to Secretário do Governo do Distrito da Zambézia, 25 December 1913; A.H.M., Fundo do Século XIX, Quelimane, Prazos da Corôa, Cx. 5 (2): Manuel Monteiro Lopes (sub-inspector), "Relatório relativo ao anno de 1895" (undated); A.H.M., Fundo do Século XIX, Governo Geral, Cx. 1 (unsigned, undated); Albuquerque, *Moçambique 1896–1898*, pp. 122–24; Ulrich, *Economia Colonial*, p. 345.

15 A.H.U., Moç., Pasta 31: António Maria da Silva Valente to Secretário Geral, 5 September 1877 (enclosed in a letter from Francisco Maria de Carvalho to Ministro e Secretário de Estado dos Negócios da Marinha e Ultramar, 4 October 1877); A.H.M., Fundo do Século XIX, Governo Geral, Cx. 11: Angelo Ferreira to Gov. de Tete, 22 February 1881; A.H.M., Fundo do Século XIX, Quelimane, Governo do Distrito, Cx. 45: José Silvestre Correira to Gov. do Distrito, 20 November 1893; A.H.M., Fundo do Século XIX, Quelimane, Governo do Distrito, Cx. 43: António Balthazar Farinha to Governador do Distrito de Tete, 18 January 1894; Ulrich, *Economia Colonial*, pp. 352–59.

16 A.H.M., Fundo do Século XIX, Governo Geral, Cx. 11: Inácio de Jesús Xavier to Gov. de Tete, 28 May 1884; A.H.M., Fundo do Século XIX, Quelimane, Governo do Distrito, Cx. 44 (1): Caetano Piedade de Souza to Gov. d'este Distrito, 3 January 1886; A.H.M., Fundo do Século XIX, Governo Geral, Cx. 20: Inspector Syndicante Henrique Lima to Governador de Quelimane, 4 December 1886; A.H.M., Fundo do Século XIX, Quelimane, Governo do Distrito, Cx. 43 (2): José Balthazar Farinha to Governador do Distrito de Quelimane, 18 January 1887; A.H.M., Fundo do Século XIX, Tete, Governo do Distrito, Cx. 189: Charles Achilles Chastings to Governador do Distrito de Tete, May 1889; A.H.M., Fundo do Século XIX, Tete, Governo do Distrito, Cx. 109: José Machado to Governador do Distrito de Tete, 1 August 1892; Francisco de Aragão e Mello, *Relatório da Inspecção A Alguns Dos Prazos do Districto de Tete* (Lourenço Marques, 1911), p. 23; Ulrich, *Economia Colonial*, pp. 352–59.

17 A.H.U., Moç., Pasta 31: Francisco Maria de Azévedo to Ministro e Secretário d'Estado dos Negócios da Marinha e Ultramar, 24 October 1878; A.H.U., Códice 1455, fol. 169: António Maria Cardoso to Secretário do Governo Geral, 21 February 1879; A.H.U., Fundo do Século

XIX, Governo Geral, Cx. 11: Inácio de Jesús Xavier to Gov. de Tete, 24 May 1884; A.H.M., Fundo do Século XIX, Governo Geral, Cx. 20: João Manoel Guerreiro d'Amorim to Secretário Geral, 4 January 1887; A.H.M., Fundo do Século XIX, Governo Geral, Cx. 11: Francisco Maria de Magalhão to Secretário do Governo de Tete, 11 December 1891; A.H.M., Fundo do Século XIX, Tete, Governo do Distrito, Cx. 20: José Gurado de Campos to Gov. do Distrito de Tete, 2 July 1891; A.H.M., Fundo do Século XIX, Quelimane, Governo do Distrito, Cx. 43 (1): Francisco Manoel Correa (undated); A.H.M., Fundo do Século XIX, Quelimane, Governo do Distrito, Cx. 43: Eigenmann E. Pereira to Gov. de Quelimane, 7 January 1898; A.H.M., Fundo do Século XIX, Quelimane, Governo do Distrito, Cx. 43: António Balthazar Farinha to Gov. da Zambézia, 19 July 1894; A.H.M., Fundo do Século XIX, Quelimane, Governo do Distrito, Cx. 44: Caetano Piedade de Souza to Secretário do Governo da Zambézia, 18 August 1898.

18 A.H.M., Fundo do Século XIX, Quelimane, Governo do Distrito, Cx. 43: Eigenmann E. Pereira to Governador de Quelimane, 7 January 1898.

19 A.H.M., Fundo do Século XIX, Quelimane, Governo do Distrito, Cx. 45 (1) (unsigned) 1892; A.H.M., Fundo do Século XIX, Quelimane, Governo do Distrito: Raphael de Mello Amaral to Secretário do Governo, 18 February 1892; A.H.M., Fundo do Século XIX, Quelimane, Governo do Distrito, Cx. 43: António Balthazar Farinha to Gov. da Zambézia, 19 July 1894; A.H.M., Fundo do Século XIX, Quelimane, Governo do Distrito, Cx. 43 (1): Francisco Manoel Correa (undated); A.H.M., Fundo do Século XIX, Quelimane, Governo do Distrito, Cx. 43: Eigenmann E. Pereira to Gov. de Quelimane, 7 January 1898.

20 Pedro A. Álvares, *O Regime dos Prazos da Zambézia* (Lisbon, 1916), pp. 45–46.

APPENDIX B: HISTORIOGRAPHICAL NOTE
ON THE PRAZOS

1 Manuel Barretto, "Informação do Estado e Conquista dos Rios de Cuama, 1667," in *Records of South-East Africa*, ed. G. M. Theal (Capetown, 1899), 3:468.

Bibliography

ORAL DATA

A copy of these tapes will be deposited in the A.S.A. oral data archives housed in the Archive of Traditional Music, Indiana University, Bloomington, Indiana.

Region of Tete

BOROMA

Gaspar Cardoso, interview July 15, July 17, July 18, 1968. Translated Tape #2, Side 1 [T.T. #2(1)], T.T. #2(2), T.T. #3(1); Edited Tape #3, Side 1 [E.T. #3(1)], E.T. #3(2).
Aleixo José, interview July 16, 1968. T.T. #1(1); E.T. #1(1).
Pedro Damião Chamualira, intervew July 17, July 25, 1968. T.T. #2(1), T.T. #4(2); E.T. #1(2), and E.T. #3(1).
Luís Gonzaga Cebola, interview July 18, 1968. T.T. #1(1); E.T. #1(1).
João Cristóstomo, interview July 18, July 25, 1968, T.T. #1(1), T.T.#4(1), T.T. #4(2); E.T. #1(1), E.T. #1(2), E.T. #2(2).
Luciano Camilo, interview July 25, 1968. T.T. #4(1); E.T. #2(2).
Conrado Msussa Boroma, interview July 28, Aug. 17, Aug. 20, September 29, 1968. T.T. #5(1), T.T. #5(2), T.T. #6(1), T.T. #6(2), T.T. #6a(1), T.T. #6a(2); E.T. #3(2), E.T. #4(1), E.T. #4(2).

VILLAGE OF TETE

José António de Abreu, interview July 16, July 22, 1968. T.T. #3(1), T.T. #3(2).
José da Costa Xavier, interview July 22, 1968. T.T. #7(1).

DEGUE

Marco Coutinho, interview July 23, 1968. T.T. #3(2), T.T. #4(1); E.T. #2(1).

Khaliche António Camundi, interview July 26, 1968. T.T. #4(1); E.T. #1(2), E.T. #2(1).

Sete Marqueza, interview July 27, 1968. T.T. #4(2), T.T. #5(1); E.T. #3(2).

CHIOCO

João Alfai, interview July 26, 1968. T.T. #7(2).

Region of Massangano

João Vicente, interview Sept. 26, 1968. T.T. #13(1); E.T. #9(2).

Domingo Kunga, interview Sept. 27, 1968. T.T. #13(1); E.T. #9(2).

António Gavião, interview Sept. 27, 1968; T.T. #13(1), T.T. #13(2); E.T. #10(1).

Chacundunga Mavico, interview Sept. 27, 1968. T.T. #13(2); E.T. #10(2).

Chale Lupia, interview Sept. 28, 1968. T.T. #13(2); E.T. #10(1).

Niquicicafe Presente, interview Sept. 28, 1968. T.T. #13(2); E.T. #10(1), E.T. #10(2).

Alberto Vicente da Cruz, interview Oct. 13, 1968. T.T. #16(2).

Region of Sena

SENA

Jasse Camalizene, interview on Aug. 6, 1968. T.T. #8(1); E.T. #5(1).

Mozesse Domingos, interview Aug. 6, 1968. T.T. #8(1); E.T. #5(1).

Mortar Nhacalazi, interview Aug. 7, 1968. T.T. #9(1); E.T. #5(2).

Gonçalves Chibante, interview Aug. 8, 1968. T.T. #9(2); E.T. #5(2).

Botão Ganunga, interview Aug. 8, 1968. T.T. #8(2), T.T. #9(1); E.T. #6(1).

Gimo Tito, interview Aug. 9, 1968. T.T. #8(2); E.T. #5(1), E.T. #5(2).

Esmail Mussa Valy, interview Aug. 10, 1968. Untaped.

Quembo Gogo, interview Aug. 11, 1968. Untaped.

CHEMBA

Renço Cado, interview Aug. 13, 1968. T.T. #9(1), T.T. #9(2); E.T. #6(1).

Tomás Chave and Oliveira Sinto, joint interview Aug. 14, 1968. T.T. #9(2); E.T. #6(2).

Lole Nhanticole, interview Aug. 26, 1968. T.T. #10(1), T.T. #10(2); E.T. #7(1).

Sete Catondo, interview Aug. 26, 1968. Untaped.

Simões Zindo, interview Aug. 27, 1968. Untaped.

António Vas, interview Sept. 13, 1968. T.T. #12(2); E.T. #9(1), E.T. #9(2).

Guiraza Passo, interview* Oct. 10, 1969. Untaped.

Bruto Sabão, interview* on Oct. 10, 1969. Untaped.

Quembo Passalampapi, interview* Oct. 10, 1969. Untaped.

Carlota Checanhanza, interview* Oct. 10, 1969. Untaped.

CAYA

João Pomba, interview Aug. 31, 1968. T.T. #10(1); E.T. #7(2).

Aleixo Jasere and José Gunda, joint interview Sept. 1, 1968. T.T. #10(1); E.T. #8(1).

Tomás Zimbaue, interview Sept. 2, 1968. T.T. #10(2); E.T. #8(1).

Zacarias Ferrão, interview Sept. 2, 1968. T.T. #11(1), T.T. #11(2).

Dauce Angolete Gogodo, interview Sept. 3, 1968. T.T. #10(2); E.T. #8(2).

Gente Renço and Quembo Pangacha, interview Sept. 4, 1968. T.T. #10(2), T.T. #11(1); E.T. #8(1).

Joaquim Anseni Saíca, interview Sept. 4, 1968. T.T. #11(2).

D. Anna Mascalenha Costa, interview Sept. 9, 1968. Untaped.

CHERINGOMA

José António, interview Sept. 7, 1968. T.T. #12(1); E.T. #8(2).

Chale Penga, Tomás Chambe, and Jamusse Guede, joint interview Sept. 7, 1968. T.T. #12(1); E.T. #8(2).

Andisseni Tesoura; interview Sept. 8, 1968. T.T. #12(2); E.T. #9(1).

Alface Pangacha, interview Sept. 9, 1968. T.T. #11(2), T.T. #12(1).

Region of Makanga

Malisseni Máuo, interview Oct. 9, 1968. T.T. #15(1); E.T. #10(2).

Simon Biwi, interview Oct. 10, 1968. T.T. #14(2); E.T. #10(1).

Capachika Chúau, interview Oct. 10, 1968. T.T. #14(1), T.T. #14(2); E.T. #10(2).

Chaparira Muiessa, interview Oct. 12, 1968. T.T. #15(1); E.T. #10(2).

Calavina Couche and Zabuca Ngombe, joint interview Oct. 14, 1968. T.T. #15(1), T.T. #15(2); E.T. #11(2).

Chetambara Chenungo and Wilson John, joint interview Oct. 15, 1968. T.T. #15(2); E.T. #11(2).

Chiponda Cavumbula, interview Oct. 16, 1968. T.T. #15(2), T.T. #16(1); E.T. #11(2), E.T. #12(1).

° Interviews collected by Jamusse Joaquim Fernandes of Chemba. They deal with questions relating primarily to the social system and to religious ceremonies.

Leão Manuel Banqueiro Caetano Pereira, interview Oct. 17, 1968. T.T. #16(1); E.T. #12(1).
Domingo Fernandes, interview Oct. 18, 1968. Untaped.

Region of Luabo

Avaringa Avarinho, interview Nov. 11, 1968. Original tape #46.
Jaime Casenga and Jorge Nhasambo, joint interview Nov. 12, 1968. Original tape #47.
António Anselmo Almeida and Inácio Petrino, joint interview Nov. 13, 1968. Original tape #48.

MANUSCRIPTS IN ARCHIVES

England

Public Record Office
   FO 84/17, 84/24, 84/31, 84/42, 84/55, 84/71, 84/84, 84/95, 84/112, 84/122

Portugal

Academia das Ciências de Lisboa
   MS 648 Azul
Ajuda, Biblioteca Pública da
   51–VI–24–29
   51–VIII–40
   52–X–2, No. 3
   52–X–2, No. 7
   52–X–2, No. 8
Arquivo Histórico Ultramarino
   Moçambique, Caixas 1–77 (1608–1826)
   Moçambique, Maços 1–38 (1739–1832)
   Moçambique, Pastas 1–32 (1834–1881)
   Moçambique, Primeira Repartição, Pastas 1–4 (1879–1888)
   Moçambique, Segunda Repartição, Pastas 1–3 (1883–1888)
   Códices 1306, 1314, 1315, 1326, 1332, 1333, 1336, 1346, 1358, 1363, 1368, 1381, 1406, 1414, 1422, 1436, 1439, 1446, 1450, 1451, 1452, 1453, 1454, 1455, 1456, 1457, 1458, 1459, 1460, 1462, 1463, 1464, 1468, 1469, 1470, 1473, 1477, 1480, 1489, 1703, 1755, 1756, 1757, 1758, 1759, 1760, 1761
Arquivo Nacional da Torre do Tombo
   Ministério do Reino, Maços 603, 604 (1750–1779)
Biblioteca Nacional de Lisboa
   Colleção Pombalina 721
   Fundo Geral 826

Mozambique

Arquivo Histórico de Moçambique
  Fundo do Século XVIII
  Fundo do Século XIX, Quelimane, Governo do Distrito, Caixas 1, 4–16, 31, 34–35, 43–47
  Fundo do Século XIX, Tete, Governo do Distrito, Caixas 1–2, 4, 6–9, 11–15, 18, 22–28, 35–42, 45–48, 58, 66, 78–79, 93, 107–114, 118–19, 123–25, 127, 129, 134, 146, 161, 163, 165, 174, 188–91, 196, 210–13
  Fundo do Século XIX, Tete, Comando Militar, Caixas 1–15
  Fundo do Século XIX, Governo Geral, Caixas 2.37, 8, 11, 13
  Fundo do Século XIX, Arquivo do Governo Geral, Caixas S. 2 Nd. 1, S.2 Nd. 4, S.2 Nd. 9, S.2 Oa. 1, 1–A–Nd. 2.
  Códices 21–168, G.F.4; 2–266, F.D.3; 2–437, F.E.6; 2–438, F.D.6; 2–439 F.E.5; 2–440, F.D.9; 2–441, F.E.9; 2–442, F.E.9; 2–443 F.E.7; 2–446, F.E.2; 2–819, M.B.7; 2–1160, F.F.7; 2–1167, F.F.1; 2–1482, G.B.7; 2–1530, G.B.12; 2–1685, G.F.10; 2–1749, F.F.5; 2–1788, A.G.1; 2–1804, G.B.1.
Boletim Oficial de Moçambique

UNPUBLISHED MANUSCRIPTS

Alpers, Edward Alter. "The Malawi Empire and the Yao: Aspects of Trade as a Factor in the History of East Central Africa." Paper read at a conference on East Africa and the Orient in Nairobi, 1967. Mimeographed.
———. "The Role of the Yao in the Development of Trade in East Central Africa." Ph.D. dissertation, London School of Oriental and African Studies, 1966.
Fernandes, Júnior, José, "História de Undi." Paper, Makanga, n.d.
———. "Narração do Distrito de Tete." Paper, Makanga, 1955.
Isaacman, Allen. "Palmares: A Study of Withdrawal and Resistance." Seminar paper, University of Wisconsin, 1966.
Langworthy, Harry. "A History of Undi to 1890." Ph.D. dissertation, Boston University, 1969.
———. "The Political and Religious Elite in the History of Undi's Malawi Empire." Paper read at a conference on African history in Kampala, 1968. Mimeographed.
Newitt, M. D. D. "The Zambesi Prazos in the Eighteenth Century." Ph.D. dissertation, University of London, 1967.

PUBLISHED SOURCES

Abraham, D. P. "The Early Political History of the Mwene Mutapa (850–1589)." In *Historians in Tropical Africa*, Proceedings of the Levehulme

Inter-Collegiate History Conference, University College of Rhodesia and Nyasaland, pp. 61–92. Salisbury, 1962.

————. "Ethno-History of the Empire of Mutapa — Problems and Methods." In *Historian in Tropical Africa*, edited by Jan Vansina, pp. 104–121. London, 1964.

————. "Maramuca: An Exercise in the Combined Use of Portuguese Records and Oral Traditions." *Journal of African History* 2 (1961): 211–25.

————. "The Monomotapa Dynasty." *NADA* 36 (1959): 59–84.

————. "The Principality of Maungwe: Its History and Traditions." *NADA* 28 (1951): 56–83.

————. "The Role of Chaminuka and the Mhondoro-Cults in Shona Political History." In *The Zambesian Past*, edited by E. Stokes and R. Brown, pp. 28–46. London, 1966.

————. "Tasks in the Field of Early History." In *Conference on the History of the Central African Peoples*, Proceedings of the 17th Conference of the Rhodes-Livingstone Institute, pp. 1–6. Lusaka, 1963.

Alberto, Manoel Simões. "Elementos Para Um Vocabulário Ethnológico E Linguístico De Moçambique." In *Memórias do Instituto de Investigação Científica de Moçambique*, vol. 7, série C, pp. 135–70. 1965.

————. "O Império do Monomotapa e os aborígenes africanos." *Moçambique Documentário Trimestral* 15 (1938): 25–48.

————. *O Oriente África Portuguesa*. Lourenço Marques, 1942.

Albuquerque, Joaquim Mousinho de. *Moçambique 1896–1898*. Lisbon, 1913.

Almeida, António Tavares de. "Notícias do Districto de Tete." *Annais do Conselho Ultramarino, Parte não oficial*, pp. 71, 89–92. Lisbon, 1863.

————. "População e Produções na vila de Sena no ano de 1861." *Annais do Concelho Ultramarino, Parte não oficial*, pp. 101–2. Lisbon, 1863.

Almeida, João Tavares de. "Carta do Governador Geral de Moçambique ao Snr. Ministro e Secretário de Estado dos Negócios da Marinha e Ultramar, 7 de Agosto de 1863." *Arquivos das Colónias* 1 (1917): 100–102.

————. "Documentos Referentes á soberánia portugueza na Manica e Quiteve, 1863." *Arquivos das Colónias* 2 (1918): 99–105.

Alpers, Edward. "The Mutapa and Malawi Political System to the Time of the Ngoni Invasions." In *Aspects of Central African History*, edited by T. O. Ranger, pp. 1–28. London, 1968.

————. "North of the Zambeze." In *The Middle Ages of African History*, edited by Roland Oliver, pp. 78–84. Oxford, 1967.

Álvares, Pedro A. *O Regime dos Prazos da Zambézia*. Lisbon, 1916.

Alves, Pe. Albano Emílio. *Dicionário Português-Chisena e Chisena-Português*. Lisbon, 1930.

Andrada, Joaquim Carlos Paiva de. "Campanhas da Zambézia." *Boletim da Sociedade de Geografia de Lisboa* 7 (1887): 714–38.

Andrade, A. Freire de. *Relatório Sobre Moçambique*. Lourenço Marques, 1907.

Andrade, António Alberto de, ed. *Relações de Moçambique Setecentista*. Lisbon, 1955.

Andrade, Jerónimo José Nogueira de. "Descripção do Estado em que ficavam os Negócios da Capitania de Moçambique nos fins de Novembro do anno de 1789." *Arquivo das Colónias* 1–2 (1917–18): 75–96, 115–34, 166–84.

Aquina, Sister Mary. "A Sociological Interpretation of Sorcery and Witchcraft Beliefs Among the Karanga." *NADA* 9 (1968): 47–53.

————. "A Study of the Vatura Kinship System." *NADA* 37 (1960): 8–26.

Axelson, Eric. *Portugal and The Scramble for Africa*. Johannesburg, 1967.

————. *Portuguese in South-East Africa 1600–1700*. Johannesburg, 1960.

————. "Portuguese Settlement in the Interior of South East Africa in the Seventeenth Century." *Congresso Internacional de História dos Descombrimentos* 5 (Lisbon, 1961): 1–17.

————. *Southeast Africa, 1480–1530*. London, 1940.

————, ed. "Viagem que fez o Padre Antonio Gomes, da Companhia de Jesús, ao Império de se [*sic*] Monomotapa; e Assistência que fez nas ditas terras de algus annos." *Studia* 3 (1959): 155–242.

Baker, Robert H. "Portuguese Words in Chimanyika," *NADA* 24 (1947): 62–64.

Baptista, João Pedro. "Cópia da derrota que fez . . . ." In *Annaes Maritimos e Coloniaes*, pp. 165–90, 223–38. Lisbon, 1943.

————. "Lembrança da partida para a terra do Cazembe . . . ." In *Annaes Maritimos e Coloniaes*, pp. 426–39. Lisbon, 1943.

Baptista, João Pedro and Amaro, José. "Journey of the Pombeiros from Angola to the Rios de Senna." In *The Lands of Cazembe; Lacerda's Journey to Cazembe in 1798*, pp. 165–244. Translated by Richard Burton. London, 1873.

Barnard, Lt. R. N. *Three Years Cruise in the Mozambique Channel*. London, 1848.

Barretto, Manuel. "Informação do Estado e Conquista dos Rios de Cuama, 1667." In *Records of South-East Africa*, edited by G. M. Theal, vol. 3, pp. 436–95. Capetown, 1899.

Barros, João de. "Extract from Da Ásia." In *Records of South-East Africa*, edited by G. M. Theal, vol. 6, pp. 1–306. Capetown, 1900.

Biker, Júlio Firmino. *Judice Colleção de Tratados e concertos de pazes que o Estado da Índia Portugueza com os Reis e Senhores com quem teve relações nas partes da Ásia e África Oriental desde o princípio da conquista até ao fin do século XVIII*. 14 vols. Lisbon, 1881–87.

Bocarro, António. "Década da Índia." In *Records of South-East Africa*, edited by G. M. Theal, vol. 3, pp. 254–435. Capetown, 1899.

Boteler, Thomas. *Narrative of a Voyage of Discovery to Africa and Arabia, Performed in His Majesty's Ships Leven and Barracouta, from 1821–1826*. 2 vols. London, 1835.

Botelho, José Justino Texeira. *História Militar e Política dos Portugueses em Moçambique*. 2 vols. Lisbon, 1934.

Botelho, Sebastião Xavier. *Memória Estatística sobre Os Domínios Portu-guezes na África Oriental.* Lisbon, 1835.

————. *Segunda Parte da Memória Estatística sobre Os Domínios Portu-guezes na África Oriental.* Lisbon, 1837.

Bowdich, T. E. *An Account of the Discoveries in the Interior of Angola and Mozambique.* London, 1824.

Boxer, Charles Ralph. *Four Centuries of Portuguese Expansion, 1415–1825: A Succinct Survey.* Johannesburg, 1961.

————. "The Querimba Islands in 1744." *Studia* 11 (1963): 343–55.

————. *Race Relations in the Portuguese Colonial Empire 1415–1825.* Oxford, 1963.

————. "Sisnando Dias Bayão: Conquistadore do Mae D'Ouro." In *Primeiro Congresso da História da Expansão Portuguesa no Mundo* 3 (Lisbon, 1938): 101–114.

————, ed. "A Dominican Account of Zambésia in 1744." *Boletim da Socie-dade de Estudos de Moçambique* 29 (1960): 1–11.

Brendon, N. J. "Chiuzunu." *NADA* 36 (1959): 19–25.

Bruwer, J. P. "The Composition of a Cewa Village." *African Studies* 8 (1949): 191–98.

————. "Kinship Terminology Among the Cewa of the Eastern Province of Northern Rhodesia." *African Studies* 7 (1948): 185–87.

————. "Notes on the Maravi Origin and Migration." *African Studies* 9 (1950): 32–34.

————. "Remnants of a Rain Cult Among the Acewa." *African Studies* 11 (1952): 179–82.

Burton, R. F. *The Lake Regions of Central Africa.* London, 1860.

Buxton, Thomas Lowell. *The African Slave Trade.* London, 1839.

Cabral, António Augusto Pereira. *Racas, Usos e Costumes Dos Indígenas da Província de Moçambique.* Lourenço Marques, 1925.

Castilho, Augusto de. *Relatório de Guerra da Zambézia em 1888.* Lisbon, 1891.

Castro, Dionízio de Mello e. "Notícia do Império Marave e dos Rios de Sena, 20 de Janeiro de 1763." *Anais da Junta de Investigações do Ultra-mar* 9, tomo 1 (1954), pp. 119–49.

Castro, Francisco de Mello de. "Atrociadades Cometidas na Zambésia." *Arquivos das Colónias* 3 (1918): 120–25; 4 (1919): 120–24.

————. *Descripção dos Rios de Senna, Anno de 1750.* Lisbon, 1861.

Chagas, Pinheiro. *As Colónias Portuguezas no Século XIX.* Lisbon, 1890.

Chilcote, Ronald. *Portuguese Africa.* Englewood Cliffs, 1967.

Chinyandura. "The Tribes of Mambo." *NADA* 24 (1947): 73–75.

Cirne, Joaquim Mendes Vasconcelos e. *Memória Sobre a Província de Moçambique.* Lisbon, 1890.

Coissoro, Narana. "O Regime das Terras em Moçambique." In *Moçambi-que. Curso de Extensão Universitária, ano lectivo de 1964–65*, pp. 367–435. Lisbon, 1964.

Conceição, Frei António. "Tratados Dos Rios de Cuama." In *O Chronista de Tissaury Periódico*, edited by J. H. da Cunha Rivara, vol. 2, pp. 39–45, 63–69, 84–92, 105–111. Nova Goa, 1867.

Cooper, J. D. Omer. *The Zulu Aftermath: A Nineteenth Century Revolution in Bantu Africa*. Evanston, 1966.

Correa Pereira, João. *João Correa: Colono Zambeziano*. Porto, 1952.

Costa, Mário Júlio Brito de Almeida. *Origem da Enfiteuse no Direito Portugues*. Coimbra, 1957.

Coupland, R. *East Africa and Its Invaders*. Oxford, 1956.

Courtois, Padre Victor José. *Diccionário Cafre-Tetense-Portugues*. Coimbra, 1900.

———. *Notes Chronologiques sur les Anciennes Missions Catholiques au Zambesi*. Lisbon, 1889.

Coutinho, João de Azévedo. *A Companha do Barué em 1902*. Lisbon, 1904.

———. *Manuel António de Sousa: Um Capitão-môr da Zambézia*. Lisbon, 1936.

Cunnison, Ian G. *The Luapula Peoples of Northern Rhodesia*. Manchester, 1959.

Cunha, Joaquim d'Almeida da. *Estudo Ácêrca dos Usos e os Costumes dos Banianes, Bathias, Pares, Mouros, Gentios e Indígenas*. Lourenço Marques, 1885.

Decle, Lionel. *Three Years in Savage Africa*. London, 1898.

Dias, Carvalho. "Fontes para a História, Geografia e Commércio de Moçambique." *Anais da Junta de Investigações do Ultramar* 9, tomo 1, (1954), p. 11–14.

Dias, Margot. *Os Maganjas Da Costa*. Lisbo, 1965.

Documentos Sobre os Portugueses em Moçambique e na África Central 1497–1840. 5 vols. Lisbon, 1962–66.

Douglas, M. "Matriliny and Pawnship in Central Africa." *Africa* 34 (1964): 301–311.

Duffy, James. *Portuguese Africa*. Cambridge, 1961.

———. *A Question of Slavery*. Oxford, 1967.

Duly, A. W. R. "The Lower Shire: Notes on Land Tenure and Individual Rights." *Nyasaland Journal* 1 (1948): 11–44.

Durão, Albano Augusto de Portugal. "Considerações sobre a Zambézia." In *Congresso Colonial Nacional*. Lisbon, 1903.

Eça, Felipe Gastão de Almeida de. *História Das Guerras No Zambeze*. 2 vols. Lisbon, 1953–54.

Elton, J. Frederic. *Travels and Researches Among the Lakes and Mountains of Eastern and Central Africa*. London, 1879.

Ennes, Ernesto. *As Guerras Nos Palmares*. São Paulo, 1938.

Fagan, Brian. "Pre-European Ironworking in Central Africa with Special Reference to Northern Rhodesia." *Journal of African History* 2 (1961): 199–210.

———. *Southern Africa During the Iron Age*. New York, 1965.

Ferão. "Account of Portuguese Possessions Within the Captaincy of the Rios de Sena." In *Records of South-East Africa*, edited by G. M. Theal, vol. 7, pp. 371–86. Capetown, 1901.

Ferreira, José Joaquim. *Recordações Da Expedição da Zambézia em 1869*. Lisbon, 1891.

Figuerido, Luís António de. "Notícia do Continente de Moçambique e abreviada relação do seu comércio." *Anais da Junta da Investigações do Ultramar* 9, tomo 1 (1954), pp. 251–67.

Foà, Edouard. *Do Cap au Lac Nyassa*. Paris, 1901.

———. *La Traversée de l'Afrique, du Zambèze au Congo Francais*. Paris, 1900.

Gamitto, António Candido Pedroso. "Algumas Superstições de Rios de Sena." *Archivo Pittoresco* 1 (1857–58): 163.

———. "Colonisação da África Oriental." *Archivo Pittoresco* 1 (1857–58): 150–51.

———. "Escravatura na África Oriental." *Archivo Pittoresco* 2 (1859): 369–72, 397–400.

———. *King Kazembe*. Translated by Ian Cunnison. 2 vols. Lisbon, 1960.

———. "Povos Munhaes do Monomotapa." *Archivo Pittoresco* 1 (1857–58): 89–91.

———. "Prasos Da Corôa Em Rios De Sena." *Archivo Pittoresco* 1 (1857–58): 61–63, 66–67.

———. "Successão e Acclamação dos Reis de Barué." *Archivo Pittoresco* 1 (1857–58): 28–29.

Godinho, Manuel. *Relação Do Novo Caminho Que fez por Terra e Mar Vindo da Índia para Portugal no Anno de 1633*. Lisbon, 1842.

Gouveia, Miguel Augusto de. "Zambésia." In *Annais do Conselho Ultramarino, Parte não oficial*, pp. 92–98. Lisbon, 1868.

Guillain, M. *Documents sur l'Histoire, la Géographie, et la Commerce de l'Afrique Oriental*. 2 vols. Paris, 1856–58.

Guyot, Paul. *Voyage au Zambèse*. Nancy, 1889.

Haight, Mabel Jackson. *European Powers and South-East Africa*. London, 1967.

Hamilton, Alexander. *A New General Account of the East Indies*. London, 1727.

Hamilton, R. A. "Oral Tradition: Central Africa." In *History and Archeology in Africa*, edited by R. A. Hamilton, pp. 19–23. London, 1955.

Hammond, R. J. *Portugal and Africa 1815–1910*. Stanford, 1966.

Hoppe, Fritz. *Portugieisch-Ostafrika in der Zeit des Marques de Pombal (1750–1777)*. Berlin, 1965.

Isaacman, Allen. "The Prazos da Coroa 1752–1830: A Functional Analysis of the Political System." *Studia* 26 (1969): 149–78.

Johnston, H. H. *British Central Africa*. London, 1898.

Junod, Henri. *The Conditions of the Natives of S.E. Africa in the Sixteenth Century According to the Early Portuguese Documents*. Capetown, 1914.

Junod, Henri Alexandre. "Notes on the Ethnological Situation in Portuguese East Africa, South of the Zambesi." *Bantu Studies* 10 (1937): 297–300.

Kerr, Walter Montagu. *The Far Interior.* 2 vols. London, 1886.
Kuper, Hilda. *The Shona and the Ndebele of Southern Rhodesia.* London, 1955.
Lacerda, Francisco Gavincho De. *Costumes E Lendas Da Zambézia.* Lisbon, 1925.
―――. *Figuras e Episodas Da Zambézia.* Lisbon, 1943.
Lacerda e Almeida, Francisco José de. *The Lands of Cazembe: Lacerdá's Journey to Cazembe in 1798.* Translated by Richard Burton. London, 1873.
―――. *Travessia Da África.* Lisbon, 1936.
Lavrádio, Marquês de. *Portugal em África depois de 1851.* Lisboa, 1936.
Liesegang, Gerhard. *Beiträge zur Geschichte des Reiches der Gaza Ngoni im südlichen Moçambique, 1829–1895.* Cologne, 1968.
―――. *Resposta Das Questõens Sobre os Cafres.* Occasional Paper, no. 2, Centro de Estudos de Antropologia Cultural. Lisbon, 1966.
Lima, Alfredo Augusto. "Prazos Da Zambézia." *Boletim da Agência Geral Das Colónias* 1 (1925): 56–64.
Lima, Augusto de and Henrique, Carlos Castilho. "Os prazos da Corôa na Província de Moçambique." *As Colónias Portuguezas* 8 (1890): 57–58.
Livingstone, David. *Livingstone's Last Journey.* New York, 1875.
―――. *Missionary Travels and Research in South Africa.* London, 1857.
Livingstone, David and Livingstone, Charles. *Livingstone's Narrative of an Expedition to the Zambesi and Its Tributaries.* New York, 1866.
Lobato, Alexandre. *Colonização Senhorial Da Zambésia.* Lisbon, 1962.
―――. *Evolução Administrativa e Económica Da Moçambique 1752–63.* Lisbon, 1957.
Lopes, Gustavo do Bivar Pinto. *Respostas ao Questionário Ethnográfico.* Beira, 1928.
Lopes, Manoel Monteiro. "Usage and Customs of the Natives of Sena." *Journal of the African Society* 6 (1907): 350–65.
McLeod, Lyons. *Travels in Eastern Africa.* 2 vols. London, 1860.
Martin, C. "Manyika Beads of the XIX Century." *NADA* 17 (1940): 18–26.
Martins, A. Rego. "Monografia sobre os Usos e Costumes dos Senas." *Boletim da Sociedade de Estudos de Moçambique* 29 (1960): 13–33.
Martins, J. P. Oliveira. *Portugal Em África.* Lisbon, 1953.
―――. *Relatório da commissão encarregada de estudar as reformas a introduzir ao sistema dos prazos de Moçambique.* Lisbon, 1889.
Marwick, M. G. "History and Tradition in East Central Africa Through the Eyes of the N. Cewa." *Journal of African History* 4 (1963): 375–90.
―――. "The Social Context of Cewa Witch Beliefs." *Africa* 22 (1952): 130–35, 215–33.
Maugham, R. C. F. *Portuguese East Africa.* New York, 1906.
―――. *Zambezia.* London, 1910.
Mazula, A. Y. "História dos Nianjas." *Portugal em África* 19 (1962): 155–66, 235–47.

Mello, Francisco de Aragão e. *Memória e Documentos Ácêrca dos Direitos de Portugal Aos Territórios de Machona e Nyasa*. Lisbon, 1890.

————. *Relatório da Inspecção a Alguns Dos Prazos do Districto de Tete*. Lourenço Marques, 1911.

"Memórias da Costa da África Oriental e Algumas reflexões uteis para Estabelecer Melhor e Mais Florente o seu Comércio." *Anais da Junta de Investigacoes do Ultramar* 9, tomo 1 (1954), pp. 217–51.

Miranda, António Pinto de. "Memória sobre a costa de África." In *Relações De Moçambique Setecentista*, edited by António Andrade, pp. 231–302. Lisbon, 1954.

Miranda, A. P. *Notícia Ácêrca do Bongo da Zambézia*. Lisbon, 1869.

Mitchell, J. Clyde. *The Yao Village*. Manchester, 1956.

Monclaros, Father. "Account of the Expedition Under Francisco Barretto." In *Records of South-East Africa*, edited by G. M. Theal, vol. 3, pp. 157–254. Capetown, 1899.

Montaury, João Baptista de. "Moçambique, Ilhas Querimbas, Rios de Sena, Villa de Tete, Villa de Zumbo, Manica, Villa de Luabo, Inhambane." In *Relações De Moçambique Setecentista*, edited by António Andrade, pp. 339–73. Lisbon, 1954.

Mota, A. Teixeira da. *A Cartografia Antiga Da África Central e A Travessia Entre Angola e Moçambique 1500–1860*. Lourenço Marques, 1964.

Newitt, M. D. D. "The Massingire Rising of 1884." *Journal of African History* 11 (1970): 87–105.

————. "The Portuguese on the Zambesi: An Historical Interpretation of the Prazo System." *Journal of African History* 10 (1969): 67–85.

————. "The Portuguese on the Zambesi From the Seventeenth to the Nineteenth Centuries." *Race* 9 (1968): 477–98.

———— and Garlake, P. S. "The Aringa at Massangano." *Journal of African History* 8 (1967): 133–56.

Oliveira, Delfim José de. *A Província de Moçambique e o Bonga*. Coimbra, 1879.

Owen, W. F. W. "Letter from Captain W. F. W. Owen to J. W. Crocker, 9 Oct. 1823." In *Records of South East Africa*, edited by G. M. Theal, vol. 9, pp. 32–35. Capetown, 1903.

————. *Narrative of Voyages to Explore the Shores of Africa, Arabia, and Madagascar*. London, 1833.

Pereira, Francisco Raymundo Moraes. "Account of a Journey Made Overland From Quelimane to Angoche." Translated and edited by M. D. D. Newitt. *Central African Historican Association, Occasional Papers, no. 14*. Salisbury, 1965.

Phillipson, D. W. "The Early Iron Age in Zambia — Regional Variants and Some Tentative Conclusions." *Journal of African History* 9 (1968): 191–211.

————. "The Date of the Ingombe Ilede Burial." *Journal of African History* 10 (1969): 199–204.

Pilar, Fr. João do and Ribeiro, Manoel António. "Edital da Inquisiçã de

Goa — Contrat Cortos Costumes e Rites da África Oriental." In *O Chronista de Tissuary*, edited by J. H. da Cunha Rivara, vol. 2, pp. 273–75. Nova Goa, 1867.

Price, Thomas. "More About the Maravi." *African Studies* 11 (1952): 75–79.

Randles, W. G. L. "South East Africa and the Empire of Monomotapa as Shown On Selected Maps of the 16th Century." *Studia* 2 (1958): 103–163.

Rangeley, W. H. J. "The Earliest Inhabitants of Nyasaland." *Nyasaland Journal* 16 (1963): 32–42.

————. "Mbona — The Rain Maker." *Nyasaland Journal* 6 (1953): 8–27.

————. "Two Nyasaland Rain Shrines — Makewana, the Mother of All People." *Nyasaland Journal* 5 (1952): 31–50.

Ranger, T. O. *Revolt in Southern Rhodesia 1896–97.* Evanston, 1967.

"Relação dos Moradores Portugueses que existem em Moçambique e seus Distritos, Julho de 1757." *Anais da Junta da Investigações do Ultramar* 9, tomo 1 (1954), pp. 151–70.

Rezende, Pedro Barretto de. "Do Estado da Índia." In *Records of South-East Africa*, edited by G. M. Theal, vol. 2, pp. 401–426. Capetown, 1898.

Ribeiro, Sousa, ed. *Regimen dos Prazos da Corôa, 1832–1906.* Lourenço Marques, 1907.

Rita-Ferreira, A. *Agrupamento e Caracterização dos Indígenas de Moçambique.* Lisbon, 1958.

————. "Os Azimbas." *Boletim De Sociedade De Moçambique* 24, no. 84 (1954), pp. 47–140; no. 85, pp. 31–61.

————. *Os Cheuas Da Macanga.* Lourenço Marques, 1966.

Robinson, K. R. "The Archaeology of the Rozwi." In *The Zambesi Past*, edited by E. Stokes and R. Brown, pp. 3–26. Manchester, 1966.

Rowley, Henry. *The Story of the Universities Mission to Central Africa.* London, 1867.

Salt, Henry. *A Voyage to Abyssinia and Travels into the Interior of That Country.* London, 1814.

Santanna, Francisco, ed. *Documentação o Avulsa Mocambicana Do Arquivo Histórico Ultramaraino.* 2 vols. Lisbon, 1964–67.

Santos, João dos. "Ethiópia Oriental." In *Records of South-East Africa*, edited by G. M. Theal, vol. 7, pp. 1–370. Capetown, 1901.

Santos, Júnior, Joaquim Norberto dos. *Contribuição para o Estudo da Anthropologia de Moçambique-Alguns Tribos do Distrito de Tete.* Porto 1944.

————. "O Marombo ou Malombo." *Revista de Garcia de Orta* 6 (1957): 1–16.

Santos, Luís dos. "Apontamentos sobre a Etnografia dos Nhúngùes." *Estudos de Antropologia* 8 (1949): 1–16.

Schapera, I., ed. *Livingstone's African Journal 1853–1856.* Berkeley and Los Angeles, 1963.

————. *Livingstone's Missionary Correspondence 1841–1856.* London, 1961.

————. *Livingstone's Private Journals 1851–1853.* London, 1960.

Schoffeleers, Mathew. "The Political Role of the M'bona Cult." Paper read at U.C.L.A. Conference on the History of African Religious Systems, 1970, Dar Es Salaam.

Selous, Fredrick Courteney. *Travel and Adventure in South-East Africa.* London, 1893.

Seyrig, M. Henry. *Rapport Sur La Situation Actuelle et L'Avenir Possible du Prazo de Gorongoza.* Lisbon, 1897.

Sicard, H. "O Propósito de Sisnando Baião." *Studia* 16 (1965): 179–87.

————. "The Rhodesian Tally." *NADA* 31 (1954): 52–54.

Silva, Manoel Galvão da. "Diário das Viagens feitas pelas terras da Manica em 1790." *Anais da Junta de Investigações do Ultramar* 9, tomo 1 (1954): 323–32.

————. "Diário ou Relação das Viagens Filosóficas, nas Terras da Jurisdição de Tete e em algumas dos Maraves." *Anais da Junta de Investigações do Ultramar* 9, tomo 1 (1954), pp. 311–19.

Silva, Pedro Augusto de Sousa e. *Distrito de Tete.* Lisbon, 1927.

Silva Rego, A. Da. *O Ultramar Portugues No Século XIX.* Lisbon, 1966.

————. *O Ultramar Portugues no Século XVIII.* Lisbon, 1967.

Sousa, Francisco De. *Oriente Conquistado O Jesú Christo Pelos Padres Da Companhia De Jesús da Província de Goa.* 2 vols. Lisbon, 1710.

Sousa, Manuel De Faria e. "Ásia Portuguesa." In *Records of South-East Africa*, edited by G. M. Theal, vol. 1, pp. 1–41. Capetown, 1898.

Stefaniszyn, Bronislaw and de Santana, Hilary. "The Rise of the Chikunda Condottieri." *Northern Rhodesia Journal* 4 (1960): 361–68.

Sullivan, C. G. L. *Dhow Chasing in Zanzibar Waters and On the Eastern Coast of Africa. Narrative of Five Years' Experience in the Suppression of the Slave Trade.* London, 1873.

Summers, Roger. "The Southern Rhodesian Iron Age." *Journal of African History* 2 (1961): 1–13.

Tabler, E. D., ed. *The Zambesi Papers of Richard Thorton.* 2 vols. London, 1963.

Termos de Vassalagem Nos Territórios de Machona, Zambézia e Nyasa 1858 a 1889. Lisbon, 1890.

Tew, Mary. *People of the Lake Nyasa Region.* London, 1950.

Texugo, F. Torres. *Letter on the Slave Trade Still Being Carried On Along the Eastern Coast of Africa.* London, 1839.

Theal, George McCall. *The Portuguese in South Africa.* Capetown, 1896.

————. *Records of South-East Africa.* 9 vols. Capetown, 1898–1903.

Thomas, Frei Manoel de Santo. "Memória dos Rios de Sena." In *O Chronista de Tissaury Periódico*, edited by J. H. da Cunha Rivara, vol. 2, pp. 43–46, 61–66. Nova Goa, 1867.

Thorton, Richard. "Notes on the Zambesi and the Shire." *Journal of the Royal Geographic Society* 34 (1864): 196–99.

Tracey, Hugh. *António Fernandes, Descobridor do Monomotapa, 1514–1515.* Lourenço Marques, 1940.

Truão, António Norberto de Barbosa de Villas Boas. *Estatísticas da Capitania dos Rios de Sena no Anno de 1806.* Lisbon, 1889.

———. "Extracto do Plano para um Regimento ou Nova Constituição Económica e Política da Capitania de Rios de Senna." *Annais do Conselho Ultramarino, Parte não oficial,* pp. 407–417. Lisbon, 1857.

Ulrich, Ruy Ennes. *Economia Colonial.* Coimbra, 1910.

Vansina, Jan. "Anthropologists and the Third Dimension." *Africa* 39 (1969): 62–68.

———. "A Comparison of African Kingdoms." *Africa* 32 (1962): 324–35.

———. *Kingdoms of the Savanna.* Madison, 1966.

———. *Oral Traditions.* Translated by H. M. Wright. London, 1965.

Varella, Joaquim José. "Descrição da Capitania de Moçambique e suas povoações e produções, pertencentes a Corôa de Portugal." *Anais da Junta de Investigações do Ultramar* 9, tomo 1 (1954), pp. 281–311.

Vilhena, Ernesto Jardim de. *Estudos Sobre a Zambézia: De Tete a Quiloa.* Lisbon, 1902.

———. *O Regime dos Prazos da Zambézia.* Lisbon, 1916.

———. *Questões Coloniaes.* Lisbon, 1910.

Wagley, Charles. *Amazon Town: A Study of Man in the Tropics.* New York, 1964.

Wallis, J. P. R., ed. *The Zambesi Expedition of David Livingstone 1858–1863.* 2 vols. London, 1956.

———. *The Zambesi Journal of James Stewart 1862–1863.* London, 1952.

Warhurst, Phillip. *Anglo-Portuguese Relations in South Central Africa 1890–1900.* London, 1962.

Wiese, Carlos. "Expedição Portugueza À Mpeseni (1889)." *Boletim Da Sociedade De Geografia de Lisboa* 10 (1891): 235–73, 331–412, 465–97.

Xavier, Ignácio Caetano. "Memórias da Costa da África Oriental e algumas reflexões úteis para estabelecer melhor e fazer mais florente o seu comércio, 21 de Marco de 1762." *Anais da Junta de Investigações do Ultramar* 9, tomo 1 (1954), pp. 217–49.

———. "Notícias dos Domínios Portugueses na Costa de África Oriental 1758." In *Relações de Moçambique Setecentista,* edited by António Andrade, pp. 139–88. Lisbon, 1954.

———. "Relação do Estado presente de Moçambique, Sena, Sofala, Inhambane, e todo o Continente da África Oriental, 26 Dec. 1758." *Anais da Junta de Investigações do Ultramar* 9, tomo 1 (1954), pp. 171–215.

Index

Abreu, Manoel de Paes de, 102
Abutua, Fair of, 70
Abutua (capital of Rozvi state), 10
Abutua (kingdom): trade with prazos, 81–82; mentioned, 84
Achikunda: conflict with colonos, 23; political role on prazos, 33–34; resistance to prazo system, 40–41; defensive role on prazos, 102; role on Prazo Makanga, 128–29; joining Prazo Massingire, 134; role on Prazo Massangano, 142–43; mentioned, 18, 22, 35, 37, 39, 42, 54, 56, 57, 63, 67, 68, 77, 78, 84, 88, 94, 104, 105, 106, 110, 115, 116, 117, 119, 124, 132, 135, 136, 138, 139, 141, 142, 143, 148, 151, 154, 156, 157
Aforamento, 96–97, 121
Afumu. See Mfumu
Agriculture: decline on prazos, 119; on new prazos, 161
Akaporo, 43, 47–51, 63, 67, 90, 157
Albuquerque, Pedro Saldanha de, 100
Alves da Silva, Governor, 94
Alvim, Ignácio de Mello: quoted, 106
Amambo. See Mambo
Angoche (place), 13
Angola, 80, 81, 86, 90
Angónia (territory), 133
Anguru (people), 134
Anões (people), 3, 4, 5
Arab traders: as middlemen, 75; mentioned, 173
Aragão, João Xavier Pinheiro de, 57
Aringa: locations of principal Massangano aringas, 229–30n99; mentioned, 135, 143
Aruangua, Fair of, 79

Badzo: political role on prazo, 34
Banda (Malawian clan), 5
Bangoma (member of royal family of Muenemutapa), 109
Bantu migrants into Zambezi, 3
Bares, 105
Barretto, Manuel: quoted, 173
Barue (kingdom): initial relations with Muenemutapa, 7–11; independence from Muenemutapa, 10–11; conquest by Lobo da Silva, 18; 18th-century succession crises, 21; attacks on Tonga and Sena, 22; relations with prazos, 110–12; holy water, 111, 112; invasion of prazos, 120; alliance with Bongas, 144; relations with Gouveia, 148–50; revolt of, 162; relations with Muenemutapa, 177–78n19; mentioned, 19, 36–37, 39, 48, 78–79, 80, 85, 91, 103, 106, 108, 109, 111, 117, 119, 146, 147, 149–50, 156
Bayão, Sisnando: relations with Quiteve, 19–20; mentioned, 18, 36–37, 57, 102, 110
Bemba (people), 81, 85
Benga (prazo), 37
Berenha (King of Quiteve), 20
Berlin Conference of 1885, 146
Bisa (people): as middlemen traders, 80–81; mentioned, 53, 77, 82, 85, 90, 129